THE STORY

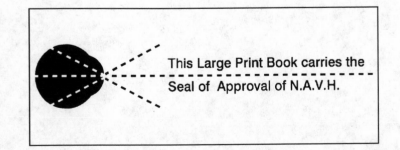

THE STORY

A REPORTER'S JOURNEY

JUDITH MILLER

THORNDIKE PRESS
A part of Gale, Cengage Learning

GALE
CENGAGE Learning·

Farmington Hills, Mich • San Francisco • New York • Waterville, Maine
Meriden, Conn • Mason, Ohio • Chicago

GALE
CENGAGE Learning®

LIBRARY OF CONGRESS CATALOGING-IN-PUBLICATION DATA

Miller, Judith, 1948–
    The story : a reporter's journey / Judith Miller.
      pages cm. — (Thorndike Press large print biographies and memoirs)
    Includes bibliographical references.
    ISBN 978-1-4104-7959-4 (hardcover) — ISBN 1-4104-7959-5 (hardcover)
    1. Miller, Judith, 1948– 2. Women journalists— United States— Biography.
3. Large type books. I. Title.
PN4874.M492A3 2015b
070.92— dc23
[B]   2015009178

Published in 2015 by arrangement with Simon & Schuster, Inc.

Printed in Mexico
1 2 3 4 5 6 7 19 18 17 16 15

*For friends, fellow journalists killed while
telling the story:
Dial Torgerson
David Blundy
Daniel Pearl
Marie Colvin
And for Bill Safire, word warrior,
who encouraged me to keep trying*

CONTENTS

7

PROLOGUE

I thought I was doing well. In the spring of
2002, a year before the invasion of Iraq, I
was at the peak of my profession. A member
of an investigative unit at the *New York
Times,* America's most prestigious newspaper, I had been part of a small team that
had just won a Pulitzer for our investigation
before 9/11 into Al Qaeda and its growing
threat to America. I had also received an
Emmy that year, for a documentary based
on *Germs,* a book I had written with Stephen Engelberg and William Broad, two
respected *Times* colleagues. I had finally
been lucky in love. For the past nine years I
had been married to a brilliant publisher, a
legend in his own profession, who was
proud of my work and tolerated my frequent
lengthy assignments often to dangerous
places, especially in the Middle East, where
I had been the paper's Cairo bureau chief
for several years.

I could not have imagined that three years later my reporting would be mired in controversy, or that some of my life-long assumptions about politics, foreign policy, and journalism would be tested and shattered.

At the start of the Iraq War in 2003, I was sent to cover it as the only reporter embedded in a secret army unit charged with finding the weapons of mass destruction that the Central Intelligence Agency and other intelligence agencies concluded Saddam Hussein was hiding. Before and during the war, it was my job to report in the most timely way on what the US government believed to be true. It sounds easy. In the hypersecretive world of national security, it isn't.

The CIA and other intelligence agencies were convinced with "high confidence" that Saddam had chemical and germ weapons programs and was actively seeking a nuclear bomb. I got scoops about some of that intelligence. I hedged the assertions with all the proper qualifiers. Eventually, over the course of America's long occupation of Iraq, more than six thousand chemical weapons or remnants of them — some containing mustard gas and sarin made before the 1991 war — were found and tragically sickened some American soldiers and Iraqis.

While the *Times* and other news outlets claimed that these were not the weapons for which America had invaded, Saddam's failure to acknowledge or account for them violated his pledges to the United Nations and was part of the administration's justification for war.

But the central, clearly newsworthy claim of some of my prewar stories was wrong. As we now know, Saddam did not have an active program to create and use WMD or stockpiles of such new, sophisticated weapons. The faulty intelligence on which the decisions of policy makers and politicians were based was used to justify a war whose consequences have thus far proven disastrous for the Iraqi people and America.

As the war began to go badly, controversy erupted not only over the government's missteps but also the media's role in publicizing the government's estimates, and my reporting, in particular. From a journalist whose boss, Bill Keller, once described as "smart, relentless, incredibly well sourced, and fearless," I was suddenly being characterized as a pushy woman reporter who would do anything for a scoop, a warmonger who had helped sell and carry out the war.

A campaign against my reporting had been launched in the blogosphere by critics, some of whom have no idea what reporting involves; I sensed that they were reacting to the ill-fated war. But the false characterizations still stung. I often didn't know whether to laugh or cry. (I did a bit of both.) Accusations that I was a closet neocon or the most gullible reporter the *Times* had ever hired quickly migrated from internet columns to ideologically linked journals, then to the so-called mainstream media, and soon reverberated throughout the global electronic universe. The accusations popped up in books by celebrated pundits, almost none of whom called me for comment; in scholarly works on journalistic ethics; and even in a book on "irresponsible work" by a Harvard professor.[1]

On WMD in Iraq, I had lots of company in government and the media. In hindsight, few of the officials whose decisions prompted the mess in Iraq understood what they were getting into — not those in 1991 who favored leaving Saddam in power, or those in 2003 who sought to bring democracy to Iraq by force. Wrong, too, were those who argued in 2007 as the war was failing that switching strategies and a "surge" of forces in Iraq would not affect America's military fortunes there. So were those who claimed that America had finally "won" in

Iraq, and those in 2010 who advocated pulling our troops out posthaste.

There is no shortage of mistakes about Iraq. Good grace, and honesty, require all of us who made them to admit error. This book is part of that process.

Over time questions about the rightness of the Iraq War both in its conception and outcome morphed in some quarters into a broad condemnation of the media and accusations that the press — not the government — had taken the country to war. The charge was both untrue and toxic to our political discourse. But with newspapers under increasing economic pressure, the charges of warmongering felt like mortal threats to an institution and a profession to which I had devoted my life.

It was into this landscape that a federal investigation was launched to determine who had leaked the name of a CIA agent whose husband had accused the White House of having lied about Iraq's WMD. I received a federal subpoena demanding that I disclose the identity of sources who may have blown the agent's cover. I went to jail to protect those sources, or so I thought.

When the officials and weapons experts finally determined that there were no WMD stockpiles and active programs to make them to be found in Iraq, I was shocked and angry. But I thought I knew *why* the CIA and other intelligence agencies made some of their mistaken assumptions and reached the wrong conclusions. I believed it was my responsibility to report this. The *Times* did not permit me to do so, and soon after I got out of jail, I felt I had no choice but to resign.

For years afterward, friends urged me to write about this tumultuous period. I hesitated. The entire episode was still too painful and confusing. But eventually, I concluded that I had to try. When journalists make mistakes about an event — or a person — we must revisit our work to report new, contradictory information or fill in the contours or holes in an incomplete story. I wrote this book because I believe that the forces that played substantial roles in my personal experience — a government that aggressively hides the truth from the public and prosecutes reporters, the collapse of the flawed but still invaluable temples of twentieth-century American journalism, and the very real threats that emanate from a part of the world that understandably frightens and exhausts us — are continuing to drive the deeply troubling decline in the quality of information available to both policy makers and the public.

I take tremendous pride in being good at my job. Correcting and completing the record are part of the pact that journalists make with readers. The book is my effort, finally, to fulfill the last of my end of that bargain.

CHAPTER 1
ANBAR PROVINCE, IRAQ

Late July 2010

As I opened the door of my flimsy CHU, the "compartmentalized housing unit" at Camp Ramadi in the Iraqi desert where I had slept after arriving from Baghdad, a gust of wind covered me with sand. The thermometer on the trailer door registered 100. It was six in the morning.

"Welcome to Spa Ramadi!" Maj. Ryan Cutchin said.

Tall, sandy haired, and army fit, Ryan loved mornings. Twenty years a soldier, he had probably been out for a run.

Summer was an insane time to visit Iraq. But I wanted to report on the US military's withdrawal before Ryan finished his final deployment here, his third in seven years. America's war in Iraq was ending. Soldiers like Ryan were leaving in what military spokesmen insisted on calling a "responsible drawdown of forces." President George W.

Bush had established the withdrawal schedule by December 2011. President Barack Obama was implementing it rigorously.

When we had first met seven years earlier in March 2003, then Captain Cutchin was serving in the 75th Field Artillery Brigade in Fort Sill, Oklahoma. The brigade had been charged with finding WMDs in Iraq. Embedded for the *New York Times,* I was the only reporter with his then-secret brigade, known as the 75th Exploitation Task Force. The XTF, as it was called, would find only traces of the weapons that the CIA and fifteen other American intelligence agencies had concluded Saddam Hussein was hiding, a nightmarish cache that the soldiers searching for them (and I with them) were convinced existed: remnants of some 500 tons of mustard and nerve gas, 25,000 liters of liquid anthrax, 38,000 liters of botulinum toxin, 29,984 prohibited munitions capable of delivering chemical agents, several dozen Scud missiles, and 18 mobile biological weapons vans — not to mention its ambitious nuclear weapons program, according to US estimates based on United Nations reports of what Iraq had made and claimed to have destroyed.[1] My bond with Ryan and other XTF members, forged during that often frustrating, infuriating, ultimately fruitless four-month search, had endured.

"We were so sure we'd find WMDs! Any day now," Ryan recalled, as we sipped coffee in the ice-cold trailer housing the Green Bean cafeteria, one of the few private contractors left at the forsaken army base on the outskirts of Anbar Province, a Sunni Muslim stronghold sixty miles west of Baghdad.

Neither of us would ever forget that maddening hunt, or the faulty intelligence that had helped justify the war, some of which I had been the first to report. When the war had begun, I accompanied Ryan and other XTF members day after exhausting day — inspecting sites on a list of more than eight hundred suspect places that the intelligence agencies had identified based on the outdated reports of UN inspectors. Most of those sites had been heavily looted by the time we arrived. At one villa in Baghdad, soldiers found a singed fifteen-page list of Iraqi front companies and individuals authorized to buy dual-use equipment in Europe and Asia suitable for conventional or unconventional weapons. The list and other weapons-related documents were smoldering in an old metal steamer trunk when the soldiers arrived. The contents had been set on fire — we never learned by

19

whom. Tewfik Boulenouar, the unit's Algerian-born translator, had salvaged some pages by stamping out the fire with his boot. Most of the time, intelligence about what was stored where were stunningly wrong.

"Remember those packets we got each morning, with the glossy pictures and a tentative grid?" Ryan reminisced. "Go to this place. You'll find a McDonald's there. Look in the fridge. You'll find French fries, cheeseburger, and Cokes. Then we would get there, and not only was there no fridge and no fries, there hadn't even been a thought of putting a McDonald's there."

One day in mid-April 2003, Ryan had raced to the city of Bayji, 130 miles north of Baghdad, to inspect a dozen fifty-five-gallon drums in an open field that soldiers had unearthed. The Iraqis buried everything of even remotely potential value, which increased suspicions about them among US intelligence agencies. Ryan, who led Mobile Exploitation Team (MET) Bravo, was told that one of the drums had tested positive for cyclosarin, a deadly nerve agent. "It turned out to be gasoline," he recalled. On another trip, his soldiers had dug up a crate containing a sofa.

In late May 2003 Ryan's friend, Chief Warrant Officer Richard "Monty" Gonzales, the head of search team MET Alpha, was sent to Basra in southern Iraq to investigate what senior weapons experts had described as nuclear equipment. What they found were industrial-scale vegetable steamers. The contents of the crates had all been clearly marked — in Russian.[2]

By the time their deployment and my embed ended in June 2003, the soldiers who had tried to remain optimistic about their mission were bitter. After promising leads had fizzled and Iraqi weapons scientists who had cooperated with the XTF were turned over to the Iraq Survey Group (the XTF's larger successor), Ryan Cutchin, Monty Gonzales, and Dave Temby, a veteran Defense Department bioweapons expert, called the suspect site list "toilet paper." They had reached another disheartening conclusion: while weapons hunters were likely to continue uncovering remnants of chemical and biological munitions, suspect chemicals, and WMD precursors, they were unlikely to find stockpiles of modern unconventional weapons that administration officials claimed had posed the "grave threat" to America. We were gobsmacked.

What we did not know then was that Saddam Hussein had been playing a double game: while he wanted the UN to believe that he had given up his WMD so that sanctions would be lifted, he also wanted Iran, Israel, and his other external and internal enemies to believe that he had kept those weapons. Moreover, as America's top weapons analysts would later conclude, even Saddam wasn't absolutely sure what was left in his stockpiles. At a Revolutionary Command Council meeting in October 2002, he had asked his senior staff whether "they might know something he did not about residual WMD stocks," Charles Duelfer, America's top Iraq weapons inspector, would write in 2013.[3] But a decade earlier, as we were crisscrossing Iraq in search of the elusive WMD stockpiles and the scientists who had produced them, all we knew for certain was that the intelligence the XTF had been given about Iraq's unconventional weapons was wrong. With this came the devastating realization that, as a result, some of my own earlier WMD stories were wrong, too.

I had not been wrong about Saddam, though. He was a mass murderer, a true psychopath. Sure, there were lots of bad people in the world, and some of them even led countries. It would have been folly for the United States to try to oust them all.

But after years of reporting in the Middle East, I considered Saddam special.

When I had first visited Iraq, in 1976, Saddam, not yet president, was already consolidating power. An American assistant secretary of state had described him at the time as a "rather remarkable person," "very ruthless," and a "pragmatic, intelligent power."[4] During my first visit to Baghdad, my suitcase was stolen. The incident would not have been noteworthy if I hadn't been the only journalist covering two US senators on a visit chaperoned by US security officials and a large contingent of Iraqi uniformed and secret police. Although I was reporting for the *Progressive,* an obscure leftist midwestern monthly, the delegation had a high profile.

I had seen my bag loaded onto a well-guarded van as we left for the airport. Still, someone, perhaps one of the many Iraqi "minders," had been brazen or desperate enough to walk off with it. The incident was telling. If Saddam was trying to build a "new socialist Arab man" — secular, disciplined, marching confidently into an oil-rich future — this petty theft was not an encouraging start.

The political climate deteriorated dramatically three years later in 1979, when Saddam assumed the Iraqi presidency in a characteristic bloodbath. He celebrated his inauguration in a giant hall in Baghdad by denouncing party members and even close friends whom he considered insufficiently loyal. As Saddam intoned their names one by one, the men were surrounded by goons and dragged out of the room. He had then called upon senior ministers, party leaders, and loyalists to form instant firing squads to kill their colleagues. After he had finished reading the list of the condemned, officials of the ruling Ba'ath Party who had not heard their names called wept openly with relief and began hysterically chanting in Arabic "Long Live Saddam!" "With our blood, with our souls," they shouted, "we will sacrifice for you, O Saddam!" (It more or less rhymes in Arabic.)

Years later, I would hear an audiotape of the astonishing assembly, the details of which Laurie Mylroie, a scholar at Harvard University's Center for Middle Eastern Studies, and I would be among the first to describe in a book we wrote and published in 1990 just before the US-led liberation of Kuwait.[5]

I had joined the *Times* in 1977 and became its Cairo bureau chief in 1983, responsible for covering most of the Arab Middle

East. I traveled to Iraq more than a dozen times to cover the Iran-Iraq war and had grown to dread those visits. The war that Saddam had launched against neighboring Islamic Iran less than a year after becoming president was not turning out as he — or the CIA — had predicted. Though weak and internally divided, Iran's revolutionary government, which in 1979 had ousted the Shah and created the world's first militant Shiite Islamic state, was fighting back ferociously. Outgunned but not outmanned, given a population some three times that of Iraq, theocratic Iran seemed at times on the verge of defeating the secular state that Arabs regarded not only as the cradle of their civilization but also the "beating heart" of Arab nationalism.

During my visits in the mid-1980s, it was still unclear which side would win. Officially, the United States was neutral. But President Ronald Reagan had secretly decided that "secular" Iraq could not be permitted to lose to anti-American theocrats who, in 1979, had attacked the US Embassy in Tehran and held American diplomats hostage for more than a year. So even after the United States received evidence that Saddam was using poison gas and other chemical weapons against Iranian forces and, later, his own citizens, Reagan extended credits to Iraq. America would also give intelligence guidance to Iraq's military to enhance the accuracy of its bombing raids and missile strikes. Once Saddam concluded that the United States would let him "get away with murder," as one scholar put it, his use of chemical weapons increased.[6]

Throughout the eight-year war, however, Washington had quietly provided, or tried to provide, covert assistance to both Iraq and Iran, reflecting what was euphemistically known as a "realist" foreign policy.

On my seventh trip to Baghdad in March 1985, I saw firsthand what our cynical policy meant for the Iranians and the Iraqis. After landing in Baghdad late at night and checking into the Sheraton, I was just dozing off when a missile struck. Its high-pitched whoosh was followed by an ear-splitting boom. The blast shattered the sliding glass terrace door of my seventh-floor room overlooking the Tigris River.

I bolted upright in bed, moving my hands slowly across the sheets. There was no glass on the bed, but shards covered much of the floor near the window. Barefoot, I inched my way across the room toward the light switch. Nothing. The blast had knocked out the power.

I had come to Baghdad to investigate whether Iran had begun firing Libyan-supplied Scud-B missiles at Iraq in retaliation for Iraq's relentless rocket attacks in the "war of the cities," the latest escalation of the Iran-Iraq war, then in its fifth year. The missiles I was trying to find almost found me.

Flashlight in hand, my duffel bag strapped over one shoulder, and my purse dangling from the other, I inched my way down the unlit emergency stairwell to the hotel's gaudy marble lobby. Its lights were still glowing brightly — a surreal scene, given the darkness and chaos above.

An Iraqi concierge, who only an hour earlier had been overly solicitous while checking me in, suddenly barked at me, *"Where are you going?"*

I was leaving the hotel, I told him as calmly as possible. My room had just been destroyed by a missile.

"You are not going anywhere," he commanded.

Seeing him reach for the bulge under his ill-fitting hotel uniform jacket, I froze as he retreated behind the front desk. Handing me a sheet of paper listing over $1,000 in charges for the night and the week I had planned to spend there, he insisted that I pay my bill, in cash. Rattled but furious, I flung two $100 bills on the desk and left. As I bolted out of the hotel, I was pretty sure he wouldn't shoot me.

While I walked to the home of a European diplomat, I thought about the Iraqi leader. In a region of brutal tyrants, Saddam stood out. *The Godfather* was his favorite film — a nugget that Laurie and I unearthed in researching our book. His role model was Joseph Stalin. "I like the way he governed his country," Saddam had told a well-known Kurdish politician.[7]

Like Stalin, Saddam had institutionalized terror as an instrument of state policy. With more than 150,000 employees of his competing intelligence agencies watching citizens in a country of fourteen million people (the population would surge to thirty million by 2010), his reliance on arbitrary punishment and the promotion of the most obsequious had destroyed Iraq's civil society and all centers of opposition. Individuals were subordinate to the whims of a state that — as noted by Kanan Makiya, an Iraqi writer and exile whom I had befriended — was synonymous with Saddam.

No one could escape his vile gaze. Thirty-foot-high portraits and smaller renditions of him — as soldier, peasant, teacher, and tribal elder — were everywhere. With his black hair and trademark mustache, his portrait graced the entrances of hotels, schools, public buildings, city squares, private offices, and even the dials of the gold wristwatches favored by the political elite. As Makiya wrote, the government had devoted an entire agency, the Very Special Projects Implementation Authority, to creating and maintaining such depictions of him.[8]

Iraqi women died for him, literally and figuratively, and men emulated his style of dress, his swagger, even the cut of his mustache. All mustaches in Iraq seemed to resemble his; I longed to see a goatee or a handlebar mustache. In the land where Sumerians had invented writing, discourse had been degraded to a single ubiquitous image.

All roads led to Saddam, the "leader-president," "leader-struggler," "standard-bearer," "leader of all the Arabs," "knight of the Arab nation," "hero of national liberation," "father-leader," and my personal favorite title, the "daring and aggressive knight" (*al-faris al-mighwar*)."[9] A scholar said that Saddam's name was mentioned between thirty to fifty times an hour in a typical radio broadcast; his TV appearances often lasted several hours a day. Makiya argued that Saddam's name and image were so ubiquitous that he had become the personification of what Iraqis perceived to be the "Iraqi" character.[10]

In Saddam's Iraq, real and imagined critics had a disconcerting way of ending up dead, in jail, or simply disappearing. Saddam had used the war as a pretext for persecuting the two groups he feared most: the Iraqi Shiites, a majority, and the Kurds, the luckless minority in northern Iraq who spoke their own language, had their own distinct culture, and constituted 20 percent of the population.

During my assignment in Cairo in the mid-1980s and my visits to the region, I had managed to interview almost every Arab leader — but not Saddam. I kept a stack of fifty rejected faxed requests for meetings with him in a file in Cairo. Saddam rarely gave interviews to journalists, especially foreigners.

On another trip to Baghdad in 1985, I had yet another encounter with a bomb. I was having lunch at the home of a British defense official with David Blundy, a British reporter for the London *Sunday Times* — a brilliant, dashing friend with whom I often collaborated. (A sniper killed David four years later, while he was covering the war in El Salvador.) As the diplomat, David, and I talked about the war, an Iranian missile struck. By the sound of the explosion and proximity of the white smoke, our host guessed that the missile had landed nearby. Since this could be a rare opportunity to see precisely which missile the Iranians were firing, we hopped in the diplomat's jeep and raced to the bomb site.

Arriving before the Iraqi police, we ran toward the smoking crater. Scud-B missiles were more than thirty-three feet long and capable of carrying 2,200 pounds of explosives, the defense expert told us. This missile was less than half that size, and the damage around it suggested that it had contained less than 500 pounds of explosives.

I snapped pictures of the crater and the surrounding damage, removed the film from my camera, put it in my purse, and inserted instead a half-used roll of film containing photos of a boring government-sponsored trip to the Iraqi front that I had taken the previous day.

The defense attaché was measuring the crater when we saw an unmarked black car with tinted windows — standard issue for the Mukhabarat, secret police — in the far distance. If we all began running, David warned, the Iraqis would surely catch us. It could be fatal for foreigners to be anywhere near such sites. David and I agreed that while we should stay, it would be riskier for a diplomat to be found there. The Iraqis might accuse him of being a spy and us his accomplices. I shoved the film roll I had just taken into his hand, hoping that he would get it out of Iraq in a diplomatic pouch. "We'll be all right," Blundy assured the Brit as he made a dash for his jeep.

The black car rolled to a halt, and three stocky men in black suits scrambled out, pistols drawn. David and I raised our hands and yelled in unison, *"Sahafi! Sahafiya!,"* Arabic for "journalists," among the first Arabic words foreign correspondents in this treacherous region learned.

The men took us to a police station in a part of Baghdad I did not know. There we were thrown into an insufferably hot, pee-stinking cell. There was no toilet, no water, no bed, and no shortage of flies. While I paced back and forth, blinking at the graffiti in Arabic on the cell's peeling walls, David spread his safari jacket out on the least filthy part of the floor and dozed off instantly. His ability to catnap through any crisis was impressive, if infuriating. "Cheer up," he yawned an hour later, restored by his nap. "It's cheaper than the Sheraton."

The hours passed slowly. I was desperate for a cigarette, and so was David, but my pack was in my confiscated purse. As an Iraqi guard walked by, cigarette in hand, David called out to him. *"Habibi,"* he pleaded, using the Arabic for "dear friend," "have you got a cigarette?"

The guard, who appeared to speak no English, moved closer to the cell. He had clearly understood, as he blew a smoke ring in David's face through the bars. "What you give?" He smiled menacingly, extracting an Iraqi cigarette from his uniform's shirt pocket and waving it in front of David.

"Ma fi lira!" David replied. "I h-a-v-e *no* m-o-n-e-y. You have my wallet," he added, dramatically emptying his jeans pockets.

"What you give?" the guard repeated. David looked at me, grinning diabolically.

"Take the woman!" David offered, pointing at me — a joke utterly lost on the guard.

Only David could make me laugh at such a moment. The mystified guard walked away, shaking his head. *"Majnoon,"* he muttered: foreigners are "crazy."

Several hours later, we were escorted to a bureaucrat's office. The garishly lit room was filled with overstuffed leather sofas, ornate, wood-carved armchairs, and plastic flowers — standard issue in Arab government offices. Seated behind a desk beneath a giant photo of — guess who? — was an officious young man in an expensive double-breasted suit and a well-practiced smile. He motioned for us to sit down. He had no mustache.

Rafik, as he called himself, had just returned from university in England. He had loved studying there, he told us, showing off his English. He was responsible for determining whether David and I were spies, he continued quite casually. Why were we at the bombing site?

We were journalists doing our jobs, David explained in a tone meant to imply that surely such a sophisticated Iraqi would appreciate what reporters do. We happened to be in the neighborhood when the missile struck.

Was there no one else with us?

David and I avoided looking at each other. If the secret police had seen the diplomat, we were in trouble. We were alone, David insisted.

Didn't we know that taking pictures of such attacks was strictly forbidden? Punishable by prison and possibly death?

"We didn't take any pictures," I lied. He

could verify that by developing the film the police had confiscated in my camera.

Rafik picked up the phone and summoned an officer. Almost twice Rafik's age, the officer groveled before his young superior. Rafik snapped an order at him. I couldn't quite decipher what he said, but the policeman looked chagrined.

Suddenly hospitable, Rafik offered us tea. A tray of sticky baklava appeared, which David and I, ravenous by now, ate quickly. An hour later, the officer returned and whispered something in Rafik's ear. From his demeanor, I sensed that the police had developed the authorized photos I had taken of Iraqi soldiers hoisting their weapons at the front.

Rafik smiled. We were free to go, he said, dismissing us. He did not apologize for having thrown us in jail. I asked for his business card. Still convivial, he said that his cards weren't ready yet. Besides, he added, while he had enjoyed our "chat," it would be better for all of us, especially us, if we did not meet again, or mention how we had spent our afternoon. In the future, he concluded, we should avoid bombing sites.

I did not write about our detention. Back then, the *Times* frowned upon first-person accounts by reporters about our professional or personal woes. Moreover, I had to continue working in Baghdad. Writing about the incident would have risked future visas for me and other *Times* correspondents. David and I hadn't been beaten or tortured. We had simply been locked up and denied water, food, cigarettes, and our freedom for a half day. That was hardly news "fit to print," as the paper's motto boasted. Especially considering what would have happened to us had we been Iraqi.

During the 1991 Gulf War to liberate Kuwait, I was in Saudi Arabia. I had been trapped there when the Saudis, without warning, closed their airspace in January on the eve of the American-led invasion. The *Times* began ramping up its prewar coverage in the fall of 1990, and Joe Lelyveld, then the paper's executive editor, had sent me back to the Middle East as "special Gulf correspondent" after reading *Saddam Hussein and the Crisis in the Gulf,* the bestseller that Laurie Mylroie and I had written after Saddam invaded Kuwait in August. I had a license to roam freely and report on the ambivalent Arab reaction to the impending invasion of the region's most powerful Arab state.

Like many of those I was interviewing, I

had mixed emotions about the impending war. On the one hand, I believed strongly that the United States and its allies had to eject Saddam from Kuwait — Iraq's "nineteenth province," as he called it — and punish him for having plundered his oil-rich neighbor. If the world failed to react to Saddam's latest aggression, respect for the sovereignty of nation-states on which the United Nations was based would mean nothing. At the same time, I had seen enough of war in the Middle East — the civil war in Lebanon, for instance — to know that wars are fiendishly hard to end.

I saw American diplomacy at its best under President George H. W. Bush before that war. Led by Secretary of State James A. Baker III, Bush's team overcame seemingly insurmountable obstacles to build an effective coalition against Iraq. Saudi Arabia's King Fahd had been persuaded to let the United States station forces on its soil — heretofore unimaginable, given the xenophobia of the kingdom's Wahhabi religious establishment. Defense Secretary Dick Cheney impressed me by flying to Riyadh armed with satellite photos showing Iraqi troops massing near the Saudi border. He convinced the king that Saddam might invade Saudi Arabia next. Only decades later would Cheney confirm why King Fahd had overruled his more cautious relatives and embraced American protection. "The Kuwaitis waited," Cheney quoted the king as having told his timorous relatives, "and now they are living in our hotels."[11]

Covering the normally reclusive kingdom during the war was thrilling. Journalist visas to Saudi Arabia had been rare during my three-year stint in Cairo. But with Saddam's forces massing near their border, the Saudis suddenly seemed delighted to host the infidel Americans.

King Fahd's review of the coalition forces was a dramatic, made-for-TV spectacular. It had begun with his visit to 1,500 American and Saudi troops assembled on a giant tarmac at Hafr al-Baten air base. The royal entourage had then raced across the desert in a fifty-car motorcade as journalists struggled to keep pace in our jeeps and vans. At King Khalid Military City, some five thousand foreign troops from over thirty coalition nations stood in formation, each battalion behind its national flag and signposts identifying it in English and Arabic. Fahd, wearing a flowing white *thobe,* a gold-embroidered, sand-colored cloak, and the traditional red-and-white-checked head scarf, had used a small footstool to hoist his enormous frame onto the floor of an open jeep. At his side was Gen. H. Norman Schwarzkopf, the beefy commander of America's ground forces. Together they drove slowly past troops assembled on the desert as far as the eye could see. Saddam had no idea what was in store for him, I thought, as I gazed at the largest international military force ever assembled for war in the modern Middle East.

Later that day, Fahd, who rarely gave interviews, spoke to me and a small group of female reporters.[12] Adel al-Jubeir, then an irreverent young press aide who would later become Saudi ambassador to Washington, had suggested this unorthodox nod to American feminism to his bosses. In a tent scented by incense and roses, Fahd held forth. About seventy-two years old — Saudis are usually vague about their age — Fahd was imposing, well over six feet tall. Seated in an ornate, high-backed chair while we stood clustered around him on luxurious Arabic carpets, he answered eight questions with a ninety-minute monologue. The king obviously had no interest in mastering the art of the press conference.

Like most of the other rulers I had managed to interview for the *Times* before the war, Fahd said that he felt betrayed by Saddam. Although he had given Iraq $25 billion in aid during the 1979 Iran-Iraq war, Saddam had repaid him by sending an assassination squad to kill him after they had quarreled over money and policy. For Fahd, this war was personal.

The same was true for Egypt's president, Hosni Mubarak, whom I had interviewed two months earlier in Cairo. A firm supporter of the war, Mubarak disclosed his heretofore secret efforts to save Saddam from himself. His account, too, was a terrifying portrait of Arab politics: lies, backstabbing, and betrayals by Saddam and other Arab leaders who had once called Mubarak their "brother."[13]

Mubarak, who led the largest, historically most significant Arab nation, had bluntly warned Saddam that war was inevitable unless he withdrew. "How can Saddam make such a miscalculation of his situation?" Mubarak wondered aloud.

Two decades later, I, too, dwelt on the puzzling consistency of Saddam's behavior. The Iraqi leader had almost always miscalculated — in failing to see that his invasion of revolutionary Iran in 1980 would solidify, not topple, the new militant Islamist regime, and a decade later, in underestimating America's resolve to uphold the sovereignty of Kuwait in 1991. After 9/11, he failed to appreciate America's fury against Al Qaeda and its supporters and President Bush's determination to prevent a hostile leader who had already used WMD against his own people from threatening to use such weapons in terror attacks against the United States, or providing them to those who would. Saddam had been the only world leader to *praise* the 9/11 attacks — America's "cowboys" were "reaping the fruit of their crimes against humanity," he declared — an insult that neither the Bushes nor Cheney would forget.[14] A bully, Saddam distinguished himself by being unwilling to retreat, even when confronted with the prospect of overwhelming retaliation.

After the 1991 Gulf War, Prince Khalid bin Sultan, the head of the non-American coalition forces, took me with him to liberated Kuwait. While he met his Kuwaiti counterparts, I interviewed Kuwaiti mothers weeping over their missing sons, visited their looted homes, and breathed the city's acrid air. I stood on a cold, deserted street in the slums of Kuwait City, taking notes about a desperate Palestinian family. Cradling a notebook on top of my elbow, I held my pen in one hand, a flashlight in the other. There was still no electricity. Because

Saddam had set Kuwait's oil fields on fire, the air was black from burning oil; it was impossible to write or even navigate the streets of the capital without a flashlight. Noon felt like midnight. Yet even darker was the evidence, everywhere, of the torture that the Kuwaitis had endured at the hands of Saddam's forces.

Prince Khalid had warned me that the allied victory might not mean the end of Saddam, then an unconventional view. By the end of February, the coalition's seven hundred thousand troops had crushed Iraq's exhausted, poorly supplied forces — the world's fourth largest army. Kuwait had been liberated in four days. Most Iraqi soldiers had surrendered or retreated to Iraq. Though Khalid and others told me that the Saudis had wanted the war to continue, Bush had declared a cease-fire when Iraq indicated it would honor the coalition's demands. One hundred twenty-five American soldiers had died; another twenty-one were missing in action. The "hundred-hour war" was hailed as a triumph for America and its European and Arab allies.

Years later, several officials who had overseen the war, Vice President Cheney among them, would regret not having forced Saddam from power. In his memoir and an interview, Cheney lamented having agreed to let Saddam's armed helicopters overfly Iraq. I had reported the consensus view among Arab and American intelligence analysts: such concessions to Iraqi dignity mattered little, as Saddam's regime would soon fall. No ruler could survive such a humiliating blow. Once again, the intelligence community would underestimate Saddam. And so would I.

In early 1993 I returned to northern Iraq after being shown samples of still-secret Iraqi documents that Kanan Makiya had helped smuggle out of Iraq with the help of US diplomats, the Iraqi opposition, and the US Air Force.[15] At an archives facility in Maryland, researchers from Middle East Watch, a private human rights group, and the US government's Defense Intelligence Agency (DIA) — groups that rarely worked together — collated, scanned, and analyzed more than four million pages of Iraqi files, proof of Saddam's genocide against Iraq's Kurds. The decade-long slaughter and repression of Kurdish Iraqis had reached its zenith between March and August 1988, but the campaign, dubbed Anfal, or "booty," had never before been substantiated by official Iraqi records.

Like the files of the Stasi, the East German intelligence agency that had trained Iraq's security police, the material described in chilling bureaucratese the "liquidations," "expulsions," and "transfers" of Kurdish victims, who were almost invariably referred to as "saboteurs," "criminals," "traitors," and "human cargo." The files included routine vacation requests, payroll records of mercenaries and informants, intercepted letters and postcards, and so on — but also page upon page of authorizations of "purifications," "liquidations," and other euphemisms for mass murder.

"Dear Comrades," stated one from the Ba'ath Party People's Command in Zakho, dated June 14, 1987. "The entry of any kind of human cargo, nutritional supplies, or mechanical instruments into the security-prohibited villages . . . is strictly prohibited. It is your duty to kill any human being or animal found in these areas." In a cover story for the *New York Times Magazine,* I wrote that the tattered, partly burned, and water-stained documents, often held together in characteristic Iraqi fashion with shoelaces and pins, constituted the best evidence to date of Saddam's genocidal campaign against his Kurdish minority.

What I saw inside the Kurdish area of Iraq

44

in 1993 was even worse. Having taken pride in America's swift expulsion of Iraqi forces from Kuwait, I was forced to confront the conflict's human wreckage. What most officials and many reporters, including me, had acclaimed as a decisive military victory for the American-led coalition, seemed decidedly less glorious as I stood next to yet another newly discovered Kurdish mass grave. The stench of human decomposition was overwhelming — a smell no one ever forgets. The remains were carefully catalogued by human rights workers to present as physical evidence at a future trial for genocide. But no nation was willing to bring charges against Iraq. Saddam's oil had let him escape justice.

Joost Hiltermann, a Dutch researcher for Middle East Watch who had spent months investigating human rights abuses in Kurdistan, estimated that Saddam's forces had leveled about four thousand villages and killed some 180,000 Kurds in Anfal — a "counterinsurgency gone wild," I wrote.[16] Thousands had been shot and buried in mass graves. Others had starved to death in desert prisons, or been gassed in Halabja, Iraqi Kurdistan, where between 3,500 and 5,000 civilian adults and children had died on a single day in March 1988. Saddam had used chemical weapons against the Shiites in the south, but his attack in Halabja remains the world's largest chemical attack against a civilian-populated area in history. When I visited the city again in 2006, the cemetery for those who had perished in chemical attacks and other Anfal victims was still the town's largest open space. Gravestones stretched as far as I could see.

What I saw in Kuwait (and later in Iraqi Kurdistan) made me ashamed that the United States was continuing to ignore Saddam's brutality because it did not affect Americans directly. As victory parades were being held in New York in the spring of 1991, Saddam's forces were draining the marshes of southern Iraq and slaughtering their inhabitants — descendants of a distinctive river culture — and mowing down other Shiite Muslims who had challenged the regime, as President Bush had urged them to do. Opponents whom Saddam did not kill had fled Iraqi terror. Tens of thousands of Kurds had huddled for weeks, hungry and homeless, in the mountains of neighboring Turkey. Saddam's depraved repression — captured on film by CNN — finally shamed Washington into establishing no-fly zones in Iraq, first in the north to protect the Kurds, and eighteen months later, over southern Iraq as well. The no-go zone was a godsend to the Kurds, who quickly began using the safety assured by American-patrolled skies to build their own independent economic, cultural, and political institutions. But by the time the no-fly zone was extended to the south, as I wrote bitterly at the time, Saddam had crushed the Shiite uprising. The Iraqi Shia, I would later learn, never forgave America for encouraging and then ignoring the uprising.

I thought about the savagery I had covered in Iraq and the hope I had felt about Bush's decision to topple Saddam in March 2003 as Ryan Cutchin and I sipped our drinks in forlorn Anbar Province and caught up on what had happened since my last trip here two years earlier.

This was Ryan's fourth deployment since we had first met — one was in Afghanistan — and my fourth trip back to Iraq since my frustrating WMD embed. But in July 2010 Major Cutchin was no longer hunting for WMDs or even seeing much combat. He was overseeing "civil affairs" work for the First Brigade, Eighty-Second Airborne Division, the "build" part of the military's counterinsurgency mantra of "clear, hold, build." He had spent the past eight months trying to win Iraqi "hearts and minds" to get intelligence about the identity and whereabouts of remaining insurgents in the area and their weapons caches. Ryan's mission, part of the 2007 shift to a counterinsurgency strategy and the surge of US forces, was to train Iraqi soldiers and police and to help civilians create new institutions, or resuscitate those paralyzed by Saddam's twenty-nine-year reign of terror and the ensuing anarchy and civil war in the wake of America's invasion. Ryan knew he would not be returning to Iraq. We were done here.

Ryan was tired. His eyes showed the strain of too many deployments in too few years. This last had begun only a week after his third child, a son, was born. The endless series of counterinsurgency campaigns had stretched American military capacity to its limits and beyond. But Ryan insisted that his mission in Anbar, the scene of half the fighting and nearly half the US deaths in Iraq, had largely succeeded. The war against terrorism in Anbar, at least for now, he told me, had "irreversible momentum."

There were few signs of Ryan's "big mo" as we drove the next day to Ramadi, the provincial capital. Ryan had succeeded in hitching us a ride in an MRAP, a heavily armored Mine Resistant Ambush Protected transport tank, to the provincial governor's compound. Taking the MRAP meant putting on protective gear in the scorching heat — an extra twenty pounds of armor that included a bulletproof Kevlar vest and helmet, protective glasses and gloves, all for a fifteen-minute ride. But Ryan said that it beat walking in the heat or getting blown up by an IED, an improvised explosive device — or as we civilians called it, a homemade bomb. At roughly $850,000 apiece, the MRAP could withstand all but the latest versions of Iranian-designed and -supplied IEDs. Soldiers told me that it was just a matter of time before "irreconcilables" in Iraq or Afghanistan found a weakness in the vehicle.

The 1.5 million people of this deeply tribal Sunni province roughly the size of South Carolina seemed to be adjusting resentfully to second-class status in Iraq led by the increasingly autocratic Shiite prime minister Nouri al-Maliki. There were no longer overt signs of Al Qaeda, which had sunk roots among the province's fellow Sunni Muslims soon after the American invasion. Anbar had been one leg of that infamous Sunni Triangle where so many Americans had died. In early 2007 Al Qaeda's black flag had flown here. Young

Muslim militants with guns had snapped orders to the proud elders of Anbar's thirty major tribes — even to the province's "paramount sheikhs." But their brutality and fanatical disrespect for Anbar's tribal ways had been their undoing.[17] Fed up with the impudent extremists — and above all, with their greedy interference with the local sheikhs' profitable smuggling — Anbaris had turned on Al Qaeda, ending what had always been, at best, a marriage of convenience.

The Sahawa al-Anbar, "Anbar Awakening," spread quickly through the Sunni heartland, stunning even the US military. By mid-2008, one hundred thousand Sunni self-designated "Sons of Iraq," many of them former insurgents, or Shia militia members, had joined the Americans. A year earlier, Gen. David Petraeus, the commander of US and coalition forces in Iraq, and his operational commanders had developed a plan that persuaded President Bush to support these new Iraqi allies with weapons and later money and to increase US forces here to help protect the people from a resurgence of Al Qaeda and extremist Shiites. The American shift in strategy from keeping soldiers on US bases to adding thirty thousand new US troops and deploying them to villages and neighborhoods to recruit Iraqis and later pay them to help destroy Sunni and Shiite extremists became known as the "surge." The gamble succeeded, at least through 2011, beyond expectations.[18]

Within the United States, Bush's belated but bold decision in 2007 to surge US forces in Iraq had been savaged by American politicians and many journalists. The Iraq Study Group headed by Republican guru James Baker and former Democratic congressman Lee Hamilton had urged Bush to accelerate the training of Iraqi forces so that America could *withdraw* all of its own forces as soon as possible. Senator Hillary Clinton had opposed the surge. So, too, had Senator Joe Biden. The "surge," he predicted, stood "zero" chance of success. "Victory is no longer an option," the *New York Times* declared after Bush announced the increase. Senator Chuck Hagel, the Nebraska Republican and former Vietnam War hero, called it "the most dangerous foreign policy blunder in this country since Vietnam." Even Secretary of State Condoleezza Rice was quietly warning the president she had advised earlier as director of the National Security Council that the surge might not work.

In Iraq, striking a balance between assuring Iraqis sufficient protection and promising to leave once the country was stable had been tough. General Mattis recalled his effort to assure Sunni Iraqis that America would not abandon them prematurely. Americans would not leave until they wanted them to go, he said; in fact, he was going to retire in Iraq. "I found a little piece of property down on the Euphrates," he told them.[19]

Despite their pivotal role in reversing the fortunes of America's ineptly prosecuted war, Iraqi Sunnis, who compose no more than 20 percent of the population, feared they were destined to be the losers of America's invasion. Those who had once ruled Iraq, repressing the Kurds and the Shiite majority, were now a relatively powerless minority. Their bitterness was palpable.

The reception hall inside the provincial governor's compound in downtown Ramadi was still a wreck from a suicide bombing less than a week before my arrival. The bomber had ignited his explosives on a Sunday — "grievance day," when widows and other women traditionally sought help here. As Ryan and I walked through the charred hallway, remnants of the strike were visible. While the largest pieces of embedded flesh had been removed from the walls, the orange-brown streaks of dried blood remained. This had been the fourth suicide bombing near or within the governor's compound that year, plus one near miss. In fact, Iraq, on any given day, still remained statistically more dangerous than Afghanistan. I was suddenly grateful that Ryan had made me wear my armor.

Deputy Governor Fouad Hikmat welcomed us in his office, undamaged by the suicide bomb. At the center of the ornate, wood-paneled, heavily air-conditioned room was a giant mock-up of "New Ramadi," a $6 billion plan for a new city, the governor's dream. Designed by a South Korean company to help win a huge construction contract, New Ramadi was to include sixteen thousand homes and villas, office space, cafés, and restaurants — even an international exhibition center. Since virtually no new housing had been built here in decades, Anbar needed at least eighty-three thousand new housing units just to meet the province's birthrate, Hikmat said.

But the grand vision demanded good security, which despite the surge of US forces, was still a challenge. Hikmat himself was proof of that. In office for only eighteen months, he had been shot at thirty times, he told us; Allah had protected him, "all praise be unto him," the translator added. But neither God nor the Anbaris' American protectors had yet provided this Sunni region with enough clean water, electricity, or real jobs to meet local needs. Anbaris averaged less than four hours of power a day. The province lacked essential services. Though Ramadi was less than sixty miles from Baghdad, security checkpoints made the trip a three-hour drive. But even if security in the province improved, as Ryan and his commanders predicted it would, "New Ramadi" seemed a pipedream.

Qasim Mohammad Abed al-Fahadawi, the dynamic fifty-five-year-old provincial governor, sounded even more bullish about Anbar's future. Prime Minister Maliki and the central government in Baghdad had routinely shortchanged his region, he complained. But somehow he would find financing for his pet project. Iraqis loved visiting Anbar, he asserted. Under Saddam, the province had been a vacation destination. Tourism would rebound, and Iraqis would vacation once more at the resort at Lake Habbaniyah.

I glanced at Ryan, whose poker face hid even a hint of skepticism. It was hard to imagine Iraqi families braving Baghdad's gauntlet of security checkpoints and still-dangerous roads to vacation at the dilapidated, rubbish-strewn, state-owned villas on a lake that was evaporating in a five-year drought compounded by upriver damming and massive overuse. Privately, American development officials were calling the ruin of a resort a "do-over." Ditto the giant state-owned glass factory on the edge of town that hadn't produced a single glass since a bombing in 2006. The government still paid salaries of the roughly 5,500 employees, but those payments would end soon. Where would they find work?

The governor had paid dearly for the lack of security. Widely admired by Americans for his role in the Sunni Awakening, he had lost his left hand in the province's deadliest suicide bombing at his compound in late 2009. The US military had saved his life. Rushed for treatment to a nearby military hospital, Qassim was later flown to the United States and given a new, state-of-the-art robotic hand.

When his compound was hit yet again on July 4, 2010, shortly before my visit, the Iraqis whom Ryan's First Brigade had trained made none of their earlier mistakes. Anticipating a second strike, the task force chief established an outer perimeter to prevent people from entering the crime scene. He left dead bodies in place: the hardest thing for an Iraqi officer to do, Ryan told me. His team ferried the wounded to medical care and collected evidence. As their American advisers looked on, the Iraqis had cased, photographed, and mapped the site, systematically collecting body parts, blast fragments, glass, wire, cement chips — anything that might help identify the bomb and its maker. The evidence was then bagged, sealed, and registered. After locating the bomber's head and upper torso, they severed his head, plucked out his eye, and sent it in an ambulance to a nearby forensics lab, also American equipped and funded. Though the iris did not find a match in a US biometrics database of jihadis, the compound's security video revealed that the bomber, clearly visible on camera, had been escorted into the compound by a provincial passport officer. This had been an inside job.

Investigators issued the first arrest warrants within twelve hours of the attack. Brig. Gen. Baha'a al-Karkhi, Ramadi's energetic police chief, told me that while the passport official had fled, six other Iraqis, four of whom also worked in the compound, had been arrested and charged — all based on evidence and not merely on what, in Saddam's day, would have been forced confessions.

A former military officer from Baghdad, Baha'a was one of those experienced Sunni army officers whom L. Paul (Jerry) Bremer III, America's viceroy in Iraq, had sent home after having officially disbanded the Iraqi army in 2003. Many in Iraq and Washington considered this among Bush's worst early mistakes in a war that was littered with them.

Focused now on completing his training mission in Anbar, shutting down operations here, and getting his soldiers home without death or further injury, Ryan Cutchin was working around such stupidity, corruption, and the waste of war. He did not complain that roughly one of every four dollars spent on contracting in Iraq and Afghanistan — roughly $60 billion over the decade — had been misspent, and mostly by Americans.[20] He dodged my questions about whether the United States had really "succeeded" in Iraq. Would Prime Minister Maliki, paranoid and dictatorial, try to cut the Sunnis and Kurds out of power, as so many Iraqis and American experts had predicted? Would long-standing sectarian tensions between Sunnis and Shia, Kurds and Arabs, Christians and Muslims explode once American soldiers were gone? Ryan changed the subject.

On the last day of my last embed, I pressed him again: Had this war been worth the cost? Had the losses throughout his three deployments — the death and wounding of friends, the far more widespread suffering of Iraqis, the interminable separations from his wife and children — been worth toppling Saddam and giving Iraq a shot at democracy?

"Am I talking to Judy Miller, my old friend," Ryan asked me, "or Judith Miller, the reporter?"

My heart sank at his implicit verdict. We hugged and said good-bye.

Polls in the summer of 2010 showed that 80 percent of Iraqis wanted American forces to leave. But many Iraqi activists who were struggling to save their country from sectarian and ideological extremism complained bitterly about what they saw as America's abandonment.

"What's your rush?" Mowaffak al-Rubaie asked when I visited him that summer in Baghdad's Green Zone, the American-guarded Iraqi Government Center. A former adviser to Maliki who had fallen out with him, as had so many other former counselors, Rubaie feared for Iraq when America was no longer there to help Iraqis navigate their treacherous new political terrain. "America still has forces in Italy, Germany, and South Korea, and those conflicts ended decades ago," he told me. I suppressed an impulse to remind him that American forces were not being targeted, maimed, and killed in Naples, Frankfurt, or Seoul.

Like so many Iraqis, Rubaie argued that only the presence of American forces, however unpopular with the average Iraqi, would prevent a coup d'état, the outbreak of another civil war, or the "Lebanonization" of Iraq — a splitting again along sectarian lines. Iraqis had "failed miserably" so far to build new state institutions, he said. Corruption was endemic. Few among the elite trusted Maliki, who cared only about perpetuating his own power and was overly influenced by Iran, they complained. His repressive Interior Ministry employed five times as many Iraqis as the Ministry of Education, yet even Baghdad was still far from secure.

The only truly secure, thriving place in Iraq was one hundred miles north of Baghdad: the Kurdish region — the "other Iraq," as Kurds relished calling their three prosperous, liberated provinces. With their own flag, their prime minister, their 175,000-man army, or Peshmerga — in Kurdish, "those who face death" — and even their own immigration stamp, the region's four million Kurds seemed to be living in a different country. This infuriated Baghdad, of course.

Kurdistan was possibly the most pro-American place on the planet in 2010. Kurds loved thanking American visitors for having liberated them from Saddam's murderous regime — something, understandably, I didn't hear often from Iraqi Sunnis. The Kurds knew that the United States was responsible for their relative success. They had been essentially running their own affairs since 1991, when President George H. W. Bush created the no-fly zone north of the 36th parallel after Saddam had crushed their US-encouraged uprising. The Kurds, at long last, were governing themselves with a determination born of vengeance.

Kurdish per capita gross domestic product had skyrocketed since Saddam's fall; illiteracy had been reduced from 56 percent to 16 percent; foreign investment was pouring into the Kurdish Regional Government — an estimated $35 billion from neighboring Turkey alone since 2003, and $5 billion from Iran. Since the KRG had ratified a liberal new foreign investment law in 2006, a half-dozen international airline carriers had begun operating direct flights to Erbil, often bypassing Baghdad. The regional government had built more than two thousand schools; there were now seven universities in Kurdistan; many schools offered English, rather than Arabic, as their second language. Though the world's thirty-million-strong Kurds considered themselves the largest nation without its own independent state, Iraqi Kurds enjoyed success that their brethren in neighboring Turkey, Iran, and Syria could envy.

Cranes vastly outnumbered minarets in this predominantly Sunni region. Majidi Mall Shopping and Entertaining Centre was mobbed, and Dream City, a new apartment complex, was selling some units for over $1 million each. Israelis were rumored to have bought several units. Unlike Iraqi Arabs, Kurds had been doing business informally with Israel for years and had few hang-ups about the "Zionist entity," as Israel was sometimes denigrated in Baghdad.

Kurdistan was safer than Turkey, its murder rate lower than Chicago's. Not a single American soldier had been killed in the region.

But Kurdistan had problems, Fuad Hussein, a key adviser to the Kurdish Regional Government, acknowledged when we met for lunch at the newly refurbished Erbil International Hotel. Corruption was still rampant: some called it worse than Baghdad's. But Kurdish officials didn't just pocket proceeds and leave their people without basic services, like their kleptocratic Arab counterparts.

Yes, Kurdish president Massoud Barzani was far too thin-skinned, given the political and economic clout he was accumulating. Although a secular opposition party called Gorran, or "Change," was taking hold, journalists and other critics who displeased the Kurdish establishment sometimes wound up in jail on trumped-up charges — or, in the case of a few critics, including a journalist, dead. Violent intimidation and honor crimes remained challenging, given the Kurds' powerful clan structure. But enlightened Kurdish officials understood that such repression was bad for business, antithetical to the "Other Iraq" brand they were striving to nurture. The Kurds were the winners in America's invasion to overthrow Saddam.

Still, Fuad worried. Why was the United States leaving Iraq "empty-handed," having invested so much "blood and treasure?" he asked me.

Americans were tired of the two wars since 9/11 that had consumed and exhausted us, I told him. With almost 4,500 American soldiers dead and 30,000 more wounded, and with the deaths of over 100,000 Iraqis, the exile or displacement of over 2 million Iraqi civilians, and over a trillion US dollars spent, America's patience was gone. Most Americans no longer cared what happened in Iraq.

"Iraq is too important and dangerous to be left to others," he warned. "How will you protect your interests here and your friends?" I had no answer. Washington would offer no guarantees. We both knew that America had betrayed them before and might do so again. Though Kurdish officials had repeatedly invited the US military to open a base in their region, Washington demurred, given the opposition of Baghdad, Turkey, and Iran, all of which feared that the Kurds might try to turn their semi-autonomous region into an independent state.

Though the geopolitical cards were stacked against them, Barham Salih, then the region's president, told me the night before I left that he hoped Kurdistan would become a "model" for what all of Iraq might be — if Iraqis could overcome their religious and sectarian differences and autocratic traditions. That was a big "if."

When I left Iraq in mid-2010, many Iraqis and American analysts were still optimistic about Iraq's future. The success of the surge in stabilizing the country, Kurdistan's dynamism, the rise of the historically oppressed Shiites, and the largely untapped potential of oil-rich Iraq — already the region's second-largest oil producer — led many Middle East analysts to defend America's war. No matter how grave the mistakes, Saddam was gone. Neither he nor his even more brutal, psychotic sons would torment Iraqis or the region again. While Iraq had destroyed its stocks of chemical and biological weapons and agents and ended its nuclear weapons program before the US invasion, chief weapons inspector Charles Duelfer said that debriefings of Saddam in prison and thousands of hours of taped conversations with his top aides showed that he had remained determined to acquire nuclear weapons and to re-create his chemical and germ weapons capabilities once sanctions were lifted. In 2008 Duelfer disclosed that, in 1998, after President

Clinton had bombed Iraq's weapons facilities, Saddam had signed a top-secret order (only three copies were made) declaring that Iraq would no longer be bound by or comply with UN resolutions. After his arrest, Saddam told his FBI debriefer that restoring his country's WMD arsenals was the only way to "reassert Iraq's place in the region" and "match the military capabilities of others."[21]

American security had been strengthened by Saddam's ouster, said optimists such as Francis "Bing" West, a former marine who had made sixteen trips to Iraq and written an influential book endorsing the war. Despite such "anomalies" as the humiliation and abuse of Iraqi detainees at Abu Ghraib prison, West argued, no nation had ever fought "a more restrained and honorable war." Former ambassador Peter Galbraith, a long-standing champion of and adviser to the Kurds, whom I had met in 1979 when he was a staff aide on the Senate Foreign Relations Committee, argued that life for 80 percent of Iraqis — not just the Kurds, but also the majority Shiites — was immeasurably better than it had been under Saddam.[22] Violence was abating. Oil exports were slowly recovering. Eager for a second term as prime minister, Maliki had secured American support in American-brokered talks by promising to share power with his rivals and abide by Iraq's new constitution. That promise would soon prove hollow, but supporters of the war took him at his word.

Still, President Obama did not claim "victory" in his speech at Fort Bragg, North Carolina, when he welcomed the last American forces home from Iraq in December 2011. Thanking the soldiers for their "sacrifice," he spoke about being proud to have left a "stable, sovereign, and self-reliant Iraq" that could take charge of its own future. Even then, given all the danger signs I had seen and concerns I had heard on my latest trip, his assessment seemed wildly optimistic. Worse, the war had strengthened Iran, a far more tenacious regional foe.

In a foreword to the US Marines' volumes on the surge and counterinsurgency, Lt. Gen. John F. Kelly steered far clear of glory. "Words like 'won' or 'victory,' " he wrote in 2009, didn't apply in counterinsurgency operations. Insurgencies grew from problems and discontents within a given society. "Solve the problems and the insurgency goes away." But, he warned presciently, it wasn't necessarily "defeated."[23]

America had only itself to blame for the

insurgency that had nearly defeated US forces in Iraq, he wrote. Whether the "humiliation" of disbanding the Iraqi army in 2003, or America's "overreaction" to "small acts of resistance or violence" by Iraqis, the "heavy-handed approach" of both US soldiers and civilians had played into Al Qaeda's and the militant Shiite militia's ugly narratives. Yes, the belated shift in 2007 to a counterinsurgency strategy, including the surge of US forces coupled with the Iraqi Awakening, had staved off defeat and enabled the United States to stabilize Iraq, curtail much of the violence in most of the country, and leave. But progress had come too late, at far too high a cost. As I left Iraq, I feared that stability would require a sustained US military presence for several more years. That, I knew, was impossible given America's exhaustion and the growing belief at home that despite the surge's success, the war had been a terrible mistake.

Negotiations in Baghdad over America's presence in Iraq soon bogged down. At Iran's behest in late 2011, Prime Minister Maliki stalled efforts to renew the so-called Security Agreement required to permit US combat forces to remain in Iraq.[24]

President Obama, eager to claim credit for having ended America's "stupid" war and withdraw all American combat forces from Iraq, rejected his military's advice that twenty-six thousand US soldiers would be needed to ensure stability and continued political progress there. His negotiators offered to leave fewer than ten thousand soldiers in place. "Maliki knew then that the US offer was not serious," said Gen. Jack Keane, a retired four-star widely regarded as a key promoter of the "surge."

Soon after the US troop withdrawal, Maliki ordered the arrest of his longtime rival, Sunni vice president Tariq al-Hashimi, forcing him to flee Iraq and eventually sentencing him to death in absentia for allegedly running assassination squads. Breaking his pledges to rival Iraqis and Washington, Maliki made himself interior minister, defense minister, and chief of intelligence, and repressed his critics, especially Sunnis.

Outraged by Maliki's crackdown, the Sunnis of Anbar and other minority strongholds rebelled again. Weekly security incidents throughout Iraq, which had dropped from an average of 1,600 in 2007 to fewer than 100 by March 2012, began rising less than three months after US combat forces were withdrawn. By the end of 2013, the UN reported that 8,868 Iraqis had been killed that year, the highest death toll since the worst of the sectarian bloodletting in 2006. Ba'athist generals and other disenfranchised Sunnis allied themselves once more with Al Qaeda's lineal successor, the new jihadis of the Islamic State in Iraq and al-Sham, or ISIS, an even more extreme, better financed, and more dangerous group that had emigrated from Iraq and planted roots in civil war–torn Syria. Stripped of competent, nonsectarian officers by Maliki, the American-equipped and -trained Iraqi army folded. Its officers, Maliki's Shiite cronies, fled their posts. In August 2014, ISIS overran the western towns of Sinjar and Makhmour, reaching Gwer, only fifteen miles from Erbil, the Kurdish capital. Kurdistan's famed Peshmerga, ill equipped and poorly trained, had also crumbled, suffering a humiliating defeat. Too many of its officers had bought the Kurdish dream and traded in their military fatigues for real estate licenses. Desperate, both Iraq's prime minister and the Kurdish region's president appealed once more to Washington for weapons with which to fight, intelligence support, and air cover. By late 2014, ISIS had seized territory in Iraq and Syria equal to that of Great Britain. In Fallujah and Ramadi, where Ryan Cutchin's soldiers had made such progress, militant Islam's black flag flew once more.

CHAPTER 2
NIGHTCLUB ROYALTY IN THE SHADOW OF THE BOMB

I was lucky. Being in the right place at the right time for a journalist has always been important.

My good fortune began at birth: I am American. Each time I return from a reporting trip to the Middle East or the Soviet Union, or Africa, I am relieved that I live in a secular country whose leaders are chosen — and can be gotten rid of — in authentic elections, and where people generally obey laws that are approved by citizens, not dictated by God or an autocrat. Though I am aware of my country's many failings, I have never doubted that the United States is a miracle.

My husband, Jason Epstein, a publisher, editor, and an intimidating intellectual, winces when I say this. His patriotism is more nuanced than mine. He believes that to be an American is, as Henry James said, a "complex fate" — more complex, in fact, than James himself could have imagined. Jason knows America's history far better than most and deeply regrets President George Bush and what his election twice reveals about the electorate.

Where does it come from, my unshakeable faith in America's basic decency? Partly from my exposure as a journalist to cruelty and corruption elsewhere. But it also comes from the other most important man in my life.

One journalist attributed what he called my "dramatic way of looking at the world" to my father's career in show business.[1] Though the writer got much about me wrong, that observation was on the mark. My father's life was nothing if not dramatic.

Bill Miller, Jewish and Russian-born, was one of those larger-than-life, self-made Americans. A vaudeville "hoofer" turned talent agent, he became a successful nightclub owner and influential entertainment impresario. If you grew up in New York during World War II, you have probably heard of, and perhaps visited, the Riviera, his Jersey nightclub on the Englewood Cliffs in Fort Lee adjacent to the George Washington Bridge, just across the Hudson from Manhattan. If you went to Las Vegas after we moved there in 1953, when New Jersey condemned the Riv to build a highway, you may have seen one of his shows in the sixties or seventies.

Nightclubs, Vegas, and show business were Mob territory. And though he insisted that he was not connected — a lengthy FBI investigation reached a similar conclusion — my father shared the reflexive anticommunism pervasive in such circles. He was conservative and a patriot. His hero was Ronald Reagan, whom he knew and considered America's greatest president.

America meant salvation. Had my grandfather not dragged him and his five siblings out of their Russian village near Pinsk, he never tired of reminding us, the Millers would have died in the gas chambers of Auschwitz, like so many of his relatives, or lived in the prison of "Communist Russia," as the Soviet Union was known in my home.

His childhood was an immigrant cliché. He came to America in 1905, a year old, and helped his poor father at the pushcart twelve hours a day, six days a week. My grandfather would rather die than work on the Sabbath, my father told me proudly. Americanized "Bill" had no such compunctions. He worked every day, but never finished high school.

My mother, Mary Theresa Connolly, was

my father's polar opposite. The Connollys, my mother's Irish-Catholic family, had immigrated to America illegally. Though my mother was born in Chicago, her entire family was deported to Canada when she was a toddler. Three years later, my grandfather got a visa to return.

My mother and father lived the American dream. The Jewish go-getter married the pretty Irish-Catholic showgirl and lived happily ever after — until their marriage ended when I was sixteen. My father's late nights, talent-scouting trips far from home, and entourage of gorgeous showgirls whose company he seemed to prefer to ours finally drove my mother to drink and despair.

Until then, my younger sister, Susan, my older half brother, Jimmy, and I knew little but privilege. There were large homes with swimming pools and rose gardens, private schools and lessons of all kinds, two ill-tempered but fiercely protective dachshunds, and a nanny also imported from Germany. I could never fathom why my father, who because of the Holocaust hated all things German, wanted German dogs and hired an austere German spinster to help raise his children. He was a complicated man.

An hour away from Las Vegas was something else that shaped my life far more than show business. The site was off-limits to most of us at the time, but living under its shadow marked me in ways I understood only later.

The dog had melted. The rumor raced through my first-grade class at John S. Park Elementary School in Las Vegas a few days after "Harry" was detonated at dawn at the Nevada Proving Ground, sixty-five miles northwest of my home.

A family in Indian Springs, twenty-five miles from ground zero, had returned home after the test to find their pet a puddle of blood and bones. The government, we were told, had supposedly suppressed news of the incident.

There probably never was a dead dog. But there were dead sheep — over four thousand, by some claims; about a quarter of the southern Utah and Nevada herds — as well as dead pigs, rabbits, cattle, and other livestock for miles southeast of the blast. Then the goats turned blue, literally.

Just before the detonation on May 19, 1953, a strong wind altered the meteorological conditions that the US Atomic Energy Commission had mistakenly anticipated. Radioactive debris of the test spread to St.

George, a tiny farming town in neighboring Utah. Rather than evacuation, which might have "alarmed" the local population, according to AEC files declassified nearly three decades later, residents were advised to "shelter in place" with their doors and windows shut until the radioactive danger "passed." On a major freeway near the site, some forty cars registered low but above-average levels of radioactivity. The AEC instructed car owners to hose down their vehicles and themselves. Neither the unusually rainy weather nor the flu-like symptoms that some residents reported were connected to the blast, the commissioners told us. Even the radioactive "snow" found as far away as Rhode Island did not stir much debate.

I remember Harry — or "Dirty Harry," as the test was eventually called. Trudy Siebenlist, our nanny, had set my alarm for a quarter to five in the morning to ensure that I wouldn't miss the historic event. It was pitch-black when I crept out of the bedroom. I slipped out the front door of the ranch house we had recently bought near the Las Vegas Strip.

I sat with our cat on our crabgrass and cactus lawn, waiting. At exactly five o'clock, night became day. Was I dreaming? Did I really see or just imagine the flash that lit up the skies? It wasn't the familiar yellow, pink, and lavender of a Nevada dawn. In my childhood memory, it was ripe red — beautiful, and irresistibly terrifying. Brighter than a thousand suns, as nuclear historian Robert Jungk wrote later.

The flash was followed by stillness, a slight smell of iron in the air, and a metallic taste on my tongue; the sensation you get from licking a spoon after the ice cream is gone. TV broadcasters said the test was visible as far away as Idaho.

I was only six and in first grade, but I sensed that the bomb was special. I knew that being so close to something so dangerous made us different: I was living next to what American officials told us was a major "battlefield" of the Cold War on the "frontier of freedom."

There was a debate in Las Vegas about whether it was wise to test nuclear bombs in the atmosphere so close to a major population center. But skeptics were drowned out by the media and our town fathers, my own among them. Nuclear testing was our patriotic duty, insisted Hank Greenspun, the influential publisher of the *Las Vegas Morning Sun.* His closeness to the AEC and Pentagon officials and access to "inside" information had influenced my father and other Vegas entrepreneurs about the need to continue testing on American soil to "maintain our lead" over the "Reds." Atoms, Greenspun said, were as "American as apple pie."[2]

People concerned about the safety of testing were unpatriotic and undermining the city's economy, Greenspun argued in his influential column, Where I Stand, which was required reading in our household. Las Vegas depended on tourists. The testing was one of the city's "natural" attractions. President Truman's designation of Las Vegas as an area "critical to national defense" made it eligible for federal funds for housing and infrastructure that were paying for its phenomenal growth. Frivolous accounts and rumors spread by a few "sensation-seeking reporters" threatened not only America's national security but also the city's welfare. When the AEC issued a press release attributing the death of sheep in Utah to "unprecedented cold weather," Greenspun warned that "panic can spread where no danger exists."

My mother said nothing, but was not persuaded. Occasionally she would confront my father about her fears. I listened to what became a familiar refrain behind their bedroom door: Vegas was no place to be raising children. The Mob, drinking and gambling, drugs and whores were bad enough, but now her children were exposed to radiation. She missed New York. She hated the sun and the sandstorms, the dry air, the cactus. She had found a dead rattlesnake in the garage. Could radiation have killed it? Had my father heard about the blue goats? Or the dog that had melted? Couldn't we move, as we did eventually, to Los Angeles?

The AEC's public relations campaign aimed at making Nevadans "feel at home with neutrons trotting around" and to encourage "local pride in being in the limelight," according to now declassified government memos written shortly before the tests began, was effective. The commission's two-pronged strategy sought to convince those near the site that the tests were safe and vital to national security. If the United States was to win the arms race against the Reds, we had to test. A March 1953 editorial in the *Deseret News,* the daily published by the anticommunist, progovernment Mormon Church in Salt Lake City, called the nuclear trials "tragic and insane." However, it concluded, "so long as we live in an atomic world, we must and will continue to learn more about this power and how to survive it." After the first test at the site two years earlier, the paper's lead editorial, mirroring those of papers throughout America, had celebrated the dawn of the testing age: "Spectacular Atomic Explosions Mean Progress in Defense," the editorial's headline proclaimed. "No Cause for Panic."[3]

Every detonation in Nevada, the AEC assured us, was being "carefully evaluated" to protect our safety. After six full years of open-air nuclear tests, the government claimed to have confirmed that fallout from the tests had "not caused illness or injured the health of anyone living near the test site."

America's arsenal of thirteen weapons in 1947 had increased to fifty by the time I was born a year later. I memorized the names of the tests the way other kids learned the names of presidents. "Able," in 1951, the first test at the Proving Ground, as the Nevada Test Site was then known, was followed twenty-four hours later by "Baker," a more powerful, eight-kiloton device that awakened much of the city. Then came "Easy" and "Fox," almost three times as powerful as "Baker," the blast wave of which had shattered show windows in two Las

Vegas car dealerships minutes after detonation.

The bomb, like the radiation, was all around us — as much a part of my childhood as jacks, roller-skating, skipping rope, and, this being Vegas, strippers. A warning poster from the Clark County Civil Defense Agency was attached by magnets to our fridge door reminding us to keep a "well-balanced" supply of food on hand and a list of telephone numbers to call in an emergency. Since most Vegas homes had no basements, my parents argued for months about whether to build a bomb shelter in the backyard. My mother won. The underground, blast-proof shelter that my father purchased from a friend — "wholesale," not "retail," as he had boasted to my unimpressed mother — was not installed and was given to a friend.

She did yield to my appeals to take us to J.C. Penney to see the display of some fifty mannequins two weeks before they were blown out of bed in a colonial two-story home, complete with aluminum venetian blinds, that had been built for a sixteen-kiloton test at the site. The plastic people were used to assess the impact of the blasts by the Federal Civil Defense Administration, which was subjecting US soldiers, animals, and plants to ever more powerful bombs to determine blast and radiation effects. The mannequins were a major attraction for the department store chain, which proudly announced that it had donated their clothing for the test. Equally popular were the "before" and "after" photographs of the "Annie" house tests published in the *Las Vegas Review-Journal,* accompanied by a warning: "These mannequins could have been real people; in fact, they could have been you. Volunteer now for Civil Defense."[4]

In 1956, ranchers who had lost sheep and other livestock sued the AEC in federal district court. The judge accepted the government's argument that the animals' deaths had been caused by "inadequate feeding, unfavorable winter range conditions, and infectious diseases." The lawsuit received little publicity.

By the late 1950s, as the novelty of atomic testing waned and alarm about safety and radiation was growing, Greenspun and other city elders tried to allay fear and generate buzz to keep visitors coming to Vegas and parking along Highway 95 to watch the tests. One of their solutions was "Miss Atomic Bomb of 1957," aka Lee Merlin, a beaming bathing beauty whose outstretched arms welcomed fellow Americans to Vegas, her swimsuit covered demurely by a mushroom cloud.

Even after our family left Vegas for Miami Beach and then Los Angeles, my fascination with all things nuclear continued. I tore labels off Kix cereal boxes to send away for atomic bomb rings and other nuclear paraphernalia. Mom drew the line on Christmas tree ornaments, refusing to let me order the silver bulbs decorated with symbols of the atom. Christmas was about peace, not death. She also nixed the salt and pepper shakers that topped the Formica breakfast tables of many Vegas families: Fat Man and Little Boy, America's bombs dropped on Hiroshima and Nagasaki.

There was little debate about President Truman's decision to drop "the Bomb," never mind two. Analysts declared that the use of nuclear weapons had forced Japan to surrender and saved a million American soldiers. Many Americans like me grew up believing that stockpiles of tens of thousands of nuclear weapons were unsettling, but essential. Only decades later did I begin to doubt their utility, and the secrecy surrounding them.

In 2005, when I went to Las Vegas to write an article for the *Times* about the new

Atomic Testing Museum, I was flooded with memories. The museum featured a collection of the iconic postcards that had drawn a record number of tourists to Las Vegas. My favorite was a black-and-white photo of the mushroom cloud rising behind Wilbur Clark's Desert Inn — the D.I., as everyone called it. I tasted my first cocktail there: a Shirley Temple with two cherries. At bars at the Sahara, the Flamingo, the Dunes, and the Sands, tourists and residents had sampled other "Atomic Cocktails" from the recipe book my mother favored, *Mixed Drinks for Modern Times.*

I was fascinated by a blowup from the June 21, 1952, edition of *Collier's* magazine. A dozen children were lying facedown in a schoolyard, hands cupped over their heads, abandoned bikes nearby. "A is for Atom," the cover declared. I instantly recalled the drills at John S. Park Elementary. We "atomic kids" sure knew how to protect ourselves against "the big one."

In the 1950s, most Americans trusted the government. Las Vegas was proud of its status as the capital of skin and sin. Vegas glorified the testing program and the scientists and technicians who worked at the Nevada Test Site, barely noticing that they had less and less interaction with the city's residents. Many of them would relocate for months on end to a top-secret test site town, appropriately named Mercury.

I spent the night in Mercury when I visited NTS as a *Times* reporter after 9/11 to report on the nation's biodefense and nuclear weapons complex. It was almost as empty as the growing list of Nevada ghost towns. Its pool hall, bowling alley, and movie theater, where scientists and other weaponeers once relaxed, were closed.

The Testing Museum displayed photographs of life at the site. By 2005, we had learned disturbing information about the tests. "Harry" was part of an eleven-shot testing series called Operation Upshot-Knothole. Beginning on March 17, 1953, and ending June 4, the climax was a sixty-one-kiloton test aptly called "Climax." The eleven blasts unleashed a total force of over 250 kilotons in less than three months — about twenty times that of the bomb that destroyed Hiroshima. Several of its "dirty" blasts had rained radioactive debris on the sparsely populated downwind towns of southern Utah and Nevada, according to an early, comprehensive account of the testing, killing about 25 percent of the sheep.[5]

In 1982, in a wrongful death suit filed decades earlier by twenty-four cancer victims and their relatives from St. George (population, 4,500), Frank Butrico, a US Public Health Service radiation safety monitor, testified bravely that the town had been doused repeatedly with "Dirty Harry" fallout, which sent his instruments "off the scales." The Nevada Test Site's staff had ordered him to report that the radiation levels were just "a little bit above normal" and "not in the range of being harmful."[6]

As more information was declassified in the late 1970s and early 1980s through congressional hearings and lawsuits, we learned that the AEC's primary concern had not been our health and safety but securing information for the weapons program that only nuclear testing could produce. The AEC had been a shameless cheerleader for a health and safety monitoring program that the Pentagon had co-opted by 1953. At a commission meeting after yet another test had rained fallout on St. George, Gordon Dean, then head of the AEC, noted that at least one commissioner had been unhappy enough with what he called the "public relations" aspects of the test to argue for a testing delay. But the tests were "so important" to national security, Dean noted for posterity in his personal diary, that "we will have to go ahead. We just have to take a chance."[7]

By 1955, Lewis Strauss, Dean's successor, was battling a Nevada legislator who had introduced legislation demanding that the program be moved out of state. Other AEC commissioners joined Strauss in protesting such outrageous interference. "We must not let anything interfere with this series of tests — nothing!" Commissioner Thomas Murray declared.[8]

As declassified documents would show, the AEC had consistently lied about the health and safety risks of radiation to between 250,000 and 500,000 American soldiers, airmen, sailors, marines, and civilians whom the Pentagon estimated were exposed to radioactive debris from the tests.[9] Published in 1980, *Atomic Soldiers,* a slender volume by Howard Rosenberg, a friend and investigative journalist for ABC, described how soldiers were ordered to conduct maneuvers right under the cloud, sometimes without protective clothing or glasses, to see how well they would perform their missions. Describing the soldiers' subsequent battles with cancer and in court for compensation, Howard's book deplored the national security elitism that "allowed a few men to make decisions that affect us all."

By the end of the 1970s, nearly a thousand people had sued the government for radiation-related damages in federal court. But records show that the Justice Department had yet to pay a penny in court-ordered nuclear-related compensation. Not until 1979 did the government concede in a federal lawsuit that there was "some risk associated with exposure to radioactive fall-out." [10]

Some twenty-five years after the ranchers filed their suit seeking compensation for their irradiated livestock, the judge who had initially ruled against them ordered a new trial held when information secured under the Freedom of Information Act suggested that the commission had known almost from the start of the program that detonation yields were unreliable and that the testing was potentially unsafe.

Due partly to growing public alarm, atmospheric testing was outlawed in 1963 by the Limited Test Ban Treaty. But the detonation of more powerful weapons continued, underground, for almost thirty more years. By 1992, when a worldwide moratorium on nuclear testing took effect, some 1,053 tests had been conducted, 90 percent of them at the Nevada Test Site. Given the paucity of epidemiological studies, we will probably never know precisely how much extra radiation the "downwinders" living so close to the site absorbed, or the nature or full extent of the damage done to us Las Vegas residents by repeated exposures.

In 1997 and 1999, reports by the National Cancer Institute determined that atmospheric tests at NTS had spread radioactive iodine 131 across much of the United States, particularly in 1952, 1953, 1955 (the years my family lived in Vegas), and 1957. The 1999 report concluded that although scientists thought the exposure levels had still been very low, the increased I-131 from the Nevada atmospheric tests would probably wind up producing "between 11,300 and 212,000" additional cases of thyroid cancer in the United States. The downwinders, vindicated by the panel's belated link between cancer and the testing, noted that I-131 was only one of scores of isotopes produced by nuclear fissioning. The studies had not examined isotopes such as strontium 90, cesium 137, zirconium, and other atomic debris, most of which had even longer half-lives than I-131. We would probably never know, wrote Preston J. Truman, who created Downwinders, an early anti-nuclear group, "how many innocent, unwitting, and unsuspecting Americans had died" because of the tests.

CHAPTER 3
THE *NEW YORK TIMES*, THE TOKEN

I got my job as a reporter in the *New York Times* Washington bureau in 1977 through affirmative action. It was the job of my dreams.

It was also a job for which, by *Times* standards, I was unqualified. But the paper hired me anyway. It needed women.

Three years earlier, seven *Times* women had filed what became a class action suit on behalf of some 550 women at the paper, accusing the *Times* of sex discrimination. Their case was rock solid. So was that of the plaintiffs in another suit also filed in 1974 — the paper's minority employees, who accused it of racial discrimination. The *Times*'s leaders, who had always thought of themselves as liberal and enlightened, were alarmed.

In their depositions and public statements, the paper's lawyers had derided the women's charges as "frivolous" and "devoid of substance and rationality" — women who protest too much were often dismissed then, and even today, as hysterical. But employment statistics did not lie, and they were devastating.

Nan Robertson, the Pulitzer Prize–winning reporter who later chronicled the paper's sexual discrimination, summarized the case.[1] No women appeared on the paper's masthead of twenty-one names at the top of the editorial page, nor were there any female vice presidents or even women in a position to advance to that post. There were no female columnists, photographers, or members of the eleven-man board. None of the twenty-two national correspondents was a woman. There was only one female foreign bureau chief: Flora Lewis, the brilliant former wife of a *Times* executive; she had just been appointed to Paris. Only 4 of the paper's 31 cultural critics were women. There was only one woman sports reporter. Four of the 75 copy editors were women. The *Times,* which employed some six thousand people at the time, had 385 male reporters, and 40 women, 11 of whom worked in the Family/Style Section. In the largest, most prestigious bureau, Washington, only 3 of the 35 reporters were women. "There were no women in the pipeline for power," Robertson concluded.[2]

But discrimination against women ran deeper. Although the paper was subject to the Civil Rights Act of 1964, the few women who had managed to win jobs at the paper were paid substantially less than their male counterparts for the same work. The gap between the average salaries of male and female reporters was $59 a week — or some $3,000 a year.

Publisher Arthur Ochs Sulzberger, known affectionately as Punch, claimed to be shocked by the evidence that the Women's Caucus presented at a meeting with him and other senior executives in the spring of 1972. Robertson described how the caucus confronted Punch with "hard truths" about the plight of women toiling on the Sulzberger "plantation." Promises had been made, she told me years later. But although several women were subsequently hired — including me — the salary disparity between male and female reporters expanded. By the time the women finally filed suit in 1974, the gap had grown from roughly $3,000 to $4,800 a year.

While such discrimination was fairly standard in the sixties and seventies, the *Times*'s record was egregious given its sanctimonious editorials blaming others for such sins. While women composed 40 percent of the American labor force, they represented only 26.2 percent of full-time *Times* employees. And according to census figures, while women held 41 percent of all "editors and reporters" jobs in the nation, they held only 16 percent of these posts at the *Times*.[3]

I had heard little about the women's suit when John Finney and I had one of our occasional lunches in May 1977 at the Army-Navy Club, a male bastion near the White House. Finney was an avuncular fixture in the paper's Washington bureau, and we talked mostly about national security. I sought his advice on a story I was writing about Stealth cruise missile technology. Finney took pride in mentoring young reporters, most of them male. He complimented me on my recent articles about the Middle East, defense issues, and nuclear proliferation threats for the *Times*'s Sunday magazine, the *Washington Post,* and the *Progressive,* the nation's second-oldest monthly, published in Madison, Wisconsin, since 1909. That surprised me, because the *Progressive,* originally an organ of Robert La Follette's Progressive Party, was left-wing, especially on national security issues. I didn't think of Finney, a Pentagon correspondent who was rather conservative, as a *Progressive* reader.

Getting a reporting job in Washington in the mid-1970s was not nearly as tough as it became later. In my case, Erwin Knoll, the *Progressive*'s Washington editor, had chosen me to succeed him when he moved back to Madison to become the magazine's editor. I had done several freelance pieces for him. The job didn't pay much, but my association with the well-established journal guaranteed me credentials at the White House and most federal agencies — almost as valuable a commodity as money in the nation's status- and access-hungry capital. Knoll, a fervent civil libertarian who was deeply suspicious of government, was close to I. F. Stone, the irreverent journalist whose newsletter broke many a story about political finagling in Washington. Stone's scoops were usually based on information contained in the thousands of documents that agencies published but that few reporters had the time or energy to read. Since I shared "Izzy" Stone's interest in Israel and the Middle East, I had sought him out for advice before my own first trip to the region. Erwin later told me that Izzy had lobbied him relentlessly to offer me the job — not the last time I would benefit from an influential man's support.

Erwin knew that I had not always been so liberal. Having grown up, like Hillary Clinton, as a "Goldwater Girl," I had inherited some of the conservative convictions of my parents. But the official lies told to protect atomic testing in Vegas and then the Vietnam War shattered much of my trust in the government. At Ohio State University in Columbus and later at Barnard College in New York, I came to believe, as did so many in my generation, that the war was not only unnecessary but also immoral — a betrayal of the country's traditions, policies, and values.

In college I devoured Herbert Marcuse, Noam Chomsky, Germaine Greer (Betty Friedan was already passé), H. Rap Brown, and Frantz Fanon. Like so many others, I smoked dope and experimented with cocaine and LSD, reveling in the self-absorption that was a hallmark of the boomer generation.

Music and the arts were then my passion. I spent part of my year abroad between Barnard and graduate school in Brussels and London with my half brother Jimmy, who had started producing what became some of the Rolling Stones' greatest hits. Jimmy

— who would tragically die at age fifty-two of heroin-related liver failure in 1994 — was a son from my father's second, brief marriage. Since we hadn't spent much time together when we were young, I loved getting to know him. Though he was only six years older, he was already establishing himself as a musical force in London, the center of the sixties music revolution.

An avid R&B drummer and composer, Jimmy had remixed what became the Spencer Davis Group's first big American success — "Gimme Some Lovin'," whose driving beat made it a megahit in 1967. When Steve Winwood broke away to form his own rock group, Traffic, Jimmy produced its albums, too, among them the rock classic *Mr. Fantasy.*

Although I had enrolled at the London School of Economics, I quickly lost interest in my courses, preferring to watch Jimmy work — usually from midnight to dawn. Unlike other producers, he rarely stayed behind the glass wall separating him and the engineer from the musicians in the recording studio. When Jimmy got into the music, a friend recalled, he would abandon his giant console where tracks were mixed and appear in the studio, accompanying the musicians on drums, singing along in harmony, or adding an original sound to a track: a washboard, a whistle, a flute, a tambourine, finger cymbals, congas, castanets, and, my favorite, the cowbell that opened the Rolling Stones' classic "Honky Tonk Women."

Eddie Kramer, Jimmy's protégé and his favorite recording engineer, said years later that my brother was a true "musical impresario," who, like our father, knew how to bring musicians together, rehearse them 'til they dropped, and excite them about their work. Jimmy was "unstoppable," he told an interviewer.[4]

Jimmy was just starting to work with the Rolling Stones when I arrived to live in London. Though the reigning dean of rock today, Mick Jagger was anxious back then about bucking the prevailing trends, Jimmy told me. Friends were showering him with unsolicited, contradictory advice about what to record next. Jimmy weighed in emphatically: stick to your roots, he told Jagger. Be who you are, advice he gave everyone he loved, which I, too, would take to heart.

As much as I loved the musical scene, I knew that it would not be the focus of my life — and I missed America. So when I had a chance to apply for a full scholarship in a master's program at Princeton University's

Woodrow Wilson School of Public and International Affairs, I leapt at it. (The school, too, was short of women grad students. My class had four women and fifty men.) Thanks to Princeton, I fell in love with the Middle East and journalism.

In the summer of 1972, Princeton sent me to Jerusalem to write a paper required for my degree. The topic was one of Israel's early grassroots campaigns to stop the government from building an ugly housing compound on a hilltop overlooking Jerusalem, the eastern half of which Israel had annexed after the '67 war.[5]

My academic paper reflected none of the excitement I felt. After I finished my research in Israel, I traveled through Cyprus — Israel was then isolated from its Arab neighbors — to Cairo; Amman, Jordan; and Beirut, Lebanon. After interviewing officials and as many ordinary people as I could, since I didn't speak either Hebrew or Arabic, I was sure there would be another Arab-Israeli war — and soon. I had seen much that wasn't showing up in the newspapers. I sent an essay to the *Progressive* about a group of Israelis who called themselves "black panthers." These young Jews from North Africa, imitating their American counterparts, were protesting Israel's discrimination against Jews from Arab lands. The magazine published it. I saw my words in print and found my calling.

Six years later, over our lunch at the Army-Navy Club, Finney told me that he was about to be the *Times*'s Washington news editor — the second-ranking post in the bureau.

He admired an article I had written for the *Washington Post* about how environmentalists had used the plight of the pink-footed booby, an endangered bird that nests on Diego Garcia, to stop the expansion of the American base on that Indian Ocean island. (I was pro-booby.) Finney, a former navy officer who had served in the Philippines, knew Diego Garcia well.

He had also read some of my other freelance articles for *Science* magazine, the *New Republic,* and even my stories for National Public Radio, where I worked part-time as a national security correspondent.

I greatly admired Finney for having infuriated government officials with articles about how scientific advisers to the government had subsequently gone to work for companies seeking government contracts. Many of the 2,500 articles that carried his byline in his thirty years of reporting focused on the development of nuclear weapons, the satellite technology that guided them, and the arms race they had produced. There was nothing that John did not seem to know about the Atomic Energy Commission and nuclear proliferation, my first obsession since Las Vegas.

Despite his criticism of government, he respected Washington's institutions and the often anonymous civil servants who sustained them. "What they are doing is so thankless," he said, reflecting an unfashionable empathy for federal officials.

Finney confessed that he enjoyed having lunch with me because, unlike most women, I did not seem to mind the permanent cloud of pipe smoke that enveloped him. A binge cigarette smoker, I liked the smell of pipe tobacco and even cigars.

Would I be interested in joining the *Times*? he asked, popping the question casually.

I tried but failed to appear equally cool. Of course!

Finney said he would recommend me to A. M. Rosenthal, the *Times*'s executive editor. I shouldn't get my hopes up, he warned, but the timing might be propitious. The paper was hunting for "qualified" women reporters, tiptoeing around the women's lawsuit. Though I was five years out of

101

graduate school, had not attended journalism school, and had not worked full-time for a wire service or a daily regional newspaper — the traditional training grounds for *Times* reporters — I might be offered a job. I would, of course, have to spend at least six months to a year on the Metro desk in New York.

My elation evaporated. I can't do that, I told him.

"Why on earth not?" said Finney, a polite man who seemed stunned by my reluctance.

The reasons were personal, I told him. I had recently become romantically involved with someone and did not want to leave Washington, I said, carefully avoiding the man's name.

"You mean Les Aspin?" he asked. Finney had heard that I had moved into the Georgetown home of the Wisconsin Democratic congressman and Pentagon gadfly, whom I had gotten to know years earlier through my work for the *Progressive.*

"Surely you would not sacrifice a job at the *Times* because of a boyfriend?" he said, a statement more than a question.

"Oh yes I would. You can't take your typewriter home to bed with you at night."

Finney suppressed a smile. Perhaps I was not such a radical, his eyes suggested as he tamped down a wad of tobacco in his pipe. Well, he added coyly after several puffs, perhaps we could work around that "constraint."

"Don't discuss your living arrangements with Abe when you see him next week," he counseled.

Finney gave me a long list of topics I was *not* to discuss with the formidable Abe Rosenthal, the brilliant journalist who had revolutionized news coverage at the *Times* but was a polarizing figure inside the paper. Abe could be "challenging," another early mentor, Bernard Gwertzman, the *Times*'s State Department reporter, had warned me.

Abe was impossible; his moods swings were a legend. He was also smart, original, and utterly committed to the paper. He was determined to keep ideology out of the news sections. He knew, of course, that objectivity is an illusion — that every story's headline, word count, and placement reflect a judgment. Bias can be evident in the stories that the *Times* chooses to print, or print for only one edition, or delay publishing, or bury in the back of the thick Sunday paper or on Saturday, the week's least-well-read paper. Abe believed in making the news columns as impartial as possible and confining opinion to the editorial and op-ed pages, where it belonged. Violations of this ethos, however subtle or unconscious, could be punished ruthlessly.

Friends had warned me that Abe could be harsh and irascible one moment, schmaltzy the next. Nan Robertson, quoting another reporter, called him "a cross between Caligula and a Jewish mother."

I flew to New York for the meeting, replaying my earlier conversation with Hedrick Smith, the debonair Washington bureau chief who was planning to offer me a job as a reporter for the paper's financial section, provided that Abe approved.

Would I take any available slot in Washington? Rick Smith had asked me.

"Absolutely anything."

"How about the SEC?"

"Sure!" I said. "But remind me: What does it do exactly?"

"Well, you are willing to learn about it, aren't you?" A declaration, not a question.

In the spring of 1977, the list of "no-go" topics reverberated in my head as I paced in front of the *Times*'s New York headquarters, then the fourteen-story Gothic building on West Forty-Third Street, just off Times Square.

I was *not* to discuss Congressman Aspin, my sometimes leftist views, or political activism. Above all, I was *not* to tell Abe about my participation in the Columbia University student strike of 1968, which had paralyzed the campus for months and upended the university's administration. Abe had written a notorious attack on the protesters who had occupied the office of Columbia's president. I hadn't occupied that office, but I had been among those more than 720 antiwar students from Columbia and Barnard, its sister institution across Broadway, who had seized and occupied four other university buildings before being removed by the police.

I shall never forget the thrill I felt pushing my way for the first time through the heavy revolving glass door into the lobby of the *Times,* which would be my home for the next twenty-eight years.

Abe was on the third floor — intense, operatic, and unforgettable. A short man whose thick, black-rimmed glasses covered shrewd, lively eyes, he received me in his sitting room at the back of his office. Decorated in Japanese style, with a shoji screen and wall scrolls, the room's décor — a reflection of his time in the Tokyo bureau — was intended to convey inner peace. But it didn't.

Abe, who had won a Pulitzer for his reporting from Poland, from which he had been expelled by the Communist regime, had a honed bullshit detector.

He seemed intrigued by my Russian-Jewish father and Irish-Catholic mother. How had that worked out? he asked.

"Not well," I replied. There was an ugly divorce that began when I was thirteen and ended when I left high school at sixteen, I told him, feeling an instant, intangible rapport.

What did I consider myself: Jewish or Catholic? he asked — his second politically incorrect question.

"Jewish, I guess," hesitating as I thought of my mother's intense attachment to her church and my years in Catholic school. "But I'm an agnostic," I added. "Secular, really."

What did I think of the new Home section, which was one of several new supplements — Sports Monday, Science Tuesday, and others — that Abe and his number two, Arthur Gelb, had created to emphasize "soft news" and broaden the paper's appeal to younger readers and advertisers? The new sections, which many in the *Times* cautious bureaucracy had resisted, saved the paper.

I hadn't read the Home section often, I confessed.

If I were ever lucky enough to join the paper, Abe said ominously, I would have to be prepared to write for *all* its sections, or at least be passingly familiar with their contents.

Why had I graduated from Barnard in absentia? he asked, approaching dangerous turf. I had studied economics overseas at an institute at the University of Brussels during my last year at Barnard, I explained, and had also worked for a firm whose only client was the European Economic Community (EEC), as the European Community was first known. My research, I babbled on, had focused on the American Selling Price system, a nasty American tariff that had raised the price of European goods made of benzenoid chemicals by as much as 172 percent in the American market.

Abe's eyes glazed over. He was clearly not riveted by details of trade negotiations in Geneva and, I suspected, financial news in general. This was fortunate, since he quickly switched topics and did not ask me why I had spent my senior year overseas rather than at Barnard. Had he asked, I would have been forced to violate a John Finney dictum and disclose that I had fled America because I was more or less on the lam.

My arrest at Fayerweather Hall in the spring of 1968 had not been my only encounter that year with law enforcement. I had been arrested twice before in antiwar protests led by Resist, whose nonviolence I preferred to the more aggressive tactics and goals of SDS (Students for a Democratic Society). Resist did not want to "off the pigs" of capitalist America but to disrupt the Vietnam War by peacefully encouraging draft-age men to destroy their draft cards and go to jail or flee the country. I had been given a warning after my first arrest for a sit-in at selective service headquarters in downtown New York. After the second, at the New York offices of Dow Chemical, the producers of napalm, I had been charged with disorderly conduct and resisting arrest for refusing to move. I had been released "on my recognizance," which meant that I could stay out of jail while the matter was being adjudicated if I did not violate the law again.

After my third arrest at Columbia, I spent my first hours in jail. The Manhattan House of Detention — better known as the Tombs, in downtown Manhattan — was filled that spring with Columbia and Barnard students arrested in antiwar protests. After my release, Resist's lawyers advised me to find someplace to study overseas until my legal situation was resolved.

Had Abe asked me, I would have told him that I never regretted my opposition to the Vietnam War, my civil disobedience, or my participating in the student strike at Columbia. Years later, when we again discussed those topics, we had become close enough that we could agree to disagree.

CHAPTER 4
THE WASHINGTON BUREAU

When I arrived at the Washington bureau, I discovered that I was not the only woman to have been hired in the paper's scramble for gender correctness. By June 1977 three far more experienced female reporters had also joined the bureau.

By that time, however, the Women's Caucus in New York had gained access through its suit to private memos in the paper's personnel files. It was not pretty: bigotry and sexism were blatant.[1] Less than a year later, the suit was settled quietly. Because both sides agreed to an out-of-court settlement, the papers and affidavits associated with the case were sealed, and remain so. While refusing to acknowledge "past or present" discrimination, the *Times* pledged to implement an affirmative action plan that would place women at the paper in key jobs and give the Women's Caucus annual status reports. The paper agreed to pay $350,000 to *Times* women, mostly for back pay — as Nan Robertson complained, a "puny amount" compared with the $1.375 million settlement that the *Reader's Digest*'s women got in their lawsuit.

Most of the caucus leaders wound up paying a high price for the suit. None ever became a manager. Before she sued, Betsy Wade, the lead plaintiff, was described in house publications as "one of the best damned editors who ever held down a place on a *Times* copydesk" and "one of the glories of the newsroom." [2] Part of the team that had worked on the paper's Pulitzer Prize–winning story about the Pentagon Papers in 1971, she ended her career writing a weekly column in the Sunday Travel section called Practical Traveler. More than thirty years later, Betsy still believes that suing the paper was the most important thing she had done professionally. "We knew at the time that we would not be the ones to benefit. The beneficiaries would be those who came after us."

Progress was painfully slow.[3] The men's resentment of women, the double standards to which we were held, remained. Not until 2003 was a woman appointed to one of the top two editorial posts at the paper. That woman, Jill Abramson, was a high school classmate of Betsy's younger son. "That's how long it took to get a woman to the position that I thought I should have," Betsy said.

The quiet resentment toward us new recruits to the Washington bureau was tolerable because the paper was in the midst of another wrenching transition. I was a novice, but an intensely competitive reporter at a time when the paper craved them. I lived for scoops, a goal often undervalued in the stately Washington bureau.

Although Rick Smith still tried to run a traditional, hierarchical shop, Watergate had shattered the bureau's independence from New York — a practice that began in the 1930s when Arthur Krock demanded autonomy as the price of moving to Washington to run the bureau. Since then, the bureau had been a "veritable duchy in the kingdom," as one *Times* observer called it. Watergate changed all that.

The bureau had gone from journalistic exaltation over its publication of the Pentagon Papers to despair from having been trounced by the *Washington Post* on the Watergate scandal, which began to unfold a year later. Under Max Frankel, the bureau had ceded the story of the century to the

Washington Post, its main rival. Backed by executive editor Ben Bradlee, two metro reporters, Bob Woodward and Carl Bernstein, had run rings around the *Times.* Their triumph had dramatized investigative journalism, which had often been undervalued at the *Times.*

The *Times* had begun in 1851 as a city broadsheet whose reporting — as implied by Adolph Ochs's description of his paper as the impartial "newspaper of record" — had relied heavily on official pronouncements. Despite some excellent reporting, the Washington bureau had traditionally seen itself as part of the establishment.

Frankel would later acknowledge that he had blown the story, remaining sluggish even after the White House itself was implicated.[4] He had believed his sources, among them White House press secretary Ron Ziegler, his occasional tennis partner, as well as National Security Adviser Henry Kissinger, and other White House officials who had dismissed the 1972 break-in at the Democratic National Committee headquarters as a "third-rate burglary" — an assessment that many of Frankel's reporters shared initially. Later, as Richard Nixon's involvement in Watergate was revealed day after day in the pages of the *Washington*

Post, the bureau began scrambling, but too late. "I was so envious of the *Post*'s lead that I allowed myself to be skeptical of some of its revelations," Max confessed in his memoir decades later.

This failure did not prevent him from becoming the paper's Sunday editor and, despite another disappointing performance, succeeding Abe Rosenthal as executive editor in 1986. Among the fraternal order of Timesmen, life was full of second and third chances. Not so for women.

After Watergate, Abe Rosenthal vowed not to be beaten again on a major story. In his book decades later, Arthur Gelb, Abe's indispensable number two, said that Rosenthal considered his decision not to remove Frankel from the Washington bureau sooner "the greatest mistake of his career." [5]

By the time I was hired, a younger, more aggressive management — though tall, preppy Rick Smith was hardly Columbo — had taken command of the bureau. Smith, and Bill Kovach, who succeeded him, began hiring or promoting some of its investigative stars: David Burnham, whose police corruption series had resulted in major law enforcement reform; Nick Horrock, a dogged corruption reporter (an editor once joked that Horrock "kept his cards so close

114

to his chest that not even he could see them"); and the relentless Ed Pound, who spent so much time reporting on FBI and drug enforcement officials that he came to resemble them. The short leash that Abe had kept on Seymour Hersh, who in 1968 had broken the My Lai massacre story in Vietnam for the *St. Louis Post-Dispatch,* was finally loosened so that he could cajole and browbeat recalcitrant sources. Long before I joined the *Times,* I had urged Sy to team up with a long-standing friend of mine from the antiwar movement, Jeff Gerth, a gifted financial reporter. Their partnership produced an impressive series on the financial shenanigans of Sidney Korshak, a notorious fixer for the Mob. Jeff, who was also hired full-time by the *Times* in 1977, eventually won his own Pulitzer Prize.[6]

My first beat produced at least a couple of hard news stories a week. After reading the latest corporate filings at the SEC headquarters and speaking to the government attorneys who were overseeing a particular company of interest, I would race back to the bureau to file my story. Deadline had its own frenetic rhythm: we would type our stories, double-spaced, on thick copybooks of typing paper separated by sheets of carbon paper. After a page was finished, we would yell "Copy!" A copyboy, invariably a tweedy young man, usually a graduate of an elite college who yearned to work at the *Times,* would rush to our desks, pick up the finished page from our "out" baskets, and deliver it to an editor at the center of the office. As we struggled to complete another page, the copyboy would bring the edited pages back to us, the editor's questions scribbled in the margins. If the questions were serious — such as, "Where is the lead of your story hiding?" — the news editor responsible for your section of the paper might call you on the phone. If there were even more serious issues, he would come to your desk. The financial desk editor, and even John Finney himself, spent a lot of time at my desk, teaching me what the *Times* expected in a news story and "news analysis" pieces, which, unlike today, were then clearly distinguishable from one another.

The bureau had never been regarded as a particularly welcoming place, and some veteran reporters made little secret of their disapproval of the relatively large group of young, ambitious female reporters.

But I soon discovered some supportive editors. I had a rocky start with one of them, David Binder, a former Bonn correspondent and Washington editor for foreign news who spoke several European languages and had written a brilliant biography of German chancellor Willy Brandt.

Soon after I arrived, I filed a story on a Saturday about how an insurgency in some remote corner of the globe was being financed. Binder came by and threw the story on my desk in evident disgust.

"The problem with you," he said, "is that you have no respect for the craft."

I was crushed. "What did you mean?" I asked meekly.

"Look at this copy," he said, ignoring me. "Look at this sentence."

The page I had submitted lacked margins and the proper *Times* formatting. More seriously, it also referred to the rebel gang in the South American country I was writing about as a "gorilla" movement.

"Is this group part of the Cro-Magnon family?" he mocked.

It was just a spelling error, I said, trying to portray my mistake as haste rather than sloppiness. "The copy editor would have caught it," I lamely added, falling back on the layers of *Times* editors who check and recheck facts, spelling, and even sentence structure.

"You make a mistake a day like this,"

Binder countered. "It's unprofessional, and unacceptable," he said, walking away from my desk. I raced out of the building to smoke a cigarette and calm down.

Several cigarettes later, I returned to Binder's desk. He was right, I told him. I neither knew nor cared much about the paper's arcane rules and traditions. I thought I had been hired to break news, but observing the *Times*'s rituals of form and content were important. Would he help me figure them out?

Binder seemed to soften. He agreed. I learned an enormous amount from him, though I doubt he ever knew of my intense admiration for him.

It was on a weekend working overtime that I met my first real friend at the paper, and, eventually, an anchor of my personal and professional lives and that of our close-knit circle of friends. One Saturday, when the bureau was mostly empty, a boyish-looking blond in tennis clothes tossed his squash racket onto the desk of the chief economics reporter, whom I still had not met. "You can't sit there," I mumbled, assuming he was a new copyboy. "That's Steve Rattner's desk," I told him.

"He won't mind," the smiling young jock replied. "I *am* Steve Rattner."

I had heard that Rattner, who went on to make a fortune in investment banking, was a wunderkind who had been a news clerk to James "Scotty" Reston, a former Washington bureau chief and executive editor and distinguished political columnist. But I was stunned at how young he looked. In fact, Steve was just a few years younger than I. He laughed and suggested a drink.[7]

Steve and I, among a handful of reporters under the age of thirty-five, quickly became a circle. Philip Taubman, who covered intelligence, and his wife, Felicity Barringer, who then worked for the *Washington Post* and would later join the *Times,* became part of the group. So did Steve Weisman, who had won a bureau slot after his superb coverage of New York City's fiscal crisis in the mid-1970s.

When the bureau moved to Connecticut Avenue and K Street, closer to the White House, a new desk appeared just opposite the economics cluster. Its occupant was a general assignment reporter who immediately stood out: he was young like us, but formally dressed, given the bureau's rather informal dress code. The cuffs of his custom-made shirts bore gold links. He wore suspenders and a bow tie. But he was friendly and very funny, and was immediately accepted by us.[8] His name was Arthur Sulzberger Jr.

CHAPTER 5
BECOMING A "TIMESMAN"

I was still covering the Securities and Exchange Commission when stories about my sharp elbows and romantic escapades began circulating. I paid little attention at first. I was determined to make news even on a beat that had little priority in Washington or New York. When I wasn't working hard, I was socializing with equal fervor. Let them gossip, I thought. What did it matter?

A child of the 1960s, I had what was then regarded as a traditionally "male" attitude toward sex: I enjoyed fairly casual encounters that neither my partners nor I assumed would lead to a long-term commitment. With rare exceptions, I remained on good terms with the men I dated.

We female boomers were blessed to have come of age when, for the first time in history, women could control reproduction with ease and certainty. I was convinced that the birth control pill belonged on anyone's list of history's great inventions — ranking alongside the discovery of fire, the wheel, the printing press, cars, penicillin, and, as someone who spent so much time in the Middle East, air-conditioning.

I was nevertheless intensely private. Long before joining the *Times,* I was determined to keep my personal life to myself. Part of that was my reluctance to share unpleasant if clichéd memories of modern American life: my parents' ugly divorce, my mother's lonely alcoholic binges, my brother's self-destructive heroin addiction. Part of it was also pragmatic: dating influential men like Les Aspin, who, for all his high public profile was shy and also deeply private, made discretion essential.

While the *Times* was in the disclosure business, it was institutionally averse back then to invading the private space of even the very public people it covered. The paper tended to be even more discreet about its own sexual and ethical lapses. The *Times,* of course, had conflict-of-interest and nepotism rules, often haphazardly enforced, almost invariably at the expense of women. Editors and other supervisors, for instance, were not supposed to fraternize with reporters or those they supervised. But a succession of senior editors often disregarded this rule: editors' dalliances with secretaries, reporters, and other subordinates were well known among the staff.

Rick Smith's decision to assign me to the SEC, I learned, was based not only on a fortuitous opening in the department but also on a need to ensure that I would not be covering national security, politics, or other areas of potential conflict-of-interest with Les Aspin. Although I had been writing about these topics long before I was romantically involved with him, I agreed reluctantly not to write about them for the *Times* as long as Les and I were living together.

The *Times* was no monastery. But male journalists were rarely, if ever, scrutinized as closely as women were. While my male colleagues would often boast about having cultivated or slept with the secretaries and assistants of powerful men they covered, women reporters who were suspected of sleeping with their sources, or who openly socialized with them, were the objects of vicious gossip. *Spy* magazine, a forerunner of irresponsible internet bloggers, profited from the fascination with the *Times* and those who worked for it. The fact that I was living with a congressman was of interest,

123

not to mention resentment in some quarters of the paper. Being linked with other powerful men whose friendship I enjoyed magnified that interest. But prior to my romance with Les and even after it, contrary to the many stories in *Spy* and other gossips, most of the men with whom I was romantically involved were fellow journalists, none of whom I worked for.

To ward off gossip, I tried to avoid discussing Les at the office. But gossip about us continued. What most of my colleagues did not know was that after only a year at the paper, my relationship with him was quietly unraveling.

Long before I began dating Les, I had admired him. A Phi Beta Kappa from Yale University who had been one of Defense Secretary Robert McNamara's "whiz kids" in the 1960s, he had a small but close-knit group of national security–obsessed friends — among them, Les Gelb, who soon became my colleague and the chief national security analyst for the *Times;* Frank Wisner, a gifted foreign service officer who served as ambassador in both Cairo and New Delhi, India; Mort Halperin, a brilliant defense and policy analyst; and Richard Holbrooke, then an assistant secretary of state for Asia. Most of them had risked their careers by opposing the escalation of the war in Vietnam, which they had initially supported.

Les had been married for nearly a decade. The marriage ended for reasons that he wouldn't, or couldn't, ever explain. We had started dating a few months after his separation.

We had much in common, apart from our Wisconsin connection. We both cared deeply about national defense and foreign policy, and we both wanted to make a difference. Elected in 1970 on a recount by only a few votes from a southern Wisconsin district, Les had been influential on defense issues since he had won his seat at the age of thirty-two. Because the First District was conservative and nominally Republican, he had to spend much of his time raising money and shoring up his political base. This meant returning to his district almost every weekend.

Early in our relationship, which began before I joined the *Times,* I accompanied him occasionally on trips to Kenosha. During the difficult '76 campaign, I spent nearly a month with him in Wisconsin, watching election politics from a vantage experienced by few journalists.

Campaigning was grueling. Whatever glamour it held for me soon dissipated as I watched Les endure the biannual ritual. I would help his staff hand out campaign literature while he schmoozed at farms, factories, schools, shopping malls, union halls, and the endless meetings of private voluntary organizations crucial to American democracy. The campaign staff was almost always with us. On those rare fall nights when we weren't eating chicken at a Rotary Club dinner, we would drive from his house on Lake Beulah, where he had learned to sail, to Lake Geneva for a late-night dinner at the Playboy Club. He was not much of a drinker: one gin and tonic, heavy on the tonic, was a big night. But he loved to dance, which, given my family background, was a godsend. Other men may have enjoyed ogling the bunnies. Not Les.

Work never seemed to end, a constant source of friction between us. While he knew how important my work was to me, Les was invariably crestfallen when I canceled a dinner or vacation because of breaking news. Though he rarely complained, his quiet disappointment was more painful than anything he could have said. I felt increasingly guilty: it was becoming obvious that I valued my job more than spending time with him, and that my relationship with this kind, intelligent man was in trouble.

It wasn't just the age gap between us — a decade did not seem all that significant. Rather, I was becoming increasingly uncomfortable with the role of congressional wife-in-training — with being the "other half" of a very public figure. A legislator's life is often thankless. Social life in Washington revolves around working dinners. Impromptu votes at all hours require one to be on the House floor, often late at night. Weekends are spent in the district or on the phone raising money.

I resented the lack of privacy. Many of Les's normally considerate constituents had little compunction about calling his home at any hour, on weekends or holidays, with complaints about government or not having gotten some government service.

Although I was breaking news on my SEC and banking beat, I missed covering national security. In summer, I would accompany Les on trips to Colorado to attend the Aspen Strategy Group, a deliberately nonpartisan group of mostly men, and an occasional woman, who would spend a week debating a national security issue in the morning and climbing mountains or biking in the afternoon. The Strategy Group was my definition of heaven, and topics ranged from how best to secure oil supplies in the Persian Gulf to prospects for the reunification of Germany. I yearned to present a paper there myself one day, which I did eventually.

Our mutual interest in national security, our friends, and trips to venues like Aspen kept my relationship with Les intact longer than it should have been. Another source of solace, and common bond, was Junket, a rescue mutt, mostly sheepdog. Junket, named for those infamous congressional outings to exotic places financed by corporations and other lobbyists, normally slept under Les's desk at the office and under the bed at home. He rarely left Les's side when he was in Washington. On weekends when Les was in Kenosha, Junket was my ward, accompanying me to the Washington bureau and virtually every other place I went.

Given my unpredictable hours at the paper, even Junket was almost more than I could handle. It was becoming clear to me that I would never have children or possibly a fulfilling marriage. But I was consumed by journalism, so that prospect did not trouble me. As my unmarried women friends watched their biological clocks anxiously, I watched deadlines. Where was my maternal instinct? I sometimes wondered. "Missing in action," Les would reply.

Though he never pressured me, I sensed that Les wanted more than I could give. As we began leading effectively separate lives, I was spending more and more time with my friends from the Washington bureau and presidential appointees our own age who worked on Jimmy Carter's White House staff or as equally coveted "deputies" of his agencies. Many of those friends were our sources, and vice versa. And some of my friends, Arthur Sulzberger and Steve Rattner in particular, disliked Les, whose reserve they mistook for indifference.

There was never a quarrel — just a calm but painful discussion. Les was sad; so was I. Junket refused to emerge from under the bed. We agreed to spend some "time apart" to see how we felt, but both of us knew that I was not coming back.[1]

Les and I remained close. We celebrated when he became chairman of the Armed Services Committee in 1985, and grieved when Junket died in 1989. I never stopped admiring his defense expertise and centrist, pragmatic, nonideological approach to military matters, which greatly influenced my own views and thinking about national security and foreign policy. Though his opposition to Vietnam had brought him to Congress, he played a key role in convincing his fellow House members to support President George H. W. Bush's 1991 invasion of Iraq, an unpopular stance among many fellow Democrats. When he became President Clinton's defense secretary in 1993, he told me that he looked forward to restructuring the defense sector in the aftermath of the Cold War. But his tenure as secretary was brief. The loss of American lives in Somalia in 1993 due to inadequate military support, which critics blamed on him, prompted his resignation, at Clinton's request. A profound blow, Les never recovered from losing the job he had wanted for so long. Having struggled for years with a congenital heart ailment, he died of a stroke in 1995, at age fifty-six. I miss him still.

CHAPTER 6
EGYPT: FOREIGN
CORRESPONDENT

"Gamal!" I yelled.

The air-conditioning had gone off again. And the lights, of course. There was no telling how long the power outage would last. The screen of my computer, installed soon after I had arrived in July 1983 as chief of the Cairo bureau, went black. I lost yet again much of what I had been writing and neglected to save.

Journalism in Cairo in the early 1980s was challenging. But I loved it. Most of the time. The first woman to cover most of the Arab world for the *Times,* I was thrilled with the assignment. What did a few blackouts matter? Or taking Pepto-Bismol with every meal?

Gamal Mohieddin, who had been the *Times*'s office manager for thirty years by the time I arrived, entered my blacked-out office with two cups of steaming tea and a pack of Cleopatra cigarettes. My latest ef-

131

fort to quit smoking was failing: in lieu of Marlboros, I smoked Gamal's Cleopatras, telling myself that bumming cigarettes didn't count and wouldn't kill me.

"You might as well quit," he said, referring not to my smoking but to my work. "It's our transformer. We won't have power for hours." A dignified man with an infectious smile, Gamal specialized in *sabr.* The word meant "patience," a virtue I lacked.

Another of those infuriating words was *bukra* — "tomorrow." *"Bukra fil mish-mish,"* my Arabic instructor had taught me: "Tomorrow there will be apricot blossoms." Which meant that something you needed yesterday would probably remain unavailable. *Mishmumkin,* or "impossible," was more definitive. It meant that the permission needed to visit a project, an official, or anything connected with the Egyptian military would not be granted. But the most infuriating staple word was *insha'allah,* or "God willing."

Would the transformer be fixed by Monday? I asked Gamal. *"Insha'allah,"* he sighed.

We laughed and lit cigarettes. Gamal was a marvel, as imperturbable as the Nile, as full of humor and forbearing as Egypt itself. A Nubian whose family came originally from the Sudan, he was tall, thin, and

132

darker than the average Egyptian. Since it was a weekend, he was wearing his white galabiya, the traditional loose-fitting robe that many Egyptian men wear at home and prefer to the Western-style shirts and jackets that officials wear to work. Gamal's was always snow-white and freshly starched and ironed.

Like many Egyptians, he was quietly but fiercely patriotic. If he had trouble accepting the fact that the *Times* had appointed a relatively young woman as his boss, I never felt it. He sensed that I loved Egypt and was endlessly curious about it, which was all that seemed to matter.

Our tea break was interrupted by Charles Richards, the *Financial Times* correspondent, with whom the *Times* shared its dilapidated office. The normally unflappable Charles was agitated. Who did we think had carried out the bombings in Beirut?

Gamal and I looked at each other. What bombings?

Charles's words tumbled out: there had been two huge explosions in Beirut at the compounds of the French and American "peacekeepers," a contingent of 1,500 American soldiers, mostly US Marines, who were trying to keep a nonexistent peace in Lebanon. Many were dead or wounded.

There had been no attribution. Was this the work of the mysterious Islamic Jihad (long before *jihad* became a familiar household term), which in April had claimed responsibility for a car bomb at the US Embassy in Beirut, killing sixty-two people, seventeen of them American citizens? Was Iran, Islamic Jihad's suspected host, to blame? Or Syria? Or Iraq? Or all, or none of them?

I tried phoning Tom Friedman, then the *Times* bureau chief in Beirut, but the lines were swamped. Tom would clearly need some help if the attack was as bad as Charles reported. Then the foreign desk called. Could I get to Lebanon?

"Tell them no," Gamal said. "Beirut airport is closed."

"I'll drive," I replied.

"From Cairo?" Gamal asked, only semi-accustomed to my often unorthodox solutions to obstacles.

No, from Israel, whose troops were still occupying parts of Lebanon. I would take the evening flight that had linked Cairo and Tel Aviv since Egypt and Israel made a cold peace in 1979. Next, I'd find an Israeli taxi that could get me north to the Lebanese border, and then a Lebanese driver willing to drive me still farther to Beirut from "Dixie," as journalists called Israel when we worked in Arab countries. The trip would probably take most of the night (and several hundred dollars in cash). Gamal rolled his eyes, handed me another Cleopatra, and started booking a flight and lining up taxis.

I arrived in Beirut on a cool October morning just before dawn. Giant strobe lights lit what was left of the four-story marine compound. Huge slabs of concrete were perched precariously like dominos. Seabees were still using picks, shovels, and their hands to remove bodies from the smoldering rubble.

An FBI agent at the site told me that it was the most powerful nonnuclear bomb anyone on his team had ever seen. The force of the explosion had lifted the building off its foundation, and then it collapsed in on itself, crushing many of those inside.[1] Had such a bombing occurred in the United States or Europe, the crime scene would have been cordoned off long ago. But this was Lebanon. So I wandered at will, unescorted, along the periphery of the blast and the stew of concrete, twisted metal pipes, shards of glass, chairs, bunks, clothes, scattered letters, birthday cards, and photographs — pictures of the marines and sailors with their girlfriends and families — all ash colored, crumbled.

Nothing in my relatively sheltered life had prepared me for such carnage. While I had written from Washington about "terrorism" and "Islamic militancy," they were abstractions. I had never seen them. Now I had.

One dust-covered marine who had been digging through the rubble suddenly froze atop a mound of concrete. He plucked something out of the debris, cradled it in his arms, and began rocking back and forth. As I got closer, I saw that it was a dented, blood-smeared helmet — his best friend's.

I stayed at the site for much of the day, interviewing soldiers, officers, military chaplains, bystanders — anyone who would talk to me — and taking notes on the largely futile rescue operation. Tom Friedman was writing a news analysis about why the attack had occurred and the mysterious group, Islamic Jihad, that had by then claimed credit for it, leaving me to report the bombing.

I saw courage and strength that day, as soldiers and civilians battled horror and fatigue to save anyone who might be alive under the rubble. I saw that not all the volunteer rescue workers were humanitarians. Toward dusk, one removed a wedding ring from a dead marine's finger and stuffed it into his pocket.

I did not mention the theft or the marine in my dry account of the bombing that night, my first front-page, above-the-fold appearance as a foreign correspondent — a grisly debut.[2] But I wrote that the timing of the attack was complicating efforts to identify the bodies. Because so many of the marines had been asleep or taking showers, they were not wearing their dog tags when the Mercedes truck rammed through the poorly defended compound's southern perimeter and into the building's lobby. By the day's end, the military estimated the death toll at 193. It would rise to 299 — 58 soldiers at the French compound two miles away and 241 American marines, sailors, and soldiers — the deadliest attack on Americans overseas since World War II.

Exhausted and shaken, I returned to the site later that night after filing my story. I still hoped, illogically, that more marines might be found alive. I managed to interview one who had been guarding the entry post with an unloaded weapon as his "rules of engagement" required when the attack occurred. The Mercedes truck was large and yellow, he recalled; its driver had an intense, thin face, a black beard. And he was smiling.[3]

■ ■ ■ ■

Though I didn't realize it at the time, that five-ton truck loaded with dynamite that the marine guard saw heading toward him in Beirut that awful morning was the future. The synchronized twin bombings marked the beginning of the age of asymmetrical mass terrorism by militant Islamists. The suicide attack — and the earlier strike in April against the US Embassy in Beirut — marked the de facto start of a war against America that would continue straight through to 9/11 and beyond. Lebanon was where it had all begun. I was present at the creation.

Ihsan Hijazi, the *Times*'s veteran local reporter, briefed me the next morning over coffee at the Commodore Hotel, where Friedman was staying after his own apartment was blown up. He predicted that we would find Iranian and Syrian fingerprints on the truck and its suicidal driver.

Syria had long controlled its neighbor Lebanon. Its forty thousand troops had occupied much of Lebanon's territory since 1976, when Damascus was invited to help end Lebanon's civil war, then in its second year. Syria opposed the May 17 agreement among America, Israel, and Lebanon's Maronite-led government, which was intended to end the war. Lebanon had agreed to normalize relations with Israel, which had invaded that country in 1982 partly in response to repeated pleas from Lebanese Christians for help in the civil war and to oust the Palestine Liberation Organization, which had used Lebanon as its base.

The UN-blessed multinational peacekeeping force of American, French, Italian, and British soldiers had arrived in Lebanon in the summer of 1982, soon after the May agreement was signed, to oversee the PLO's withdrawal from Lebanon and to bolster the Christian-led government. Damascus had not been asked to participate in the May 17 talks and would not accept its terms. The rejection of the accord by Syrian president Hafiz al-Assad, in turn, prompted Israel to ignore its commitment to withdraw, since its removal of troops was contingent on the withdrawal of Syrian forces. Without Syrian participation, the May agreement was worthless, Ihsan told me. But the Americans refused to acknowledge this reality. Iran, too, wanted to see the United States, the "Great Satan," humbled in Lebanon, and these events had brought Tehran and Damascus together in a vengeful embrace.

Ihsan, a Palestinian Sunni Muslim and Lebanese citizen since 1958, loved his adopted homeland but had few illusions about the region's violent politics. He knew Washington almost as well. Syria would not abandon Lebanon, but the Americans would leave, he predicted.

He did not criticize me for having quoted President Reagan's vow to stay in Beirut in the lead of my story. After all, our tough-talking president had declared that terror would "never" force the United States to abandon its peacekeeping mission in Lebanon.

Ihsan smiled wearily. Words were cheap, coffins expensive, especially as the 1984 US presidential election approached. America would leave Lebanon. The West's peace-keeping role had been doomed from its creation: there was no peace to keep.

Shiite Muslims had long ago become the country's largest sect; Sunni Muslims were second, and Maronite Christians a distant third. The civil war that erupted in 1975 had obliterated Lebanon's fragile cohesion. The dynamic, prosperous country I first visited in 1971 as a graduate student at Princeton's Woodrow Wilson School and aspiring reporter was no more. By 1983,

Beirut was a physical and political wreck.

Ihsan urged me to report outside the "city-state" of Beirut. Lebanon's future was being written beyond Beirut's mutilated borders. Demography could not be denied forever. The country's Shia Muslim majority was being mobilized throughout southern Lebanon. "Their day is coming," he said.

In Jibchit, then a town of fourteen thousand, their day had already come. Fewer than forty miles southwest of Beirut, Jibchit was a planet away. As Ali, the Shiite driver Ihsan had hired for me, steered his battered yellow taxi deeper into southern Lebanon, I saw that Ihsan was right. In Jibchit, the idea that a country as secular, materialistic, and religiously diverse as Lebanon could ever become a theocratic state of any kind, much less an Islamic republic like Iran, seemed less preposterous.

This was the Lebanon of men like Sheikh Ragheb Harb, a young Shiite mullah known for his fierce opposition to Israel's occupation and his determination to turn Lebanon into an Islamic state. This Lebanon had none of the immaculately coiffed women of Beirut in their clinging silk blouses and high heels. Even young girls in Jibchit wore Islamic garb. There were few street or shop signs in English. The town looked more Iranian than Lebanese. Posters of Iran's glum Ayatollah Ruholla Khomeini stared down on the main square from dozens of roadside signs.[4]

Sheikh Harb helped me understand more about the still-nameless suicide bomber who had attacked the marine compound. Posters featuring the bombed ruins of the compound were being prepared in the sheikh's outer office by young men with scraggly beards who had just returned from military training in Iran. One of them shoved a headscarf into my hand, insisting that I wear it during my interview with the sheikh. "He's with Iran's Revolutionary Guard," Ali whispered. "Do what he says."

Sheikh Harb, the first Islamic militant I would interview, was squat, with a sparse beard and a bulldog face. Lebanese Shiites considered him charismatic; his appeal eluded me. Raspy voiced and glowering, Harb (which means "war" in Arabic) explained that the marine barracks were an "appropriate" target because America supported Israel and its occupation of Lebanon. The strike was a "defensive" action. The bomber had gone straight to paradise not for having committed suicide, which is forbidden in Islam, but for having died as a holy warrior, a *jihadi,* a *shahid,* or "martyr," to Islam. In heaven, seventy-two virgins and all of life's sensual pleasures that he had denied himself on earth awaited him. Hence his smile.

Israel, he lectured in a monotone, was a "cancer" that Shiites have a religious duty to destroy. A Jewish state had no place in what the holy Koran designated as the *Dar al-Islam,* the "Abode of Islam," where Muslims were meant to rule. Neither he nor any other observant Muslim would ever accept the presence of a Jewish state here. Israel would have no peace, he warned me. And as long as Americans helped them, neither would we. "Mark my words carefully," he said, ending our interview. I did.

In village after village, Iran's influence was unmistakable. Almost every town had a cleric who, like Sheikh Harb, was a frequent visitor to Tehran. In a village not far from the Shiite stronghold of Nabatiye, I met a kindergarten teacher, another returnee from Iran, who marched his young students up and down a hill like soldiers. Wielding wooden sticks as if they were rifles, the children were no more than five or six years old. He was training them to be "martyrs," he boasted. They, too, might have the honor of dying for Islam.

The Iranians were seeding the infrastructure and culture of terror in the very presence of Israel's occupying army. Did Israel not understand the implications of its occupation?

I posed that question to the deputy commander of Israel's military headquarters in Tyre, near the Lebanese-Israeli border. This time Ali, my driver, had not accompanied me. Genial and accommodating until our arrival at the Israeli base, he became enraged when I asked him to drive into the compound. How could I possibly meet with *them,* he yelled, his country's occupiers? How could I enter a place where Lebanese and Palestinians had been detained and, he said, tortured? He must have found my response — that journalists must interview people on all sides of a conflict — naive or disingenuous. It neither convinced nor calmed him. Dumping my luggage and me at the compound entrance, he drove off.

I lugged my bag up the unpaved road that led to the compound's high steel gate. Beyond was another steel fence enclosing the same rock-filled barrels and cement Delta barricades I had seen at the US Marine compound in Beirut. But here many more soldiers and Arabic-speaking paramilitary border police were on guard. The place appeared impregnable.

Tracking down the base's deputy commander, I got permission to interview his intelligence officer, who confirmed my fears about the growing Shiite militancy in southern Lebanon. Israel's occupation of the south, he had repeatedly told senior officers in Tel Aviv, was jeopardizing not only Israel's forces in Lebanon but also its broader goal of peaceful coexistence with the Shiites, Lebanon's single largest and increasingly militant religious community. Although the Lebanese Shiites had initially welcomed Israel's help in ridding their towns and villages of the arrogant PLO intruders, Israel was now the alien body that had to be expelled. Attacks on Israeli forces in southern Lebanon were rising. He had sent numerous warnings to his bosses, he told me. But policy makers in Jerusalem resisted his conclusions.

Echoing Ihsan Hijazi, the Israeli intelligence officer told me that he, too, was certain that the US Marine and French army compound bombings were the work of Shiite militants from southern Lebanon, with the connivance and/or support of Iran and Syria.

I left the Israeli post at Tyre in an Israeli army supply truck, the ride procured for me by the officer's young female aide. A few hours later, I reached the American Colony Hotel, the favorite haunt in East Jerusalem of journalists who cover the Arab world. Dog tired, I slept badly, images of the bombing reverberating in my head. I dreamed about the sneakers I had abandoned at the Commodore Hotel in Beirut. I left them in the closet when I was unable to remove the caked-on grime and bloodstains from the bomb site.

The sound of the muezzin at the mosque next to the American Colony interrupted my nightmare. Still groggy, I turned on the BBC. "In the wake of the suicide bombing attack at dawn today on Israel's military headquarters in Lebanon at Tyre," the announcer said, Israel was implementing tougher security measures throughout southern Lebanon. "At least thirty-nine people have been killed in the suicide bombing attack . . ."

I dressed quickly, grabbed a notebook, and raced to Beit Agron, Israel's press center in West Jerusalem. There was as yet no list of the dead from this latest attack; this, too, claimed by Islamic Jihad. Hours later, I learned that the death toll had risen to sixty. The officer who had briefed me was unhurt. But the young soldier who had helped find me the ride back to Israel was dead. She was eighteen.

From our bureau in Jerusalem, I sent a message to Ihsan that I was out of harm's way. Having helped hire Ali to accompany me, Ihsan was partly responsible for my safety. Though we knew that foreign correspondents are not immune to the violence we cover, most of us did not yet consider ourselves targets. Normally, all sides, even Islamic militants, tried to use us to get out their message. "Terrorists want a lot of people watching, not a lot of people dead," my friend Brian Jenkins, the Rand Corporation's premier terrorism expert, had written before Islamists decided they wanted both.

We all knew that reporting on Lebanon was increasingly perilous. Our safety depended on avoiding undue risks and on the eyes and ears of the Ihsans and Gamals and the *Times*'s other local representatives throughout the Middle East who had helped school dozens of correspondents in the ways of their region.

While our editors in New York would occasionally remind us to be careful, reporters who took wildly unnecessary risks were rarely chastised. Getting the story first was what mattered. Bill Farrell, my predecessor in Cairo, for instance, was a fast, vivid writer who had covered Egyptian president Anwar el Sadat's assassination in 1981. He had spent almost two weeks introducing me to his friends and sources in Cairo. One steamy night when we both had a lot to drink, he told me about having been detained and terrorized by militiamen in Lebanon. A lanky, gentle man, he described having been locked for hours in a coffin-like box — a harrowing experience for anyone, but especially for Bill, who was claustrophobic. He needed some time off and counseling after the ordeal. But in the macho style of foreign correspondents, he had insisted on returning to work immediately. The *Times* did not object. After a struggle with alcohol, Bill died of cancer in New York two years later in 1985. He was forty-eight.

The surge of Islamic militancy added another challenge to Middle Eastern journalism: religious extremists and their violent movements had to be covered, but in a way that did not risk making reporters the accidental story.

In such a climate, the competence and loyalty of a paper's foreign staff were critical. If our office managers, stringers, translators, or drivers were untrustworthy, we could be betrayed and our sources compromised. In authoritarian regimes, the situation is doubly complex. Several of us had long suspected that local *Times* staff members were forced to cooperate with their respective intelligence services. In Cairo, I would often wonder whether Gamal cooperated with the Mukhabarat, Egypt's secret police. I never asked.

On December 12 the determined and now seemingly omnipresent Islamic Jihad struck again. It claimed credit for having detonated car bombs in a ninety-minute coordinated strike on six American and Arab targets in Kuwait, killing six people and injuring sixty-three. Canceling my Arabic lessons in Cairo once more, I was on a plane and back on page one covering yet another synchronized terror attack.

In the initial strike at the American Embassy, a dump truck carrying forty-five cylinders of gasoline and plastic explosives crashed through the embassy's flimsy sheet-metal gates and demolished the northern half of its three-story administration annex. An hour later, a car parked outside the French Embassy exploded, leaving a forty-foot hole in the embassy's security wall but, miraculously, no casualties.

The living quarters for employees of Raytheon Company, which was installing a new Hawk surface-to-air missile system for Kuwait, had an equally close call. So did Kuwait International Airport, where one person was killed in a car bomb explosion beneath the control tower, and another at Kuwait's main oil refinery and its major water desalination plant. Had the refinery been hit, production from one of the world's largest oil exporters would have been crippled. And without water, Kuwait's estimated 1.4 million people, 600,000 of whom were expatriates, would have lasted less than a week.

David Good, the US Embassy's chief public affairs officer, told me that had the truck hit the chancellery building where most of the Americans work, the death toll at that site alone would have rivaled that of the Beirut bombing. Because the administration building had not collapsed for ninety minutes, security officials had time to evacuate — a miracle.

After the devastating attacks on the US Embassy and the marine compound in Beirut, I assumed that US Embassies around the world, and surely in the Middle East, would urgently improve security. Yet in Kuwait, the perpetrators pulled off another synchronized attack with virtually identical tactics to those employed with such deadly effect in Lebanon. How was that possible?

Although additional security measures were taken after the Lebanon attacks, others had not been because of a lack of priority or money. The State Department's chargé d'affaires, Philip Griffin, told me that Washington had funded the embassy's plans to move its main entry gate to the back of the compound, where it would have bordered an open field, not a public road. But the Americans were still negotiating with Kuwait about closing the road when the militants struck. Although the embassy had increased security after the Beirut bombings, neither the Kuwaiti guards outside the embassy, nor the six marines inside it, had weapons powerful enough to stop such a large, speeding truck. No shots at all had been fired. The guards had no time to react.

If American facilities in the Middle East had failed to heed the warning of the Lebanese attacks, how would Americans in other regions or even in the United States prepare for the grave new threat we faced?

By mid-December, I reported what we knew about the attacks in Lebanon and Kuwait in an 1,800-word analysis of the emerging militant Islamic trend that Abe

Rosenthal put on the front page. Almost five years after the Islamic revolution had toppled the Shah of Iran, I wrote, "a resurgence of religious fundamentalism is unsettling the Moslem world from Africa through the Middle East and into Asia." Quoting unnamed Western diplomats and Arab officials, I reported that Tehran was said to be training thousands of militants in facilities near the clerical city of Qom and elsewhere, and distributing diatribes against the West and corrupt Arab governments through radio broadcasts and, as Iranian militants had done under the Shah, on cassettes that were circulating widely in the region. I had collected over a dozen in my office in Cairo.

Although the new Islamic government in Tehran drew its inspiration from Ayatollah Khomeini, a Shiite Muslim, his example had inspired many Sunni Muslims, the overwhelming majority of Arabs as well, I wrote. Islamic purists, whether Sunni or Shiite, were seeking to replace secular governments, which they saw as "corrupt" for having deviated from the "straight path of Islam." True Islamic governments did not distinguish between church and state.

Though the bombings in Beirut and Kuwait were the ostensible news "peg" for such a lengthy analysis, I wrote that Sunni militants had also resorted to violence: the assassination of Egypt's Anwar Sadat two years earlier was still raw enough to be shocking, and the two-week siege of the Grand Mosque of Mecca in 1979 in conservative Saudi Arabia — the self-proclaimed protector of Islam's two holiest shrines — had slowed Riyadh's tentative efforts to loosen what was the strictest and the least tolerant of region's Sunni-led governments.

The bombings and other violence were just one weapon in the campaign to return Islamic nations to an idealized, purer past. Equally significant, if not more so, was the political pressure that nonviolent militants like the Muslim Brotherhood were putting on pro-Western Arab governments to become more "Islamic": to ban pork and alcohol, expel Christians and other religious minorities, force women to wear the *hijab*, and to abandon secular legal codes in favor of sharia, or Islamic holy law.

When I later reread that 1983 article after 9/11, I was intrigued by how early I began grappling with questions about the origins and evolution of Islamic extremism. The article suggested that many scholars who studied Islamist movements believed that this latest wave of fundamentalism had been encouraged by the effects of the oil boom of the 1970s. The tremendous wealth accumulated by a few Arab countries created envy throughout the region and charges that the money had not been spent for the Muslim good. The arrival of millions of foreigners, many of them Western, also increased resentment of the infidel.

My friend Saad Eddin Ibrahim, a professor of sociology at the American University in Cairo, told me that this latest wave of Islamic militancy was rooted in growing political and economic frustration. Fundamentalists, he argued, tended to come not from poor but from lower- and middle-class families that were affected most adversely by inflation, limited opportunities for social mobility, and the region's vast disparities of wealth. Those forces were strongest in cities, where foreign influence was most apparent. Saad would not have been surprised by 9/11 hijacker Mohamed Atta's middle-class origins, but such arguments were unusual when I first wrote about them. Saad would be jailed in 2000 for advocating democracy and for criticizing President Hosni Mubarak.

When Washington announced in February 1984 that it was "repositioning" its multinational forces out of Beirut, I called Ihsan

Hijazi to congratulate him for having pre-dicted that the United States would leave. There would be no overt American military retaliation against the Hezbollah barracks in the Syrian-controlled Bekaa Valley, where Iran had set up a terrorist training camp. By pushing out the Americans after President Reagan had vowed to stay, the Lebanese factions aligned with Syria and Iran had won. The collapse of the Lebanese army in February gave Reagan the rationale he wanted: the multinational peacekeeping force no longer had a mission.

Soon after the *Times* published my front-page analysis on the spread of Islamic militancy, the Pentagon released a high-level study of the marine compound bombing. Headed by retired admiral Robert L. J. Long, the commission concluded that major failures of command, intelligence, and policy had all contributed to what it called the "catastrophe" and "an overwhelming success" for the terrorists.[5]

Although it had no mandate to investigate Washington's decision to send the marines there, the commission supported Defense Secretary Caspar Weinberger's desire to withdraw them. There was an "urgent need" for a reassessment of "alternative means to achieve U.S. objectives in Lebanon" and "reduce the risk" to the marines, it concluded. Peacekeeping in Lebanon had become impossible. "No sense of national identity" united the Lebanese or "even a majority of the citizenry"; Lebanon had become a "battleground" where armed Lebanese factions manipulated and were manipulated by the foreign forces surrounding them. If Syrians and Iraqis wish to kill one another, the report said, "they do so in Lebanon." If Israelis and Palestinians wanted to fight over the land they both claim, the venue was Lebanon. "If terrorists of any political persuasion wish to kill and maim American citizens, it is convenient for them to do so in Lebanon."

The Long Commission also concluded that the lack of HUMINT, or intelligence from agents and other human sources, resulted from a policy failure: specifically, from decisions by senior officials to "reduce the collection" of such information worldwide due to budgetary constraints and America's overreliance on satellites and other technical collection methods.

Two decades later, the 9/11 Commission would identify depressingly similar failures within what officials called the "intelligence community," which remained a battleground among warring agencies.

The Long Commission cited other failings: a poorly defined mission; inadequate communication among top officials; inappropriate "rules of engagement," which, among other things, barred marines from keeping their weapons loaded and ready for use; and the command's decision to locate most of the marines in a single building.

But if the commission had a bottom line, it was this: America had failed to appreciate that we were at war. The report's "most important message" was that the marine compound attack was "tantamount to an act of war using the medium of terrorism." "Terrorist warfare sponsored by sovereign states or organized political entities to achieve political objectives" was becoming an ever-greater threat to the United States. In effect, Muslim extremists, often backed by states, had declared war against America on a worldwide, decentralized battlefield on which our traditional weapons and tactics were often useless or counterproductive. America did not yet understand the challenge.

CHAPTER 7
FROM THE NILE TO THE SEINE

"Paris!"

Abe was calling me in Cairo from his office in New York. The connection was poor. "I'm sending you to Paris — as correspondent."

"Gosh, Abe," I said, momentarily speechless. Then I thanked him for rewarding my tour in Cairo with a promotion.

"You don't sound thrilled."

"I'm delighted," I replied too quickly. "But there's no news in Paris."

Correspondents would kill for this job, he replied curtly. I could feel his anger. He was offering me the number two slot in Paris, a big step up in the *Times* hierarchy. Why did I hesitate?

Then he chuckled. "You are the only woman in the world who would rather stay in Cairo than spend the next three years in the world's most romantic city."

Abe loved delivering good news, a rare

enough event in 1986, the finale of his brilliant if tumultuous reign as executive editor. My lack of enthusiasm had spoiled the moment for him.

"I'm really grateful for the new job," I lied.

What I didn't say — at least, not then — was that I feared I might find France a letdown after Egypt. Richard Bernstein, my shy friend and a gifted writer, was the Paris bureau chief who would cover the big stories. I would be left with the rest.

Cairo had been a thrilling initial assignment. In just over three years, I had reported from seventeen countries and was more or less my own boss, driven by my own definition of the beat. As Abe had predicted, I was drawn most to the rise of what was slowly beginning to be called "Islamic fundamentalism" and would later be known as "militant Islam" — a trend within Islam as old as Islam itself which was slowly taking hold yet again, this time as a postcolonial response to the dictatorships that ruled in the name of Arab nationalism and independence.

I discovered much about the Arabs, and even more about myself, during that initial tour. For one, while the competition for a story in Washington is exhilarating, being a foreign correspondent is far more so. There had been so many magical moments: sunset sails on the Nile; wandering through the Damascus bazaar with its exotic scents, colors, and sounds; and walking alongside a riverbank on the outskirts of Khartoum, Sudan, as fishermen scrambled ashore from an old wooden trawler at sunset, falling on their knees, bowing toward Mecca.

There were also moments of intense sadness, fury, fear, and frustration. My decision, for instance, to equip the bureau with primitive computers at a time when frequent power outages required us to send important letters and requests for interviews by messenger had been folly. So, too, was jogging in the streets. After I was tracked by a pack of wild dogs, I stopped. Gamal Mohieddin banned me from driving after I wrecked our already dilapidated car three times. I survived an elevator crash in my building by hanging from the lamp embedded in the lift's ceiling as the elevator plunged. Food poisoning nearly killed me twice — once after sampling "local cuisine" on Ethiopian Air. But such challenges were related to my job, not my gender.

Abe was understandably proud to have sent a woman to head the Cairo bureau. He wanted *Times* readers to learn about the many subtle and significant ways in which Arabs, and women, in particular, were affected by the growth of militant Islam. Since I was increasingly convinced that the treatment of women strongly correlates with a society's development and prosperity, I was happy to focus on discrimination against Arab women and the fear that led to it.

However badly women are treated in some Arab countries — and their status varies dramatically from country to country — working for the *Times* in the Arab Middle East was advantageous for me professionally. For one thing, Islamic militants and other fanatics were still relatively chivalrous then: they didn't intentionally kill or kidnap women in Lebanon and other war zones where my male colleagues were perpetually at risk.

For another, I could befriend Arab women, which was far trickier for male reporters. If a minister refused to see me, I would enlist his wife's help over lunch or tea. Only a foolhardy husband would willingly incur his spouse's wrath for stiffing her friend. While Arab women are often portrayed as victims, many wield enormous power. Upper-class Egyptian women, especially, were then, and remain today, as tough and sophisticated as Parisians or New Yorkers, but warmer. Many are tyrants in their own homes, deciding where their children go to school, when and whom they marry, whether their husbands accept new jobs. They know who has married whom and why, and who is sleeping with whom — invaluable gossip in any society but particularly in closely knit Egypt. They know why someone's idiot nephew, rather than a more qualified candidate, has a plum job or contract. Back then they knew what Mubarak ate for breakfast or dinner, and why this or that minister was really fired. Moreover, my Egyptian women friends usually heard the best political jokes first.

Because I was a Westerner, the official and informal rules that restrict Arab women seldom applied to me. Keenly aware of them, however, I sometimes profited from the virtual invisibility of women in the most restrictive Arab countries and used it to gain access to places from which men were barred. In Saudi Arabia, I wrote about riding in the back of a public bus in the stifling rear compartment to which women were relegated.[1] Wearing an *abayeh,* the head-to-toe black cloak that Saudi women wear in public, and pretending that I was a Saudi woman visiting a relative, I tricked my way into a Saudi prison from which my male colleagues would almost surely have been barred. I filed a front-page story on how several American workers for Aramco, the all-important Saudi-American oil company, had been abused and tortured by Saudi police in one of the kingdom's jails.[2]

Finally, status usually trumps gender in the Arab Middle East. Almost everyone I dealt with professionally was aware of my newspaper's clout. That alone usually assured me a cordial reception, though I was also helped by the tradition of Arab hospitality and the awareness that I was genuinely interested in the people I covered.

Relationships matter in the Middle East. I met Jordan's King Hussein when I first interviewed him as a graduate student. In official interviews over the years, he made important policy statements. He was even more candid speaking on background over coffee and cigarettes. Once, during a break at an Arab summit, he tried, but failed, to teach me to water-ski — harder than making peace between Arabs and Jews, he joked. I wrote a condolence letter when his beloved wife, Alia, was killed in a helicopter crash in 1977, and got the first interview with Lisa Halaby, the shrewd, charming American woman who became Hussein's fourth wife in 1978 and his last queen — "Noor al-

Hussein," he named her ("Hussein's light," in Arabic.) Though I interviewed many Arab leaders repeatedly during my decades of work in the region and though he made several terrible mistakes during his forty-six-year reign, King Hussein's decency; his relatively just, tolerant rule; and his desire for peace distinguished him.

I also began to sense my limitations as a reporter. Despite Egypt's love of revolutionary slogans and rhetoric, it was a deeply conservative society, with strong divisions. Although I tried hard to report on the lives and frustrations of the poor, I had far less contact with the *fellaheen,* Egypt's long-suffering farmers and working poor. While I wrote many stories about their plight, the Egypt I knew best was one of Savile Row suits and Dior dresses in Cairo and Alexandria. Social life in both cities revolved around dinner parties at people's homes. Conversation flitted among French, English, and Arabic. My French was tarnished by creative grammar and an American accent. And my Arabic remained primitive. But Egyptians were ready with translations and explanations.[3]

Personally, the job also took a toll. Being single at age thirty-five in Egypt was as much a curiosity as my gender. Most Arab women my age had been married for years. The officials I interviewed would invariably ask about my husband and I was unprepared for the alarm that telling them I was not married evoked. Half of the ensuing interview would invariably be devoted to questions about whether I was lonely on my own, or to other topics that Americans considered intensely private. Those officials were not making a pass or avoiding tough questions. For Arabs, family is the center of life, particularly for women. That a woman should be deprived of its protection is profoundly disturbing to many Arab men and women.

So, soon after my arrival in Cairo, I decided to acquire a husband and two children as a guise. My fictitious husband, George, lived in Washington. I neglected to name my mythical children, select their gender, or decide why George and the kids were not with me in Cairo. Few Egyptians were curious about any of that. What counted was their presumed existence. A husband and children ensured that I was not alone: George was looking out for me.

After a particularly boisterous lunch in Alexandria, Frances Cook, then the American consul general there, and a few Egyptian friends who were in on the ruse accompanied me to the souk to buy a proper wedding ring. George, the kids, and, above all, my new diamond-encrusted snake ring had the desired effect: they eliminated further personal questions and saved time. When I would finally marry twenty years later, I wore that ring, which by then had been accompanied by much good fortune.

I loved foreign reporting, but part of the mission did not suit me, and this, too, had little to do with being a woman. Mainly, it had to do with the way people, male or female, react to war. Some women may be cut out to be war correspondents. Not me.

The discovery came in the summer of 1983 in Lebanon after the devastating Marine Corps bombing in Beirut. After years of covering the civil war, Tom Friedman had grown cautious. When I unpacked a bulletproof vest the foreign desk had provided, he chided me. "If you need that," he said, "you're too close." But some reporters, like John Kifner — a talented veteran of several Middle Eastern posts, who would succeed me in Cairo — seemed to relish that part of the assignment. Kif, as everyone called him, never forgave me for urging Abe to pull him out of Beirut after several of his colleagues there were kidnapped.

I was afraid much of the time in Beirut,

and afraid to acknowledge that fear to my editors or even my colleagues, most of them male. Instead, I would drink away the day's trauma with friends like David Blundy and Liz Colton — a correspondent for *Newsweek* who later became a foreign service officer in Afghanistan and other challenging posts — and diplomats at the Hotel Commodore, which was thriving on the war's misery. It was always full, thanks to the rotation of reporters looking in on war. Innocents like me were routinely offered a choice of rooms: Would I prefer the shelling or the car bomb side of the hotel?

Lebanon's endless violence should have been enough to make anyone flee. But it was covering the evacuation of Christians from the Lebanese mountain town of Deir el Qamar that taught me that a war correspondent's life was not for me.

Inga Lippman, a freelance photographer in Beirut, interested me in a planned evacuation of the town, arguing that it would help show that almost nothing is black and white in a civil war like Lebanon's. Yes, some twenty-five thousand Christians who sought refuge in the town from fighting in their own villages had been encircled for two months by Druze soldiers and prevented from leaving. The Druze, an eleventh-century Muslim sect, an offshoot of an offshoot of Islam that had fought a civil war with the Maronite Christians in 1860, still resented the Christians. But members of the Phalange, militant Christian militiamen, took refuge among the town's civilians, and the Druze refused to lift the siege unless they surrendered. As I would see repeatedly in other Middle Eastern conflicts, civilians were being used as pawns. When the Druze finally agreed to let the Red Cross remove women, children, and the elderly from Deir el Qamar, Inga and I headed there.

It took us about two hours of chatting and drinking tea at a series of checkpoints variously manned by Christian, Lebanese Army, and Druze militias to reach the outskirts. At the final station, three-quarters of a mile from the town center, logic, charm, threats, pleas, bribes, and feminine wiles all failed. There was sniper fire along the road, the Druze captain warned us. If our car's tires were shot out, the evacuation would be impeded.

"Then we'll walk," I told him. Inga stared at me in disbelief.

Certain that two unarmed women would never take the dare, the captain grinned. "If you please," he said, motioning us toward the town.

I heard the first bullet about two hundred yards down the road. After the fourth shot, I knew I had made a terrible mistake. Since Inga would not permit me to take such a risk alone, I had endangered both of us needlessly. I told her we were turning back.

"The hell we are," she snapped at me. It was as dangerous to turn back as to go ahead at that point, she said. We were going into town if she had to drag me. "So shut up and count the rifle shots," she said. "You'll need it for your story."

There were seventeen. It was a good story; the *Times* put it on the front page.[4] But it hadn't been worth the risk. I had let my hunger for a scoop prevail. I turned out to be just as susceptible to the adrenaline of war as any of the macho male reporters I disparaged, perhaps more so. As a woman, I felt I had to prove to editors who had resisted sending me to Lebanon and to the region in general that I could deliver the goods. But no story was worth such recklessness. It was a lesson I would have to learn repeatedly. Journalism's incentives — the prizes, praise from editors and peers, promotions — rewarded risk, not caution.

To avoid clashing with Richard Bernstein, the Paris bureau chief whom I greatly admired and whose friendship I still cherish, I decided to stake out new reporting territory in France that avoided foreign policy and national security. So I wrote about art heists, the fashion industry, and the nobility of truffles.

Abe loved the stories. "Off to a great start! More! More!" said one "hero-gram" that Anne Aghion, the bureau manager, dropped on my desk. Yes, this was a plum assignment, a step up on the paper's professional ladder. But after the heady turbulence of the Middle East, this was not the way I imagined spending the rest of my career.

All too soon, however, the Middle East reached out to me in Paris. Only a few weeks after my arrival, I found myself covering a series of terrorist bombings that risked turning Paris into Beirut. That December, I returned to Egypt to help with our coverage of the *Achille Lauro* crisis, the now infamous Italian cruise ship that had been seized by Palestinian terrorists sailing between Alexandria and Port Said, Egypt. The hijackers had killed a disabled American-Jewish passenger, Leon Klinghoffer, and thrown his body overboard from his wheelchair. They then agreed to abandon the cruise ship in exchange for safe conduct and flew to Tunis, Tunisia, aboard an Egyptian jetliner, eluding capture by America. It had been a terrible but fascinating story to cover.

The story that would change my life and lead to my first book also had nothing to do with fashion, contemporary French politics, or even the Middle East, but, rather, with history, memory, and the obligation of civilized people to confront evil — themes that along with terrorism and national security came to dominate my work.

Soon after I had moved to Paris from Cairo, I was asked to write about a court ruling affecting Klaus Barbie, the infamous Nazi Gestapo chief in the occupied city of Lyon during World War II. The so-called Butcher of Lyon had been languishing in a French jail for four years while the courts sorted out for which crimes he could be tried in France. In late December 1985 a French appeals court ruled that he could be charged with having killed or deported not only Jews but also French Resistance fighters.

Critics of the decision argued that by permitting Barbie's crimes against the Resistance to be heard in the same trial as his crimes against the Jews, the courts had blurred the traditional French distinction between "war crimes," or crimes against combatants, and "crimes against humanity": those committed against civilians for reasons of race, religion, or political views. Simone Veil, an Auschwitz survivor, a former president of the European Parliament, and then among France's most distinguished conservative politicians, called the decision "shocking." In an interview, she told me that the inclusion of the Resistance victims was a "denial of the specificity of Hitler's genocide against the Jews" and a "terrible banalization of the Holocaust." Alain Finkielkraut, a prominent writer, warned that neofascists in France were already accusing Jewish critics of the ruling of trying to "monopolize" the status of victim. "They are saying that this is the Jews' new greed," Finkielkraut told me over lunch. This was the "modern face" of anti-Semitism in France, Europe's ancient scourge. And it had come bubbling to the surface most vividly in France's discomfort over the impending Barbie trial.

I sensed that the French feared that the trial would raise awkward questions about those who had collaborated with Barbie in Lyon and with the collaborationist Vichy Government during the war. From France's defeat by the Germans in 1940 until liberation in 1944, the Resistance had been a relatively small movement. Most of the

French were either pro-Vichy or just keen on survival. After the war, French historians had grossly exaggerated the numbers and achievements of the "glorious" Resistance, which, until 1942, had fought a largely lonely battle against the Nazis.

I attended some of the trial in Lyon, France's third-largest city, that began in the spring of 1987. A vast ornate hall in the Palais de Justice had been renovated at a cost of more than $2 million to accommodate the more than nine hundred reporters, hundreds of witnesses, forty attorneys, and throngs of spectators. At the end of the two-month trial, despite thousands of pages of reporting and commentary, the Barbie conviction skimmed the surface of French society. Lyon was not Paris. What happened there didn't matter as much as events in the capital. And Barbie was German, not French. So his prosecution never became, as many had feared it would, the trial of France itself. The trial did not rewrite French history, at least not for the next decade: it had not forced a confrontation with the past or with the racism that had led to the deportation of sixty-five thousand Jews, the vast majority of whom had fled to France from the Nazi threat.

Abe Rosenthal and Arthur Gelb encouraged my inquiry. Earlier, Arthur had over-ruled a ban on "first-person" pieces in the paper to permit me to write for the Sunday magazine about being a woman reporter in the Middle East. (I led with "George" and our two kids.)[5] I learned later that Abe and Arthur supported the magazine editor's desire to put on the cover my essay about the eruptions of memory of the Holocaust which events like the Barbie trial were prompting in France, Germany, and Austria. They even let Ed Klein, then the editor, commission an original drawing for the cover by Larry Rivers, an artist much in vogue.[6] The article was the origin of my first book — *One, by One, by One: Facing the Holocaust* — and led to a contract for another with Alice Mayhew, the legendary editor at Simon & Schuster, who has wound up publishing virtually all my books and has become a lifelong friend.

My research into Holocaust revisionism prompted me to think about my Jewish roots, as well as my views on human rights and the obligation to oppose evil. After the disaster in Vietnam, "realists" of my generation argued that America should intervene militarily only when immediate national security interests are at stake. We can't police the world. Until my assignments in

Cairo and Paris, I largely shared that view.

For me, the Holocaust had been an abstraction. But immersing myself in the world of survivors and those who studied them was powerful and painful. I discovered that most members of my father's extended family who hadn't immigrated to America from the Pale had perished in Nazi death camps. How had so many Germans, with their advanced culture and civilization, participated in or condoned the first industrialized mass slaughter? Why had there been so little resistance to the Nazis and the Holocaust throughout Europe?

After I wrote an article which my editors entitled "Erasing the Past: Europe's Amnesia About the Holocaust," I became powerfully drawn to the question of what we owe vulnerable people in physical or political peril, and what we should do about places where the rule of law and the protection of civilians are collapsing. I found myself favoring the humanitarian intervention I had resisted after Vietnam. Europeans and Americans were ignoring challenges to our common humanity: Saddam's use of poison gas against the Kurds in the 1988 Anfal campaign; the slaughter in Srebrenica and other Balkan cities and villages, which killed some three hundred thousand people between 1991 and 1995 in the former Yugoslavia — at Europe's doorstep — and the 1994 mass murder of some eight hundred thousand Tutsis by Hutus in Rwanda. President Clinton would later call his failure to intervene there the worst mistake of his presidency.

In *One, by One, by One,* published in 1990 on the eve of the first Iraq war, I wrote that before the Holocaust was understood as a national and international catastrophe, it was an actual tragedy for millions of innocent individuals. "Abstraction is memory's most ardent enemy." "The Holocaust was not six million. It was one, plus one, plus one. . . . Only in understanding that civilized people must defend the one, by one, by one . . . can the Holocaust, the incomprehensible, be given meaning."

CHAPTER 8
"BE CAREFUL WHAT YOU WISH FOR": WASHINGTON NEWS EDITOR

I had been in Paris only a year when Max Frankel, who succeeded Abe Rosenthal as executive editor, asked me to be the Washington bureau's news editor and deputy bureau chief. I was thrilled but puzzled. I barely knew Craig Whitney, the designated bureau chief, and had no idea why Max had chosen me, since I had never been an editor and was underqualified for so senior a job. I had spoken to Max at length only once when he was chief of the editorial page. I had gone to see him about the article that had led to my Holocaust book. His family had been driven out of Germany and been separated for seven years: his father in Russia, he and his mother in America. She had barely managed to support the family as a seamstress in Brooklyn.

Max told me that my youth and enthusiasm would help energize a staid bureau. Washington reporters would relate to me, he added, since I had recently been one of them. And I was a woman. Max, acting in sync with Arthur Sulzberger's stated commitment to gender and ethnic diversity, had already promoted several women and minorities to senior jobs.★

But I was an anomaly; Max and Abe had been fierce rivals — the "not Abe," Max called himself in his memoir.[1] I was the only woman he promoted whom Abe had favored.

I was puzzled, but didn't hesitate. While I loved being a foreign correspondent, how could I resist? No woman had ever been Washington news editor and deputy bureau chief. And I was not yet forty.

But was I cut out to be an editor? Mary McGrory, a liberal columnist at the *Washington Post,* whom I deeply admired, warned that I was making a terrible mistake. "You're a writer," she told me. "Why on earth do

★ Soma Golden became national editor, the first *Times* woman to head a major department; Carolyn Lee was assistant managing editor, another female first; and Angela Dodson was named Style editor, making her the first African American woman to head a major *Times* department. Sulzberger became assistant publisher at roughly the same time.

you want to herd cats and fix other people's work?" I feared she was right. I stopped in London to discuss the job with Howell Raines, a strong-willed southerner and gifted writer who had shaken up the Washington bureau during his controversial tour as its deputy. I knew that Howell had wanted the top Washington job.

Managing reporters would be tough, especially for me, Howell predicted over bourbon that we drank from teacups at the paper's London bureau. The Washington bureau was a mixture of what he called "savants and nerds," a "cross between the Faculty Club and the Junior Electrons Science Club." Under Max, the bureau had been scooped repeatedly on Watergate by the *Washington Post* and still suffered from what Howell called an "entrenched culture of indolence" that afflicted the entire paper.[2] Since senior reporters usually held the best beats, the bureau's average age was older than that of the New York staff. Many reporters didn't work hard enough and were fiercely territorial, willing to destroy a junior reporter assigned to help cover a story they were missing. Editors were turf conscious and reluctant to edit stories outside their expertise. The bureau did all too little investigative reporting, he complained, and broke few stories.

As news editor, I assumed that I would help launch investigations into competitive stories and decide which reporters were best suited to pursue them. The bureau didn't work that way, Howell warned me, chuckling at my naiveté. Editors in New York, not Washington, often made such crucial decisions. My job as news editor would be to ensure that the reportorial trains ran smoothly, that reporters didn't fight too often or bitterly over turf, and to set a positive, encouraging tone with reporters. The job, he said, was part traffic cop, fact-checker, and cheerleader, and, because I was a woman, full-time den mother. Howell was too diplomatic to say what we both knew: none of those roles suited me, particularly den mother.

I soon discovered that the bureau had remarkable strengths. I already knew that Jeff Gerth, among my oldest friends at the paper, was an amazing investigator. But there were other gems. Gerald Boyd, an African American senior correspondent, rare at the paper, excelled as a White House correspondent, covering Reagan with Bernard Weinraub, another savvy *Times* veteran. They rarely quarreled over top billing. B. Drummond Ayres Jr., a genteel, wickedly

worth of weapons to Iran in violation of the embargo. Obviously she knew that the contras, who opposed the Marxist Sandinistas in Nicaragua, had received a portion of that money, a violation of a congressional ban, which was why some senators were demanding that Reagan be impeached. Surely she knew enough about the scandal to interview Bud? No, she replied. She had barely followed the story that had rocked the Reagan presidency and consumed Washington for over a year.

Craig and I had a choice: we could send a reporter familiar with the scandal or try to tell her enough about it to conduct the interview. I stuck with my gut.

As we waited for the limo that would take her to McFarlane's house for dinner, I told her the who, how, when, what, where of the plot that had scarred the president and destroyed the careers of several high-ranking officials. I suggested several questions for Bud. Whatever he said was bound to make headlines.

Maureen wrote a riveting account of Bud's ordeal. McFarlane, she wrote, had tried to kill himself not because he was depressed about having to testify before congressional committees and a special presidential panel, or because he was embarrassed by the exposure of his role in the Iran affair. He had done so because the scandal made him feel that he had "failed the country."

Maureen's portrait of a dedicated, well-meaning man who had broken the law was brilliant. It was among my proudest moments as an editor in Washington. Her story, which I helped edit, told us more about what ambition and pressure can do to people than all the stories about Iran-contra that we had run on the front page. It also solidified her status as a star.

That high point was overshadowed by many failures and disappointments. As Howell had warned me, the bureau had plenty of "dead wood" — what Max Frankel called "unproductive reporters." We were still being beaten on high-profile stories, and Max made clear to Craig, Johnny, and me that we had to force out nonperformers. The *Times* newsroom in New York then had over a thousand reporters and editors, many of whom would "kill" to work in the Washington bureau, he told us.

Craig, retiring by nature, often asked me to deliver bad news. I was uncomfortable with this task and soon dreaded going to work. I missed reporting and writing. I also found myself criticizing stories that I thought were thinly sourced, factually flawed, or politically slanted. I felt that a left-of-center bias — the paper's natural drift, given the political views of the overwhelming majority of its staff — would be harmful for the paper, particularly in President Reagan's Washington. Republicans tended to view the mainstream press, especially the *Times,* as the enemy. Regarded by many as a public trust, the paper could ill afford to ignore that perception.

I was sensitive to any political agenda in a reporter's copy. Confronting reporters' stories understandably generated resentment. With an average of twenty stories filed each day, I rarely had time to be deft or subtle. We often had only minutes to edit and fix copy filed on deadline and send it to other copy editors in New York on separate news desks, and then to a third rung of senior "backfield" editors who worked near Max's office.

I realized gradually that I was wrong for the job I was honored to have been offered and confessed my misery to *Times* columnist Bill Safire, whom I trusted as a friend and adviser. I had often worked with Bill when I was a reporter in the bureau. Though a conservative, Bill broke news about scandals affecting liberals and conservatives alike. He was a generous colleague, sharing tips of potentially good news stories with me and other reporters, a rarity among columnists. He had encouraged me to accept the editing job in Washington. So over lunch one day, I told him that the idea of helping run the bureau had been far more exhilarating than actually running it. Surely I was not the only reporter to have discovered that I disliked editing and managing reporters. Bill sympathized, to a point. But he reminded me that failing as an editor at the *Times* meant the end of a potentially rewarding career. The *Times* was an editor's paper. Did I want to betray my generation of reporters, especially younger women, by giving up so easily? Keep trying, he told me.

There was another issue: sexism. Both Howell and Bill Kovach, Howell's predecessor as bureau chief, had impressive tempers. And while both were inspiring editors, reporters had told me about instances in which they had scolded reporters in front of their colleagues. Several recalled that Howell had once chewed out Stephen Engelberg, one of the paper's best reporters and later its investigations editor, for having missed a hearing that had ended before his arrival. "Either you get me the story, or I will find someone who will!" he had shouted in the newsroom.[3] Male editors were quickly forgiven for such tantrums. But my own frustrated outbursts quickly became an issue. Reporters who would cower before Craig Whitney, our soft-spoken bureau chief, and even avuncular Johnny Apple, showed me little deference. If I made an assignment they disliked, or sent back their copy with questions, reporters would often complain. Sensitive to the gender bias against me, Craig usually supported my call, even when he doubted it. Not so Mr. Apple, a huge talent but a true diva, who barely hid his displeasure at having to share the deputy bureau chief's title.

The bureau needed a broad shake-up, Max Frankel decided, and Craig, Johnny, and I agreed. At his request, we had drawn up a list of recommended shifts. A few reporters were to be reassigned to New York; others would trade beats within the bureau; a couple of outsiders would be brought in from New York or other domestic or foreign bureaus to help us in areas where our reporters were lagging. Max and Joe Lelyveld, his deputy, pushed us to add more names to the list. After approving the staff changes, they came down to Washington to congratulate us for having taken difficult but essential steps to enhance the bureau's competitiveness. Despite their praise, I was unhappy. I sensed that the staff changes would be bitterly resented and resisted. And they were.

By the summer of 1987, I was more miserable. Not only did I dislike managing reporters, I surprisingly found little joy in being responsible for decisions about the priority of news stories. Despite Bill Safire's hopes for me, I realized that I didn't want to run the *Times.* I just wanted to write for it again.

After finishing the first of several drafts of my Holocaust book, I needed a break. Craig urged me to take a vacation that I had long planned in the South of France. En route home to Washington, I was scheduled to stop in London for a black-tie dinner to mark the opening of an exhibit at the Tate art gallery that Arthur "Punch" Sulzberger, the publisher, was also attending.

In Paris the night before my flight to London, Jeff Gerth called from Washington. What did I think about the news? he asked me. Was I all right? I had no idea what he was talking about. Craig was being transferred to London, he told me; Howell Raines was returning to DC to become bureau chief, the job he had always wanted. Johnny would retain the deputy bureau chief's title but return more or less full-time to reporting. Craig was being exiled in a palace putsch. Howell had won. There was no mention of my fate.

I barely remember the rest of the trip to London. I was sad for Craig, who had worked so hard to improve the bureau. I also fretted about my own prospects. Although I yearned to return to writing, I did not want to be demoted. The shifts in the bureau were an unexpected blow. Craig later assured me that he had known nothing about them when he had urged me to take my vacation.

As I entered the museum, still in semi-shock, I saw Punch and his wife, Carol. Both greeted me warmly. It was a lovely party, wasn't it? The exhibit was superb. London's weather was uncharacteristically clear and warm. Why did I look so upset? Punch asked, wrapping his arm around me protectively. The transfers were for the best, he told me. And they didn't affect me. "You still have your job in Washington."

Chapter 9
The Gulf War

I owed my liberation from editing to Saddam Hussein.

I had left Washington in 1988 for another editing job in New York. Though I had wanted to return to writing, editors had more status and were paid better than even veteran reporters. While Joe Lelyveld was trying to create a career path for reporters that would ensure them comparable status and pay, he had not succeeded yet.

By 1990, I had spent two years in New York as deputy editor of a new Media section that covered publishing, journalism, and other sectors of the news business. Then Saddam invaded Kuwait.

I learned of the invasion from Jason Epstein, the man I would eventually marry. I had slept late that morning at his home in Sag Harbor, Long Island, on Friday, August 3, 1990. He had already read the papers.

"Does it matter that Iraq has invaded

Kuwait?" he asked me.

He had to be mistaken, I told him, pouring myself some coffee. I hadn't heard anything about trouble on the Iraq-Kuwait border when I left my office earlier that week.

No, he corrected me, barely glancing up from the crossword puzzle. Iraq had definitely invaded and occupied the tiny oil-rich emirate.

It mattered hugely, I told him as I reached for the phone. If the Iraqi dictator annexed Kuwait, he would control a fifth of the world's oil reserves. If Saddam could not be persuaded to withdraw, America would probably be drawn into a war.

"How soon?" he asked, still absorbed in his puzzle.

The White House would need at least six months to mobilize and deploy forces, I estimated.

Jason despises war, but Alberto Vitale, who was then the head of Random House, sensed a publishing opportunity for an "instant" book on the Iraq crisis. Jason, who had been the company's editorial director, proposed me as the writer. I knew Iraq and the Middle East well, he told Alberto, and was accustomed to working on deadline. Vitale asked me to produce a seventy-five-thousand-word book in six weeks for Steve Wasserman, the editor of Times Books, then a Random House imprint.

Wasserman showed me an article that Laurie Mylroie, the Iraq specialist, had written for the *Wall Street Journal,* arguing that Saddam's motive for invading Kuwait was primarily financial. His eight-year war against Iran had bankrupted his regime. Iraq was $90 billion in debt and needed Kuwaiti oil. Laurie agreed to write the book with me.

With a month's leave of absence and my year's vacation time, I cloistered myself in my New York apartment and threw myself into the project.

Saddam Hussein and the Crisis in the Gulf was published on time in October 1990 to favorable reviews. The paperback sold respectably — about thirty thousand copies a month — until December, when President George H. W. Bush doubled the number of American troops to be deployed in the Gulf. By the time American soldiers invaded Kuwait in January, our paperback had become a number one bestseller.

I was not around to enjoy the publishing triumph. When the *Times* began ramping up its prewar coverage in earnest, Joe Lelyveld, who had succeeded Max Frankel as

192

executive editor, freed me from editing and sent me to the Middle East. He had named me a senior writer, one of those supercorrespondent jobs he had finally created, and called me the special Gulf correspondent, a vague enough title to let me roam and report freely on the Arab reaction to the impending war against Iraq. I wanted to explore why so many Arabs opposed, or were ambivalent about, a war to liberate Kuwait. Polls and interviews showed that poorer Arabs detested and envied the Kuwaitis' wealth, indolence, and arrogance, and admired Saddam's pugnacity.

As America edged toward war, I had exclusive interviews with many of the key Middle Eastern players in the conflict — starting in Jordan with King Hussein, who opposed the war and, like me, was chain-smoking again. Jordan imported roughly 90 percent of its energy requirements from Baghdad at heavily subsidized rates. And for reasons that only a psychiatrist could fathom, the king had a strong personal attachment to Saddam. Interviews with Yemen's president, Morocco's king, and Hosni Mubarak of Egypt followed.

Exhilarated but exhausted, I returned home for Thanksgiving to meet Jason. I looked forward to seeing him after two months on the road. I consoled myself when the weekend ended without a marriage proposal: perhaps Jason's reticence was for the best. I was hardly marriage material. The "story" would always come first, as my constant travel for the *Times* suggested. I went back to the Middle East, but not before I had persuaded him to join me at Christmas for a farewell cruise up the Nile planned by Frank Wisner, our ambassador in Cairo, who was assuming a new post in Manila, the Philippines.

Wisner's cruise from Luxor to Aswan was magical. Jason was enthralled by Upper Egypt's beauty, the gentleness of our guides, and their vast knowledge of the Pharaonic sites we visited. Frank and Jason also liked each other, a great relief, since Frank was still among Les Aspin's closest friends.

After Egypt, we went to Jordan to visit Petra, the ancient trading city that the Nabateans had built three hundred years before Jesus was born. Set deep within a mountainous fold at the edge of the Great Rift Valley, the terrain resembles Arizona at the approaches to the Grand Canyon. The young Arab director of antiquities at Petra drove us in his jeep later that night through the narrow, winding mountain passageway into the famed ancient "rose-red city half as old as time." With war so imminent, there were few tourists. We were virtually alone in one of the world's most breathtaking ruins. Around a small campfire near the entrance to the cave in which he was born, the young Jordanian archeologist recounted how his government had sent him on scholarship to study archeology at the University of Michigan. Homesick for Jordan and his family, he returned early and began working in Petra's antiquities ministry. He owed everything to King Hussein, he confided.

I did not cover the war. Johnny Apple, who was coordinating the paper's war coverage from Dhahran, did not invite me to join his team. So I worked alone, concentrating on how the war was affecting Saudi Arabia.

The thousands of American forces on sacred Islamic soil had turned this puritanical society topsy-turvy. Though I had reported from the kingdom many times, I had never really gotten to know the Saudis. Visas were rare, one's time in the kingdom limited, and a reporter's contacts intensely monitored. The Saudis were suspicious of foreigners — especially journalists. But war had forced King Fahd to open up. More than 1,500 reporters were covering the war that involved 700,000 troops from thirty-seven countries.

Fearing Saddam's revenge, prosperous Saudi men had sent their wives, mothers, and children to Mecca and other safe places they thought Iraq would not target. With their families away and business at a virtual standstill, Saudi men could now spend hours visiting one another, particularly at night, debating the war and the kingdom's future in the Bedouin-style tents that so many had pitched next to their houses in the Riyadh suburbs. Goat herders would have been stunned by these modern-day Bedouin fantasies lit by crystal chandeliers and decorated with Oriental carpets, outdoor stoves for brewing hot, sweet tea, and tiny refrigerators to chill ice for such *haram* refreshments as vodka and the unofficial Saudi favorite, Chivas Regal.

To avoid insulting foreign soldiers, journalists, and other infidel "guests," the king had temporarily grounded the dreaded *mutawa* — the religious police — old, salaried conservatives and young, fanatical volunteers who patrolled the streets, hotels, and shopping malls, telling women to cover their faces and young men to pray. Now young Saudis could suddenly entertain women, even reporters, and speak freely as never before. The war provided an exhilarating window into one of the Arab world's most insular societies, temporarily on holiday.

Throughout the war, Saudis, for the first time, passionately, publicly debated their future without fear of being stigmatized as *kafir,* nonbeliever, or worse, as heretic. Many Westernized Saudis were demanding more freedom and participation in decision-making, and greater accountability, if not Western-style democracy. They were also asking to hear more from their reclusive king and for an end to the widespread corruption he tolerated.

They faced powerful opposition from the religious establishment. The conservative, xenophobic Wahhabists were demanding a return to the old order; they wanted their suspended powers back. In their view, the war, foreign troops, and even worse, Western journalists, had defiled sacred Islamic soil. Though I was homesick, I regretted leaving Arabia that spring of 1991 after three months in the kingdom, knowing that an intense political battle would surely erupt *baad al azimah,* or "after the crisis" — the words I heard so often. Determined to write what I had seen and heard, including complaints about the corruption among members of the royal family that so infuriated the middle class, I knew that getting another visa would be unlikely once Saudi gratitude to America had dissipated.

What would the ruling family do next: open Saudi society still further, or crack down? King Fahd did both, striking a balance between liberals and conservatives. To satisfy the young technocrats, he created a *majlis al shura,* or consultative council, a baby step toward greater public participation and accountability, but hugely important in a country that had tolerated neither. Many Saudis still credit the Gulf War with having introduced "modern" politics in the kingdom.

The king also tried to sever aid to militant Islamic groups that had supported Saddam inside the kingdom and abroad. Two years later, the government announced a ban on collecting money within the kingdom for Muslim causes, then estimated to total at least $1 billion a year, without an Interior Ministry permit. But individual contributions to many radical Islamic groups continued.

To placate the politically indispensable religious establishment, Fahd increased the budget of the *mutawa* — those guardians of moral virtue — by $18 million for "training." The virtue police returned to public venues to uphold religious rules and strictures.

The war ended only a hundred hours after the ground campaign began, with Iraq's expulsion from Kuwait. Despite the coalition's swift victory and the rapid departure of most foreign forces, many Saudi conservatives remained furious at the king for letting "infidel" American forces "occupy" Saudi soil. One wealthy, young Saudi financier had persisted in using his royal access to try to withdraw the invitation to foreign forces. It was the first time I heard the name Osama bin Laden. The rich, young firebrand was known then mainly for his passionate support of militant Islamic causes, especially the Afghan rebels — some of whom the CIA had armed in America's war against the godless Soviets. Shortly before the Gulf War, Bin Laden had marched into the offices of several princes with maps and flowcharts to demonstrate how the kingdom could defend itself without infidel forces.[1] The Saudi prince who told me about young Bin Laden's meetings had mocked his presentations.[2]

But Saudi intelligence was not amused. After the war, the government revoked Bin Laden's citizenship — a rare action, since the Bin Ladens were a prominent Saudi family. Osama's Yemeni-born father had built palaces and facilities for the king and other Saudi royals. But Saudi security was more concerned about reports that Bin Laden was financing militants intent on targeting ruling Saudis and other Arab royalty. Among his beneficiaries was Muhammad's Army, which had attempted to kill then Prince Abdullah, who is now Jordan's king. Expelled from Riyadh, Bin Laden was reduced to shuttling between London and Khartoum with a passport that Sudan's radical Islamic government had issued him. Over time, his denunciations of America, his country's "master," and of his native Arabia as a kingdom of "heretics" would grow more vehement.

Warren Hoge, then the debonair editor of the paper's Sunday magazine, ran my article about the war's impact on Saudi Arabia on the cover — a totally black page, save for the golden eyes of a veiled woman shrouded in black. I was thrilled with the space he gave me and the display, and even happier when Joe Lelyveld named me, a recently minted senior writer, the magazine's staff writer in 1992.

Though I did not know it then, the Gulf War had dramatically improved prospects for peace between Israel and its Arab neighbors. Saudis and Israelis had been targeted by Iraqi Scuds, and Israeli strategists had concluded that air power and technology were more important than territory in winning wars and ensuring security. PLO chief Yasir Arafat, whom I had interviewed many times, realized that he needed a political victory after the collapse of his chief patron, the Soviet Union, and his catastrophic decision to back Saddam in the Gulf War. After the war, Saudi Arabia and the Gulf states withheld funds for his PLO and prompted a mass exodus of Palestinian refugees. The Gulf no longer wanted Palestinians who had sided with Saddam. The refugees blamed Arafat for their woes.

Unknown to us in the press, Israel's pragmatic new prime minister, Yitzhak Rabin, had blessed a secret effort to test Arafat's willingness to make peace by authorizing direct negotiations with his PLO. As peace talks sponsored by Secretary of State Jim Baker ground on in Madrid, Israeli and Palestinian negotiators were secretly meeting under Norwegian auspices in Oslo, bonding over meals of smoked fish and vodka. My friend Uri Savir, who worked for Shimon Peres, whom Rabin had put in charge of the secret back channel, attended many of the meetings, which began in January 1993. Though we spoke often by phone during those tense months, I had no idea what he was doing.

I was pursuing my own post-Kuwait preoccupation: the growth of militant Islamic forces, especially Hamas, which means "zeal" in Arabic. Hamas was growing stronger in the occupied West Bank and Gaza. Created in late 1987 after the outbreak of the Palestinian uprising in the Israeli-occupied territories, Hamas was committed to the annihilation of the Jewish state in Palestine and any peace treaty with the "Zionist enemy." It also challenged the PLO's status as the "sole" representative of the Palestinians. Israel had come to view Hamas and other militant Islamist groups — which had begun killing Israeli civilians in terrorist attacks and suicide bombings — as more dangerous than the PLO. But in yet another bitter Middle Eastern irony, the Israelis themselves had initially encouraged the formation of such groups as Hamas to counter the PLO in its more radical phase. They quickly regretted such support.

Prime Minister Rabin became increasingly frustrated by Washington's unwillingness to block financing from the United States for Hamas and like-minded groups. The State

Department, FBI, and CIA denied the existence of such financial links, despite intelligence that Israel shared with them. Rabin, I learned, might be willing to share this information with an American journalist. An Arab American used-car salesman from Bridgeview, Illinois, Muhammad Abdel-Hamid Salah, had been arrested in Jerusalem in January and was accused of being a Hamas courier, carrying money for Hamas from US donors. Ehud Ya'ari, an Israeli reporter, had written an op-ed in the *Times* asserting that Hamas's command center was in the United States and that the group had an extensive donor network in America. While I believed the Israelis, I knew that finding evidence about a Hamas presence in America would be challenging.

I had met Rabin in 1971 during my first trip to Israel when I was a student, but I did not know him well. He apparently knew my reporting from the Arab world. When he offered me an interview and exclusive access to Yaakov Perry, chief of Shin Bet, Israel's internal security service, Clyde Haberman, our gracious Jerusalem correspondent, encouraged me to follow up in Israel. This was really an American story, we agreed. Whatever I heard in Jerusalem would have to be confirmed in Washington.

After talking to Clyde, Joe Lelyveld approved my trip to Israel, though reluctantly. A turf-obsessed bureaucracy, the *Times* resisted reportorial big-footing. And Joe knew that Israel's allegations, though newsworthy if true, were likely to spark controversy and greater tension between the Jewish and Muslim communities.

Rabin told me that the United States was the source of about $30 million a year in funding for Hamas and its terror attacks. Some of the money was Iranian, he said, but American banks were being used as conduits. Some of the money was simply carried in cash by messengers such as Muhammad Salah.

As I pushed for more evidence, Shin Bet chief Perry produced photocopies of checks and bank records showing money transfers from the United States to Hamas affiliates, travel vouchers, and copies of intercepted internal communications between Muhammad Salah and top Hamas figures in London and Springfield, Virginia, allegedly Hamas's American headquarters. The evidence seemed persuasive that this forty-two-year-old used-car dealer, now in an Israeli prison, was, in fact, a senior Hamas activist who had traveled to Jerusalem, his fourth such trip to Israel, to provide money and strategic advice to the group.

Checks and bank transfer records could be forged, I told Perry; travel vouchers and telephone intercepts, fabricated. How could I know that Salah was cooperating freely with Israeli officials, as they alleged? Was he being tortured, as his lawyer had told me?

American officials, moreover, were still insisting that Hamas had no network in America. I needed more evidence. Once again, I met with Rabin. Before I could write a story, I told him, I had to see Salah myself and hear him discuss Hamas's structure in the United States. Rabin flashed his trademark crooked smile. I was, as he had been warned, a "pushy broad," he told me. I took it as a compliment.

Days later, I was sitting in a small room in the Governor's Building, Israel's highest-security prison in the occupied West Bank, next to the room in which Muhammad Salah was being interrogated. Though Salah did not know it, I was watching him on a television monitor as he spoke with his Israeli interrogator.

For the next hour, I heard Salah discuss in English and Arabic Hamas's structure in America, his role in the group, and its operations. He said he had given Hamas agents in the occupied territories $130,000 in cash in one week, of which $110,000 was intended for arms purchases, the building of new safe houses, recruitment of members, and assistance to fugitives. His superiors had authorized him to spend up to $650,000 on this trip, and they had deposited $600,000 into various bank accounts for him to purchase weapons or whatever Hamas needed.

The group's American political command, he told the interrogator, was the United Association for Studies and Research (UASR), an ostensible Arab think tank in Springfield, Virginia, less than an hour's drive from Washington, DC. Its political chief was Mousa Abu Marzook, in Springfield, a Palestinian refugee who had an engineering degree in the United States and founded the think tank in 1989. Another key figure was the institute's head, Ahmed Youssef, a writer whose code name was Abu Ahmed.

While Marzook would not grant me an interview, despite numerous requests, he had repeatedly denied through spokesmen like Youssef that he was involved with Hamas or other Islamic groups that endorsed violence. As of August 2014, Marzook was still representing Hamas as a key leader in the cease-fire talks that Israelis and Palestinians were conducting in Cairo following the latest Israeli-Gaza war.

Ahmed Youssef, too, had repeatedly denied links to Hamas. His center, he said, simply conducted research on Middle Eastern and Islamic topics and was supported by private donations and the studies it sold. Its journal listed as "editorial advisors" several prominent academics, among them John Esposito, who then headed Georgetown University's Arab-funded Center for Muslim-Christian Understanding, and Yvonne Haddad, of the University of Massachusetts, whom the think tank had listed as a board member despite her refusal to join the advisory board, she later told me.[3] Only after Hamas beat Yasir Arafat's PLO in parliamentary elections in the Palestinian territories in 2006 did Youssef move to the territories and openly acknowledge the affiliation he had long denied. He was then, and remains, a key adviser to Hamas leaders.

In retrospect, the FBI and other government intelligence agencies had been clueless about Hamas and the highly active American base that Israeli leaders and a few Islamist watchers maintained existed. Few journalists believed Israel. Some who did were afraid of being branded bigots or "anti-Muslim." Such fears among federal investigators and journalists enabled men like

Marzook and Youssef to use America's political freedoms to support and finance networks that had killed dozens of Israeli civilians. Only in 1997 was Hamas added to the State Department's terrorist list.

My front-page story in the *Times* reporting that Hamas had drawn "critical financial support and political and military guidance from agents in the United States" was published in mid-February 1993.[4] It caused a firestorm. Under my agreement with Rabin, which the *Times* had approved, I could not reveal that I had visited the security center or witnessed Salah's interrogation, which enabled some journalists and academics to accuse me of having been duped by the Israelis.

Peter Jennings, the ABC broadcaster who had spent years reporting on the Arabs, was one of the few to give me the benefit of the doubt, though begrudgingly. Over drinks days after the story was published, he asked me to explain why I thought that the Israelis had not manufactured the evidence I had been shown. Though I wanted to tell him the truth, I had to protect my sources: among them, Prime Minister Rabin. I told him only that I had reasons to believe Israel's claims about Hamas which I could not share with anyone. "If the author of this piece had been anybody but you," he told me, "I would not believe it." It was the nicest backhanded compliment a colleague had ever paid me.

My warning about the rise of Hamas and even more violent Islamic groups in America was soon vindicated. On February 26, nine days after the story was published, American-based Islamists bombed the World Trade Center, killing six, injuring over a thousand, and blowing a hole the size of a football field in the tower's basement. The State Department and intelligence agencies could no longer deny the danger that such fanatics posed. But still the FBI failed to grasp the implications of the terrifying attack that had foreshadowed 9/11.

By the fall of that year, I had decided to write a book about the rise of Islamic militancy. I asked for and got a yearlong book leave, the first the *Times* had given me. Joe Lelyveld, who had written two books, was sympathetic.

I was thrilled to receive an invitation to attend the results of the secret Oslo meetings: the ceremony on the White House lawn on September 13, 1993, to watch Israel and its long-standing enemy, the PLO, sign the Declaration of Principles. The next day, Israel and Jordan would initial an "agenda for peace" at the State Department.

It was a beautiful autumn day. As I chatted with the Americans, Israelis, and Arabs who had struggled for peace for so long, several of them said it would be a day they would never forget. Students of the region and Middle Easterners themselves had cause to be skeptical, but skepticism was suspended on the lawn that day when Yasir Arafat and Prime Minister Rabin signed the accords with the fifty-cent Bic pen that Eitan Haber, Rabin's speechwriter, adviser, and my friend, had handed his boss. When President Clinton wrapped his long arms around the shoulders of Arafat and Rabin and gently pushed them together for a handshake (which Rabin clearly resisted), the audience of several thousand cheered. If these two men could shake hands and begin making a peace, anything was possible.

Six days later, I was standing on another lawn in Sag Harbor, taking my own giant leap of faith. From the White House lawn, I had called Jason. After five years of resistance, we decided to get married, immediately, while my Arab and Israeli friends were still here.

I can't quite recall whether or when Jason had finally asked me to marry him. A few months earlier, we had applied without a future commitment for a license. An older man arrived at the Southampton Town Hall about the same time. When he told us that he had come to buy a clamming permit, we let him move ahead of us in the short line. Clamming couldn't wait, Jason joked.

My long absence during the Gulf War had been a turning point in our complicated relationship. Jason, it turned out, had missed me after all. He had called me often in Riyadh to see that I was safe, only to endure long conversations with a Filipino desk clerk who reported that I was still out conducting interviews well past midnight, Saudi dinnertime. Though we had vaguely agreed to marry, we had not set a date.

I decided the time had come as I watched Clinton, Rabin, and Arafat at the White House. After the ceremony, I told Smadar Perry, an Israeli journalist and my first friend there; Marie Colvin, a friend since our correspondent days together in Paris; Fouad Ajami, the Lebanese-American intellectual; and a few others at the White House ceremony that I hoped they would travel to Long Island on Sunday for my wedding. Smadar and Marie were stunned. How could I possibly marry someone they had never met? Both wondered whether Jason or I would show up. Several other friends seemed hesitant to change their plans for an event that seemed as unlikely as Arab-Israeli peace: Jason's marriage to an adamantly independent journalist who shared few of his many talents. I hated to cook, didn't garden, and was on the road as often as I was home.

At noon the judge that we had recruited on short notice read a statement that Jason and I had edited down to the fewest words required to make the marriage legal. The bride wore a cream-colored Armani suit with power shoulders and a flowing skirt and a cream-colored, broad-brimmed vintage hat that a fashionista friend from Sag Harbor had bought me. The groom wore a blue work shirt, khaki pants, and Top-Siders. When asked whether he would take me as his lawfully wedded wife, he replied: "I guess so." Ten minutes after the church bells of Sag Harbor marked noon, Jason and I sealed our improbable union — with a handshake.

CHAPTER 10
TERROR IN TINY PACKAGES

The Russian pilot was drunk. I could smell the vodka as he strapped me into the Mi-8 helicopter. The Soviet-era copter seemed older than its pilot, but sturdier.

It was June 1999, and I was by then an investigative reporter tracking down a sensitive story known only to the paper's senior editors.

The pilot and I were on our way to Vozrozhdeniye, an island in the Aral Sea shared by Uzbekistan and Kazakhstan, independent after the Soviet Union crumbled in 1991. I had spent more than a year arranging this visit to an island that a source had first told me about in a whisper over coffee near the Pentagon. The trip had fallen through so many times that I didn't much care if the pilot was plastered. I was finally touring the place where the Soviets had secretly buried tons of the deadliest weapons-grade anthrax, a potent strain they had made years ago during the peak of their secret bioweapons effort.

I would be the first journalist but not the first American to visit this barren biological burial ground. A CIA team had been there several times starting in 1995 to collect samples of the buried anthrax. Back at the US Army Medical Research Institute of Infectious Diseases at Fort Detrick, Maryland, the army's main biodefense research facility, scientists were still analyzing the anthrax spores to discern what the Soviets had produced, whether the spores were still lethal, and if America's vaccine would destroy them.

I became obsessed with visiting "Voz," as biowarriors called the island, after having been shown a photo that someone close to the American team had taken. Holding up an American flag, four members of the interagency group — a scientist, intelligence analyst, and two Special Forces operatives — were unrecognizable in their white, head-to-toe biocontainment suits. They looked like astronauts celebrating a lunar landing. The photo was a macabre souvenir of a top-secret mission never intended to be disclosed publicly. I was the first American reporter to learn of its existence.

As the helicopter flew toward the island,

signs of life rapidly vanished. Because of foolhardy Soviet irrigation, the Aral Sea surrounding this island was shrinking. The former seabed was cracked and dry. As we prepared to land, I put on a biological mask and rubber gloves.

Voz Island was the culmination of nearly two years of reporting on biological weapons that *Times* science reporter Bill Broad and I had done. Bio was WMD's neglected stepchild. Many of the intelligence analysts who studied it were women. Men worried about nukes; "bio" was for girls. Never mind that a gallon of anthrax in tiny doses could theoretically kill every man, woman, and child on the planet, or that a thimble of smallpox could spread across the earth in weeks. Unlike anthrax, smallpox is highly contagious and kills a third of unvaccinated victims. Smallpox epidemics had already killed a half billion people before 1980 when it was officially declared eradicated, more than all the world's wars combined.

Bioweapons, the oldest and most conventional of unconventional weapons, received a fraction of the resources allocated to nuclear and other WMD threats. President Nixon had ended America's germ warfare program in 1969 and, along with the British and Soviets, drafted a treaty banning such weapons. By 1975, when the treaty came into force, over a hundred countries had ratified it, Washington and Moscow first among them. So why worry?

My interest in this seemingly arcane corner of national security was triggered, yet again, by Iraq. In December 1997, six years after the Gulf War had ended, the Pentagon announced it would start vaccinating 2.4 million soldiers and reservists against anthrax. Steve Engelberg, the investigations editor with an incomparable nose for news, found the terse announcement intriguing. Saddam's covert germ weapons program had been disclosed more than two years earlier. What had changed? Why had the Pentagon decided to give American soldiers a six-shot vaccination and a yearly booster — a time-consuming, expensive task? Was there new intelligence about the Iraqi program or some other country's germ weapons? Steve asked me to work with Bill on a story about what had motivated the decision, which led to a book that the three of us wrote called *Germs: Biological Weapons and America's Secret War.*

While Bill and I were trying to learn what had happened to Iraq's anthrax program, I watched Diane Sawyer, then at ABC's

Primetime Live, broadcast an astonishing interview with a Soviet scientist who had defected to the United States in 1992. Kanatjan Alibekov, a Kazakh, had worked for seventeen years inside the Soviet biological weapons program and had risen to become the number two at Biopreparat, the biological war machine that American intelligence agencies had been trying to track for years.

Alibekov, who had Anglicized his name to Ken Alibek, told Diane that the Soviets had repeatedly violated the germ weapons treaty by putting germs that cause anthrax, smallpox, tularemia, and plague into warheads that until recently had been aimed at US cities. He said that the Russians were still developing such weapons at secret lab sites. Diane had broadcast part of her report from Stepnogorsk, a gigantic factory in Kazakhstan that Alibek had once headed. But the plant, which she alleged had been among the largest Soviet anthrax production facilities, would not let her in.

Surprised that her broadcast scoop seemed to have interested so few others, we tracked down an address for Alibek and went to Washington to meet the man the CIA was finally permitting to talk to journalists. Stocky, with a thick Russian accent, Alibek told us about illicit programs he had never discussed in detail with reporters before. Sawyer's report had only scratched the surface, he said. Before the Soviet collapse, scientists had weaponized at least a dozen lethal agents and genetically altered pathogens and viruses to make them deadlier and sturdier so they could be stored for years. Some had been altered to overwhelm American vaccines and antibiotics. These invisible weapons were relatively cheap and easy to make: they left no fingerprints and could not be traced. This was the Soviet Union's Manhattan Project. Almost every Soviet ministry and important institution had been involved in the program, he told us. Even the KGB had its own germ centers to develop better pathogens for assassination. The Soviets had sold equipment to Cuba, India, Libya, Iran, and Iraq, and helped them develop similar programs, he suspected. He told us that Iraq had never abandoned its germ weapons program. It was just a matter of time before such technology spread to rogue regimes and terrorist groups. He was writing a book, he told us.[1]

On the shuttle back to New York, Bill and I discussed the implications. We knew that relying on defectors was tricky, given their obvious interest in playing to the gallery, but if half of what Alibek alleged was true, we could be writing a series on the growing threat posed by germ weapons; perhaps even a book, I suggested.

Our next stop was to meet Bill Patrick, the man who had debriefed Alibek for the CIA to assess his information and his veracity. After attending one of his lectures at a biodefense conference, Bill and I wrangled an invitation to Patrick's home atop a wooded hill in Frederick, Maryland. The modest house was not far from Fort Detrick, where he had worked for over thirty-five years, first making bioweapons, and then, after Nixon banned them, defending against them. He led us downstairs to his basement office to give us a tutorial on how germ weapons were made, stored, and distributed. Near the end, he held a garden sprayer and pumped it several times, producing a cloud of fine particles that hung in the air like fog. If these were anthrax spores, he told us, we would all soon be dead. He then put a vial of simulated anthrax in my purse and scribbled his home number on the stationery of his one-man consulting firm, Biothreats Assessment. It was topped with an image of the Grim Reaper. A skull and crossbones were engraved on his business card. Call anytime, he said merrily.

He had issued the same invitation to Alibek after debriefing him for the CIA in 1992. The American germ warrior and his former nemesis had become unlikely friends — fellow bioweaponeers turned biodefenders. I would see the pattern often: American germ warriors bonding with their former Soviet rivals. It made sense. Relatively few people could understand their work or the secret lives they had led. The same characters would turn up in story after story.

Bill Patrick, for example, was part of our initial story on Iraq's bioweapons programs. The United Nations Special Commission, UNSCOM, had recruited him to help conduct inspections at suspect biofacilities around Baghdad. A mix of diplomats, scientists, and former military and intelligence officers, many of them former Cold War adversaries, UNSCOM was responsible for verifying Iraq's progress on its postwar pledge in 1991 to destroy its WMD and dismantle related programs. In 1992 Patrick visited Al Hakam, Iraq's main germ production facility about thirty miles southwest of Baghdad. Iraq insisted that the gigantic plant had produced only animal feed and biopesticides. But Patrick warned fellow inspectors that Al Hakam's fermenters, given their design and configuration, had probably produced something far more sinister.

Patrick had no proof, but his instinct was right. In July 1995, Iraqi scientists were finally forced to acknowledge not only that they had produced thousands of gallons of anthrax and botulinum at Al Hakam but also that they had made enough deadly microbes at some thirty facilities to wipe out much of the planet's people under the proper conditions.

Patrick had worked closely with UN-SCOM inspectors who had long been convinced that Iraq was lying about its WMD programs, its bio effort in particular: Richard Spertzel, who, like Patrick, had worked as a top germ specialist at Fort Detrick; David Kelly, a British microbiologist and Britain's top germ weapons expert; and their boss, deputy UNSCOM commissioner Charles Duelfer, an American intelligence analyst with extensive knowledge of Iraq and unconventional weapons. All of them would play key roles in our germ series for the *Times* and my future WMD reporting.

While most accounts of Iraq's belated disclosure of its covert germ weapons programs attributed Iraq's sudden candor to the defection to Jordan of Lt. Gen. Hussein Kamel, Saddam's son-in-law, who had managed its germ and other WMD efforts, Bill and I reported in February 1998 that UNSCOM's inspectors had forced Iraq's hand even before Kamel's defection.[2] The inspectors' repeated visits to Iraqi facilities and persistent inquiries had gradually demolished Iraq's cover stories.

In our first, 4,700-word chronicle of the seven-year hunt for Iraq's secret germ arsenal, we described how the inspectors' patient probing had proven that Iraq had lied consistently about having destroyed its germ weapons and other aspects of its biowarfare activities. Our "special report" — lengthy even by the paper's standards at the time — opened with Rod Barton, an Australian scientist and bioweapons expert, confronting Rihab Taha, or "Dr. Germ," as she would later be known, with two pieces of paper that Israel had given UNSCOM. The sales slips showed that in 1988 Iraq had bought twenty-nine tons of media (microbial food used to grow germs), and, in the years leading up to the 1991 Gulf War, ten more tons of the material from a British company. But Iraq could show that it had used only two hundred kilograms of the media in its hospitals and civilian programs. What had happened to the rest?

The Iraqis offered preposterous explanations. The material had been lost. Some of it had fallen off a truck during shipment. Records of its fate had been destroyed in an unfortunate fire that had engulfed a single file cabinet in a government office. Material had been lost in postwar riots in which Iraqis attacked local research facilities and looted only the growth media.[3] The only explanation they didn't invoke, David Kelly remarked, was that their dog had eaten the media.

As political pressure mounted over the inspectors' findings, the cover crumbled. After years of denials, Dr. Taha finally acknowledged to inspectors in the summer of 1995 that Al Hakam had been built to produce anthrax and botulinum for germ weapons. And yes, she conceded, Iraq had systematically misled inspectors about the program that had made enough pathogens to endanger the planet. But, she added in tears, the weapons and the lethal pathogens produced at Hakam had all been destroyed. Our story reported that even then, few inspectors or US officials believed her. Most concluded that Baghdad was still hiding not only missiles and germ weapons but also the means to make both.

Steve Engelberg's hunch about the anthrax vaccinations of soldiers had paid off.

223

Our reporting showed that the Pentagon's concern about germs had been triggered not only by UNSCOM's reports about Iraq but also by the implications of what Alibek and others had told Western intelligence agencies about the Soviet germ program.

In March 1998 I accompanied an inter-agency American team to Stepnogorsk, a city in the midst of the windblown Kazakh steppe, which, in Soviet times, had been closed to all but a few Soviet citizens. The biocomplex here was built in 1982 to develop a new, more lethal anthrax. Moscow's most advanced germ warfare production plant, Stepnogorsk was the only major germ facility outside of the Soviet heartland. Eager for American help in cleaning up the biological debris and finding peaceful work for the 180 scientists who still worked there, the Kazakh government had permitted Andy Weber, then a young diplomat at the American Embassy in Almaty, to tour Stepnogorsk in the summer of 1995. Three years later, I was accompanying his team on yet another visit — the first Western journalist to gain such access.

At his new post at the Pentagon, Weber told me that in Soviet times, Stepnogorsk had been listed on no map. Its address was a post office box, no. 2076. Although the CIA had deduced correctly from satellite photos of the configuration of the plant's more than fifty buildings that it had been designed to produce biological agents, spy agencies had little idea how serious a threat it posed until two senior Soviet scientists had defected.

As Andy and I stood in front of Building 221, the main production area, I was stunned by the size of what was now a decaying wreck. The ten fermentation vats towering four stories above us could each hold twenty thousand liters of fluid. The building itself was two football fields long.

Working at full capacity, the vessels could brew three hundred tons of anthrax spores in a production cycle of 220 days, enough to fill many Intercontinental ballistic missiles. Since one hundred grams of dried anthrax was theoretically enough to wipe out a small city, the product of this plant alone, if dispersed under ideal conditions, was more than enough to have killed the entire American population. And Stepnogorsk was just one of at least six Soviet production facilities — a standby plant that could produce mass quantities of anthrax if an international crisis arose.

Month by month, lab by lab, I negotiated

access through friendly Russian scientists and sympathetic officials to other components of the Soviets' biowarfare program, which at its peak had employed over sixty thousand scientists and technicians at over a hundred facilities throughout a country with eleven time zones. Sometimes I accompanied American officials; more often I was on my own. The Soviets had studied more than eighty biological agents and prepared more than a dozen others for war. The United States may have had a military-industrial complex, as I wrote later in our book *Germs,* but the Soviet Union *was* a military-industrial complex.

It took months to arrange to meet Lev Sandakhchiev, the Soviet director of the State Research Center of Virology and Biotechnology, at a conference in Washington. But after we met, he emailed me a rare invitation to his center, known for short as Vector, a name worthy of a James Bond film. Located in Koltsovo, a remote corner of Siberia, Vector had been a crown jewel of the Soviet germ warfare program. For almost two decades it specialized in weaponizing the world's deadliest viruses, including smallpox.

Weber and his team had outmaneuvered government skeptics, especially at the

Pentagon, and forged an agreement with Sandakhchiev for access and assistance to Vector after he and other experts had visited the complex and concluded that it appeared to have stopped illicit germ research after the Soviet Union's collapse. Sandakhchiev confided to Weber that he had received little funding from Moscow since 1991. But he couldn't simply abandon the hundreds of people on his staff. Where would they go? For whom would they work? He had 2,200 scientists to house and pay — half the number at its peak of operations — a lab to run, and monkeys and research supplies to buy.

There was both danger and opportunity in Vector's desperation. Iraq, Iran, or North Korea would surely offer jobs to financially strapped scientists. Vector was already selling diagnostic kits for hepatitis, and antivirals and other medications to Tehran. If Sandakhchiev was as committed as he seemed to transforming Vector into an open, international viral research center, his dream would only advance America's own security interests.

Washington initially gave Vector about $3 million — "chump change," as Andy Weber's boss called it. But to cash-strapped Sandakhchiev, the money was roughly half his annual budget. It not only ensured his center's survival but also that his scientists would be less likely to be lured away.

In September 1999 Weber and I traveled to Siberia for Vector's twenty-fifth anniversary. The World Health Organization had designated this remote center as one of the world's two repositories of the now eradicated smallpox virus — the other being America's Centers for Disease Control and Prevention (CDC) in Atlanta. Moscow had worried Western scientists by secretly moving its deadly smallpox stockpile from a lab in Moscow to Vector in 1994 (supposedly to safeguard it against radical Islamist terrorists). The Russians were storing 120 smallpox isolates at Vector — the world's largest collection, twice the size of America's — as well as 10,000 of the world's most exotic viruses and strains of other lethal pathogens Soviet scientists had tried to weaponize: Marburg, Ebola, Lassa fever, and others that cause the most deadly, contagious hemorrhagic fevers.

Sandakhchiev stressed his concern that such strains might fall into jihadi or Iranian hands. An Armenian, he feared that the insurgency in the former Soviet state of Chechnya was a warning of things to come in Russia. Andy, known at the Pentagon for his calm demeanor and fluent Russian, tried to assure Lev that the best guarantee against the spread of such weapons and expertise to Muslim fanatics was cooperation with Washington. I was struck by the trust Sandakhchiev seemed to place in Weber, with whom he spent much time in the *banya,* or sauna — and also by Weber's ability to elicit from him some of the deepest secrets about germ warfare.

Why were Sandakhchiev and other Soviet scientists willing to speak freely in the sauna's confines? Andy smiled. Probably because there were no watchful eyes and ears in such places, he said; listening devices were hard to hide in the towels they wore into the *banya,* and the rooms were too hot to bug.

It wasn't long before I encountered signs of the Iranian germ-hunting teams that Sandakhchiev feared. In December 1998 I was visiting the All-Russian Institute of Phytopathology in Golitsino, just west of Moscow, an institute that in the Soviet era had made germs for killing crops. Since the Soviet Union's collapse, the institute had struggled to stay afloat through peaceful research. The facility was so poorly heated that I wore my scarf and coat. But despite having reduced its staff from 1,200 to 276, many of whom were paid intermittently, Golitsino still excelled at manipulating plant genes to resist herbicides, insects, and disease.

As I chatted over tea with Yuri Spiridonov, a crop expert who headed the lab's herbicide department, he mentioned that a five-man team of Iranian scientists had visited Golitsino the previous year. The head of the delegation was Mehdi Rezayat, whose business card identified him as the director of Tehran Medical Sciences University's pharmacology department and also as a "scientific adviser" for Iran's then president, Mohammad Khatami. Dr. Rezayat, who spoke fluent English, had expressed great interest in scientific exchanges. He claimed to have already visited most of the former Soviet labs and met their directors and top scientists.

Spiridonov had been suspicious of his Iranian guests. For one thing, several delegation members seemed to be clerics, not scientists. "They just sat there most of the time, saying nothing, sitting on their hands," he said. For another, Rezayat was studiously ambiguous about precisely what he wanted the Russian scientists to do when and if they accepted Iran's invitation to visit or work there. Finally, a few members of Rezayat's team had shown particular interest in learning about microbes that could be used in war to destroy or protect crops, and in "dual use" genetic engineering that could be used in legitimate research but also to make deadly pathogens for which there were no antidotes.

More than one US intelligence official had already told me that Mehdi Rezayat was a senior Iranian intelligence officer — a recruiter of technology and talent for Iran's WMD programs, especially its germ weapons program. No CIA official was willing to be quoted about him, but Ahmad Hashim, a Middle East expert who consulted for the US government, let me quote him as saying that Rezayat's branch of intelligence was well known for its "relentless pursuit" of equipment and expertise in deadly weaponry, and not just in Russia.[4] The same branch was also responsible for public health, a convenient cover.

Dr. Spiridonov claimed to have declined several invitations to visit Tehran, but said that three of the institute's scientists had gone there. Who could blame them? Rezayat was offering germ weapon scientists $5,000 a month — more than Russian scientists made in a year given Russia's increasingly chaotic economy.

I always seemed to be two steps behind the peripatetic Dr. Rezayat. But on a trip to Moscow in December 1998, scientists at a lab he had visited gave me a copy of his business card. Rezayat had left the lab that morning and was still in Moscow, staying at a hotel not far from mine. His business card in hand, I raced to his hotel. The concierge told me that Rezayat had just left. When I reached him later that day by phone (at a number he had scrawled on the back of his card) and asked to meet him, he sounded flustered. Realizing that I might not have another chance to seek direct comment from him for my story, I asked him bluntly whether he was helping recruit Russian scientists for Iran's germ warfare program. Regaining his composure, Rezayat said calmly that such charges were both common and false. He was willing to meet me to discuss the matter further, he added, but not without Tehran's approval. He promised to seek permission. A day later, his assistant called to say that Dr. Rezayat was no longer in Russia.

Now in June 1999, I wondered whether Dr. Rezayat had discovered Voz Island, the place where germs went to die, as I double-checked my mask and rubber gloves. The

Russian helicopter pilot smirked at my precautions, his bloodshot eyes focused with amused disdain on the plastic bottle of Purell and one small baggie of dried bleach I had stuffed into my knapsack, just in case. He had been to the island many times, he told me. Nothing lived here.

That was not true. As I walked toward the vast laboratory complex from the island's germ test range where the chopper had landed, a tiny lizard slithered by one of the telephone poles from which detectors had measured germs and to which animals had been tied during open-air testing. The telephone poles, about a kilometer apart, stretched as far as I could see.

The laboratory and its high-containment unit where the deadliest of tests were conducted had been stripped bare of their equipment, pipes, and even their floor and wall tiles. Only a few remained. The once shiny light-green mosaics were decorated with a fish motif — a nice touch, I thought. Such tiles were a hallmark of germ labs: they were easy to wash down and decontaminate with bleach. Intelligence experts told me that what the Soviets had left behind, scavengers — apparently impervious to fears of contamination — had stripped away for sale at bazaars in the Uzbek cities of Nukus and faraway Tashkent. They had done the same at the nuclear test site of Semipalatinsk, in Kazakhstan, where I had reported on the closing of one of the tunnels the Soviets had built inside the mountain range to conduct underground nuclear tests. Thanks to the smugglers' ingenuity, radioactive copper was now being sold in markets and bazaars throughout Central Asia.

The vivaria that once housed thousands of smaller animals killed in germ tests — rabbits, guinea pigs, white mice, and hamsters — and larger animals such as horses, sheep, donkeys, monkeys, and baboons, were now empty, their windows smashed or missing, roofs collapsed.[5]

In one bungalow, obviously a storage room, hundreds of small cages were stacked. Next to them was a room containing a human-sized cage — apparently for what scientists call "nonhuman primates." Hundreds of all-too-human primates had died hideous deaths, sometimes in a single experiment, Ken Alibek and Gennady Lepyoshkin, Stepnogorsk's current director, had told me.

Both scientists adamantly denied that the Soviets had ever experimented on people. I had no way of knowing whether that was true. But the KGB, which had its own labs for developing germ weapons for assassinations, had apparently not been as fastidious. Bill Broad, who had focused on Soviet efforts to use genetically engineered germs and toxins to cause psychological and physiological changes in still-murky programs named Bonfire and Flute, was told that KGB scientists had experimented on human beings as part of these programs.

There were rumors that the Soviets had even tested smallpox here on Voz Island. Uzbek and Kazakh officials had often complained about having been the Soviet Union's nuclear and biological dumping ground. Voz Island's sad history was emblematic of Moscow's disdain for the citizens of the Muslim "stans."

In the spring of 1988, as President Mikhail Gorbachev had grown ever more nervous that evidence of the illicit germ weapons program that he had approved and doubled in size might be uncovered, Russian germ scientists had been ordered to dispose of the evidence. But where could hundreds of tons of dried anthrax be buried? Moscow had selected Voz, over a thousand miles away from Sverdlovsk, where much of the anthrax had been made, and Zima, near Irkutsk, where it was stored.

Working in haste and total secrecy, scientists had transferred tons of the germs into stainless-steel canisters that were loaded onto a train two dozen cars long and sent on a long journey to Voz. At the edge of the test range, Soviet soldiers had poured bleach into the canisters to decontaminate the deadly pink powder, dug huge pits, and poured the sludge into the ground, burying the decontaminated spores, and so, Moscow hoped, a serious political embarrassment.

Andy Weber's team, which had dug up some of the anthrax and sent it back to America for testing, had discovered that some of the hardy little spores were still alive. Tests of soil samples from six of the eleven burial pits showed that although the spores had been soaked in bleach at least twice and buried for almost a decade under three to five feet of sand, some remained potentially deadly. But the tests had also shown that the anthrax vaccine being given American military personnel was effective against the strain found on Voz.

The discovery had further alarmed Kazakh and Uzbek officials. Because the Aral Sea was shrinking, officials feared that the spores might escape their sandy tomb and be carried to the mainland by lizards like the one I had seen, rodents, and birds.

American officials feared that as access to the island became easier, the buried anthrax could also be dug up by terrorists. Doctors Without Borders told me that people in the Uzbek and Kazakh regions near testing areas like Voz were chronically ill. In desperation, Uzbek and Kazakh officials had turned to Weber and the Americans for help in cleaning up the biological debris.

En route back to the chopper, I stopped at the northern part of the site. Less than a mile from the lab stood the three-story barracks, homes, kindergarten, and cafeteria that Russian scientists and their families had used — about a thousand people in all. I took pictures of the children's playground with its swings and a jungle gym — an eerie reminder of those who had once called this forbidding place home. Gennady Lepyoshkin had told me that most of the children who lived here had not been vaccinated against the agents that were tested just a few miles downwind. They hadn't tested unless the wind was blowing south, away from their living quarters, he told me.

Lepyoshkin spoke almost nostalgically of his weeks here in the mid-1980s, testing Stepnogorsk's "products." The watercolors he had painted when he was not working with deadly microbes, playing volleyball, or drinking vodka still hung on the walls of his small flat in Stepnogorsk. The island was smaller and more beautiful then, he told me. From his bedroom, you could see the sea.

As I thought about Voz Island, I concluded that Ronald Reagan had been right about at least one thing: there was only one word to describe the systematic creation of disease by the ton — *evil*.

Moscow had turned science on its head. While most scientists struggled to cure the sick and defeat disease, the Soviets had secretly spent billions creating and mobilizing disease for war. The Soviets had harnessed their best brains, virtually unlimited resources, and Russian science to the mass production of epidemics.

Weber and officials like him were promoting programs to understand what Moscow had achieved. Such programs were essential to understanding the Soviet program and how to protect Americans against such pathogens, he argued persuasively, despite the risks. And America, if necessary, might be justified in using force to stop nations such as Iran and Iraq, or rogue groups like Al Qaeda, Hamas, and Hezbollah, from acquiring similar capabilities.

The United States faced new WMD-based threats, especially twenty-first-century bio-weapons that most Americans knew little about. Saddam, I recalled, had continued lying about his germ weapons activities long after he had closed down his nuclear program. And as the Soviet Union was collapsing, its scientists were still struggling to weaponize Marburg and Ebola viruses — which had no proven vaccines or antidotes. Ken Alibek and other defectors had warned us that Russian scientists were still conducting secret work in labs to create new bio-weapons, including new "chimera" pathogens that combined several types of microbes. Russia, for instance, had not abandoned its effort to blend the Ebola virus with smallpox, mankind's greatest scourge. If I did nothing else as a journalist, I had to write about what I had learned from the foreign scientists and officials who had helped create the germ threat and those who were committed to stopping it. If I did nothing else.

CHAPTER 11
AL QAEDA

In the Oval Office on an icy day in January 1999, President Bill Clinton reached out and touched the cast on my leg. He said that he, too, had torn a ligament several years ago. He said it had hurt like hell. Was I in pain?

He won me over at hello.

Having hurt my leg snorkeling over Christmas, I had limped into the White House on crutches alongside Bill Broad to interview the president — the first interview he had given since the Monica Lewinsky scandal a year earlier. We had been trying for months to interview him about the growing threat of biological weapons. His aides had finally, if reluctantly, agreed but insisted that Clinton would address only that issue.

During our interview, Clinton's lawyers were at the Senate defending him at impeachment proceedings. But he seemed relaxed and focused on germ weapons. A fire burned softly in the Oval Office. A portrait of George Washington gazed down at his successor. The room was quiet, tranquil.

Clinton predicted, presciently, that a biological or chemical attack in America in the next few years was "highly likely." While a chemical attack would be terrible, a germ attack would spread contagion, particularly if the perpetrators used a pathogen that could not be quickly identified and treated. He said it would be "the gift that keeps on giving." Bioweapons were cheap, easy to make, and left few fingerprints. They were what kept him awake at night.[1]

Clinton added that even worse would be a terrorist getting his hands on bioweapons, especially someone like Osama bin Laden, who had been accused of masterminding the bombings of the US embassies in Kenya and Tanzania the previous August, in which 224 people had died, 12 of them Americans. Clinton told us that terrorists were more likely than rogue states to use WMD against Americans. Rogue states were likely to hesitate for fear of retaliation. He asserted that Bin Laden had tried to make chemical weapons and "may have" tried to weaponize germs.

Bill Broad and I looked at each other. We

had seen intelligence reports that Bin Laden was recruiting Pakistani scientists to develop such weapons. We would discover only after 9/11 that Al Qaeda had already opened a small lab in Kandahar, Afghanistan, to produce anthrax. Later, experts told me that Al Qaeda's scientists had failed because they had been unable to acquire appropriate "seed cultures" for *Bacillus anthracis:* the starter germs needed to make anthrax. Given more time, they probably would have succeeded.

We were impressed by how much the president knew about unconventional weapons that might fall into terrorist hands and sensed that he would do whatever he thought was necessary to prevent such an attack. Only the month before, he had ordered four days of air strikes against Iraq's missile and suspected WMD sites, Operation Desert Fox, with over a thousand air strikes on some one hundred suspected chemical, germ, and missile sites. Clinton would later write in *My Life* that his national security team was "unanimous in the belief that we should hit Saddam . . . to minimize the chances that Iraq could disperse its forces and protect its biological and chemical stocks."[2]

The political backlash against Clinton's

preventive campaign was fierce. Senior Republicans insisted that Clinton had attacked to delay the House vote on impeachment: Desert Fox was *Wag the Dog.*[3] White House reporters called it "Monica's war."

Bill and I tended to believe Clinton. We had already spent a year investigating Iraq's efforts to hide its germ weapons programs. By the time of the December attacks, Iraq had spurned many attempts by Washington and UNSCOM to close the WMD file. Washington had tried almost every foreign policy tool to counter Saddam's aggression and secrecy: engagement, diplomatic isolation, inspections, sanctions, travel bans, trade embargoes, no-fly zones. Nothing had made Saddam honor his pledges. Baghdad was still denying UNSCOM information about its WMD efforts. Saddam's thugs were also harassing and threatening the agency's inspectors. Only after the UN inspectors had caught Iraqi officials in a series of lies had Baghdad admitted to having loaded botulinum toxin into sixteen warheads, anthrax germs into five warheads, and aflatoxin (which causes liver cancer) into four warheads. Baghdad had also belatedly acknowledged having filled 157 aerial bombs with the same deadly agents and having conducted research on tricothecene mycotoxins (which cause nausea, vomiting, and diarrhea), wheat cover smut (which ruins food grains), agents that cause hemorrhagic conjunctivitis (which causes extreme pain and temporary blindness), rotavirus (which causes acute diarrhea that can lead to death), and camel pox (a version of smallpox). The UN inspectors said that Iraq, belligerent and uncooperative, had accounted for only 25 of those 157 germ bombs and offered no convincing evidence that even those 25 had been destroyed.

The inspectors came from many different countries, not all of them friendly to the United States. If Saddam wasn't protecting WMD stockpiles or ongoing programs, why would he reject full inspections?

As Desert Fox got under way in December 1998, Bill and I wrote an article that, in effect, defended Clinton by explaining why most arms control experts doubted Baghdad's claims. Our story quoted anonymous UN inspectors who told us they suspected that Saddam might be hiding two to five times more deadly germ agents than Iraq had admitting making, plus the warheads to deliver them.[4] In his speech to the nation, Clinton said that he had ordered the raids solely "to help contain Saddam's WMD." While he had not been "eager" to use force, he asserted, he would not hesitate to do so to protect America's "vital interests."

Clinton's December strike was the second time in a year that he had acted against what he believed to be a WMD threat. On August 20, 1998, thirteen days after Al Qaeda destroyed American embassies in Africa, he authorized cruise missile strikes not only against Bin Laden's camps in Afghanistan but also against the Al Shifa pharmaceutical company in Khartoum. The plant was run by a government entity in which Bin Laden had invested. Based on information that the intelligence agencies had gleaned from highly sensitive sources and methods — both human and electronic, I was told, but asked initially not to print — administration officials believed that the plant was trying to make ingredients of VX, the deadly nerve agent, for Al Qaeda. Critics pounded Clinton for the Sudan strike — arguing that the evidence of illicit chemical weapons activity at that particular plant was contradictory. Having interviewed Sudan's militant Islamist ruler Omar al-Bashir, who boasted about his warm ties to Bin Laden, whom he was hosting, I believed Clinton and my sources on his National Security Council. Soon after the strike, I coauthored a front-page story reporting that intelligence officials had concluded that senior Iraqi scientists were helping the Sudanese try to produce VX ingredients at the plant.[5] But the controversy over the accuracy of the intelligence and Clinton's motives persisted.

After Clinton's 1998 missile strikes, Russia, China, and France, all of which did considerable business with Iraq, succeeded in disbanding UNSCOM and replacing it with a weaker UN inspection agency[6] known as UNMOVIC (United Nations Monitoring, Verification, and Inspection Commission). Sensing that the Lewinsky scandal had weakened Clinton at home, Saddam turned what should have been a military defeat into a political victory. "What is an intern?" Tariq Aziz, Saddam's foreign minister, asked Charles Duelfer, UNSCOM's deputy director, during a visit to Baghdad in early 1998 as the scandal was unfolding, incredulous that a president's dalliances with a young woman could have so disrupted American foreign policy.

By 1999, national security officials in Washington recognized the threat from Osama bin Laden. But that was not true three years earlier when I returned turned to the *Times* from an eighteen-month leave of absence to write *God Has Ninety-nine Names,* a report of the growth of militant Islamist movements. Published in early 1996, the book contained a single paragraph about the young Saudi who had financed the Afghan rebels and other radical Islamist causes. A 1997 National Intelligence Estimate (NIE) on terrorism, the last of the intelligence community's secret and most authoritative assessments of the terror threat distributed before 9/11, mentioned Bin Laden only briefly.

Joe Lelyveld, the paper's executive editor, had assigned me to unpromising investigative work on the culture desk in 1996 after my book leave. This was not my first or even second choice. In a memo to Lelyveld and Dean Baquet, then the national editor and now the paper's executive editor, I had proposed creating a beat to cover what I called the "new national security threats" which defied the paper's traditional beats and postings — cyberterrorism, bioengineering, the theft of American intellectual property, assaults on "critical infrastructure," and the proliferation of "weapons of mass destruction." "While we have reporters who cover the State Department, the Pentagon, or the FBI, and the CDC in Atlanta," I wrote, no one was responsible for systematically covering such technologically based unconventional threats to national security "not from a particular building or place but as a theme." Nor had we written consistently about "the civil liberties challenges inherent in many of the new projects aimed at protecting Americans from such threats." I never heard from either senior editor. Steve Engelberg, who had recently been appointed investigations editor, knew that I missed covering national security and was irrepressibly competitive. He was helping supervise a team of reporters who were tracking the explosion and crash of TWA Flight 800 off the coast of Long Island in which 230 people died. Many reporters and even senior editors believed that terrorism was to blame. Steve persuaded Joe to let me help Jeff Gerth, who was still in the Washington bureau, write a broader story on terrorism.

Fourteen months into the investigation of the TWA crash, the FBI announced it had found no evidence of terrorism. But our inquiry led Jeff and me to spot an important shift in the pattern of terrorist attacks. In August 1996, a month after the disaster, we wrote a front-page story asserting that counterterrorism officials were now as worried about terrorist groups and their wealthy financiers, especially from Saudi Arabia and the Persian Gulf, as about Iran and Libya. The emergence of "sophisticated, privately financed networks of terrorists" posed new, even more daunting challenges for the United States, we wrote. Wealthy Muslim businessmen in the Gulf, for instance, had helped finance Ramzi Yousef, enabling him to carry out the first World Trade Center attack in February 1993, as well as another plot called Bojinka to blow up a dozen American airliners on Pacific routes. Only later would investigators link Yousef to his uncle: Khalid Sheikh Mohammed, the "principal architect of 9/11," as the 9/11 Commission called him.

Jeff and I learned that American intelligence agencies were focused on one terrorist financier in particular, Bin Laden. The State Department called Bin Laden "one of the most significant financial sponsors of Islamic extremist activities in the world." In the summer of 1996, when Jeff and I wrote about the government's shift of focus from rogue states to wealthy groups and individuals, our article was the first major exposé of Bin Laden's role in jihadi violence.

A few reporters took note. Peter Bergen of CNN, who had been covering militant Islam since the 1993 World Trade Center attack, followed up on our article in Afghanistan. The first, and one of only a handful of reporters, to interview Bin Laden for an American news outlet, Peter often credited our assessment as groundbreaking in his own superb reporting.[7]

Jeff and I had tried unsuccessfully to get Bin Laden to comment. In his earlier interviews with reporters, he had denied any involvement in terrorism. We quoted his spokesman in London, Khaled al-Fawwaz, as describing the terrorism charge as "rubbish."

In 1992 I had tried to interview Bin Laden for my book on the resurgence of militant Islam. When I was covering a meeting of Arab extremists hosted by the militant Islamist regime in Khartoum, my interpreter and I drove out to his compound on the outskirts of the capital to try to meet him. But guards with Kalashnikov assault rifles turned us away. I left my business card with some of his aides, one of whom was an associate of Khaled al-Fawwaz. I offered to return to Khartoum to see Bin Laden whenever he liked.

I thought little about my offer until 1996, when Jeff and I were trying to get Bin Laden to comment on our story about him. Fawwaz had promised to relay the request to him in Afghanistan, but we never heard back. Two years later, in the spring of 1998, Fawwaz called me. Was I still interested in interviewing Bin Laden?

Normally, I would have jumped at the invitation. But I hesitated. Richard Clarke, Clinton's chief counterterrorism adviser, and other officials I trusted had warned me that Bin Laden was becoming more aggressive by the day and his militant networks ever more violent. Bin Laden was no longer a mere financier of terror but a key operator. His goal was to unite disparate militant groups under the single banner of the group he had founded and funded: Al Qaeda, "the base." He had issued a fatwa calling on all Muslims to kill Americans wherever and whenever they could.

The *Times* did not like reporters poaching on others' beats. I had written terrorism stories, but one of our correspondents closer to the region could have interviewed Bin Laden and would have resented my doing so.

What's more, I was more apprehensive. Perhaps it was the trip's logistics. I was to fly to Islamabad, Pakistan, and then on to Peshawar, near the Afghanistan border. Someone from Bin Laden's group whom Fawwaz would not identify would meet me at an as yet undesignated hotel and drive me across the border to Bin Laden's location at an undisclosed place in the Afghan mountains. I was to tell no one outside the newspaper about the purpose of my visit and take no electronic items with me except a cell phone.

This unnerved me. While Bin Laden had probably not read my book, numerous articles about it and me were on the internet. They would know that I identified myself as Jewish and considered Islamic militants dangerous. I was uneasy enough about the offer not to pursue it with Steve Engelberg or others in the paper's chain of command. I feared that Bin Laden might decide that killing this particular messenger would send a more powerful message than anything I could write.

Fawwaz didn't tell me at the time that he had also extended a similar invitation to a colleague: John Miller, no relation, who was then at ABC. John later became the FBI's spokesman and New York City's deputy police commissioner for counterterrorism. When I watched his superb interview with Bin Laden on TV in May 1998, I was delighted for him, and also envious. If I had been braver, or better positioned within the paper, I thought at the time, the *Times* and I could have shared the scoop.

■ ■ ■ ■

In the fall of 2000, two years after I had turned down the chance to interview Bin Laden, I was en route to Afghanistan to interview Ahmed Shah Massoud, the charismatic military leader of the Northern Alliance, the major Afghan opposition to Bin Laden's Taliban hosts.

I was deeply involved by then in a series about Bin Laden, Al Qaeda, and the growing jihadi terrorist threat. I felt it was important to understand why young Muslim men had traveled to this forlorn land to fight for the self-declared Islamist state. Since 1996, when the Taliban had seized the Afghan capital, Kabul, the so-called "students" of Islam had turned their country into a nightmare.[8] Yet their rule was admired by thousands of foreign-born Muslims who had come to Afghanistan to fight for them. I wanted to understand why.

I had second thoughts about my decision soon after the helicopter lifted off an airstrip near Dushanbe, Tajikistan's capital. The Northern Alliance's Soviet chopper was even older than the one I had taken to Voz Island a year earlier. The Afghan opposition had only four of these vintage vehicles left.

The fifth had crashed a few weeks earlier, killing all on board. As I glanced out the mud-splashed window, I saw nothing below us but jagged mountain peaks.

I was relieved when we touched down north of Kabul at a makeshift Massoud camp. But the mortars I could hear seemed awfully close. After offering me tea, an anxious aide told me we had to leave immediately. The Taliban were attacking. Three nerve-racking hours later, our convoy of jeeps and ancient cars arrived in the Panjshir Valley at one of Massoud's many headquarters. Although it was the end of summer, the house was freezing. There was no heat or power. Later that night, I interviewed the commander by candlelight.

An ethnic Tajik with expressive brown eyes, a well-clipped mustache, and a white-tipped beard, Massoud was very different from the Arab leaders I had covered. He had no interest in small talk, flattery, or inquiries about one's health, staples of Arab conversation. He spoke fractured French, not English — the result of a few years' education in a French lycée. And he quickly acknowledged his mistakes. He accepted partial blame for the terrible civil war among Afghanistan's many Islamic sects and ethnic groups after the Soviets were driven out in 1989.

Despite financial aid and weapons from Iran and Russia, he said, his alliance was losing ground to the Taliban. They had often tried to kill him, he told me. (On the eve of 9/11, they would succeed.) The soldiers Massoud had fought earlier that day — the so-called Fifty-fifth Brigade — had been assembled by Bin Laden himself, and included some seven hundred Arabs and other militant Muslims. His forces had captured some brigade members whom he called seasoned fighters. I asked to interview them, but he refused. His security had not yet interrogated them. But he agreed to let me interview some of the 120 foreign Muslim fighters whom he was holding among his 1,200 Taliban prisoners. These young foreign fighters — Pakistanis, Yemenis, Britons, and Chinese Uighurs, among others — were in a remote prison that was accessible only by helicopter.

An eternity later, as the helicopter rounded a set of craggy cliffs, with the prison and our landing spot in sight, its rotor sputtered. The chopper tipped sideways as we began to plunge. One of Massoud's aides pulled a Koran out of his flak jacket; another rapidly fingered his worry beads. A few seconds later, the chopper righted itself but came down hard about a half mile from our intended landing spot. Even the pilot, who must have been accustomed to such emergencies, looked relieved.

Over the next two days, I came face-to-face with several of the young men Bin Laden had inspired. Muhammad Khaled Mihraban, a Pakistani from Lahore, was only twenty-six, but he claimed to have killed at least one hundred people. He had an "Islamic ideal" to fulfill, he told me. Afghanistan under the Taliban was the pure land he had been seeking. If ordered to so do, he would travel to New York to kill women and children for Islam. He would not hesitate.

I heard similar words from other prisoners. Obeida Rahman, twenty-one, a Yemeni from Sana, one of ten children, had been sent to Afghanistan by teachers at his madrassa, the religious school. They had paid for living and training expenses in Afghanistan and, against his family's wishes, encouraged him to fight. Abdul Jalil, twenty-one, from Kashgar in Xinjiang Province, China, said that despite his capture, he yearned to create an Islamic state "all over the world, God willing." When released, he would return to China to expand the jihad.

The young men being held here were a

sample of what the CIA estimated were between fifty thousand and seventy-seven thousand militants from fifty-five countries who had been trained in recent years at a network of camps that the Taliban hosted. Arab officials had estimated that as many as five thousand recruits had passed through camps that were operated by Bin Laden. Two terrorism experts I trusted — Mike Sheehan, the former US Army Ranger who had worked for President Clinton as the co-ordinator of the State Department's counterterrorism office, and Richard Clarke — said that participants in nearly every plot against the United States and its allies in the past decade had learned the arts of war and explosives in such camps. Bin Laden used the most closely guarded of them for advanced training on suicide bombs and mass attacks. The 1998 US Embassy bombings in Africa had been rehearsed on a model built to scale at a Bin Laden–run camp. Another, Abu Khabab, was being used to experiment on chemicals, poisons, and toxins.

I was planning to fly to Faizabad in the northeastern tip of Afghanistan, where three of the world's most forbidding mountain ranges converge. There I would wait in a guest house for a private relief group's weekly supply flight to Dushanbe in a more reliable, fixed-wing Cessna. The chopper that was to fly me to Faizabad was the most dilapidated yet. Its cracked windshield was covered in masking tape. Its fuel tank was leaking; the rusty cabin smelled like a gas station. A pipe carrying fuel to the rotor was wrapped in burlap. The pilot, who was smoking under the helicopter when I arrived, seemed disoriented. It was insane for me to board. But I had no choice. This junkyard dog of a chopper was my only way out of Afghanistan.

Mine was a telling panic. I had surely come closer to being killed in my reporting career. But I had obviously changed since those near misses. I was no longer the daring young foreign correspondent who had ventured into Khartoum's Kobar prison yard in 1985 amid several hundred impassioned Muslim believers to cover the hanging of an intellectual "heretic." By the end of 2000, I had a lot to live for: Jason, good friends, and the life I loved in New York.

Given my growing aversion to senseless risk, it was doubly ironic that four months later I would be pleading with Steve Engelberg to let me return to Afghanistan — this time as a guest of the Taliban.

Laili Helms was a soccer mom and mother of two who lived in New Jersey. An Afghan-American who had married the nephew of former CIA director Richard Helms, she was the Taliban's improbable unofficial spokesman in America.[9]

I was fascinated by Laili. A granddaughter of two former Afghan ministers in the late monarchy, she never seemed to tire of putting the best possible face on a regime whose human rights abuses were exasperating Washington. It was also clear to me that she loved Afghanistan and thought that the Taliban were the country's best hope of reestablishing security after a brutal civil war that had ruined what the Soviets hadn't destroyed.

In November 2000 she helped me interview the Taliban foreign minister, Wakil Ahmad Mutawakil, who had adamantly denied that his regime was hosting terrorist training camps. (Intelligence sources had already shown me satellite shots of such facilities.) He had also denounced American pressure to expel Bin Laden as "insulting and useless." Bin Laden had helped expel the Soviets. He was their guest. Finally, while some non-Afghan "volunteers" from the 1980s war against the Soviets remained in Afghanistan because they were not permitted to return to their countries, they were not being "trained" in "jihadi" training camps. There was none in Afghanistan, he insisted. Nothing was "hidden" in Afghanistan. I should come see for myself.

How could we refuse such an offer? I begged Steve. Thanks to my interviews with the opposition's Taliban prisoners in northern Afghanistan and information that I had from Western intelligence officials, we knew the names and locations of at least a dozen Bin Laden camps. The trip would provide the natural conclusion of our series on Al Qaeda and militant Islamic terrorism, I said. After a year of research, travel, and nonstop interviews, most of the articles for our series on the growing militant Islamist threat were almost finished, and a portrait of Al Qaeda and Bin Laden's terror network had emerged. All we needed was on-the-ground information about his camps. This was our best shot at getting it, I argued.

"Forget it," Steve Engelberg said when I first proposed the trip. "Dead reporters can't write stories."

Gradually I wore him down with daily justifications for the trip. The Afghan code

260

of hospitality, which even the Taliban shared, would protect me, I argued. If the Taliban refused to expel their "guest" Bin Laden, they were unlikely to kill or jail a reporter whom they had also invited to Kabul and were honor bound to protect. Besides, I had persuaded Laili to accompany me as translator and guide. Would the Taliban murder or imprison their best American advocate? Reluctantly, Steve agreed.

Clarke, Washington's counterterrorism chief, was less encouraging. Was I mad? he asked. Unlike Bin Laden, I wasn't paying the Taliban an estimated $40 million for its "hospitality" — money that had bought off local warlords and secured weapons. Dick was especially concerned about my determination to visit Abu Khabab camp. "Don't even think about going there," he warned me.

I didn't share Clarke's advice with Steve. In mid-December 2000 Laili and I left for Afghanistan. True to his word, Mutawakil welcomed us at his ministry with tea and sweets. After he discussed the interviews he had arranged, he asked us what we would like to see. I handed him a list of the Bin Laden camps I wanted to visit. The list contained a dozen names, locations, and ostensible specialties. The minister's face darkened. He twisted the end of his turban. There were no Arab Afghans at these locations, he said firmly. Yes, there were camps in some of the places on my list, but they were Taliban facilities for Afghans only. Of course I would be welcome to visit them.

The next day, armed with my list and a global positioning monitor to determine precise location, Laili and I set out in a Foreign Ministry car with a guide from the Interior Ministry, which conducted surveillance.

Our first stop was the Qargagh Division camp near the former tourist town of Paghman, twenty minutes north of Kabul. At the entrance, the guards told us that no one could enter without written authorization from the Defense Ministry. The Interior Ministry's permit was useless, they said, much to our Interior Ministry guide's embarrassment. The guards said there were no Arabs in the camp, but when we stopped for tea in Paghman, villagers told us there were lots of Arabs in Qargagh, as well as Turks, Africans, Tajiks, and, of course, "Punjabis" — the local term for Pakistanis. The foreigners had been there a long time, they said. Our Taliban guide insisted that they were mistaken.

Having failed to enter Qargagh, we tried later that day to visit a compound that had been closed a few months earlier through Pakistani pressure but was recently reactivated: Rishkoor, twenty minutes south of Kabul. There, too, guards denied us entry. The camp commandant had gone to Kabul to pray. No one could enter without his permission. We would wait for his return, I replied. That might take several days, they told me. Once again, villagers and relief workers near the camp told us that whenever the Taliban feared that the United States might be planning to target the camp, many of the Arab and other non-Afghan residents who lived there had moved to Kabul or other towns temporarily.

So it went, day after day, with Mutawakil promising to eliminate obstacles. Afghan officials later told Laili and me that he and the Taliban defense minister had argued over whether we should be admitted and that Mutawakil had even tried to persuade Mullah Omar, the Taliban's de facto ruler, to expel Bin Laden. As we waited in the Taliban guest house, Mullah Omar decided that only a UN commission would be granted entry to military installations because of the ongoing civil war. Humiliated and overruled, Minister Mutawakil became inaccessible.

On our fourth day in Jalalabad, a Foreign Ministry official appeared suddenly and promised to escort us to the Darunta complex, housing Abu Khabab. He had full authorization to do so, he said. Laili brightened. Mutawakil had prevailed after all, she said. The official asserted that Abu Khabab was not a military camp at all but an "agricultural and technical training area" where chemicals and other fertilizer ingredients were stored. Yet shortly before we were scheduled to leave, the embarrassed diplomat reappeared: the trip was off, he apologized. The provincial governor had disapproved our visit. He hoped that we had enjoyed our stay in Afghanistan, he added, politely inviting us to leave the country later that day. He would escort us to the border.

As our car headed for Pakistan, I saw a sign indicating the turnoff to Darunta. "Turn here," I instructed the driver, as Laili gasped, and the young diplomat protested. "I'm not leaving Afghanistan without seeing the Darunta dam," I told them. Based on a map I had gotten from Western intelligence officials, I knew that a few miles farther down the road was a bridge that led directly to the Abu Khabab camp. We had made it, I thought.

Soon after we made the turn, several heavily armed, bearded men suddenly appeared out of nowhere and surrounded our car. Laili blanched. So did the Taliban diplomat. One of the guards was carrying a rocket-propelled grenade; the other approached the driver's side of the car, pointing his Kalashnikov straight at us through the half-open window. Neither of them spoke, but their motion for us to turn the car around was unmistakable.

I didn't know who these men were, but judging from their appearance and dress, they weren't Afghans. Our status as "guests" of the Taliban riding in a Foreign Ministry car meant nothing to them as they barred our way.

I looked hard at the guard pointing his rifle at me. He returned the stare. I had seen those sinister eyes before: at Islamist militant rallies in the Sudan; in the jihadis in cages being tried after having killed Egypt's Anwar Sadat; at the prison in northern Afghanistan earlier that year. This man, whoever he was, meant business. I told our driver to turn the car around.

CHAPTER 12
ASHES AND ANTHRAX: THE SHADOW OF 9/11

Was it preventable — that terrible day?

The bipartisan 9/11 Commission, whose staff was headed by Philip Zelikow, the historian and policy analyst who had worked for President Bush, thought so. Based on interviews with 1,200 people in ten countries and a review of 2.5 million pages of documents containing national security secrets, the commission's devastating indictment blamed almost every branch of government, as well as the press, for appalling failures.

Published nearly three years after the catastrophic attack, the report made heartbreaking reading.[1] The CIA had lost track of two of the hijackers in Bangkok, Thailand, and failed to prevent them from entering the country. Although the agency had done more than any other to prevent the attacks, it had downplayed huge failures, such as its lack of sufficient intelligence and paramilitary ability to strike Al Qaeda at its base in Afghanistan. It had not produced a National Intelligence Estimate on terrorism since 1997, despite the growing number and lethality of attacks. Paul Pillar, the intelligence officer responsible for the Middle East and drafting national intelligence estimates on the region, had published a book arguing that terrorism had to be managed, not "won" and that Washington's "preoccupation" with capturing Osama bin Laden was a "misallocation of attention and resources."[2] Director George Tenet had declared "war" on Al Qaeda in 1998 after the US Embassy bombings in East Africa, almost no one in government had mobilized, including his agency.

In 1996 the CIA had established a special unit in a nondescript building in a Virginia suburb to monitor Bin Laden.[3] But even some of their colleagues regarded the unit as "alarmists." Resources for counterterrorism were not increased significantly. The CIA, responsible for monitoring enemies overseas, and the FBI, charged with tracking them down internally, resented each other. Rules and perverse traditions also prevented them from sharing information. The Federal Aviation Administration had not received names on the terrorist watch list. The State Department had ignored Saudi financing of militant Islamist groups.

The crucial weakness, though, was a lack of "imagination." America's leaders had failed to grasp "the gravity of the threat," the report said, echoing the Long Commission's bottom line in its report on the US Marine compound bombing in 1983. "The terrorist danger from Bin Laden and Al Qaeda," the 9/11 Commission report concluded, "was not a major topic for policy debate among the public, the media, or in the Congress."

The *Times*'s three-part series, published eight months before 9/11, was called "Holy Warriors." The project I helped launch, report, and write had warned explicitly of Bin Laden's militant terrorist network in Afghanistan. It described in detail the web of extremist Muslims that Al Qaeda was mobilizing to wage jihad against America and the West. It reported that Afghanistan had become "an essential base of operations, a reservoir of potential suicide bombers and a battle front where crucial ties were forged and plots being crafted." It disclosed that Al Qaeda trainers were believed to be experimenting with chemicals — and perhaps biological agents, poisons, and toxins

— at a complex of camps at a place called Darunta. It warned of plans for a major attack against America, though not precisely where or when it would come, or what form it would take. The series was among the most ambitious, expensive national security investigations the *Times* had ever published.

It had almost no impact.

The days after the 2001 attack were a blur. Dozens of *Times* reporters had raced to the site. I lived less than a mile away and had just gone around the corner to vote in the city's mayoral primary when the first plane struck the North Tower. I could see the flames and the smoking towers clearly. I tried to call John O'Neill, a trusted source and former FBI counterterrorism head who had become chief of security at the Towers, but could not reach him.

When I got to the office, Howell Raines and Gerald Boyd were mobilizing the *Times* army. Having led the paper for less than a week, they would send out three hundred reporters and fifty-four photographers that day to produce a comprehensive report on the attacks.[4] In the ensuing weeks and months, they followed up with a daily section of stunning quality. I had never been so proud to be a foot soldier in that *Times* army.

I spent much of that first day frantically trying to reach sources in Washington. Since this was surely an Al Qaeda attack, I would be more useful working my sources by phone from Forty-third Street than reporting from the site. I sent an email to Roger Cohen, the acting foreign editor. "Whoever is claiming credit," I wrote, "I think we need to focus on Bin Laden's networks."

I reached almost no one. Dick Clarke, his counterterrorism team at the White House, and experts at the Pentagon had been evacuated. Cell phones didn't work.

Our apartment downtown was a constant reminder of the tragedy. I had begged Jason to move in with friends uptown. The air where we lived — twenty blocks from the smoldering debris — was foul. Jason refused to leave, so I gave him a biomask from the stash I had used to tour Voz Island and warned him not to leave the apartment without wearing it. I did not believe, as officials assured us, that the air was safe.

I soon learned that John O'Neill had died in the attack he had warned us about for so long. John had seen it all: the bureau's successful apprehension of Ramzi Yousef in Pakistan to stand trial in New York for the

1993 World Trade Center bombing; the 1998 embassy bombings in Africa; Bin Laden's 1998 fatwa declaring war on America; the attack on the US Navy destroyer Cole in Yemen in 2000. How I would miss his knowledge and instincts, his "bullshit" barometer on all things Al Qaeda.[5]

Less than a month later at my desk, I opened a letter from Florida containing a mysterious powder initially thought to be anthrax, triggering more trauma for colleagues who were already under enormous stress. The office was evacuated, except for me, who was quarantined near my cubicle. I shall never forget the sight of those moon men in their tan head-to-toe biosuits and gas masks: public health and law enforcement officials who were sealing off the investigative unit with yellow crime-scene tape and moving noiselessly through our normally bustling newsroom. Reporters' computers were still on, but the third floor was silent save for the ringing of unanswered phones. Health officials prescribed the antibiotic Cipro for colleagues who were near me when I opened the letter, just in case the powder turned out to be deadly. It wasn't.

Once transport was reestablished in the

northeast, Howell Raines's deputy, Gerald Boyd, called me into his office. He wanted me to go to Washington to do "whatever it takes" to help keep us ahead on the story. I described his instructions to David Barstow, the star investigative reporter whose cubicle was next to mine, and Matt Purdy, then the investigative unit's deputy. I was worried, I told them, about Gerald having told me literally to "run amok" in turf-obsessed Washington. David and Matt were sympathetic. "I can just hear the wailing from the bureau," I told them. " 'Here comes little Miss Run Amok,' " a phrase I coined in self-mocking jest.

I spent much of the fall of 2001 and most of 2002 commuting between New York and Washington, where Jill Abramson, the bureau chief, negotiated what she called the "Osama bin Laden rate" at the Ritz-Carlton Hotel, within walking distance of the paper. The hotel had the best gym in Washington. I spent so many nights there in 2002 that the hotel embroidered my initials on the pillowcases in my room.

Having failed to give Al Qaeda sufficient priority in the first eight months in office, President George W. Bush's national security team was determined to compensate by embracing a fierce "war" on terror. In a speech to Congress nine days after the attack, the president declared war on Al Qaeda and on terrorism itself. Many analysts mocked his declaration of war on a "tactic" rather than an enemy, but National Security Adviser Condoleezza Rice and other senior officials were arguing that the counterterrorism campaign had to be waged against both the tactic "to delegitimize its use" and the people who practiced it.[6] Defining the enemy broadly empowered Washington to forge alliances against anti-Western Islamist groups that were only loosely linked to Al Qaeda: Hamas in Gaza; Hezbollah, Iran's proxy in Lebanon; the Islamic Group and Islamic Jihad in Egypt; Abu Sayyaf in the Philippines; and Jemaah Islamiyah in Indonesia, she argued, persuasively, I thought.

In an interview with David Sanger, the *Times*'s White House correspondent, and me in December 2001, and years later in her memoir, Rice had explained the decision to define the antiterror campaign broadly as a "global" war on terror. Neither of us knew what she knew during our interview: that Bin Laden had escaped to Pakistan from his mountain refuge in Tora Bora, Afghanistan. Rice seemed alternatively combative and apologetic. Before 9/11, she told us, President Bush had characterized earlier efforts against Bin Laden as "swatting at flies."[7]

I understood the frustration. For years, I had watched terrorists and American enemies conclude that America was weak and unwilling to defend its interests. Now the fanatics I had covered for so long would understand that a price would be paid. But I questioned whether the CIA was up to its mission. The agency had failed to tell the Clinton and Bush administrations when, where, and how Al Qaeda planned to strike the United States.

Only after 9/11 did the intelligence community's failings become a legitimate topic of debate yet again in Washington. I coauthored several front-page articles about the failures resulting in 9/11 as part of the *Times*'s "Terror and Response" series, part of the articles for which the paper would win a Pulitzer. The CIA had no sources inside Al Qaeda; nor did it have a CIA employee in Afghanistan. It had not sent agents to Darunta, where Al Qaeda was supposedly testing chemical and perhaps biological agents. Such failures made senior officials nervous.[8]

While White House officials struggled to

project competence and calm, I suspected that both were wanting. The anthrax letter attacks within weeks of 9/11 had dramatically intensified anxiety. Vice President Cheney would tell me that both he and President Bush had been vaccinated against small-pox and anthrax. But Condi Rice gave no hint of an even more terrifying incident that she would later recount in her memoir. Less than a week after the death of the first anthrax letter victim, she wrote, White House germ detectors had registered the presence of botulinum toxin, the deadly nerve agent for which there is no known antidote. For twenty-four hours, as tests on lab mice were being performed, President Bush, Vice President Cheney, Colin Powell, Rice, and other senior officials who worked in or visited the White House did not know whether they were infected. Only when the lab mice came back "feet down" did security aides conclude that the warning had been a false alarm, one of many.[9]

Some senior officials and journalists were convinced that the anthrax letters were, as Rice feared, "Al Qaeda's second wave." Several blamed militants tied to other Islamist causes, or Iraq, or both. At least two of my most reliable sources for *Germs* — Bill Patrick and Dick Spertzel — suspected the source was foreign: Russian or, more probably, Iraqi. Spertzel, the former UN inspector who had uncovered evidence of Iraq's covert germ weapons activities in 1995, was willing to be quoted saying that he was convinced that Saddam was to blame.

Senior Bush officials had signaled before 9/11 that Iraq was unfinished business. If Iraq were linked to the anthrax attacks, there would be no more "fly swatting." Bush identified Iraq as the leading suspect. "After all, he gassed his own people," he told another reporter. "We know he's been developing weapons of mass destruction . . . and so we're watching him very carefully." Sources had told me that Cheney and neoconservatives — the Pentagon's Paul Wolfowitz and Douglas Feith, among them — had been quietly pushing the president even before 9/11 to overthrow the regime, and unilaterally if necessary. I figured that Saddam had to know that, too. Would he risk so wildly provocative an attack? He was ruthless, but I doubted he was suicidal.

In mid-December Scott Shane, then at the Baltimore *Sun,* published a front-page exclusive that also helped defuse the pressure to finger Iraq. He reported that tests showed that the anthrax spores in a letter sent to Senator Tom Daschle were genetically identical to those made by US Army scientists at the Dugway research facility in Utah. The evidence pointed to a domestic terrorist rather than an Iraqi or other foreign perpetrator.

Contradictory information kept emerging, as it usually does in competitive stories, especially those involving secret government intelligence. So the narrative on the nature of the source shifted as we pried loose tidbits about the attack and the state of the government's inquiry. In an essay in the *Times* in October 2001, Richard Butler, the Australian diplomat who had headed the UN inspectors charged with monitoring Iraq's weapons activities, identified Iraq as his top suspect. He cited no evidence but asserted that bioweapons were "closest to President Hussein's heart" because "it was in this area that his resistance to our work reached its height." Because Iraq had thrown inspectors out of the country in 1998, it was "impossible to know what further steps" Saddam may have taken to perfect his anthrax arsenal. But "all the signs are that he has remained in the bioweapons business," Butler wrote. He suggested that an unidentified Iraqi official may have given anthrax spores to 9/11 plotter

Mohamed Atta in Prague in June 2000 — an idea that former CIA director Jim Woolsey, a neoconservative, was promoting in the British press.

I thought this sounded unlikely, but clearly such a public accusation in my own paper from an experienced Australian diplomat who had headed the UN agency charged with monitoring Iraq's compliance with its pledge to disarm itself of WMD could not be ignored. Reporters who covered intelligence or the UN knew that Butler had access to sensitive information that he would not be at liberty to disclose. Since there was a WMD angle to the charge, I wanted to pursue it. But days after Butler's op-ed, John Tagliabue, an experienced foreign correspondent reporting from Prague, wrote that Czech officials said they did not believe that Atta, the 9/11 plot ringleader, had met any Iraqi officials during his brief stop in Prague. A week later, Tagliabue and Pat Tyler, a national security reporter from the Washington bureau, reported that the Czech interior minister had reversed himself: Atta had met an Iraqi intelligence agent named Ahmed Khalil Ibrahim Samir al-Ani in Prague in the summer of 2001. Security experts in Germany were investigating claims by Israeli intelligence that Iraqi agents had given Atta anthrax spores, which he was then said to have carried to the United States in his luggage.

The CIA was furious, as Jim Risen, who covered intelligence, would report. The agency did not believe that Iraq was behind the anthrax letters or 9/11, and was pushing back hard on such allegations. Several of my sources also disputed the alleged Iraqi connection to the 9/11 hijackers and to anthrax terrorism. So Bill and I wrote that while the FBI could not rule out a foreign state or Islamist group as the likely "perp," most government experts favored the theory that the anthrax culprit was probably a domestic "insider."[10]

In mid-December 2001 we got a tip indicating that soon after the first anthrax victim died in October, the administration launched an intense, unsuccessful effort to find evidence linking Iraq to the anthrax letters. The hunt for Iraqi fingerprints had continued even after scientists concluded that the lethal germ in the envelopes was Ames, an American strain that the US military, among others, had used.

Normally, I would have pursued that story with Bill and David Johnston, who covered the Justice Department. But I was busy investigating another tip about possible Iraqi WMD that had nothing to do with anthrax. The quest would send me halfway round the world to meet a controversial Iraqi defector. The story I wrote would spark a sustained campaign against me and my reporting.

CHAPTER 13
THE DEFECTOR

I spotted Ahmad Chalabi, the Iraqi opposition leader, at the US Air shuttle baggage area in Washington, DC, one morning in early November 2001 as he was retrieving his leather overnight bag. My battered canvas tote came off last. Like me, he traveled light, but in grander style. Neither of us would have checked a bag if the newly established Transportation Security Administration (TSA) hadn't insisted on it. I was flying to Washington to get to an interview for "A Nation Challenged," the series that Howell Raines had assigned to explore the weaknesses in pre-9/11 intelligence. Since Chalabi was then based in London, I had not expected to encounter him.

Why was he visiting Washington? He said that he was seeing administration officials and legislators on the Hill to express condolences over 9/11.

And promoting regime change in Iraq?

"Of course!"

Long before 9/11, Chalabi had been pressing his long-standing allies in Washington for their support in ousting Saddam. The day after President Bush's inauguration in January 2001, Richard Perle, an influential defense expert whom I had known for many years, had hosted a brunch for Chalabi and a small group of neocons who would soon occupy key national security posts in the incoming Bush administration to discuss how best to persuade the new president to overthrow Saddam.[1] I hadn't known about the brunch at the time. But soon after 9/11, I was told that the president had flatly rejected a proposal from Paul Wolfowitz, the deputy defense secretary, to strike Iraq and the Taliban in Afghanistan simultaneously.

I mentioned to Chalabi two *Times* stories that seemed to have his fingerprints all over them. The more explosive was about a defector: an Iraqi general who had allegedly seen his officers train Arab fighters to hijack airplanes without weapons at a camp near Salman Pak in Iraq. The story suggested a link between Iraq and Al Qaeda — and, hence, between Iraq and 9/11. Had he been responsible for that story? Yes, Chalabi confirmed; he had connected my *Times* colleagues and others to the general, as well as other defectors.

In Washington, Chalabi was widely known for his fervent advocacy of regime change in Iraq. Within the Arab world, he was known for having been convicted by a Jordanian military court of stealing millions of dollars from Jordan's Petra Bank and having fled Amman in the trunk of a car to avoid jail. He insisted that the charges had been trumped up because of his opposition to Saddam, on whom King Hussein depended economically. Remembering the king's impassioned defense of Saddam before the 1991 Gulf War as a "deep thinker" and "strong leader," I gave Chalabi the benefit of the doubt.

As my bag appeared on the carousel, I asked him if he had any new information about Iraq's efforts to acquire illicit WMD components or expertise. His smile vanished. "We really don't have much on that," he said. "Your people keep asking us to provide WMD defectors and information. But solid information on this is hard to get and even harder to verify."

I hadn't thought much about that chance encounter when Zaab Sethna, one of Chalabi's top aides, called me in early December 2001. "Ahmad says hi," Zaab said. "We have someone he thinks you should meet."

The "someone" was an Iraqi defector: an engineer who claimed to have refurbished facilities throughout Iraq to enable Saddam to store radiological and other unconventional weapons and material safely. He had copies of government contracts to substantiate his claims, Sethna told me. The Iraqi National Congress, Chalabi's opposition group, had partially vetted him — which meant that it had decided he was who he claimed to be and was known to at least one or more INC members. He seemed to be the real deal, Zaab said. American intelligence agents were eager to interview him. Could I travel abroad soon?

On December 9, 2001, less than a week later, I was on a plane to meet the Iraqi in Bangkok. Zaab said the engineer had flown to Thailand after Saddam's thugs had tracked him to Damascus and threatened to kill his family members in Iraq if he talked about his work.

My editors were enthusiastic about the story but concerned that it would take me away from my other competitive assignments: the anthrax investigation, ongoing terror threats, and our inquiry into the intelligence failures that had led to 9/11. But

Chalabi had offered the defector to the *Times* as an exclusive, too tempting to turn down.

If Saddam's stonewalling of the UN unconventional weapons inspectors was an annoyance to the Bush administration before 9/11, it became an obsession once the towers fell. After routing the Taliban so easily, Bush was ready to turn his attention to Iraq and the potentially dangerous nexus between rogue states and WMD terrorism. So were newspapers. If this mysterious engineer had evidence that Iraq had refurbished facilities to store or work on nuclear, chemical, or biological materials, the trip would be well worthwhile.

Before agreeing to go, I tried verifying what Chalabi's aides had told me: where the engineer had worked and what he claimed to have done for Iraq's Military Industrialization Organization, which had, indeed, organized and served as a cover for many of Iraq's earlier WMD activities. High on my list of experts was Charles Duelfer, who had recently resigned as the deputy chief of UNSCOM, the WMD inspectors for Iraq. Duelfer, who would eventually head the US WMD hunt in Iraq, was skeptical but curious. The Iraqi's biography sounded "credible," he said. The contract that Zaab Sethna had faxed me seemed legit — not a forgery, at least. But there was no way to assess the defector's veracity without meeting him. When a Pentagon source confirmed that the DIA wanted to debrief the defector and that CIA analysts were also arranging to see him, I decided to try to get to him first, before the intelligence community snatched him away to an undisclosed location. If the *Times* was unwilling to hear him out, other newspapers or TV networks would surely do so.

Though I had met Chalabi briefly soon after the 1991 Gulf War, I got to know him better after human rights activists began crediting him with having helped smuggle out of Iraq the official documents about Saddam's use of poison gas against the Kurds in 1988. I had depended on those records for my 1993 *New York Times Magazine* cover story on the massacre.

In 1998 Clinton had made regime change in Iraq official US policy after becoming the second US president to sign a secret lethal finding authorizing Saddam's overthrow.[2] The 1998 Iraq Liberation Act had authorized $97 million to help Iraqi dissidents — most of which had gone to Chalabi and his coalition, much to the consternation of the State Department and the CIA. Both had long regarded him as corrupt and duplicitous and his information useless. The bitterness was mutual. In March 1995 Chalabi was furious at the CIA and the Clinton White House for refusing to support an insurrection against Saddam that Chalabi's forces and the far more numerous Kurdish Peshmerga guerrillas had staged in the Kurdish zone patrolled by US jets in northern Iraq. A year later, in June 1996, as *60 Minutes* producer Rich Bonin would report in his book on Chalabi, *Arrows of the Night,* Saddam foiled a CIA-planned coup by arresting some two hundred Iraqi army officers involved in the plot, executing eighty of them. He also tortured to death the three sons of the coup's leader, who was orchestrating the insurrection from the CIA station in Amman, Jordan. Forging a temporary alliance with a Kurdish leader with whom Chalabi had quarreled, Saddam sent his army into northern Iraq to destroy Chalabi's headquarters and his CIA-funded infrastructure. More than two hundred of Chalabi's men were lined up and shot; the CIA airlifted another six thousand INC members from Turkey to Guam for safe-keeping.

Chalabi said that he had tried to prevent

the debacle. At a meeting in Washington in March, he had warned CIA director John Deutch that Saddam's Mukhabarat had penetrated the plot. Agency officials were furious, convinced that Chalabi had exposed the CIA's plans to prevent them from replacing Saddam with a dependable Sunni general instead of him. The agency would learn only after the 2003 invasion, as Bonin disclosed, that the culprit of the leak was an Egyptian smuggler — one of the agency's own couriers. But Chalabi's relations with the CIA had soured by then.

At the end of 1996, the CIA had tried to shut down the INC, issuing a "burn notice" on Chalabi personally.[3] But he refused to quit and began raising money privately, spending some of his own to nurture his diverse if fractious coalition of Iraqi opposition groups: Kurds, Shiites, Sunnis, secular and religious critics. In Washington, he had ties to conservatives, neocons, and liberals on Capitol Hill and in the White House.

Chalabi and I first spoke at length in August 1998. I called him to confirm a story I was pursuing with Jim Risen, the paper's new intelligence reporter, about an Iraqi whom the CIA then considered the highest-ranking scientist to defect from Iraq's nuclear program: Khidhir Abdul Abas

Hamza. I had learned of Hamza's existence from David Albright, a Washington-based physicist and former inspector for the International Atomic Energy Agency, the UN group that had surveyed nuclear sites in Iraq. He had hired Hamza after the CIA had finished debriefing him. They were planning to write a book on Iraq's nuclear program when David offered me the chance to be the first reporter to interview him.

Risen and I wrote a front-page story — an Iraqi's account of the inner workings of Saddam's three-decade effort to build a nuclear bomb. The fifty-nine-year-old Hamza told us that on the eve of the 1991 Persian Gulf War, Iraq, despite Israel's attack on its sole reactor a decade earlier, had completed the research and testing needed for an atomic weapon and was scrambling to make at least one crude bomb using uranium. The effort might have produced a bomb in a few months, he told us, had it not been disrupted by the allied bombing campaign.

Before the Gulf War, the CIA had assured policy makers that Iraq was at least a decade away from producing a bomb. Based partly on Hamza's information, the agency acknowledged having underestimated not only Iraq's nuclear capabilities but also Saddam's determination to resume his bomb program once UN inspections ended and economic sanctions against Iraq were lifted. Before leaving the nuclear program in 1990 and defecting in 1994, Hamza told us, he had helped train young Iraqi scientists who were working on nonnuclear projects but could quickly resume work on weapons if Saddam ordered them to do so.

The second part of Hamza's story particularly intrigued us: he claimed to have nearly slipped through America's fingers because of CIA bungling. After fleeing to the Kurdish safe haven in 1994, Hamza said, he had sought out Chalabi, who, like him, had graduated from the Massachusetts Institute of Technology and was then working with the CIA. He said that Chalabi had put him in touch with the agency. But the CIA had dismissed the scientist as a fraud after a cursory telephone interview; it had not sent an agent to vet him in person. So Hamza had sought shelter first in Turkey, and then in Mu'ammar al-Qaddhafi's Libya — the oil-rich rogue state with its own nuclear ambitions, which had tried unsuccessfully to recruit him for its own fledgling nuclear program. He fled Libya in 1995 after the Iraqi secret police sent his eldest son to Tripoli to persuade him to return to nuclear work in Iraq. Iraqi agents had tried to kill his son twice, he told us. Hamza again reached out to the United States, this time successfully.

Chalabi confirmed Hamza's tale of how an intelligence coup for the CIA had nearly become a bonanza for Qaddhafi. He gave me a quote for our story about Langley's mishandling of Hamza.

My editors were pleased with both stories.[4] Chalabi's information had proven correct. On subsequent occasions, what Chalabi told me had also panned out. So although I knew that the CIA, State Department, and Israeli intelligence loathed and mistrusted him, I thought he had been straight with me.

Adnan Ihsan Saeed al-Haideri reminded me of Khidhir Hamza when I met him in a hotel in Bangkok. Both were slightly pudgy, their thinning hair slicked back, comfortable in cashmere V-necks and tailored shirts with their initials embroidered on the pocket. They wore a lot of aftershave.

I was surprised to learn that Haideri, who was sipping tea with Zaab Sethna when I arrived, was a Kurd. Why would Saddam employ someone from a suspect ethnic minority group for such politically sensitive work? And why would a Kurd work for Saddam? In a corrupt, autocratic regime like Saddam's, Zaab said, money was a great leveler — as well as a tempting incentive. Being connected to the inner circle would protect a vulnerable Kurd, in addition to making him rich. And with a steady, lucrative government contract for his work, Haideri had prospered.

Unlike Hamza, Haideri seemed nervous. I couldn't blame him. I had interviewed Hamza in a comfortable apartment in Virginia four years after his defection. The CIA had given him a green card, compensation for his cooperation, and assurances of his safety. Haideri had none of these and was to be interviewed the following week by US intelligence officials who would decide his future.

If he had been coached by the INC about what to say, there were few signs of it. There was no coherent narrative. He seemed accustomed to keeping secrets, hesitant to volunteer anything beyond what I had asked him.

He claimed to have personally renovated secret facilities he was told were for biological, chemical, and nuclear weapons. He was careful to say that he had never seen such weapons at the twenty places he had visited or helped refurbish. Iraqi military officials had told him that the sites were intended to store such weapons. He could think of no alternative plausible reason why such rooms would need to be lined with lead-filled concrete and made waterproof. He gave me copies of contracts from the Military Industrialization Organization and a front company called Al Fao that had paid for his work. The storage areas were built alongside wells, in private villas, and even under the Saddam Hussein Hospital in Baghdad. He described how Iraq used foreign companies to circumvent the sanctions aimed at preventing it from acquiring barred equipment and technology. He named companies he had worked with and provided contracts for these deals, too. He drew detailed maps of the locations of the storage areas where he said he had worked or visited. He told me that Saddam's "presidential sites" from which UN inspectors had been barred in 1997 were being used for concealment.

Over the next two days, I grilled Haideri repeatedly about the names of Iraqi civilian and military officials he claimed to have worked with, the type of work he had done before and after his contracts with the military, the details of his family's background. He had relatives in Australia, he told me, and if the Americans didn't believe him, he would try to flee there. He also had family in Iraq, so at first he asked not to be named in my article. It would be impossible to remain anonymous, I told him. If he wanted his story publicized, he would have to be identified by name.

About a week later, the story was about ready to run. It seemed solid. The head of Leycochem, a German construction materials company based in Cologne, confirmed that he had worked with Haideri in Iraq. He denied that he or his firm had any connection to WMD. Charles Duelfer had shared copies of Haideri's contracts with some of his former inspectors. The contracts and maps seemed authentic, they told me. Duelfer agreed to be quoted. Zaab and I talked by phone. A joint CIA-DIA team had interviewed Haideri twice and was attempting to verify his claims. Haideri had told him and the US intelligence analysts something he had not mentioned to me: that Iraq had tested chemicals and germ agents on Shiite and Kurdish prisoners at undisclosed sites in the desert in 1989 and 1992. Finally, Zaab said that Haideri would, though reluctantly, be named in the story.[5] The US team had now taken him to a secure location. In Washington, a military intelligence officer I trusted confirmed this, adding that the analysts' tentative conclusion was that Haideri's information seemed reliable.

My story appeared on the front page. Haideri's account was "consistent with other reports" that continued to emerge from Iraq about unconventional weapons activities, Charles Duelfer was quoted as saying. "The evidence shows that Iraq has not given up its desire for weapons of mass destruction."[6] The story also quoted Richard Butler, the former UNSCOM chief, who called Haideri's claims "plausible." The places and projects that Haideri had identified were "known to, or suspected by, his inspection commission," I quoted him as saying.

Given the potentially explosive nature of Haideri's charges, editor Steve Engelberg and I made sure that the story was heavily qualified. There was "no independent way to verify Haideri's account," I wrote. I disclosed in its fourth graph that my interview had been arranged by Chalabi's INC, "the main Iraqi opposition group, which seeks the overthrow of Mr. Hussein." If verified, I wrote, Haideri's allegations would provide "ammunition to officials within the Bush administration who have been arguing that Mr. Hussein should be driven from power partly because of his unwillingness to stop making weapons of mass destruction, despite his pledges to do so."

CHAPTER 14
PHASE 2: IRAQ

I never had an opportunity to interview senior White House officials about the decision to invade Iraq and the role that Iraqi WMD played before the war began. I have never met George Bush. I did not discuss the war with Dick Cheney until the winter of 2012, when I was seated next to him at a dinner in New York, years after he had left office. I interviewed him about that decision in January 2013. While I would have relished an opportunity to interview either of them before the war, the administration's passion for secrecy and its aversion to the media made that unlikely. So did the paper's traditions.

The *Times* has always been a tribal, turf-ridden organization. David Sanger, a collegial White House correspondent, would have vigorously resisted my trespassing. The Pentagon was covered by two able correspondents. I had worked on several intelligence stories with Jim Risen, but the decision to oust Saddam was being made at the White House, not at Langley. The CIA's role was to provide assessments of Iraq's links to terror and its WMD actions and capabilities. Its conclusion, that Iraq was continuing to hide chemical and biological weapons and had an active nuclear program, turned out to be wrong, but it was widely shared even by foreign intelligence agencies of governments that opposed the war.

I was a lead reporter on a part of the prewar buildup: what the Bush administration knew, or thought it knew, about Iraqi WMD. Even this aspect was not mine exclusively. I would not have written a story about WMD that involved the CIA without asking Jim Risen if he wanted to join forces. A beat reporter had contacts and context that roving investigators like me lacked. Their input made our stories richer and usually more accurate. For that reason, I had long campaigned for joint bylines years before the executive editor allowed them. When I joined the paper, only one reporter's name could appear on a story, a policy that had stoked a reluctance to cooperate. Having been big-footed by senior reporters, I knew what it was like to be frozen out of front-page stories. Citing anonymous *Times* staff, several critics would later write that some reporters had refused to work with me because they doubted my reporting. But my stories both before and after 9/11 were mostly joint bylined.[1]

Still, I sensed even early in 2002 that my near-constant presence in the Washington bureau was causing resentment. But during those frantic months after 9/11, I had little time to dwell on *Times* internal politics. I agreed with Howell Raines, Gerald Boyd, and Steve Engelberg that the paper had a historic duty to publish as much information as quickly as possible about Al Qaeda, the source of the mysterious anthrax letters, the pre-9/11 policy misjudgments and intelligence lapses that had resulted in the death of thousands, and what the Bush administration was doing to prevent the next attack. And the administration was doing plenty.

Having campaigned for president with a cautious foreign policy critical of his predecessor's humanitarian and nation-building interventions, President Bush had radically altered his outlook and policies after September 11. "I had just witnessed the damage inflicted by nineteen fanatics armed with box cutters," he wrote in his memoir. "I could only imagine the destruction possible if an enemy dictator passed his WMD to terrorists."

As Vice President Cheney stressed in public statements and interviews, America had to act to thwart such threats if there was only a "one percent chance" that Al Qaeda might get a nuclear bomb or a germ weapon of mass destruction.[2] The two of them began each day in the Oval Office with a parade of potential horribles: the CIA's "Presidential Daily Brief." The PDB's terrifying tips, reports, and rumors of plots about to unfold, many of them involving WMD, seemed "a frighteningly real possibility," Bush wrote. Between 9/11 and the middle of 2003, the CIA reported an average of four hundred specific threats a month and tracked more than twenty alleged large-scale plots against American targets. FBI Director Robert Mueller told Bush in late September 2001 that there were 331 potential Al Qaeda operatives inside the United States.[3]

Less than three weeks after 9/11 came the anthrax letter attacks, which Bush feared might be the start of Al Qaeda's "second wave" — a "sickening thought," he wrote. One of the "best intelligence services in Europe" had told them that the letters might be the work of Saddam. While others suspected Al Qaeda, what terrified Bush was the realization that the intelligence community had no clue about the perpetrator's identity.[4]

In October 2001 the detection of the presence of deadly botulinum toxin by White House biodetectors, for which there was no reliable antidote — though a false alarm — had further upset senior officials. That month, CIA director Tenet told Bush and Cheney that Pakistan had arrested two nuclear scientists who had been in contact with Osama bin Laden, possibly to help Al Qaeda build a bomb — "heart-stopping news," as *Times* reporter Peter Baker would later call it. In December, Richard Reid, a British citizen, tried to blow up an American Airlines flight carrying 197 people from Paris to Miami by detonating an explosive in his shoes.

George Tenet later called his community's intelligence reports chilling enough to "make my hair stand on end." In his memoir, he wrote that the daily PDBs for the White House were more "assertive" than the National Intelligence Estimate on Iraq's WMD capabilities.[5]

Lisa Gordon-Hagerty, an NSC expert on biological and nuclear threats for the Bush administration who had also worked for

Clinton, said that if anything, the administration had downplayed the dire warnings
the CIA delivered each day after 9/11 and
the anthrax letters. She called the PDB daily
warnings "bone-chilling scary."

"What haunted the president," Michael
Anton, a former NSC official, agreed, years
after the war, "was the prospect of a nuclear
9/11: WMD terrorism."

Such intelligence reports, false alarms,
and foiled plots, coupled with Iraq's continued stonewalling of UN WMD inspectors,
led Bush to re-evaluate the threat posed by
Saddam. "Virtually every major intelligence
agency in the world," Bush wrote, was
convinced that Saddam was hiding unconventional weapons and programs to make
them. After 9/11, he wrote, "the stakes were
too high to trust a dictator's word against
the weight of the evidence and the consensus of the world." The lesson he had drawn
from 9/11, Bush wrote, was "if we waited
for a danger to fully materialize, we would
have waited too long."

Support for such preventive action was
strong, too, on Capitol Hill, and not just
among Republicans. Dick Gephardt, the
House Democratic leader, called the intelligence exchanged at the weekly breakfast
meetings that Bush, Cheney, and senior

staff held with the Republican and Democratic leadership terrifying. "It's easy to forget a decade later the mood after 9/11," he told me years later. "We all feared there would be another attack, possibly with WMD. The chilling reports of Al Qaeda activities — throughout Europe, the Middle East, and South Asia — gave us goose bumps. All of us were focused on doing everything we could to prevent such an attack — whatever was necessary."

Prominent Democrats such as Hillary Clinton, John Kerry, Joe Biden, and Al Gore, among others, agreed with the neocons and now their new convert, President Bush, that Saddam had to go. "We know that he has stored away secret supplies of biological weapons and chemical weapons throughout his country," Gore said in February 2002. "We are perfectly capable of staying the course in our war against Osama bin Laden and his terrorist network while simultaneously taking those steps necessary to build an international coalition to join us in taking on Saddam Hussein in a timely fashion," he said in September 2002. Bush had to be "prepared to go the limit" against Saddam, Gore declared. "Failure cannot be an option."[6]

Bush's speech at West Point in June 2002

endorsing preventive war was formalized in the fall of 2002 in a new national security strategy. The thirty-three-page document asserted that the United States would "not hesitate to act alone" and "preemptively" to thwart dangers from hostile states or terrorist groups "armed with, or seeking, nuclear, biological, and chemical weapons."[7]

After the invasion of Afghanistan in 2001, a rift had developed within the administration over whether the global war on terror's next target should be Iraq. Hardliners clearly thought so. Among the most influential were Cheney and his staff, as well as Secretary of Defense Donald Rumsfeld and his two neocon deputies, Deputy Secretary of Defense Paul Wolfowitz and Under Secretary of Defense for Policy Doug Feith; Richard Perle, then chairman of the Defense Policy Board, an important advisory post; several other senior national security officials; and, most critically, the president himself. Nowhere else were US planes being fired upon as they enforced the no-fly zone. Saddam had not only invaded and bullied his neighbors but also used chemical weapons against his own people. He had tried to kill President Bush's father. Finally, as Peter Baker wrote, "the last time America went to war with him, intelligence agencies discovered that he was further along in his nuclear program than they had known."[8]

Secretary of State Colin Powell and his senior staff feared that ousting Saddam, who was not responsible for 9/11, risked a protracted war and an occupation of an Arab country with unpredictable and possibly dire consequences. Iraqi threats could be contained. Though Powell warned the president about some of them in a private dinner in August 2002, he did not oppose an invasion explicitly but, rather, urged Bush to let the UN try to resolve the problem before resorting to war.[9]

By the summer of 2002, I concluded that the hardliners had won. My notes do not contain a single interview or conversation in which I was specifically told that Bush had decided on war if Saddam refused to disarm and honor his other pledges, and in his memoir, he asserts that he did not decide to invade Iraq until the spring of 2003. But soon after 9/11, a giant map of Iraq appeared on the wall of Cheney's conference room during foreign policy and terrorism discussions, recalled a White House communications official on Cheney's staff.[10] And the president, in his public statements, his body language on TV — his post-Afghanistan swagger — seemed ever more determined.

In October 2002 Congress authorized the use of force. The vote was 296 to 133 in the House, including 81 Democrats. The Senate vote was 77 to 23, with 29 Democrats in favor of war.[11]

The decision for war triggered a second internal battle within the administration. Powell and fellow "realists" fought a rearguard action not to stop the war but to make it more legally legitimate.[12] They criticized Bush's preemption doctrine against WMD threats — his preventive war[13] strategy — and his stated willingness to go it alone if necessary. They pushed for a return to the UN to seek another resolution authorizing the use of force if Saddam would not readmit international inspectors and abide by his pledges.

The realists won — at least on the key tactical choice of the path to war.[14] Bush embraced Powell's argument that the United States needed another UN resolution to enforce the sixteen earlier ones. Senior officials later wrote that Bush overruled Cheney and the other hardliners and backed the realists partly because British prime minister Tony Blair had warned that his government would not support the war without explicit UN support.[15]

The decision to adopt a multilateral approach through the UN, however, locked Bush into justifying the war based largely on alleged violations of Iraq's WMD disarmament pledges: nine of the sixteen Security Council resolutions focused on Baghdad's apparent violations of its WMD commitments.[16] As a result, most of Secretary Powell's nearly three-hour speech to the UN concerned Iraq's alleged violations of international law. Powell would later publicly regret the speech as filled with errors and unintentionally misleading. But at the time, Powell and the realists downplayed other justifications for removing Saddam: his well-documented support for militant Palestinian and other terrorist groups, his murder and repression of domestic opponents, and other violations of human rights. Also downplayed was a favorite neocon theme: the need to promote stability in the region by spreading the rule of law and democracy as an alternative to the secular autocracies whose repressive iron rule fed Islamic militancy. Though "neoconism," as scholar Frank Harvey later called the theory that a powerful neoconservative cabal had pushed the country to war, would prove stubbornly enduring, on the key issue of why and how to go to war, the neocons lost;

the realists prevailed.

I don't recall precisely when I first concluded that war with Iraq was inevitable. I remember telling Gerald Boyd in early February 2002 that I was convinced President Bush was preparing to confront Saddam. After dozens of telephone interviews and rushed coffees with Pentagon, State Department, and White House sources at what was known as the "NSC Starbucks" a half block away from the Executive Office Building, I told Gerald that not only the neocons but also many officials I interviewed did not consider killing or dispersing Al Qaeda's leadership and ousting the Taliban from Afghanistan sufficient "payback" for 9/11. To deter future attacks, they said, the administration would have to topple a rogue state with WMD.

Mostly I just connected the dots, as did many other reporters. An early indicator was the State of the Union address in late January 2002. After citing America's rapid overthrow of the Taliban in Afghanistan, President Bush warned that even if Bin Laden was killed or captured, the broader war on terror would not end. He focused specifically on states that constituted an "axis of evil," which could provide unconventional weapons to terrorists. He would not "wait on events while dangers gather."

Another early indication came in early February 2002 at dinner in New York with the leader of a delegation of Kuwaiti parliamentarians. Muhammad Jassem al-Saqer, chairman of the Kuwaiti Parliament's foreign affairs committee, whom I had known since Cairo, praised President Bush for vowing to act against Iraq, Iran, and North Korea for developing WMD. Calling Iraq the "richest, most dangerous state" in his region, he told me that he had urged officials in Washington to act quickly. "The longer you wait, the more dangerous Saddam will become."

Based on his conversations in Washington with Secretary Powell and Deputy Defense Secretary Wolfowitz, al-Saqer was convinced that Bush would oust Saddam. That assessment got my attention. My story about his impressions appeared deep inside the paper.[17]

The administration's public pronouncements became ever more bellicose, particularly those of Vice President Cheney. In late March he told CNN — incorrectly, it turned out — that Saddam was "actively pursuing nuclear weapons at this time." He told a group of Republican senators that

309

the question was no longer if the United States would invade Iraq, but when. Then in June came the president's commencement address at West Point: "We must take the battle to the enemy, disrupt his plans, and confront the worst threats before they emerge." America, Bush promised, "will act."

The president's warning was not missed or misinterpreted by the media, as some would later contend. The *Times* described it as a "toughly worded speech that seemed aimed at preparing Americans for a potential war with Iraq."

Once I concluded that the president was probably set on war, I decided to concentrate on trying to learn why administration officials seemed sure that Saddam posed so grave a threat. What intelligence was driving this choice? Were the collapsing UN sanctions deepening Bush's concern about how long Saddam could be "contained"? Was new information about Saddam's weapons activities responsible?

I also decided to position myself to ensure that I would not be excluded from covering the next Iraq war as I had been during the 1991 Gulf War. Despite my extensive experience in the Middle East and decade-long focus on terrorism, the news stories that I had broken before the 1991 invasion, and the publication of a bestselling book on Saddam's regime that I had coauthored, I had been sidelined. It would not happen again if I could help it.

I was in New York on April 8, 2002, when the Pulitzers were announced. The jury awarded the *Times* an unprecedented seven prizes for its coverage in 2001 — half of all the prizes it gave that year. Our stories on Al Qaeda's global network and the government's underestimation of its threat, which I had coauthored with a small team of reporters and Steve Engelberg, who had edited the series, won the coveted prize for "explanatory" reporting.

It was the most satisfying day of my professional life. The militant Islamist threat I had been so determined to highlight, the stories I had struggled so hard to research and write, were recognized. The award went to the "staff" of the paper, not to the lead writers by name. But Steve assured me that our early stories on Al Qaeda had been dispositive in the Pulitzer jury's decision. Until the day the *Times* abandoned its historic home at 229 West Forty-third Street, a photo display of those of us who had produced the series hung on the paper's Pulitzer row flanking the editorial writers' offices on the tenth floor. The prize, an unassuming crystal triangle, still sits proudly on my bookshelf.

Later that day, Howell Raines mounted a wooden platform beneath the spiral staircase that connected the third and fourth newsroom floors to thank the staff. Abe Rosenthal, who hadn't set foot in the paper since Arthur Sulzberger had broken his heart by canceling his column two years earlier, gave me a bear hug. "I'm so proud of you," he whispered. "I was so smart to hire you!"

Several days later, Arthur threw a bash for the staff at a funky hotel on the West Side. At the start of the party, he announced that he was suspending his one-martini-a-night limit in honor of the paper's triumph: he would drink one martini for each prize. He and I hugged and drank and even attempted a disco dance — something we hadn't done since our days in Washington. I had missed Arthur. But those of us who were close to him in Washington knew that he was determined to distance himself from us once he became publisher. His father had given his friends top jobs at the paper, a practice that the staff resented deeply; Arthur was determined not to be accused of such favoritism. Despite my regrets about the wisdom of his keeping the peers who knew him best at arm's length, I respected his decision.

Three martinis or so into the evening — we all began losing count — he toasted Steve Engelberg and me for making Al Qaeda's life "miserable." Pulling me aside and thrusting his arm around me, he said he had always loved my "passion" for the paper and for journalism. "So what will you do for us next year?" he joshed.

A month later at the Pulitzer award luncheon in May, Steve Engelberg revealed that he had decided to leave the paper. Why on earth? I asked him. This should have been the pinnacle of his career, he later confided. But as he contemplated a future of unending quarrels with Howell Raines over story ideas and how hard he was pushing reporters, he had grown ever more depressed. He and Howell were "fire and ice." Howell never seemed to appreciate Steve's creativity or the loyalty he commanded from reporters like me. If seven Pulitzers were as good as it got, Steve had concluded, he was in the wrong job.

Losing Steve, a friend and cowriter as well as an editor with perfect pitch, whose judgments the investigative reporters trusted, was a loss not only for me but also for the *Times*. Steve had a knack for making stubborn reporters rethink our assumptions. He had written some of the most challenging chapters of our book *Germs.* He had been an inspired intelligence reporter and gifted writer who worked as hard as his staff. When he told me that he was accepting an offer to start an investigative unit at the *Oregonian* in Portland, where his wife had grown up, I was devastated. The loss of an editor who I thought might lead the paper one day was a harbinger of tumultuous upheavals. Though I didn't know it at the time, a staff revolt was brewing against Howell and Gerald that would reshape my career and the paper.

CHAPTER 15
"WHERE'S WALDO?" THE HUNT FOR WMD IN IRAQ

The abandoned ammunition storage dump in southern Iraq near Karbalā' was in the middle of nowhere. Late one night in early April 2003, flashlight in hand, I inched through the derelict buildings and sheds. Desert dogs howled in the distance.

I was freezing. I had left my down jacket back at the base at Camp Udairi in northern Kuwait, the launching pad of the military's WMD-hunting brigade, the 75th Exploitation Task Force — the 75th XTF — to accompany Mobile Exploration Team Alpha, one of the brigade's units that were surveying suspect sites. This was supposed to have been a three-hour mission to Mussayab, a town where buried barrels of suspicious-looking liquids had turned out to be gasoline. That was ten days ago. Ever since then, MET Alpha and I, the brigade's sole embedded reporter, had been moving from one site to another, and, finally, to this abandoned facility. The unit members had hosed down the floor of a building in the complex and were sleeping on its icy floor.

I had stopped carrying my gas mask. So had other members of MET units Alpha and Bravo, both of which were led by enthusiastic young officers still hoping that any day now we would find traces of the elusive WMD that had brought us all here.

Col. Richard R. McPhee, forty-seven, who commanded the eight-hundred-person XTF, had insisted I wear a uniform if I wanted to travel with his METs. A reporter in civilian clothes was a natural target, he said. He was not going to be the first commander in Iraq to get his embed killed. Eventually we compromised. Wearing my own beige cargo pants and white T-shirt, I borrowed desert boots and an army jacket, which warmed me against the cold. Where was the weather that the military had warned would be too hot to fight in?

For the past ten days, Chief Warrant Officer Richard "Monty" Gonzales's ten-man unit had maneuvered its way up from Camp Udairi through southern Iraq past a series of ancient towns and villages — Nasiriya, Samarra, Najaf, Hilla — near the ruins of Babylon. Because we had assumed we would be back at Udairi by evening, I hadn't brought a sleeping bag or a change of clothes. To top it all, the mosquitos were ravenous.

Although more than 775 reporters and photographers were embedded in US military units at the start of the war, I was the only reporter with the military brigade that was charged with hunting for WMD. That was no accident.

As it became clear in the fall of 2002 that President Bush was heading for war, the media were clamoring for access to soldiers and "action." When I learned in November that administration officials were apt to grant "embed" slots, I asked my Pentagon contacts whether I could embed with teams searching for WMD. I had trouble learning much about the Pentagon's plans for its WMD hunt. Later I would discover that the secrecy masked not the mission's sensitivity but the lack of serious planning.

When a senior Pentagon official asked me to inscribe a copy of *Germs* to Defense Secretary Rumsfeld, I attached a letter to the man I had never met asking to embed in the WMD-hunting units. I heard nothing. In early January I explored the idea with Torie Clarke, the Pentagon's spokesperson, who said she found it "interesting." That is Washington bureaucratese for "Get lost." Finally, I wrote to Paul Wolfowitz. If WMD were found in Iraq, I wrote, the presence of an "independent" journalist with the American team could only "enhance the administration's credibility." I heard nothing.

In late February 2003 I left for Erbil, in the Kurdish region of northern Iraq, via Turkey, to cover the Iraqi National Congress's first meeting on Iraqi soil in a decade, a watershed. After the Gulf War, in 1992, Chalabi, with financial help from the CIA, had founded the diverse coalition of Shiites, Sunnis, Kurds, Islamic fundamentalists, secularists, democrats, monarchists, nationalists, and former military officers in Vienna, Austria, to help oust Saddam. Chalabi had wanted to assemble the group months earlier on Iraqi soil to declare the existence of a provisional government run by Iraqi dissidents, but the State Department objected. They also slow rolled the INC's request for American military training for coalition fighters who would be able to provide post-invasion security. (By the end of February, the United States had trained only forty Iraqi volunteers at a military base in Hungary.) Against all odds, the meeting was about to be held.

The long-postponed gathering in the

Kurdish region was electrifying. I was preparing for interviews I had arranged when my sat phone rang — an unusual event, given the cost. It was the Pentagon: my request for an embed had been granted. While the 75th Brigade had already left for Kuwait, I was to return to Washington immediately for briefings and immunization against anthrax, smallpox, and other potential biological hazards. I was to tell no one about this except my direct supervisors.

Now all I had to do was persuade my editors to let me go.

Before I raised the idea with the Pentagon, I had discussed it with Gerald Boyd, Howell's number two. He confirmed that I was not being considered for one of the paper's embed slots. Neither the foreign desk nor the Washington bureau had selected me. The new acting foreign editor, Roger Cohen, was no fan of mine, and I was not on Jill Abramson's list of reporters from the Washington bureau she led. If I could negotiate my own arrangement, I should try, Gerald told me. I suspected that he was humoring me.

"I have just spent the last week in Washington discussing a special assignment that I proposed to the Pentagon last fall," my memo to Arthur Sulzberger Jr., Howell, and

Gerald began. We were being offered a "rare chance to chronicle a unique mission." Never before had the US military "attempted to forcibly disarm another state of weapons of mass destruction during ongoing combat operations."

I would have access to most of the search activities. The only major restriction would be one that applied to all embeds: I would not be allowed to publish material that jeopardized operational security. And the Pentagon would insist on the right to review copy before it was filed, a requirement for all embedded reporters in sensitive posts.[1]

I compared the opportunity to that given William L. Laurence, the paper's science reporter, who had secretly been assigned to Los Alamos, New Mexico, to chronicle the development of the atom bomb during World War II. The articles he wrote after the bomb was used at Hiroshima had not only helped Americans understand the scientific and political significance of the weapon that had been created but also remained a valuable source of material for future historians. Such access in Iraq would enable us to tell "a rich story of a great challenge" comprehensively and with nuance, I wrote. "And it will be a great story whether or not the administration is able to find the weapons of mass destruction it claims Saddam Hussein has hidden."

Howell approved the embed. Seven days later, my arm still aching from the vaccines I had been given, I was at Camp Udairi, fifteen miles from the Iraqi border. The next day, March 20, American land forces crossed into Iraq. The invasion had begun.

The early days of my assignment were frustrating. While I had been warned that Colonel McPhee would be crucial to my assignment's success, the XTF's leader made it known that he was not thrilled to have a reporter embedded on such a sensitive mission. McPhee was traditional, and set in his ways. Concerned about exposing female soldiers to unconventional weapons, he had assigned none to the MET teams, much to their chagrin, as they had quickly told me. Would I not prefer to write about the army's support activities that his wife was leading back at Fort Sill, Oklahoma?

He initially resisted letting me accompany his MET units anywhere, even on training missions. He had also barred me from entering the tactical operations center: the cluster of trailers where key meetings were held. He kept me out of the battle update assessments each morning and the video-teleconference meetings conducted from the task force's HQ in Kuwait City, essential to understanding how the XTF's mission fit into the military's plans and operations.

No reporter was going to see the "classified" maps and mission statements posted in the TOC without higher authorization, McPhee ruled. Cajoling, joking, and pleading failed with him, so I appealed to the Pentagon's public affairs office in Washington. My embed would be disastrous unless McPhee gave me access.

He gradually relented, but only after a senior officer whom he wouldn't identify reassured him that Secretary Rumsfeld was aware of this unusual embed. Poor Colonel McPhee. I was bombarding him with requests for interviews and other access. Though the task force headquarters had sent the XTF a marine experienced in working with reporters to review stories that might risk compromising operations, McPhee insisted on reviewing them personally as well. Though he usually rose before dawn, I routinely filed late at night. So my copy rarely reached him until well after midnight, when his aides would have to rouse him to read it. I was exhausting the guy.

■ ■ ■ ■

A turning point in our relationship was a serendipitous meeting in late March with a senior military officer who became a supporter not only of the WMD mission but also of my own journalistic integrity when it came under fire a few years later: Maj. Gen. David Petraeus.

I had never heard of General Petraeus, who was commanding the 101st Airborne Division (Air Assault) when Colonel McPhee invited me to accompany him to the general's temporary HQ an hour's drive from our base. Petraeus had received his doctorate at Princeton's Woodrow Wilson School a few years after I had gotten my master's. He admired *Germs,* he told me, and asked pointed questions the book had raised. He also asked me what biological agents I thought we were likely to encounter in Iraq. I asked him why had we found so little trace of WMD to date. He didn't know, either.

Colonel McPhee seemed impressed that General Petraeus had read my book. From then on, our relationship was usually "pure goodness," his favorite phrase.

■ ■ ■ ■

Almost every day, the generals who chaired
the morning battle update assessments
warned of impending chemical or biological
attack by forces loyal to Saddam, particularly as US forces crossed what was considered the regime "red line": Al Kut, the last
city before Baghdad, crucial to its defense.
This was consistent with what the military
had been predicting ever since setting up its
command, the so-called CFLCC, or Coalition Forces Land Component Command,
at Camp Doha in Kuwait City, where my
colleague Michael Gordon was embedded.
"The IRAQI Ministry of Defense (MOD)
will use WMD early but not often," concluded a secret sixty-page planning memo,
signed by Gen. David D. McKiernan, the
coalition commander, and dated February
1, 2003, which I would later be shown. The
"probability" of WMD use would increase
"exponentially as Saddam Hussein senses
the imminent collapse of his regime," the
memo stated.[2]

On March 27, a week after American land
forces crossed into Iraq, my notes quote a
senior commander at CFLCC headquarters
as saying that the "use of WMD" remained

"likely within the next 48–96 hours." The officer said that Hussein al-Shahristani, a prominent Shiite Iraqi nuclear scientist and Ba'athist foe, had warned the military that if Saddam was going to use WMD, he would probably do so as US forces closed in on Baghdad. I had interviewed Shahristani before the war in London and had stayed in email contact with him. Saddam had imprisoned and tortured him at Abu Ghraib for twelve years for refusing to work on Iraq's nuclear weapons program.[3]

Over dinner one night at Camp Udairi, Cpt. Ryan Cutchin, who then headed MET Bravo, told me that soldiers were finding stockpiles of chemical protective suits and gas masks, as well as large quantities of atropine. I perked up at his mention of the nerve agent antidote. The previous November, I had written a story asserting that Iraq had ordered a million doses of atropine, most of it from a Turkish company, as well as seven-inch auto-injectors that could be plunged into a person's thigh. An official had said that Washington was trying to block the sale, which is probably why news of it had leaked. I reported that while atropine had several benign uses — hospitals and clinics used it to resuscitate heart attack patients — the auto-injectors Iraq had ordered contained five times the amount of atropine that was normally administered intravenously. Frederick R. Sidell, a chemical expert at the Army Medical Institute of Chemical Defense, had told me there were "virtually no peaceful uses for that much atropine." There was no convincing peaceful explanation for so large an order, agreed Dave Franz, a former director of the army's biodefense lab at Fort Detrick, Maryland, whom I had also quoted and consulted while writing *Germs*.

Atropine is highly effective at blocking nerve agents such as sarin and VX, both of which Iraq acknowledged having made and stockpiled but claimed to have destroyed. American intelligence agencies doubted it had done so. My story stated clearly that it was unclear how much of the drug, if any, had been delivered. So I was intrigued when Ryan told me that unit commanders were finding large amounts of it.[4]

American military planners feared that Iraq had ordered the atropine to protect its own soldiers against the chemical weapons it was planning to use against US forces. But more than a year later American weapons inspectors would conclude that Iraqis feared the opposite — that America might use the nerve agent against Iraqi troops. US officials had distributed fliers and made numerous statements on Arabic-language broadcast networks insisting that America did not have and would not use chemical weapons in Iraq, but "mirror imaging" — or believing one's enemy would do something we would not do — was apparently not just an American intelligence failing.

By early April, the XTF's officers and I were both beginning to wonder whether we would ever find the WMD that had brought us all to war. McPhee and other officers suspected the hunt did not have military priority. Two of the four METs that were supposed to be hunting for unconventional weapons had already been assigned other tasks, such as investigating human rights abuses. METs Alpha and Bravo were constantly short of everything: gasoline, food, water, power, and even detergent and toothpaste, which soldiers wound up buying with their own money from local Iraqi merchants. Humvees had to be begged or borrowed from other army units.

Reporting conditions were tough. Though I had held on to my Thuraya phone against XTF orders, I found it harder and harder to get a satellite signal to talk with Howell and Gerald or to file copy through my phone to New York. Part of my laptop's computer screen had been smashed in transport from Udairi to Karbalā'. Almost a third of the screen was a black ball the size of a tangerine, making reading a story playback or the occasional email that managed to get through to me almost impossible. Given Colonel McPhee's obsession with operational security, I could discuss potential stories I would file only with the paper's top executives: Howell or Gerald.

As days passed, the XTF's frustration was boiling over. Iraqis seemed to have buried everything of potential value — barrels of gasoline, air conditioners, refrigerators, vacuum cleaners, an entire jet plane — but not, apparently, WMD.

On April 5 I wrote a story with Doug Jehl, a national security correspondent in Washington, saying that the hunt for WMD was a mess. US forces had searched fewer than a dozen of the 578 WMD "suspect sites." Disclosing that none of the searches had uncovered evidence of illicit weapons, Pentagon officials were starting to say that the WMD hunt was in "a distant second place" to the fighting. The lack of priority had resulted in the destruction of WMD-related materials through looting and organized attacks. The soldiers told me that

Colonel McPhee disliked the story, but he did not complain to me about it.

The war was nineteen days old when MET Alpha got a tip that would change the XTF's mission and operations and cause no end of controversy. MET Alpha had just finished searching another dry hole near Karbalā' when Monty Gonzales heard that an Iraqi claiming to be a scientist with evidence of Iraq's chemical weapons program had passed a note offering cooperation to soldiers in his town. Tired of unearthing barrels of gasoline and touring heavily looted suspect sites, he decided to pursue the tip.

The note had been passed from one unit to another until it had wound up in the 101st Division's Second Brigade headquarters, under General Petraeus's command. It had never been sent to the "fusion cell," the analysts at the operational headquarters in Kuwait who were supposed to vet such information and provide the METs with WMD intelligence tips.

The letter that Gonzales showed me was tantalizing. "I am a senior Iraqi scientist," it said in the sprawling Arabic script that filled a single piece of rumpled paper. Identifying himself as Fadil Abbas al-Husayni, a chemist who claimed to have worked in "secret labs," he asserted that stocks of chemical weapons had been destroyed between the mid-1990s and up until a week before the war. He also claimed that information about unconventional weapons programs had been "hidden" from UN inspectors and that he had worked on "other projects" that would interest the Americans. He asked for protection and immunity from prosecution.

On April 17, a week after he had given the letter to an American soldier in a convoy passing through his town, MET Alpha tracked him down and staked out his house. I sat in the unit's Humvee outside as Gonzales and the unit's translator talked to him at home. When the soldiers escorted him to their vehicle behind ours, he was wearing sunglasses and a baseball cap the soldiers had given him as a disguise.

Gonzales was excited by what he had told them. Repeating his claim that the Americans were unlikely to find WMD, since the chemical stockpiles had been destroyed, the Iraqi said that Saddam had tried to "preserve Iraq's ability to return to making chemical, biological, and nuclear weapons" by transferring some sensitive equipment and materials to Syria, and focusing its recent activities on "small-scale research projects that were virtually impossible for international inspectors, or even American forces coming through Iraq's giant weapons plants, to detect," Gonzales wrote in an after-action report to Colonel McPhee and the XTF weapons experts. Abbas also told them Iraq had started cooperating with Al Qaeda, but provided few details about the nature of that cooperation or at what level it was supposedly occurring.

The Iraqi gave Gonzales's team the names of at least a dozen intelligence officers and scientists who he said were involved in the chemical program. He led them to what he said were banned equipment and samples of chemicals he had buried in his backyard and elsewhere. He claimed to have worked part-time in a lab in a warehouse on the outskirts of Baghdad. He would take Gonzales there if they promised not to detain him and to protect his family.

Why did they believe him? I asked. Because the Iraqi had confessed that he had not been fully candid about his job in his note, Gonzales told me the next day. Though he had been trained as a scientist, as he had initially told the soldiers, their translator, and the intelligence experts who interviewed him for a second time the next day, he was also a military intelligence officer who had overseen part of his agency's chemical program.

After several more meetings with Abbas, the experts deemed his allegations "credible" — which in intelligence parlance means that they did not seem to be an obvious fabrication. After they made their determination, I positioned myself outside the communications room they had set up in one of the Karbalā' complex buildings and listened quietly as Gonzales and the experts gave a lengthy report on the Iraqi's allegations and steps they were taking to verify them. I was told that the report was being sent to senior officials at the Pentagon and the White House. By flashlight, I took careful notes.

The Iraqi's account was clearly news, and I was determined to publish it. But how? Colonel McPhee pointed out that naming the Iraqi or identifying his former job or current location might compromise the XTF's mission, endanger him, and get me "disembedded." To make matters worse, the able public affairs officer who had helped mediate disputes between McPhee and me had returned to Kuwait and been replaced by an army reservist, Sgt. Eugene Pomeroy, a substitute English teacher from Albany, New York. Most of the XTF's officers, usually a tolerant bunch, considered him incompetent and cut him out of their units' information flow.

Meanwhile, the Pentagon and the CIA had begun fighting over who would debrief the new source, as they had fought over almost everything since the start of the WMD search. Although Gonzales considered the Iraqi official his most promising find, the CIA believed that all human intelligence sources (HUMINT) were its responsibility. So did Task Force 20, the Special Operations forces working closely with the CIA who were pursuing Iraq's most wanted regime leaders and WMD scientists. Task Force 20 not only wanted sole access to the source whom MET Alpha had found and cultivated, but it also wanted to keep the Iraqi at one of its detention facilities near Baghdad airport. Gonzales warned that the Iraqi would stop cooperating if he was detained and his family left unprotected.

Colonel McPhee opposed my publishing anything about the Iraqi, the still-top-secret Task Force 20, or the bureaucratic struggles between the CIA and the military. He had also ordered MET Alpha back to Tallil, an eight-hour drive, where the bulk of the XTF was deployed. That would have effectively barred me from writing about the Iraqi's claims. This was unacceptable. I hadn't spent weeks roaming around the desert to ignore such a development.

Standing outside in the moonlight later that night, the wind howling, I called Howell and Gerald in New York on my Thuraya to discuss my limited options. If the army insisted on suppressing the story, I could voluntarily disembed and join John Burns and the other *Times* reporters at the Palestine Hotel in Baghdad. Gerald opposed this. Why should the paper give up a unique embed just as it was starting to produce news? Howell agreed, he told me.

They were right. I had to do whatever it took to stay in Karbalā', remain embedded with the XTF, and get the news published without endangering the Iraqi or compromising national security. I would find a way, Gerald said encouragingly.

I decided to take my dilemma to General Petraeus. He quickly understood that I could write a story of discord and bureaucratic warfare over a promising source, or a more positive story about MET Alpha's discovery and a potential breakthrough in the WMD puzzle. He told me he would vet my story about the Iraqi to ensure that I was not inadvertently compromising sensitive sources or methods. Later that day, he discussed Gonzales's work with Colonel

McPhee and the reasons why he thought I could publish the news without collateral damage. The Iraqi would be handed over to Task Force 20, along with MET Alpha's three weapons experts, to continue the debriefing, while Gonzales would remain in the Baghdad region and report to a military intelligence unit to search for new information about unconventional weapons. The compromise seemed to please everyone.

The next day, General Petraeus awarded Gonzales a bronze star for his performance. Then he vetted my story, which made no mention of Task Force 20. If the Iraqi's information was verified, and he and his family could be protected, I could write more about him later, which I did. Petraeus changed almost nothing and gave me a strong quote. The potential of MET Alpha's new source was "enormous," he told me, echoing what military experts were reporting to the Pentagon. Though much work remained to validate the Iraqi's assertions, I quoted him as saying, if it proved out, it would "clearly be one of the major discoveries of this operation, and it may be the major discovery."

On April 21 the *Times* put the story on the front page.

■ ■ ■ ■

Three days later, less than a week after the Iraqi had met with American military and intelligence officials in Baghdad, and White House officials had been given a report about his claims, President Bush said publicly for the first time that "perhaps" the military might not find Iraqi unconventional weapons stockpiles because they had been destroyed.[5]

I called Gerald Boyd to discuss MET Alpha's plans and mine. I needed a break, I told him. I had been in Iraq since February and with the military since early March. I had assured Jason that hunting for Iraqi WMD would probably require only a couple of weeks. That was almost three months ago. Jason, who had always opposed the war, was understandably puzzled and annoyed. A break sometime in May would be fine, Gerald agreed.

Gerald seemed distracted. He and Howell were having a "problem," he told me. A plagiarism scandal was about to break wide open. It would embarrass the paper and was personally painful to him. Had I met a young reporter on the metro staff named Jayson Blair?

CHAPTER 16
THE REVOLT

I was still in Iraq in early May 2003 when I learned that Howell and Gerald would publish a 7,500-word story on how Jayson Blair, a twenty-seven-year-old reporter, had plagiarized and fabricated news during his four years at the *Times,* producing stories that were, literally, too good to be true. It would be accompanied by a 6,500-word account correcting mistakes in the six hundred stories he had written.

The articles, published on Sunday, May 11, called Blair's invention or plagiarizing of at least thirty-six articles he had written as a national correspondent a "profound betrayal of trust" and a "low point in the 152-year history of the newspaper." It was the talk of the trade.

When I returned from Iraq and entered the newsroom the next day, nobody was thinking or talking about WMD or Iraq. Gerald and Howell were in lockdown, meeting reporters and editors in small groups to discuss the collateral damage to the paper and growing complaints about their leadership.

The gravity of their situation was evident at a dramatic staff meeting at Loews Astor Plaza movie theater. Arthur Sulzberger accompanied Howell and Gerald to the theater near the *Times.* The street was jammed with reporters from other papers and camera crews yelling questions at the trio. Paparazzi pranced in front of them. It was a zoo.

Arthur opened by pulling a toy stuffed moose out of a bag and throwing it playfully to Howell. *Times* executives used stuffed animals as props at retreats, he explained, to signal the discussion of difficult, potentially embarrassing issues. I cringed. Arthur must have learned the technique from one of those management gurus he found so persuasive. It fell flat; Howell quickly put aside the stuffed animal.

The paper had not handled the Jayson Blair affair well, Arthur began. "We didn't do this right. We regret that deeply. It sucks."

It sucked? I glanced at Geraldine Fabrikant, a business reporter and friend who was sitting in the back of the theater with me. She had closed her eyes.

The focus on Jayson Blair and dignified expressions of regret from Howell and Gerald quickly morphed into an attack on the paper's leaders. Alex Berenson, a business reporter, asked Howell a question he said he would ask any boss in such straits: Was he going to resign?

I gasped as reporters applauded Berenson. Resentment was palpable. Staff members lined the aisles, waiting their turn to complain.

The room grew silent as Joe Sexton, one of metro editor Jon Landman's deputies, took the microphone. (Landman had flagged several concerns about Blair in the past months but had not been heeded.) Sexton lit into his bosses. Howell and Gerald governed by fear. "People feel less led than bullied," he declared. The staff no longer felt that editorial decisions were being made fairly or "properly." At a "deep level," he told them, sprinkling his indictment with words the paper couldn't print, "you guys have lost the confidence of many parts of the newsroom."

No one rose to support Howell and Gerald, including me. Did I think that some of these grievances were well founded? Yes, Howell could be cruel and mercurial. But under their leadership, the *Times* had won seven Pulitzers. And the paper seemed to function best under an autocrat. Abe Rosenthal had been equally ruthless.

Why did I remain silent? Was I disoriented by having just returned from another planet — Iraq? Surely. But witnessing the depth of my colleagues' fury, I was also wary of speaking out. I feared that they would interpret a defense as toadying up to senior editors who had let me "run amok." I was silent as men I respected were torn apart. But I was heartsick for them and ashamed of my own cowardice.

I turned to Geri, who also seemed shocked. "Can I go back to Iraq now?" I said.

I returned to Baghdad soon after that ugly session, but my return was not easy. Roger Cohen, the acting foreign editor, suddenly opposed the rules governing my embed. During my break in New York, he had sent me to Washington to ask the Pentagon to drop its insistence that my stories be vetted first. As I had predicted, the Pentagon spokesman refused. To allay Roger's concern, I suggested that he run a disclaimer at the bottom of my articles informing readers of the military censorship. But Roger still opposed my return.

I made my case to Gerald. I needed to go back to Iraq not only to finish my embed with the 75th XTF. I had begun hearing that the trailers that senior Bush officials had touted as proof of the existence of Saddam's illegal mobile biolabs were not WMD related at all. In February, Secretary of State Powell had emphasized the labs in his speech to the UN. If the mysterious trailers were not used to produce germ weapons, a major part of the administration's WMD indictment of Saddam and justification for its invasion would collapse. This was obviously crucial. The XTF's experts would surely know. But I needed to talk to them in person, privately, not over a satellite phone.

Gerald agreed, but he seemed distant. He had obviously been shaken by the staff revolt. I told him I suspected that Roger's sudden objection to the embed ground rules masked a broader anxiety about my reporting and the failure so far to find WMD in Iraq. I understood his frustration, I said. I, too, was surprised that the XTF had not found any weapons. My email in-box was filled with questions and complaints about the paper's WMD coverage, and several of my stories in particular. There were messages from bloggers and reporters from mainstream papers seeking comment for articles they were writing about my sourcing.

Some of the criticism focused on allegations that I had relied too heavily on Ahmad Chalabi. While I dismissed this charge from incendiary bloggers, I was dismayed when Howard Kurtz, the *Washington Post*'s media critic, in late May printed portions of my email exchange earlier that month with John Burns, our Baghdad bureau chief, over who would write stories about Chalabi. Kurtz suggested the emails showed that Chalabi was "using the *Times* to build a drumbeat that Iraq was hiding weapons of mass destruction."

This was Bart Gellman's work, I thought. Soldiers in the XTF had told me that Gellman, a *Washington Post* reporter close to Kurtz, resented the fact that I was embedded with weapons hunters. They said that Gellman and his editors had complained to the Pentagon so often about the exclusive access granted the *Times* that Defense Department officials had finally let Gellman spend a few days with the XTF in Iraq.[1]

My email exchange with Burns was hardly unusual. Reporters, not just at the *Times,* often fought over turf. A seasoned media reporter should have recognized the exchange as a classic bureaucratic spat. John had scolded me for having written a story about Chalabi without having cleared it with him. "We have a bureau here; I am in charge of that bureau until I leave," he had written. "It was plain to all of us to whom the Chalabi story belonged." My decision to write a story without his permission or advance knowledge was not "professional" or "collegial."

What John had written was not correct. Due to the sensitive nature of my embed, Howell, Gerald, and I had agreed that I should report directly to New York, not his bureau. But seeking peace, I apologized. At the same time, I let John know that he would not stop me from writing about Chalabi, whom I had covered for a decade. I thought I had the editors' support. On April 10 I had cowritten a lengthy, somewhat unflattering profile of Chalabi that was published just after Saddam's regime collapsed.[2]

Early in the war, American forces had flown Chalabi and dozens of his supporters into Iraq but dumped them unceremoniously at an abandoned warehouse near the southern Shiite stronghold of Nasiriya, not far from where MET Alpha was camped. Chalabi had held a rally that attracted thousands of Iraqis. But veteran reporters Michael Moss, Lowell Bergman, and I wrote that State Department officials considered Chalabi "divisive" and had predicted that after years in exile, he would attract little popular support inside Iraq.

Chalabi's supporters in the Pentagon — deputy secretary Wolfowitz and adviser Richard Perle — called him a "courageous and charismatic proponent of democracy" whose vision for Iraq was consistent with the Bush administration's and would help "transform autocratic, tradition-bound Arab culture," we wrote. But State Department and CIA officials dismissed him as "erratic and egomaniacal." They regarded his desire to transform Arab political culture as "flaky" and warned that it was potentially destabilizing Iraq and also other Middle Eastern autocratic regimes that were longtime American allies.

Our article challenged the assertion that White House officials had put Chalabi's group at the center of its planning. In fact, we reported, as "plans to topple Mr. Hussein developed in Washington," White House officials had "kept Mr. Chalabi at a distance," inviting him to consultations with National Security Adviser Rice and Vice President Cheney, but "never allowing him to play a significant role in conceiving a new government." We quoted an administration official who had scoffed at Chalabi's argument that the United States would need no more than thirty thousand troops to overthrow Saddam, because Chalabi would lead other exiles back into Iraq and quickly inspire an uprising by millions of Iraqis. After that, we wrote, some officials began referring to Chalabi as "Spartacus."

My email exchange with Burns made no mention of that lengthy article. But it did explain that the army unit I was embedded with was spending time at Chalabi's headquarters to use the INC's "Intel and document network," a reference to thousands of documents that Chalabi's men had taken from the Iraqi secret police headquarters. So of course I was talking to Chalabi, almost daily.

The *Washington Post,* meanwhile, Kurtz's own paper, had published allegations about Iraqi WMD and Saddam's terrorism links with Islamic militants based on tips from Chalabi. But Kurtz used my email exchange with Burns to attack the *Times* and to suggest an ideological motivation to my stories. His story encouraged other reporters and a stampede of anti–Iraq War bloggers to repeat the charge.

Even more troubling to me was that someone at the *Times* had leaked the email exchange to a rival paper. However unpopular I may have been with my colleagues, the leak risked damaging the paper. Assistant managing editor Andrew Rosenthal, Abe's son, whom Howell and Gerald had designated to work on some of my WMD-related stories, lashed out at Kurtz, saying that it was "a pretty slippery slope" to publish competing reporters' private email and "reveal whatever confidential sources they may or may not have." "Of course we talked to Chalabi," he wrote Kurtz. "If you were in Iraq and weren't talking to Chalabi, I'd wonder if you were doing your job."

Rumors of my alleged dependence on Chalabi were reinforced by Colonel McPhee's and General Petraeus's thinking in April that MET Alpha's time would be better spent working with Chalabi's INC and other Iraqi opposition groups than surveying more entries on the Pentagon's worthless suspect site list.

They made that call after Monty Gonzales tracked down Fadil Abbas al-Husayni, the Iraqi "baseball cap scientist" who turned out to be a senior military intelligence officer and a chemist who was still cooperating with the United States. Although Chalabi had nothing to do with Abbas, Gonzales's initiative in locating him had impressed his bosses and led to his reassignment.

It also seemed natural for MET Alpha to have begun working with the INC, given Chalabi's long-standing relationship with the Pentagon. Defense Intelligence Agency liaison officers were already working with the INC at the group's temporary headquarters at the Hunting Club beyond the Green Zone, a once fashionable, now run-down sports club that had been favored by Saddam's Ba'athists.

Gerald overruled Roger Cohen, instructing me to return to Iraq to finish my embed.

My bureaucratic victory proved fleeting.

On a hot and humid midnight late in May, Gonzales picked me up at the military sector of Baghdad International Airport. The Special Forces soldiers attached to the XTF no longer considered some roads near the capital safe. But the mood around the lake at XTF headquarters was calm, almost jubilant, as the brigade prepared to return to Fort Sill. The status briefing that Colonel McPhee gave the day after my return focused on vehicle safety. Too many soldiers were being injured in vehicle accidents, he told us. We had to fasten our Humvee seat belts.

Colonel McPhee seemed pleased to see me. I was relieved to be back in Iraq. Although I had lost over twenty pounds during my first three months covering his brigade, slept little, and worked incessantly, I had found the war within the *Times* more emotionally taxing than my embed in a war zone.[3] The increasingly poisonous politics of the paper frightened me, and I had missed the soldiers' camaraderie and sense of purpose. I had also come to understand better the pressures and disappointments that the colonel had faced in a WMD hunt which was shaping up as a true "mission impossible." Despite his frustration, McPhee promised to give me an interview about the XTF's strengths and weaknesses after the brigade returned to Fort Sill. He was understandably proud to be bringing home all his soldiers. The XTF had suffered no losses or severe casualties. He must have sensed that the task force was leaving just in time.

McPhee's calm was infectious, but days later, my own was to end. Iraq was a cauldron, but so, too, was the *Times.* One night, on a fraught call with Jim Wilkinson, chief of public affairs for Central Command in

Doha, he gave me shocking news. I had called to renegotiate the terms of my embed for the umpteenth time at Roger Cohen's instructions, when Wilkinson said, "Haven't you heard the news?"

Howell Raines and Gerald Boyd had been fired.

CHAPTER 17
THE WAR WITHIN

I thought about Howell and Gerald on the long military flight home from Iraq in June 2003. At some level, I wasn't surprised. But I was depressed and heartsick for them.

Deputy investigations editor Claudia Payne, who was closer to Howell than I was, told me that she had concluded they were doomed as soon as she heard Sexton's curse-filled accusation that they had lost the newsroom's confidence. Howell would admit a decade later that he had sensed he would not last soon after the Jayson Blair exposé was published, indicting not only the reporter but also the newsroom's management. I thought, naively, that if Arthur continued to back them, they would survive.

Gerald wrote a wrenching book about his experience as an African American at the *Times*.[1] After thirty years at the paper, he was given only hours to leave. Gerald's wife, Robin Stone, a former *Times* reporter, called Arthur's dismissal of him "swift, and brutal, and ugly." He would die of cancer, still heartbroken, less than three years later, at age fifty-six. His memoir was published posthumously.

Shortly after he was diagnosed, we had lunch together at an Italian restaurant near the paper. Gerald never hinted that he was ill. But he told me that his ordeal's most painful moment had been in the theater when none of his friends or colleagues defended him. "Not one," he said. I looked down at my pasta. My cowardice had broken a bond between us.

The revolt transformed the paper. Having gauged as weakness Arthur's capitulation to the board, which had insisted that Howell and Gerald be fired, some reporters and editors were triumphant; others were simply relieved. Reporters in Washington boasted of having deposed the "Taliban."[2]

Bill Safire, the paper's conservative columnist and my longtime mentor and friend, was glum. From then on, he told me, the staff would have a de facto veto over an executive editor's decisions. Arthur would ignore them at his peril.

I came back from Iraq with a list of story ideas to pursue or share: the impact of the looting and theft of weapons from the Karbalā' complex, where MET Alpha had spent time, and from other Iraqi arsenals; the army's faulty body armor; the growing tension between the returned Iraqi exiles and L. Paul Bremer, America's "viceroy" in Baghdad; the transformation of the liberation of Iraq into a despised occupation; the growing corruption among Iraqi officials but also Americans. But of greatest concern to me was what looked increasingly like a colossal intelligence failure with respect to Saddam's WMD arsenals and the army's hunt for them. Before the first Gulf War, the CIA had severely underestimated Saddam's WMD capabilities. Had intelligence analysts grossly exaggerated them this time?

I sent the list to Roger Cohen, the foreign editor, and to Jill Abramson, the Washington bureau chief. I heard nothing. When I went to the bureau, Jill did not mention the list, but she asked me to help examine intelligence and policy failures in Iraq. I began writing an account of my three-month embed with the 75th XTF and the hunt for WMD, which, as of June 2003, was fruitless.

Still uncertain whether WMD would be found in Iraq, I had raised the possibility that the hunt would come up empty with senior editors, and publicly, as early as May in a commencement speech I gave at Barnard College during my brief break from Iraq. My alma mater was honoring me with a medal of distinction, and I spoke about Iraq. I had "very mixed feelings about this war," I told the graduates. Mostly, I had questions, chief among them whether the war was "justified." Yes, Saddam was a "monster." Deposing him had been "a good thing for Iraq." But the Bush administration's mishandling of postwar security had "puzzled and depressed" me, I told them. Iraqis had expected us, the "American invaders, to protect them after the war." But "we have failed to do that." Everyone knew by now that Americans could blow things up. But did we have "staying power" or a clear vision of how Iraqis or Afghans could "build a better future"? Would the weapons hunters find the "WMD programs that were cited repeatedly as the major justification for the invasion? . . . Were the concerns about nuclear and anthrax clouds over our cities exaggerations? Were they justified by what we knew then, as opposed to now? Was the intelligence that produced them politically distorted? Were those who wanted to go to war deceiving themselves about Saddam's capabilities? Was the war really necessary, not just for Iraq, but for American national security?"

I was at my desk early on July 19 when a news alert flashed across my computer screen. A British scientist involved in a scandal over whether the British government had "sexed up" prewar intelligence on Iraq's WMD to strengthen the case for war had been found dead near his home in Oxfordshire. It was being called a suicide.

I prayed that the scientist was not shy, self-effacing David Kelly. But it was.

Bill Keller, recently appointed executive editor, asked me to his office for our first meeting since his promotion to discuss Kelly. When he saw how upset I was, he said that he was sorry about David's death. But this was not a condolence call. What did I know about the scientist's state of mind? he asked.

I had come prepared. I showed him printed copies of the most recent emails David had sent me, the last written hours before his death. He was under enormous stress because the British government had identified him as the source of a charge by a BBC reporter that Prime Minister Tony Blair had "sexed up" the prewar WMD intelligence assessment, I told Keller. David told me he had spoken to the BBC reporter but claimed not to have been the original source of his story. He had been misquoted, he insisted. "I would never have used the phrase 'sexed up' to a reporter," he joked. In response to an email I had sent him, David then replied that "many dark actors" were "playing games" — a reference, I surmised, to jealous officials within Britain's Ministry of Defense and the intelligence agencies with which he had often fought over interpretations of intelligence. He would wait "until the end of the week" before judging how his appearance before the committee had gone, he wrote.

David was clearly worried about facing further scrutiny over his interactions with reporters, but he had not seemed unduly depressed. He had often told me how eager he was to return to Baghdad and participate in the US Iraq Survey Group's inquiry into the missing Iraqi WMD. He wanted to interview the Iraqi WMD scientists with whom he had once sparred, several of whom were then imprisoned at Camp Cropper, not far from where the 75th XTF weapons hunters and I had been based.

No one knew Iraq's biowarfare scientists better than Kelly, I told Keller. Having long argued that those Iraqis were key to figuring out what had happened to the missing chemical and biological stocks, he hoped that the scientists he had known for so long would open up to someone they considered their peer.

I recalled our first meeting in 1998, when Bill Broad and I were researching our account of UNSCOM's seven-year hunt for Iraq's hidden biological program. David, a Welsh microbiologist who was one of the world's top bioweapons experts, was one of the four UN weapons inspectors — the "gang of four," they had christened themselves — whose detective work had forced Iraq to acknowledge that it lied after the 1991 Gulf War about not having germ weapons.[3] In 1995 their persistence forced Baghdad to admit that, since 1974, Iraq had explored at least a dozen pathogens as potential weapons. David's area of expertise was biological research and development, an inherently "dual-use" endeavor that made understanding intentions vital. "If David Kelly were a tax inspector," wrote Tom Mangold, the author of a fine early account of the Soviet biowarfare program, "he would recoup Britain's entire national debt."[4]

David and I shared another interest: the former Soviet Union's secret germ weapons program. In 1989 he had toured Soviet bio-labs and facilities and had been one of the first two British scientists to debrief Vladimir Pasechnik, then the most senior Soviet bio-warrior ever to defect from Moscow's top-secret program. His assertions that the Soviet Union had developed long-range missiles to deliver germs, and a genetically modified version of plague that was impervious to some vaccines and antibiotics, had astonished and alarmed Western intelligence officials. Though his CIA counterparts had long argued that the Soviets had no sophisticated bioweapons program and had initially doubted Pasechnik's claims, David's work helped persuade them that Moscow was hiding what turned out to be the world's largest, most ambitious germ weapons effort, a blatant violation of the 1975 biological weapons treaty.

David was also concerned about a possible connection between former Soviet germ warriors and Iraq. After Pasechnik's revelations in 1989, both Britain's MI6 and the CIA had attempted to monitor the movement of Soviet microbiologists and Moscow's bioexchanges with Iraq, Iran, North Korea, Libya, and other countries of concern. He had tracked such movement ever since 1991, when he told me that MI6 had spotted at least one scientist in Baghdad.

David was among my first calls after a scientist who had attended a World Health Organization conference in Lyon, France, in August 2002 told me that Iraq might have obtained a virulent strain of smallpox from a Russian scientist who had worked in a Moscow lab in the Soviet era and was thought to have visited Iraq in 1990. Another scientist identified that Russian as Nelja N. Maltseva, a virologist who spent over three decades at the Research Institute for Viral Preparations in Moscow before her death in 2000. Because her institute had once housed what Russia claimed as its entire national collection of some 120 strains of smallpox, British and US intelligence officials were concerned that she might have given or sold the Iraqis a version of the virus that could be resistant to vaccines or transmitted easily as a bioweapon.

Having spent months visiting decaying former Soviet labs and ill-equipped, poorly heated research institutes, and having seen one of the world's most dangerous plague strains stored in a used pea can, I knew how tempting Iraqi money would be to desperate Russian scientists. Intelligence officials were concerned that Iraq was among those rogue states trying to benefit from their financial distress.

When David confirmed that intelligence analysts in London and Washington were investigating the Maltseva report, which he stressed to me was uncorroborated, I flew to Geneva to comb through World Health Organization records of scientific exchanges. The records, plus interviews with scientists there, indicated that Dr. Maltseva had visited Iraq at least twice in the early 1970s as part of the global campaign to eradicate smallpox. But had she visited Baghdad in 1990?

By the winter of 2002, I had pieced together intriguing information about Maltseva's activities and what intelligence analysts thought they knew about them.

On a trip to Russia the previous autumn for a bioconference, I had tracked down Maltseva's daughter, a physician in Moscow. She told me that she did not believe her mother had *ever* been to Iraq. Neither did the scientist who had been her deputy in the Moscow laboratory. Neither claimed to know about a secret trip she had made in 1971 to Aralsk, a port city in the then Soviet republic of Kazakhstan. Recently declassified records, however, showed that Maltseva had traveled there as part of a covert Soviet mission to stop a smallpox outbreak that Moscow had failed to report to the WHO. The documents indicated that she had taken tissue samples of the so-called Aralsk strain back to her lab. In interviews that fall in Moscow, Russian biologists insisted that the dangerous material was later destroyed. Western experts had no evidence of that. And Russia remained secretive about the illicit Soviet biowarfare effort as well as ongoing research and development activities.

When I learned in December 2002 that the CIA was concerned enough about the possible transfer of a Soviet smallpox strain to Iraq to have briefed President Bush, I decided to write a story. The president's briefing, if not the CIA's inquiry itself, would surely leak, especially because the administration was preparing to announce the number of American soldiers who would be vaccinated against anthrax and smallpox, an officially eradicated disease. My editors agreed we could no longer wait. I reported that the CIA was investigating whether Iraq had obtained a highly lethal smallpox strain from the old Soviet Union's germ weapons program. David Kelly agreed to be quoted on the record, as did several other sources I had interviewed on background. I quoted him as saying that UN weapons inspectors had noticed a "resurgence of interest" in smallpox vaccine in Iraq back in 1990, "but we have never known why."

The story was long but appeared deep inside the paper, since I stated clearly that Dr. Maltseva's alleged trip in 1990 was uncorroborated and that the CIA was still investigating it.[5] Many of the sources I interviewed were identified by name. And the story contained numerous caveats about what the agency knew and did not know about the allegation. So I was upset when critics of my WMD reporting began listing this story, among others, as examples of high-level White House leaks to me that I had rushed into print to scare Americans into going to war.[6] Anyone who knew anything about germ weapons — or investigative reporting, for that matter — should have grasped how much time and effort this cautiously worded article about WMD-related intelligence had required. I had spent almost five months searching documents and conducting interviews in Russia, Switzerland, London, New York, and Washington to write the smallpox story.

As I sat with Keller that sultry day in July, I did not tell him how crucial a source David had been on so many other stories I had written, especially my prewar WMD stories. I said nothing because I never discussed the sources of sensitive stories with anyone, even editors, unless I was asked specifically. The focus of much of my WMD and terrorism work required the trust of people who saw classified information. Most could have been fired simply for talking to me without proper authorization. So I guarded their identities, limiting discussion of them to senior editors who asked about them and had a need to know.

Perhaps I also hesitated because I no longer felt comfortable with Keller. Unlike other senior editors, he had not been supportive initially, in public or private, when critics began attacking my reporting on Iraq and WMD. The ferocity of the blogger-led assault after the Iraq invasion had stunned me. True, Keller was a columnist and not executive editor when Kurtz published my private email exchange with John Burns. But he had not asked me about it, either.

Most of my colleagues had dismissed Kurtz's initial blast. But some were more troubled by his second attack a month later. Published in late June 2003 on the front page of the paper's much-read Style section, he alleged that I had "hijacked" at least one of the XTF's weapons-hunting units that I had covered. I had "crossed the line" from reporter to serving as a "middle man" between the unit and Chalabi. Quoting Sgt. Pomeroy, the disgruntled soldier, and anonymous military sources, he wrote that I wore a military uniform throughout my embed and helped debrief one of Saddam's sons-in-law. I had also supposedly bullied General Petraeus into forcing the XTF leader, Colonel McPhee, to rescind an order recalling MET Alpha back to the brigade's temporary base near Tallil.

None of this was accurate. MET Alpha's chief Gonzales, fed up with what he called the Pentagon's worthless "suspect site" list, had received his commander's approval to reach out to Iraqis who might help locate Iraqi WMD scientists. His commander, McPhee, had given me permission to accompany MET Alpha during that period. He had approved Gonzales's request to work with Chalabi, to whom a DIA liaison officer was already assigned. As for Saddam's son-in-law, I never met him. And I occasionally wore an army jacket because McPhee had barred me from covering MET missions unless I "blended in" with the units. Since he had assigned no women soldiers to the METs, I was already visible enough, he said.

I took special exception to Kurtz's assertion that I got Colonel McPhee to rescind an order pulling MET Alpha back from the search by complaining to General Petraeus and threatening to write a "negative story" about his decision. Kurtz quoted excerpts of a note I had written to Colonel McPhee informing him that I intended to stay in the Baghdad area even if MET Alpha rejoined the rest of its brigade in Tallil. What Kurtz apparently did not know was that I had discussed this course of action with Gerald Boyd, via satellite phone in New York. Gerald urged me to find a way to stay near Karbalā' to follow up on the front-page story I wrote in April about the Iraqi scientist whom MET Alpha had found, and who claimed to have seen chemical weapons and precursors destroyed shortly before the war. The Iraqi source was in great potential danger, especially after I had reported that he was not a scientist but a military intelligence officer who was cooperating with the United States. At the time, I knew little more about him. But since he was willingly providing a small group of MET Alpha and US intelligence officers with leads, McPhee's decision to withdraw the soldiers he trusted seemed to epitomize the problems inherent in the army's WMD hunt.

Gerald had asked me to prepare a story that focused on that decision as a reflection of the task force's weaknesses. We would publish it immediately if the colonel pulled back MET Alpha and refused to let me stay on in Baghdad.[7] "Try not to get yourself disembeded," Gerald told me. "But stay with the story!"

McPhee had quickly reversed course after consulting on a secure line with MET Alpha's chief, General Petraeus, and other brigade officers. He instructed MET Alpha to continue working near Baghdad. Nothing I said or did affected that decision. Officers routinely changed orders based on new information, or new facts on the ground. And the "negative" WMD story Kurtz said I had "threatened" to write was, in fact, published at length, but in July, three days after David Kelly's death and a month after I ended my embed with the XTF and returned to New York. While my story praised the task force for persistence and creativity in what seemed to be a hopeless mission, I argued that the WMD hunt had been crippled from the start by a lack of resources, too little real-time intelligence, and, oddly, given the administration's repeated claims about the existence of Iraqi WMD to justify the war, a lack of priority.

Even if there were hidden stockpiles of unconventional weapons in Iraq, I wrote, the XTF would have been unlikely to unearth them.[8]

Had Kurtz been reporting from Iraq rather than Washington, he might have learned that the sole military source quoted in his story — Sgt. Eugene Pomeroy, the former substitute teacher from Albany — was problematic at best. Two of the four MET chiefs had banned him from accompanying them on sensitive missions. Senior officers in the task force decided that he was not knowledgeable enough to review my stories. Since I was the brigade's only embedded reporter, he essentially had no job.

I refused to talk to Kurtz because he had published my private email exchange with John Burns a month earlier, but Andy Rosenthal did. He called Kurtz's allegations "idiotic" and "baseless."

"She didn't bring MET Alpha anywhere," he told Kurtz. "She doesn't direct MET Alpha, she's a civilian . . . a reporter. She's not a member of the US armed forces. She was covering a unit, like hundreds of other reporters for the *New York Times, Washington Post,* and others. She went where they went to the degree that they would allow."

"We think she did really good work there," Andy Rosenthal was quoted by Kurtz as saying, having examined at least some of the twenty-four stories I had filed about the XTF's work. "We think she broke some important stories."

When Monty Gonzales and several other XTF officers involved in the hunt read Kurtz's story, they wrote letters to the *Washington Post* flatly denying Kurtz's account, which they copied to me. The *Post* eventually published excerpts from two of them, but declined to run a retraction.[9]

While I was furious, General Petraeus seemed bemused by the flap. He dismissed the story and urged me to do the same. "Quite a hatchet job," he wrote me in an email. "Sounds like the *Post* was desperate for news . . . Trust me: You never pushed me around!" he joked.[10] "Keep your chin up."

Despite such support, I knew that Kurtz's story was a problem. It was one thing for little-known bloggers to accuse me of "hyping" the WMD threat by noting that I had written more stories than other reporters about WMD intelligence regarding Iraq, Ahmad Chalabi, the Iraqi opposition, and the administration's post-9/11 concerns driving its decision to go to war. But Kurtz was published by the *Washington Post,* widely read and respected in our profession.

All this preoccupied me as I sat with Keller the day David Kelly died. I told him that we needed to write an obit describing Kelly's extraordinary career as a scientific biowarrior and hero of the US-UK's non-proliferation campaign. He assigned me to write it. For whatever reason, I left without telling him about my last meeting with Kelly, when I had stopped in London to see him three months earlier in March en route to Iraq before starting my embed. I had wanted to learn what he thought I might find in Iraq.

Over dinner at one of his favorite vegetarian restaurants, David told me he had little doubt that Iraq was hiding some pre–Gulf War era chemical or germ-related materials, and perhaps some older weapons whose alleged destruction it had not documented, as the UN required. He believed, he said, that Iraq had active chemical and biological programs, and perhaps even in the nuclear arena, too. But he was concerned about the quantity and quality of British and American intelligence underlying their official estimates. "Not enough hard evidence to support . . . logical conclusions," he told me, according to my notes of our discussion that night. Though he refused to be specific, he described the intelligence so far as "thinner" than he had hoped or expected.

David was briefly silent when I asked about the United Kingdom's claim, in a WMD dossier it had published in September 2002, that Iraq could launch chemical- and bioready rockets and missiles within forty-five minutes, an assertion that received widespread publicity and alarmed many in Britain and the United States.[11] He had not written that part of the dossier, he told me after a pause, unwilling even off the record to challenge openly his government's official assessment. David was utterly loyal to a government that would prove unwilling to return the favor. Little reliable new evidence had been collected since he and other UNSCOM inspectors were ejected from Iraq in 1998, he complained. Given the limitations on their activities, the inspectors who had followed them there were unlikely to find whatever Saddam had chosen to hide, he told me.

Finding Iraq's WMD scientists was key to understanding what had happened to its WMD programs, David said. "Find Taha," he said, referring to Dr. Rihab Taha, known in the United States as the notorious "Dr. Germ," the former head of Saddam's biowarfare program. "Find Amir Saadi and Dr. [Nissar] Hindawi," he counseled, referring to leading Iraqi weapons scientists about whom I had written for years. If the US military focused instead on visits to the Pentagon's suspect site list, "you'll be in Iraq for a very long time," he predicted.

Did he doubt that we would find WMD in Iraq? I asked as we finished our meal. "I'm sure you'll find something of interest," David said, evading a direct answer. "Just find the scientists," he urged me, "and you'll find what you're looking for."

David hailed a cab for me and wished me luck. Looking back at the notes I had scribbled during our dinner, I realized that he had not repeated George Tenet's cavalier assertion that finding Saddam's weapons and materials would be a "slam dunk." Unlike so many other analysts, including me, David had not equated the absence of evidence confirming Iraq's claim to have destroyed its banned weapons with proof of such weapons' existence. Yes, he *believed* that Saddam was lying and was hiding such weapons, he told me. But he could not be certain. He said that he hoped we would soon enjoy another dinner together — next time along the banks of the Euphrates.

"My treat!" I replied as I climbed into the spacious black taxi.

CHAPTER 18
CORRECTING THE RECORD

Diane Ceribelli, Bill Keller's assistant, called me on Friday afternoon, May 21, 2004. Could I stop by Bill's office before I left for the weekend?

Could it wait until Monday?

No.

Her tone was grave. This can't be good, I thought. Kind and resourceful, Diane never forgot a birthday. So if she sounded worried, it meant trouble.

Seeking insight, I called Bill Safire. He had just heard that Bill Keller and Jill Abramson were planning to run an editor's note — a mea culpa — on the paper's prewar reporting about Iraq. He didn't know what it would say or when it would run, but he urged me to be prepared.

Prepared for what?

"For anything."

Keller and Abramson were waiting for me

in his office. Most reporters had already left by six o'clock, so the newsroom was still. Jill was seated, unsmiling. Keller was pacing, clutching papers.

Surely I was aware of the controversy surrounding the paper's pre–Iraq War reporting, he began.

Of course. How could I not be? Since soldiers had failed to find WMD in Iraq, and a bloody insurgency had taken hold, opposition to the war had intensified. So, too, had attacks on the paper's prewar coverage, especially my reporting, since it was by far the most extensive. WMD, terrorism, and the Middle East were all part of my beat, and I had written more stories about these subjects than other *Times* reporters. Bloggers and other media critics were portraying me as either a closet neocon bent on taking the country to war, or a credulous dupe spoon-fed by Ahmad Chalabi and White House "shillsters" — a "useful idiot," one assistant professor from the University of Michigan called me.[1] I had "blood on my hands," the email declared.

Keller said that after Howell and Gerald left the paper, he first wanted to "heal the wounds" they had inflicted and "move on." But continuing criticism of the paper's prewar reporting — and of my work, in particular — had forced him to examine our coverage and publish an editor's note acknowledging our "collective" failings. The paper had an obligation to "set the record straight."

A note had been drafted, he said, handing me the papers he was shuffling. It would run on the front page, Sunday. In two days.

I was stunned. The schedule meant that space on the coveted front page of the Sunday paper, with our largest circulation, had already been allocated. Without having asked me a single question about my sources, the circumstances under which the articles were published, or the editors who had handled them, the paper was going to publish what read like a front-page indictment mostly of my articles. The editor's note was a done deal.

The draft note impugned unnamed "senior editors" — a slap at Howell and Gerald — for having allowed my stories into the paper. It implied that I had written only stories that supported President Bush's assertion that war was justified because the intelligence community had concluded that Saddam was hiding unconventional weapons. Attached to the note was a list of my prewar stories about Iraq, showing my ostensible dependence on Chalabi. The list was lengthy. However, it included stories that mentioned or quoted Chalabi as an opposition leader but had nothing to do with WMD. Nor was it comprehensive.

"If you run this," I said as coolly as possible, "you had better prepare a second editor's note to correct the errors, omissions, and unsupported innuendos in this version. And you'll also have to explain why I'll be denouncing my own paper on CNN."

Keller asked me to identify the errors. First, I told them, I had not relied heavily on Chalabi or his prowar, neocon American allies, as the note asserted. Chalabi was the source of only one of my prewar WMD stories — the interview in Bangkok with Adnan Ihsan Saeed al-Haideri, the Iraqi engineer — and that meeting had taken place in December 2001, before CIA agents were even tasked to seek information about Iraq's WMD programs.[2]

I was not the only *Times* reporter who had written stories based on prewar intelligence that turned out to be wrong, I reminded them. Why was there no mention of Pat Tyler's and John Tagliabue's front-page exclusive in October 2001 about the alleged meeting between 9/11 hijacker Mohamed Atta and an Iraqi diplomat in Prague before

9/11?[3] Or another Tyler front-page exclusive, "Intelligence Break Led U.S. to Tie Envoy Killing to Iraq Qaeda Cell"? Published in February 2003, the story virtually declared the existence of a crucial, direct link between Saddam and Al Qaeda. Why had they not included a story by Jim Risen, our intelligence reporter, and David Johnston, who covered the Justice Department? Their page-one scoop challenging the alleged link between Iraq and Al Qaeda asserted that there was "broad agreement within intelligence agencies that Iraq has continued its efforts to develop chemical, biological, and probably nuclear weapons" and was "still trying to hide its weapons programs from United Nations inspectors." Would Keller's note mention that Pat Tyler had hired Chalabi's niece to run the *Times* bureau he had opened in Kuwait before the war? Or Chris Hedges's forever-exclusive scoops on Iraq's alleged camps for training Al Qaeda recruits to hijack airplanes? His articles had relied on *three* defectors provided by Chalabi.

Here were the facts, I told them, pulling out my list of prewar stories. Yes, I had written more stories about WMD and the Iraqi opposition than other *Times* reporters: those topics were part of my beat. If I had not gotten such exclusives, I wouldn't have been doing my job. I had written a total of ten stories about intelligence on Iraqi WMD in the year before the war. Only one mentioned Chalabi by name. None of the others relied on him as an unnamed source. In that same year, I had written thirteen stories about the Iraqi opposition, from Turkey, Iraq, London, and Washington. And yes, those articles had focused on Chalabi, not WMD, because he was the leader of the INC, the largest Iraqi dissident coalition. Moreover, ten of those twenty-three stories about various aspects of the impending war were collaborations with other *Times* reporters.

I said that Keller's and Abramson's list also omitted articles I had written or coauthored that cast doubt on the WMD intelligence, or had warned of crippling disputes within the Iraqi opposition, and by implication, the wisdom of the Iraq invasion.

"Such as?" Keller pressed, according to notes I made later that night.

Most significantly, I replied, his note overlooked my exclusive interview in January 2003 with Hans Blix, the Swedish chief of the UN chemical and biological weapons inspectors for Iraq, who disputed President Bush's stated rationale for war. Blix then said that he did not believe that military action was needed "to avoid the risk of a September 11–style attack by terrorists wielding nuclear, biological, or chemical weapons." Written with UN bureau chief Julia Preston, the interview challenged several of the administration's most cherished assertions about Iraqi WMD cheating. Blix said he still endorsed disarmament through "peaceful" means and that it would be "terrible" if the standoff with Iraq ended in war. What I had assumed would be a front-page story was cut and run on page ten.

Keller's draft implied that my stories had a political agenda; that I had written them to build a case for war. That was false, I told him. Having covered Saddam's brutal regime for so long, I had privately hoped that President Bush would oust him and end the Iraqi people's misery. But I had never peddled WMD to advance the case for war. And I had never taken a public position on the war, a mortal sin for a *Times* reporter. When journalists or book critics had pressed me about Iraq or our book *Germs,* which contained a chapter on Saddam's bioweapons program and deceptions, I had laid out arguments for and against the war.[4] My earlier book on Saddam had raised questions about the wisdom of our invading Iraq in 1991.

I had never publicly identified myself as a "reluctant hawk," referring to an article Keller had written on the eve of the war. His op-ed in February, entitled "The I-Can't-Believe-I'm-a-Hawk Club," endorsed arguments by Britain's Tony Blair, American Middle East expert Kenneth Pollack, and Hans Blix, who, he asserted, "without endorsing war" had demonstrated "Iraq's refusal to be contained."[5] He was "hard pressed to see an alternative [to invasion] that is not built on wishful thinking," Keller wrote.[6]

"I know you weren't around then," I said, referring to the fact that he had become executive editor after my articles were published and my embed in Iraq had ended. But Abramson was Washington bureau chief at the time.

"Yours were investigative stories — edited by the investigations editor, not Washington," she interjected.[7]

Another error was the draft's implication that I was solely responsible for the paper's erroneous stories about Iraq's mobile germ labs — the vehicles that Colin Powell had featured in his UN speech, which had been widely praised, including by the *Times,* but was now seen as exaggerated.

I had written three stories about the discovery of the trailers during my embed in Iraq in the spring of 2003. Keller's note made no mention of Sabrina Tavernise's initial article for the paper about the vans. Nor did it indicate that Bill Broad had coauthored two of the trailer articles with me. Worse still, I pointed out, the note made no mention of the final story that Bill and I wrote on June 7, 2003, after Gerald Boyd approved my return to Iraq. The article was the first to challenge in detail the administration's claim that the trailers were intended to produce germ weapons.[8] It corrected our own earlier front-page report that had repeated the CIA's claim in a white paper that the trailers were intended to produce pathogens for bioweapons.[9] The story might have received more attention if Howell and Gerald had not been fired on the day we filed it.

Finally, none of my mobile lab stories had come from administration officials or neocon sources, I told them. I had interviewed Paul Wolfowitz only once since President Bush took office, and Doug Feith, his deputy, twice, both times on the record. I had not written about or relied on "Curveball," the fraudulent Iraqi source whose testimony supported the CIA's claim that Iraq was making germs for weapons in mobile vehicles. The story that Broad and I wrote was sourced to intelligence experts who had refused to be named, but they had either been with me in Iraq or had reviewed the trailers themselves or seen videos, photos, and read descriptions of their specifications. The earlier stories were wrong because the initial intelligence assessments we reported were themselves mistaken — not lies or exaggerations. We had been first to report the final verdict.

My embed in Iraq had prevented me from revisiting my earlier WMD reporting, I reminded them. Camped for weeks in bombed-out or abandoned weapons facilities with neither running water nor reliable power, linked to the outside world by only a satellite phone and episodic access to the internet, I could not reach independent experts or sources I had relied on at home. Nor could I receive or read most of the heavily edited "playbacks" of stories that would run the next day under my name.

Bill Broad, who had faced none of those constraints, had not encountered intelligence dissenters on WMD back in New York and Washington. Nor, apparently, had Jim Risen. Jim and I had worked together on several intelligence exclusives, but he had not published a single story that questioned the intelligence community's WMD estimates before the war.[10] Though we had talked at length about the paper's refusal to run several of his stories, he never told me that he doubted the CIA's WMD estimates or my reporting on them. And while the CIA had tenaciously battled the White House's claim of an operational link between Saddam's Iraq and Bin Laden's Al Qaeda, there had been no comparable dispute about WMD.

The failure to find WMD in Iraq had prompted some rewriting of history by politicians, analysts, and journalists. Before the war, a majority of Republican and Democratic politicians and many independent analysts asserted that Iraq was hiding some of its older chemical and biological weapons and was trying to reconstitute its nuclear program — or, at very least, trying to preserve an ability to do so quickly when sanctions were lifted. President Clinton made that claim. So, too, had four of the six Democratic presidential hopefuls who tentatively supported the war. Iraq's search for WMD, Al Gore said, "has proven impossible to completely deter, and we should assume that it will continue for as long as Saddam is in power."[11] "We have known for many years that Saddam Hussein is seeking and developing weapons of mass destruction," Senator Ted Kennedy said on the Senate floor, though he opposed the US invasion. "All US intelligence experts agree that Iraq is seeking nuclear weapons," said Democratic senator John Kerry of Massachusetts.[12]

Most foreign intelligence agencies — British, French, Canadian, Israeli, Australian, German, and even Russian — thought that Saddam had retained weapons and had active unconventional weapons programs, even those that did not believe such violations of UN resolutions justified war. So did Hans Blix, the UN chief Iraqi weapons inspector, according to our interviews and his book about the UN's effort to disarm Iraq of WMD.[13] So, too, did most influential nongovernmental organizations that specialized in nonproliferation, including the Carnegie Endowment for International Peace and the London-based International Institute for Strategic Studies. Both had published estimates of Saddam's hidden WMD arsenals and programs similar to the administration's.[14]

Colin Powell, the cautious author of the much-quoted "Pottery Barn" rule — "If you

383

break it, you own it" — was convinced enough to have staked his personal credibility on his WMD presentation to the Security Council six weeks before the invasion. While Col. Lawrence Wilkerson, Powell's former chief of staff and one of his closest aides, asserted after the war that Powell had long harbored doubts about the estimates, Powell and other aides contradicted that claim. In his 2012 book on leadership, Powell recalled the four "frantic" days and nights when his team of experts had put aside the "prosecutor's brief" that Cheney's aide, Scooter Libby, and NSC deputy adviser Steve Hadley had given them at President Bush's request and instead assembled their own "airtight" case for Saddam's possession of WMD. Will Tobey, a team member who participated in vetting its key claims, later told me that Secretary Powell and all of his team considered the UN presentation "rock solid."[15]

Powell wrote that he was "annoyed" years later when he heard former CIA officials bemoan in articles and interviews the "unsupported claims" in his speech. "Where were they when the NIE was being prepared months earlier," he wrote, "or when the same claims were being written into the president's January 2003 State of the Union address?"

Powell declined my requests for an interview on Iraqi WMD (before, during, and after the war). But I shared his criticism of the analysts' self-serving historical revisionism. I, too, had tried to find specific examples of flawed intelligence from dissenters on the WMD estimates before the war. Even had I thought they were wrong, I would have published their concerns.

"But what about the aluminum tubes story?" Keller asked. How could I explain *that* intelligence and reporting debacle?

I was, by now, exhausted. No story had been more professionally or personally traumatic for me.

Michael Gordon and I were drowning in work in late August 2002 when a Washington desk editor conveyed Howell's request for a comprehensive account of why the Bush administration believed that Saddam was hiding WMD. He wanted the story in two weeks.

Earlier that week, Vice President Cheney had given a bellicose speech at the Veterans of Foreign Wars national convention in Nashville, declaring there was "no doubt" that Saddam was hiding WMD and was prepared to use such arms against the

United States. The administration had to protect the nation by taking preventive action. The speech was widely regarded as the strongest signal yet that the White House was determined to go to war.

The request for a story on what the US intelligence community knew about Saddam's WMD effort was certainly warranted. Michael and I, however, were both committed to other ambitious projects with short deadlines.

Somehow we would have to juggle it all, Abramson told Gordon and me. But we all knew there was not enough time to do the reporting that such an extensive report required. If we were lucky, we would probably restate what had already been published and top it with a few new facts. Michael would pursue new intelligence about nuclear weapons; I would hunt for fresh information about Saddam's chem-bio activities.

I made countless calls to sources and came up dry. A relentless reporter, Michael kept picking up rumors of new intelligence about Iraq's nuclear efforts but couldn't nail it down. We were both gloomy on the Thursday before our Sunday story was set to run. The only new information I had about Saddam's chem-bio program came from an Iraqi military officer I had interviewed the previous summer in Istanbul who claimed to have worked in Iraq's chemical warfare program. I had met him through the Iraqi Officers Movement, an opposition group that the CIA preferred to Ahmad Chalabi's INC. While several intelligence experts deemed much of what he told me "credible," his allegations were uncorroborated. I did not feel they merited a "stand-alone" story.

Then Michael hit pay dirt: a trusted source let slip a reference to an order of aluminum tubes that the Iraqis planned to use to enrich uranium for nuclear bombs. Michael called the White House, which refused comment. He was slowly filling in details of the program, but we needed the White House to give us some reaction, if only a "no comment."

With time running out, I called Robert Joseph, President Bush's senior adviser on proliferation. I bluffed. Michael and I were writing a front-page story about the tubes whether or not the administration would discuss them. He promised to get back to me.

With Condi Rice's blessing, Joseph and his deputy, Susan Koch, met us on Friday morning at his office in the Old Executive

Office Building and confirmed much of what Michael had unearthed. He outlined the administration's concerns about Iraq's purchases within the past fourteen months of tens of thousands of high-strength aluminum tubes that CIA officials believed were intended as components of centrifuges to enrich uranium. The specifications of the tubes had persuaded American intelligence experts that they were meant for Iraq's nuclear program, he told us. While several efforts to ship the aluminum tubes to Iraq had been blocked or intercepted, he declined to say who had sold them, where they had come from, or how or where they had been stopped. We suspected there was far more to this story, but this was the first time that any senior official had discussed any aspect of the tubes for publication. Indeed, the administration had only recently become confident enough of its assessment to begin briefing the relevant congressional oversight committees.

After that meeting, Michael and I continued our frantic hunt for more details about the tubes. I called David Albright, the former International Atomic Energy Agency (IAEA) weapons inspector whose Institute for Science and International Security often consulted for the government and whose expertise and judgment I trusted. No answer. I left messages everywhere for him, stressing our urgent need to reach him.

Michael and I wrote through the night on Friday. His byline was first. The tip on the tubes was his. When our 3,500-word story appeared Sunday, September 8, with an assertive headline, "U.S. Says Hussein Intensifies Quest for A-Bomb Parts," I was okay with it. The story contained numerous caveats. The sixth graph, for instance, warned that there was "no indication" that Iraq was "on the verge of deploying a nuclear bomb" anytime soon. It also noted that the "hard-liners in the Bush administration" were using intelligence like this "to make the argument that the United States must act now."

I was still comfortable with our effort until I watched the Sunday talk shows. Vice President Cheney and National Security Adviser Rice both trumpeted the tube story, attributing it to the *Times* rather than to their own intelligence agencies. Rice paraphrased a line that another analyst had given us. The administration was unwilling to wait till the first sign of a "smoking gun" was a "mushroom cloud."

Both Michael and I were uncomfortable with the administration's use of our story.

But while neither of us had wanted our work to become fodder in a campaign to justify war, a lead article on the front page of the nation's most influential newspaper made that inevitable.

David Albright called back Tuesday. He had been overseas when he read our "tube" story. "There is a problem," he told me. The government's experts were divided about whether the aluminum tubes were intended to enrich uranium in a nuclear program or, rather, as several experts at the nation's nuclear labs believed, intended for use in conventional artillery rockets. Either way, he acknowledged, Iraq had failed to report the tube purchases as the UN required. But there was obviously a significant difference between a failure to report equipment for conventional and unconventional arms.

I called Michael. We had to write a follow-up to our tube story. There might be a conventional use for the tubes. Michael was not pleased. Home with a son who was ill, he was about to travel overseas on a Pentagon trip. I volunteered to do the legwork. Still, he asked, why would we want to undermine our own scoop?

"Because it might be wrong," I replied as breezily as possible in a conversation still etched in my memory and recorded in my notes. If there was a plausible, less ominous purpose for the tubes, we should be the first to say so. He agreed quickly.

Having spent the past three years researching bioweapons, my nuclear sources were rusty. Scientists I trusted at Los Alamos and Livermore National Laboratory said they had heard nothing about a dispute over aluminum tubes. They weren't in the "tube loop." I called back David Albright. My sources were coming up cold, I told him. He suggested that I quote him about the tubes. Not without a second, confirming source, I replied. I begged him to call a few friends at the labs and urge them to talk to me. I assume he did and that none of them would.

In search of nuclear dissenters, I took a taxi to the home of an intelligence analyst, a curmudgeonly skeptic who had occasionally been helpful on other nonproliferation issues. I felt like a journalist cliché, pacing outside his house for over an hour till he returned from work. He was not thrilled to see me. I never got to finish a sentence. He shot me a "Sorry." He couldn't help me.

Bill Harlow, the CIA spokesman, confirmed that the agency stood solidly behind its assessment. The CIA had "high confidence" that the tubes were for nuclear centrifuges, he told me. He refrained from answering my questions about whether other intelligence agencies might have an alternative view but made a point that struck me as important: despite their dissenting views about the purpose of the tubes, none of the fifteen intelligence agencies or the Department of Energy had contradicted the NIE's "key finding" that Iraq had reconstituted its nuclear program and was trying to acquire a bomb. I would learn later that the most skeptical of the intelligence agencies, the State Department's Bureau of Intelligence and Research, had asserted that the evidence was "insufficient" to conclude that Saddam was reconstituting its nuclear program. But even INR, as the bureau is known, did not assert that Iraq was not doing so.[16] So differences over the tubes hadn't affected the intelligence community's bottom-line conclusion about Saddam's nuclear intentions, he said.

I was getting nowhere. Working from home, Michael wasn't having much luck either. On Wednesday, September 12, the White House published a paper repeating the CIA's assertion that the tubes were hard evidence that Saddam was still trying to make a nuclear bomb. I called Michael. We couldn't wait. If we mentioned the tubes again, we had to write whatever we knew about the dispute over their purpose, which wasn't much.

With our deadline approaching, I called Bob Joseph again. Analysts and scientists were telling us that the tubes were meant for conventional arms, not nuclear centrifuges, making David Albright's still-unconfirmed report more solid than it was. Why hadn't he told us about this fierce intelligence dispute? Joseph seemed taken aback. The agency had assured him "at the highest levels" that the tubes could not have been used for anything other than centrifuge rotors. Yes, some analysts disagreed. That was not unusual in intelligence assessments. But the CIA was adamant, he stressed. "Judy, they *have* the tubes," he said. Physical possession of the tubes meant that their assessment was based not on vague defector tips, or purchase orders, or satellite photographs, but on an examination of the equipment in question.

I was torn between experts I respected who disagreed. I had dealt with Bob Joseph on many stories. As far as I knew, he had never misled me. Though David Albright was a physicist and a former inspector, he had never examined an actual tube. In fact, as he had told me, he hadn't participated in any of the intelligence community's debates about it. Michael and I had the CIA on the record, plus the White House's most senior nonproliferation official, on background, standing solidly by the claim. Albright's anonymous allies had refused to talk to either of us. Finally, whatever the experts' differences on the tubes, most of them had endorsed the CIA's conclusion that Saddam was back in the nuclear game.

On deadline, I wrote a first draft of our follow-up story. It led with the new White House paper on WMD. The sixth paragraph disclosed for the first time the existence of a dispute about the tubes' intended purpose. Although the CIA was "adamant" in its view that the tubes were evidence of a nuclear bomb hunt, we wrote, the Energy Department and experts at State believed that the tubes were intended for "multiple launch rocket systems."

The story noted the government's enormous "sensitivity" about suggestions that the intelligence community was divided about the tubes and Iraq's intentions, because Saddam's pursuit of WMD, we wrote, was "the centerpiece of the argument for planning a military campaign to topple him."

Finally, we wrote, the "dominant" view

among the most senior analysts was that the tubes were for Iraq's nuclear program and that they were only one of several indications that Iraq was reconstituting and expanding its effort to acquire nuclear weapons. "This is a footnote, not a split," I quoted an unnamed "senior administration official" — Bob Joseph — as saying. The story was 880 words long and ran on page 13.

David Albright's objections to the administration's tube claims did not appear in the final version. Perhaps his name was cut for space — or by me or the Washington bureau or foreign desk editors. I no longer remember or have the original draft. He was furious. Why had we suggested that the most experienced experts had sided with the CIA? And why hadn't I quoted him?

In October 2004, almost two years after our initial story was published, David Barstow, Bill Broad, and Jeff Gerth — friends as well as colleagues — wrote a 10,000-word dissection of the tube disaster based heavily on the Senate Select Committee on Intelligence's 550-page report on the Iraqi WMD intelligence failure. Their front-page article, which Michael and I were not shown until shortly before it was scheduled to run, contained details about how officials had repeatedly failed to disclose the "contrary views of America's leading nuclear scientists" and how officials and experts alike had "overstated even the most dire intelligence assessments of the tubes," while minimizing or rejecting the Energy Department's view that the tubes — the only physical evidence the United States had of Saddam's alleged nuclear weapons drive — were "too narrow, too heavy, too long" to be of practical use in centrifuges.

Years later, Bob Joseph, still at a loss to explain some of the worst WMD intelligence failures that had helped pave the path to war, recalled that George Tenet had personally and repeatedly assured him that the CIA was right about the tubes.[17] John McLaughlin, Tenet's deputy, had carted part of a tube around the White House and the offices of congressional Iraq War skeptics. "I told you exactly what I had been told about the tubes," Joseph asserted in June 2013, over coffee near his government think tank in Virginia. "I never lied to you."

The complexity of such intelligence disputes — and the difficulty inherent in writing about them — was described in a book about intelligence failures published in 2010 by Robert Jervis, a professor of international relations at Columbia University and a former consultant to the CIA. Jervis, who had participated in an internal CIA review of the prewar intelligence failures, pointed to a plausible explanation of the CIA's adamancy on the tubes, one that had not appeared even in the meticulous *Times* account. The army's National Ground Intelligence Center (NGIC), which DIA and CIA analysts traditionally relied on for technical expertise, had found the tubes, from a technical standpoint, "poor choices for rocket bodies." In other words, the army's main center of expertise had concluded that the tubes were probably not intended for the most plausible conventional use.

Jervis argued that the army center's verdict might also help explain why Secretary Powell, who hailed from the military, had embraced the CIA's view over that of his own agency's intelligence division in his UN presentation.[18] The importance of the army center's view was not noted in the paper's reconstruction of the intelligence disaster. But it was cited earlier by the Commission on the Intelligence Capabilities of the United States Regarding Weapons of Mass Destruction, the bipartisan committee chaired by former Democratic senator Charles Robb of Virginia and the conservative judge Laurence H. Silberman. After spending a year reviewing thousands of intelligence documents and interviewing hundreds of intelligence officials and experts, the Robb-Silberman commission concluded in its March 2005 report that the army center's finding had played a key role in the intelligence community's conclusion with "moderate" confidence that Iraq was reconstituting its gas centrifuges for a nuclear weapons program. The verdict on the tubes, in turn, was bolstered by Iraq's reported attempts to purchase such "dual-use" items as "magnets, 'high-speed balancing machines,' and machine tools," by claims that Saddam had " 'reassembled' many scientists, engineers, and managers from Iraq's previous nuclear program," and by reports of suspicious activity at sites formerly associated with Iraq's pre-1991 nuclear weapons program.[19]

Powell himself would not comment on the evolution of his thinking about the tubes. But interviewed almost a decade after the intelligence mess, Carl Ford Jr., who headed the State Department's intelligence unit that had challenged the CIA's view of the tubes, agreed that the army technical center's view had deeply affected his boss Powell. "He was clearly impressed with that," Ford recalled. "I just wasn't persuading him. And in intelligence, persuasion is everything."

Another crucial factor was the tube dissidents' endorsement of the intelligence community's broader claim that Iraq was reconstituting its nuclear program. David Albright, who later said he had opposed the war, appeared to believe that Iraq was trying to acquire a bomb. Four days after Michael's and my initial tube story appeared, Albright and a colleague published a paper suggesting that new activity at Al Qaim in western Iraq might be part of the regime's secret effort to make atomic weapons.

Above and beyond all the intelligence challenges was the fact that Saddam had long been playing a double game with respect to his WMD. As Bob Woodward reported in 2006 in *State of Denial: Bush at War,* part 3, David Kay, the second chief of the weapons hunt, had informed a dispirited President Bush in January 2004 that US intelligence on WMD failed because "the Iraqis actually behaved like they had weapons."[20] Saddam did not have WMD, but he wanted his foes to believe that he did. Many of his own officers and officials thought that Iraq's ostensible arsenal of chemical and biological weapons — and one day, *insha'allah,* atomic bombs — would thwart an American invasion.

None of this was known when Michael and I disclosed Iraq's purchase of the aluminum tubes on September 8, 2002, or when we wrote our follow-up article disclosing a dispute about their purpose five days later. And most of this was still not known in May 2004 when Keller and Abramson tried to blame the paper's alleged reporting failures on me.

I was recalling Michael's fury over the media criticism of our tube story when Keller asked: Why had I not pressed harder for a more in-depth look at the tubes later in the year? Why had I not insisted on going deeper into the intelligence dispute?

"We did return to the tubes before the war," I reminded him. In January 2003 Mohamed ElBaradei, head of the IAEA, publicly sided with the experts who claimed that the tubes were for conventional rockets, not nuclear centrifuges. Michael Gordon wrote about ElBaradei's stance.

Others had written better, more comprehensive stories about the dispute, Keller said. Jonathan Landay of the McClatchy newspaper chain, for instance, had written in greater detail about it in October. Why hadn't I?

I recalled that Landay's story was published about a month after ours. It had quoted one source by name: David Albright. At the time, no editor had mentioned it to me or Michael.

Exhausted after almost five hours of defending my reporting, I struggled for words.

"I didn't pursue it again before the war began," I said, picking up my notes to leave, "because my father died."

At ninety-eight, my father had outlived most of his friends and three beloved Yorkies. He had survived a series of strokes. But toward the end, he would rant in Yiddish and Russian, neither of which Denise, his fourth wife, spoke. He had never warmed to my husband, Jason — too "lefty," too "critical" of America. And America, of course, along with Israel, could do no wrong. Only in America could the son of a pushcart owner — or a "building tradesman," as his *Times* obit had diplomatically called my grandfather's profession — become wealthy and a legend in show business. It was useless to argue — to explain that Jason's criticism was meant to be constructive, or that Jason was no less a patriot than my father, who believed that Ronald Reagan, whom he called a "second-rate" actor, had not only been a first-rate president but the "best president *ever*." I went alone to the funeral in Palm Springs, California.

Dad was no fan of my newspaper either: "too liberal." Its entertainment coverage was too "skimpy" and "lousy" — his version of the classic Yiddish joke "such bad food and such tiny portions!" Plus, the *Times* didn't pay me enough. He was right about that; though, like many women, I never complained or asked for a raise.

The *Times* had sent flowers to the synagogue — Diane Ceribelli's thoughtful touch again.

As I stood at his grave, I felt guilty about the birthdays, dinners, and family trips I had missed because of my work. Luckily, I had married the one man on the planet who seemed proud of my all-consuming passion for reporting and had never tried to change me, perhaps because he sensed he would not succeed. But that week, rather than write yet another story on the tube controversy that no editor wanted, I went home to Sag Harbor.

Controversy over the prewar WMD reporting reignited in February 2004 when the *New York Review of Books* published a lengthy attack on the press's performance in the run-up to the invasion, calling me the poster child for the media's "submissiveness" to the government line on intelligence before the war. Michael Massing's eight-thousand-word article, titled "Now They Tell Us," lambasted the nation's major newspapers, particularly the *Times* and me, for failing to warn the country about the Bush administration's "deceptions and concealments" of critical information about Iraq prior to the war.

The article was especially problematic for me, as Jason and his former wife, Barbara, had cofounded the *Review* in 1963 during the New York press's printer's strike. Barbara had remained coeditor until she died in 2006. Jason continued to write regularly for it. So did his daughter.

When Massing called before publishing his essay and read me a long list of questions — most of them hostile about how reporters dealt with sensitive national security issues — I warned Jason that things could get "ugly." But he urged me to talk to Massing, whose writing struck him as "fair-minded."

The results were disastrous. By the time he called me, Massing was wedded to a view that the press had not only "failed" by not having stopped the invasion of Iraq, but also was "complicit" in having "sold" the war to a fearful American public. He accused the press of having held back information and of succumbing to a "pack mentality."

Robert Kaiser, the *Washington Post*'s associate editor and senior correspondent, rejected Massing's charges as "laughable." Listing several *Post* stories that challenged the administration's prewar assertions, Kaiser said that his paper had not suppressed news of bitter intelligence disputes.[21] Journalists may have learned slowly that the administration's WMD claims about Iraq were "almost all wrong," in chief US inspector David Kay's memorable phrase, Kaiser wrote. "But literally no one outside Iraq knew that before the war. . . . Still today," he wrote on March 25, 2004, "we have no smoking-gun evidence" that the administration engaged in "deliberate deception."

Kaiser accused Massing of doing what he accused the Bush administration of: cherry-picking "examples that suit his thesis" and dismissing articles that contradict it. Moreover, he added, Massing had not acknowledged his antiwar view.

In his response, Massing avoided the issue of whether he had opposed the war. But in an essay in January 2003 in the *Nation,* a left-of-center weekly, he had criticized intellectuals who favored ousting Saddam to end his systematic human rights abuses. While they probably meant well, he allowed, invasion was unjustified. "Despite his brutal record," Massing wrote, Saddam was not then "carrying out the type of mass slaughter he did against the Kurds in the late 1980s." Iraq was not Rwanda in 1994, when Hutus slaughtered Tutsis, nor even Bosnia in the early and mid-1990s. Massing wrote that he would oppose war with Iraq even if the Security Council authorized such action.

Two years earlier in late 2001, Massing had complained about me in two articles in the *Nation.* In October he criticized an article that Steve Engelberg and I had written soon after an anthrax-filled letter forced the evacuation of the Senate office of Majority Leader Tom Daschle. Accusing the press of "monolithic and unquestioning coverage" of the anthrax strikes, he wrote that we, and the *Times* especially, had hyped the story and tried to blame Iraq for the attack. But the front-page story that Steve and I wrote, as Massing acknowledged, reported that Iraq was only one of several potential suspects, and that it was far too early to hold anyone responsible.[22] A second Massing article in December essentially accused Steve, Bill, and me of hyping the attacks to sell our book *Germs,* a serious charge. Our "alarmist language" and "strong suggestion of state sponsorship" had contributed to a "sense of panic in the land."

The powder-filled letters ultimately killed five, infected seventeen, put over ten thousand Americans on antibiotics, and closed several post offices throughout the Northeast and a Senate office building. They triggered the largest, most complex FBI investigation in US history. A *Times*/PBS documentary based on that reporting for our book, *Germs,* won an Emmy in 2002.

I wanted to write a detailed response to Massing's highly selective account of the press's prewar coverage, as Bob Kaiser had done, but I didn't. For one thing, as Jason reminded me, the *Review* gave its own writers the last word. Knowing that the social media would revel in a lengthy, angry exchange with Massing, given my husband's continuing involvement with the *Review,* I decided to complain only about being misquoted in my response to his questions. I counted on Michael Gordon, who told me he was writing a response to Massing's critique, to set the record straight and defend not just his own work but also the paper's prewar reporting, including certainly what we had written together.

Michael's letter listed *Times* stories that had challenged the administration's case for war that Massing had ignored.[23] He went toe to toe with Massing. My concerns about Massing's rebuttal turned out to be well founded. His response to Michael's two-thousand-word letter was almost equally long.

In his response to my letter, Massing asserted that I was "simply wrong" about his misquoting me, though he offered no evidence to support that claim. He was relying on memory, as was I, but his quote of what I had supposedly said made no sense. Moreover, it was "revealing," Massing added, that I had not contested the other "serious shortcomings" he had identified in my work.

Massing was surely aware of my awkward position. My decision not to respond, however, was a mistake.

CHAPTER 19
SCAPEGOAT

I was at a biology conference in New Orleans on May 26, 2004, when the *Times* published its unsigned editor's note, "The *Times* and Iraq."

Initially I was relieved. At 1,145 words, it was half as long as the draft Keller and Jill Abramson had shown me five days earlier. It ran on a Wednesday, not the Sunday paper; on A-10, not the front page. It did not name me or any other reporter. It blamed prewar coverage that was "not as rigorous as it should have been" and "insufficiently qualified" on anonymous "editors at several levels who should have been challenging reporters and pressing them for more skepticism" who were "perhaps too intent on rushing scoops into the paper." Those unnamed editors had bannered "dire claims" about Iraq on page 1 and "buried" more skeptical stories inside the paper.

Though being accused of trying to "rush

scoops into the paper" was usually not considered a transgression, the criticism seemed to be aimed at Howell Raines, who had complained often that the paper's "ingrained complacency" had resulted in a "slow response to competition."[1]

The note also blamed a "circle of Iraqi informants, defectors and exiles bent on 'regime change' in Iraq," especially Ahmad Chalabi, an "occasional source" since 1991. Chalabi, a "favorite" of Bush administration "hard-liners" and "a paid broker of information from Iraqi exiles," had "taken in" administration officials and many news organizations with his "misinformation . . . in particular, this one," the note stated.

"The *Times* and Iraq," the note "From the Editors," asserted that the paper had produced some good reporting that had accurately reflected "the state of our knowledge at the time." It acknowledged the possibility that chemical or biological weapons might still be found in Iraq.[2]

I thought of that session the week before. It had taken me almost five hours to persuade Keller and Abramson that their original version of the note was wrong, but a great deal was at stake. An editor's note is not just one of those standard corrections published on page 2. It is the paper's equivalent of a papal bull: an acknowledgment that something terrible has happened. Two months earlier, Keller had rejected a request for a review of the paper's Iraq War–related reporting from Daniel Okrent, the *Times*'s newly minted "public editor." Soon after becoming executive editor, Keller wrote Okrent an email that Okrent subsequently put online, saying that he had reviewed my WMD coverage and had not seen a "prima facie case for recanting or repudiating the stories." Charges that our coverage had been "insufficiently skeptical" were "an easier claim to make in hindsight," he wrote. Keller had called me a "smart, well-sourced, industrious and fearless reporter with a keen instinct for news, and an appetite for dauntingly hard subjects." My early Osama bin Laden coverage was "uniquely foresighted before 9/11" and had been "at least partly responsible for one of our Pulitzers." Like many "aggressive reporters," I had sometimes "stepped on toes," but that was hardly "grounds for rebuke."

Publisher Arthur Sulzberger Jr. defended me, too. Challenged about my Iraqi WMD reporting in March 2004 at a college newspaper convention in New York City, he said that he had known me "for decades" and that I had "fabulous sources."[3] "Were her sources wrong? Absolutely," he said. "Her sources were wrong. And you know something? The administration was wrong. And when you're covering it from the inside like that, you're going to get things wrong sometimes." He blamed the Bush administration for "believing its own story line."

While I welcomed Arthur's defense, I had not parroted the administration's line. I had struggled to verify every published tip. Still, I was pleased that Arthur was unwilling to let antiwar critics scapegoat me for the intelligence community's failure.

So what had changed between March and May of 2004? After months of criticism of my reporting and that of others at the *Times,* why had Keller — and, by implication, Arthur, since such an institutional statement would have required his approval — decided that an editor's note was needed? And why the sudden rush?

I had urged Keller to examine more closely what the paper had published. I had sent him and Abramson copies of memos and emails I hoped would shake their conviction that my reporting had been unduly credulous and reflected a prowar bias. I included an example of a headline, crafted by editors, that had contradicted my

411

story. The headline, "U.S. Experts Find Radioactive Material in Iraq," ran over the article, which asserted, at its top, that the discovery was "very unlikely to be related to weaponry." I attached copies of unanswered emails to foreign editor Roger Cohen and a memo I wrote to several editors, before the invasion, suggesting stories that had questioned the rush to war and the administration's competence.

I included a memo I sent two senior editors on January 28, 2003, listing ideas I hoped to pursue alone or with other reporters. First was the interview with Hans Blix, the UN's Iraqi WMD inspections chief. Another concerned the Bush administration's "Lack of Day-After Planning" in the run-up to the invasion. A third challenged the oft-repeated assertion that international inspections could not be prolonged because soldiers who had already been deployed to the region could not be kept there "for weeks and months on end." Keeping them there would be expensive, I wrote, and there would be some degradation of capability over time. But military sources had assured me that the US forces could remain deployed "thru next September without a significant loss in war-fighting capability." I proposed a more detailed look at the antiwar movement at home. A Michigan paper had reported that "42 cities across the nation" had already approved resolutions opposing the war — impressive, I thought, and undercovered by the *Times*.

I also suggested a deeper look at Condi Rice's dysfunctional decision-making at the NSC. "People leave principals' meetings unsure of what has been decided," I quoted a senior source as having remarked about the White House's Cabinet-level meetings. They seemed to resolve few disputes, especially those between Rumsfeld's Pentagon and Powell's State Department — America's "Sunnis and the Shiites," as Charles Duelfer had called their notorious rivalry. "So everyone goes off and does his own thing," I wrote in my memo. Could this continue "if the nation is at war?"

I proposed exploring the apparent policy contradiction between administration officials who, on the one hand, wanted to transform Iraq into a pro-Western democracy, and, on the other, claimed to be "instinctively resistant to nation building." How would the president resolve this inconsistency?

While I interviewed Blix with UN bureau chief Julia Preston days after sending the memo, neither Abramson nor any other editor had asked me to pursue my other suggestions. Occasionally I would see stories by *Times* reporters on similar themes. But I had no idea whether my memo had helped trigger them.

Recalling Keller's original draft of the editor's note, I felt less distressed than I had anticipated when I read the note in New Orleans, until I called Safire. He was furious. Had I not noticed that I had written, or coauthored, four of the seven "problematic" stories that had accompanied the paper's online version of the note?[4] "You've been trashed, kiddo."

"You should have seen the original version," I replied. Besides, my battle over the note had not been totally in vain. Keller had told me before the note ran that once the issue was behind us, the paper would explore in depth the Iraq War intelligence, policy, and operational failures that so preoccupied me. He had finally decided to assemble a team of reporters to investigate the alleged WMD intelligence lapses and the poorly managed postwar occupation, the type of inquiry at which the *Times* excelled. I would be part of that team, he assured me. Excited about the prospect of revisiting issues and experts I had written about before the war, I agreed to go to

Washington as soon as possible to start reporting on the sudden end of the Pentagon's relationship with Ahmad Chalabi.

Launching such an investigative series meant that I would be able to figure out whether the paper and I had been misled and to interview officials who were normally off-limits, given the paper's preoccupation with turf, particularly at the Washington bureau.

Keller had insisted since September 2003 that I clear each trip to DC in advance with him. The desk in the Washington bureau that I once regularly occupied had been given to another reporter. I felt increasingly like a nonperson during my visits.

Safire knew that Keller had quietly urged me that fall to avoid Iraq War topics, especially WMD, until criticism of me in the blogosphere had subsided. Why, he asked me, would Keller suddenly launch such a controversial series now? And why would he risk more criticism by including me on such a reporting team? Washington bureau reporters came by each day to chat with him. Safire spoke often with Phil Taubman, the new Washington bureau chief, who had been a friend of mine since our reporting days in Washington and a champion of investigative reporting. But neither Phil nor any of his reporters had mentioned such an ambitious project, Safire told me.

That was odd, I agreed.

It didn't take long for media critics to pounce on Keller's editor's note as "too little, too late." Why had the *Times*'s "mini culpa" not appeared on the front page? demanded Jack Shafer. Writing for *Slate,* Shafer had been complaining about my WMD reporting for almost a year.

Okrent, the paper's public editor, weighed in on the *Times*'s Iraq War reporting on Sunday, June 30, four days after the editor's note. Okrent, who had taken the ombudsman's job only five months earlier, was still learning how the *Times* operated. Three days before his column was published, we discussed my work for an hour over coffee. Because he seemed to have his mind made up, I declined to discuss in any detail how my stories had been written or the identity of my sources.[5]

Okrent's 1,850-word essay in the Sunday paper reflected Keller's apology. He, too, concluded that the paper's "flawed journalism" had been "not individual, but institutional." While he cited two of my articles about defectors' claims in his list of "flawed" stories — my prewar article based on Adnan Ihsan Saeed al-Haideri's allegations and the postwar story based on the claims of Fadil Abbas al-Husayni, the Iraqi military intelligence officer — Okrent concluded that critics' effort to pin the paper's "failure" on me was "inaccurate and unfair." He blamed unnamed editors for questionable story assignments, placement, length, headlines, and the lack of follow-up.[6]

Okrent's note helped explain why Keller had seemed so determined to publish an editor's note quickly. Okrent disclosed that he had told Keller on May 18 that he would be writing about the paper's failure to revisit its Iraq intelligence coverage. Keller had replied that an independent inquiry was already under way. Their discussion took place three days before Keller and Abramson showed me their first draft of the editor's note.

I was pleased that one of Okrent's main complaints was the lack of follow-up on controversial stories. But he repeated Keller's assertion that our stories were wrong because we had fallen for "misinformation, disinformation, and suspect analysis." While I couldn't rule out the possibility that some intelligence analysts had altered their conclusions under White House pressure, or told their bosses what they thought they wanted to hear, two major studies after the invasion discounted the existence of such political pressure and endorsed a less conspiratorial conclusion. The reports about the WMD intelligence debacle by the Senate Select Committee on Intelligence and the Robb-Silberman commission found that the analysts were wrong, but not because they wanted to go to war. Some did; some didn't. Rather, the studies concluded, the analysts had erred because of sloppy tradecraft, bureaucratic rivalries, failures of communication, and because they feared the consequences of underestimating a WMD or terrorist threat in the wake of 9/11, as many had done so often before the September attacks. State Department intelligence chief Carl Ford argued that such 9/11 fears had been reinforced by the intelligence community's underestimation of Saddam's nuclear weapons program before the 1991 Gulf War.[7]

After the editor's note and Okrent's column were published, I contemplated the damage. Though Keller's note had not named me, and Okrent had explicitly concluded that it was inaccurate and unfair to blame me alone for the paper's alleged "failings," their essays scarred my reputation. In attempting to restore the newspaper's editorial integrity, they had taken my twenty-seven-year prize-filled career, as Bill Safire had complained, and trashed it. I was not a perfect reporter. I had broken quite a few rules in my thirty years of journalism and committed my share of journalistic sins. As a foreign correspondent, I had occasionally drunk too many martinis in too many hotel rooms on the road after eighteen-hour-long reporting days. I had yelled at colleagues who I thought had failed to carry their weight on a story or endangered our sources. I was perpetually late filing expense accounts. I had sharp elbows. I resisted being cut out of stories. I failed to appreciate the importance of building a network of friends inside the *Times.* While I had a few close pals at the paper, I tended to regard time spent at the coffee cart with colleagues as goofing off since I was not reporting. But I had never lacked skepticism. Nor had I twisted or ignored facts to achieve a political outcome. Yet that was the crime of which I was accused.

In accusing me, however, Keller, Abramson, and Okrent were accusing the *Times* as well. Nor did their notes quell the growing media fury over the paper's prewar coverage of what was becoming a disastrous war.

Suggesting that reporters and the paper had been insufficiently skeptical incited the paper's critics. From then on, such critics would point to the notes as proof that the *Times* and "mainstream media" could not be trusted.

Howell, who feared the impact of Keller's note on the institution he had led, attempted damage control. In an interview with the *Los Angeles Times,* he denied that our Iraq stories had been rushed into the paper to get scoops. "In 25 years on the *Times* and in 21 months as executive editor," Howell wrote, "I never put anything into the paper before I thought it was ready." Any of the "30 or so people who sat in our front-page meetings during the run-up to the Iraq invasion and the first phase of the war can attest to the seriousness with which everyone took the story." Neither Keller nor Okrent had contacted him about how such controversial stories had been handled, he told me.[8]

The editor's note and Okrent's essays refocused attention on Ahmad Chalabi, who had become a target of the war's critics. A man on a mission, Chalabi made it his business to be well informed, and to share what he had learned, or suspected, with journalists. Talking to him was essential. But his allegations had to be double- and triple-checked.

When Chalabi sat behind Laura Bush at the president's State of the Union address in January 2004, few would have predicted that four months later, an American-assisted Iraqi police raid would descend on his Baghdad HQ, or that the administration would soon sever the $340,000-a-month payment to his INC opposition group. The raid on his well-fortified compound was preceded by even more stunning news: Chalabi, according to *Newsweek,* was alleged to have given Iran information about top-secret American surveillance of Iran's communications. Rich Bonin, a *60 Minutes* reporter and producer, asserted that Chalabi and a top aide had informed senior Iranian intelligence officials in March that US intelligence had broken Tehran's encryption code and was monitoring its diplomatic cables.[9] Chalabi took to the Sunday talk shows to deny the charge: George Tenet was trying to smear him to shift blame from the CIA's faulty prewar intelligence, he said.

Long before this, pressure had been building on Keller and Abramson to distance themselves and the *Times* from Chalabi. The American press had published 108 articles based on information that Chalabi's INC had provided. (I had written one of them.) In our meeting before the editor's note was published, Keller kept returning to Chalabi. Hadn't I relied excessively on him?

No, I hadn't, I insisted. Chalabi had provided information or quotes for two of the stories I had written before the war about Iraq's WMD capabilities and only three of some twenty-four stories I wrote during my embed with the 75th XTF in the spring of 2003. Only one of those three concerned the hunt for WMD.

Yes, the 75th XTF's MET Alpha unit I had spent the most time monitoring had worked closely with Chalabi for part of its mission in Iraq. So, too, had a team of DIA analysts working out of the INC's headquarters at the Hunting Club. One of them was an agent whom I had come to trust. Code-named "Jim Preston," he had recently returned to Washington from Baghdad.

I did not know whether the reports of Chalabi's extensive lies and double-dealing were true, I had told Keller and Abramson. Like so many of the charges and counter-charges swirling around the Iraq War mess, this one would remain murky. Military and intelligence analysts would remain divided over Chalabi. MET Alpha's soldiers and other DIA analysts who had worked with his group most closely, including "Jim Preston," had praised some of Chalabi's information. Richard Myers, then chairman of the Joint Chiefs of Staff, had told Congress that information provided by Chalabi's group had "saved American lives."

Chalabi was at very least a convenient scapegoat for the intelligence community. Had his group "coached" defectors? Several reports and investigations said so. Others defended him. Whatever the case, the dispute over the impact of Chalabi's information diverted attention from the CIA's and the intelligence community's grave shortcomings.

I was thinking about Chalabi's sudden fall from grace as I entered the DC steak house where "Jim Preston" was at the bar, nursing what was apparently not his first beer. I was alarmed by his appearance. Like all of us, he had lost a lot of weight in Iraq. He looked exhausted. His blue eyes sat deep in their sockets; his pale cheeks were flushed. He was jittery.

"The beer's a lot colder here than in Baghdad," he greeted me. I smiled and hugged him.

"You look awful," I told him. "What's

wrong?"

Nothing, he protested.

For an intelligence official schooled in the art of deception, Jim was a poor liar. The cause of his misery soon tumbled out. Ever since his return from Iraq, he told me, FBI counterintelligence agents had been grilling him about whether he was the source of the intelligence leak to Chalabi about the NSA's secret surveillance of Iran's diplomatic cables.

Jim protested that he had not known about the program, which was classified top secret. He said he had just been poly-graphed. And he was not alone. FBI agents had gone to Baghdad to "poly" other DIA colleagues who were working with Chalabi, he told me.

Fearful of being blamed as the source of the leak, he had hired Plato Cacheris, a lawyer whose clients included such high-profile defendants as the spy Robert Hanssen and White House intern Monica Lewinsky. The investigation was costing him his extra combat and hardship pay in Iraq, but it was necessary. Before telling me what was wrong, Jim made me promise that I would not publish or reveal his name. Journalists were then competing to report what federal investigators were doing to identify the source of the Chalabi leak. If his real name was published, the FBI would assume that he had talked to me.

When I returned to New York the next morning, I met briefly with Keller and Abramson to tell them what I was learning about prewar intelligence and to discuss my reporting plans for our series. Jill mentioned that the bureau was scrambling for information about whom the FBI was targeting in its inquiry into Chalabi's leak to Iran. I told them that a sensitive American source who had been ensnared in the dragnet had told me that the FBI was focusing on him and other civilian military intelligence analysts at the Pentagon, as well as other contractors who had worked with Chalabi in Baghdad.

Who was my source? Keller and Jill asked.

Senior editors have the right to know the identity of such sources, but I hesitated. Stressing that my source was desperate and that I had promised to protect his anonymity, I said his name was Jim Preston, using the code name. He had hired Plato Cacheris as his lawyer, I added.

By the time I returned to Washington the next day, Jim had called my cell phone several times. He was frantic. Why had I betrayed him? he shouted.

What was he talking about?

David Johnston, the *Times* Justice Department reporter, had just called Cacheris to ask whether he had a client named Jim Preston whom the FBI suspected of having leaked sensitive information to Ahmad Chalabi. Could Cacheris confirm the report? Did he have any other clients who were also targets in the inquiry?

Keller and Abramson had obviously passed on my source's name, employer, and lawyer to David. Since they knew only Jim's code name, Cacheris told David Johnston, accurately, that he had no client by that name. Fortunately, I had worked with David long enough to know that he was among the more discreet reporters in Washington. I stopped by his desk to explain the sensitivity of Jim's involvement and to share what little more I knew about the FBI's probe. David, a pro, wrote a story about the inquiry that protected my source.

When I confronted Keller and Abramson about the incident the next day, Abramson said that she hadn't understood that my source was quite so sensitive. Keller told me that his broader obligation to the paper had prompted him to pass along Jim Preston's name, without a reference to me, so that David could pursue what was obviously a competitive story. But Keller had neglected to tell me what he had done, I said. As a result, I hadn't alerted my source or his attorney. Jim Preston's confidence in me, not to mention my flagging faith in my senior editors' discretion, was shaken. The protection of sources was essential to investigative reporting. We were nothing without people who trusted us enough to risk their careers to help us inform our readers.

Some sources risked more than their careers in talking to journalists or the US government. They risked their lives. After what happened with Jim Preston, I was determined to say nothing to anyone about my efforts to learn the fate of Fadil Abbas al-Husayni, the "baseball cap" scientist who had been cooperating with the US army at great personal peril since MET Alpha had tracked him down.

Over time, I had learned more about his alleged WMD activities. While some of his claims to me were later described as wrong or exaggerated, or could not be verified, I was told that Abbas was, as he had claimed, privy to information about a very sensitive, secret part of the chemical weapons effort that would never be fully understood. Charles Duelfer's final report on Iraq's WMD, issued in September 2004, identified the Iraqi I had written about as a member of an elite group of senior military intelligence officers who had supervised a unit that made poisons and chemical agents for assassinations and other small-scale operations in the late 1980s and early 1990s. The ISG report noted that while this secret, twelve-man "chemical preparation division" within the Iraqi intelligence service's M16 directorate was not producing toxic chemicals or poisons at the time of the invasion, it may still have been conducting some small-scale research and development. The report said that while the M16 directorate did not appear to be an attempt to keep a core group of scientists together to restart a larger chemical warfare production group when and if sanctions were lifted, sources had told the ISG that the M16 division had plans to "produce and weaponize nitrogen mustard using CS rifle grenades" and to make and ship "sarin and sulfur mustard" in perfume bottles to the United States and Europe. The plans were "extremely difficult to corroborate," the ISG reported, "because they were not carried out" and because so few people within the Iraqi intelligence directorate were aware of them.

Still later, a former intelligence officer told

me that Duelfer's report should not have mentioned Abbas by name because he had been an important source for the American weapons hunters. The disclosure of his name, which appears but once in Duelfer's three-volume, fifteen-hundred page report, had been a mistake, the official disclosed. Unaware of his status at the time, I had identified him in a draft of a story because the army's translator thought that the name he had given MET Alpha in his written offer to cooperate was a pseudonym. I was mortified to discover that it wasn't. While his name was deleted from most of the paper's editions, I had inadvertently endangered an Iraqi who was cooperating with the United States. After consulting with Gerald and XTF officers, we decided that the best way to deflect attention from my innocent error was not to answer press questions about him. My silence allowed critics to charge that I was embarrassed by the story I had written. That was not true. Having inadvertently identified him, I feared that he would be targeted by forces still loyal to Saddam. He was, after all, a Shiite who had worked with Saddam's dreaded intelligence service — a "traitor" to his fellow Muslims, some of the more fanatical Shia might conclude.

At a press conference in December 2003, David Kay told reporters about the danger faced by Iraqis who were working with the Americans. He mentioned that at least one scientist had been shot and badly wounded as a result of such retaliation. Kay declined to discuss the matter further — and declined to be interviewed by me. But an intelligence officer told me that Kay had been referring to an attempt on Abbas's life.

I never stopped asking experts on Iraq and WMD whether they knew where he was and what had happened to him. In my subsequent trips to Iraq, I kept searching for Fadil Abbas al-Husayni. I never found him.

On Friday, June 4, 2004, I was back in Keller's office in New York with Jill Abramson. Agreeing to "cut right to the chase," as I had requested, Keller said that a week ago, he thought that after the editor's note had run, he could assemble a team of reporters, including me, to pursue an investigative series about prewar intelligence, its impact on Iraq policy, and mismanagement of the occupation. He had changed his mind, he said. Whatever I wrote about Chalabi, Iraqi WMD, or the war would lack "credibility." I would not be covering any of them in the future. In fact, he did not want me to cover national security.

I was astonished.

Like the editor's note, this was a fait accompli. Bill Safire's hunch had been right. The paper would publish several excellent stories that examined specific instances of alleged failures in prewar intelligence, but there would be no in-depth investigation into this spectacular intelligence failure. I realized then that there was never going to be. Even if there was one, I would not be part of it. As Safire had suspected, Keller and Abramson had dangled the prospect of my working on subjects I cared about so deeply to buy my silence in advance of the editor's note, which I had agreed not to discuss in print, on radio, or on TV.

I came close to rage in his office that day. The record suggested that I was committed to the pursuit of the truth, however complex, no matter where it led, I told him as calmly as possible. Since returning from Iraq a year earlier, I had helped break stories about problematic prewar intelligence and policies that were unflattering to the administration.

I could understand his decision to remove me from Iraq War reporting, I told him, though I thought that was a mistake, given my expertise. But why was I being barred from all national security? How could that possibly be in the paper's interest?

"Because all national security involves Iraq and those same sources," he replied, according to my contemporaneous notes of the meeting. "People inside and outside of the paper are now suspicious of your reporting," he said. The paper could not tolerate such doubt. He had to defend its "integrity."

He had publicly defended my reporting, I reminded him. The editor's note had called our "flawed" stories an "institutional" failure, rejecting individual blame. Why was I now being singled out? And what signal would it send the paper's critics — many of them motivated ideologically — to know that if they complained loudly enough about a reporter's work, no matter how inaccurate or reckless their complaints, the paper would bar that reporter from a story or a beat — indeed, from an entire area?

I would not be sidelined, I told them. Their decision would surely leak. I could not allow what remained of my professional integrity to be besmirched unjustly. I would consider an assignment outside of national security tantamount to being fired. I would leave the *Times* and write the book on intelligence failures and the hunt for WMD, which I had begun researching with Charles Duelfer, the inspector.

By the end of the meeting, Keller and Abramson were almost as angry as I was. We agreed to consider our options over the weekend. "It was, without a doubt, the ugliest meeting I have ever had with any senior editors at this paper," I wrote in a notebook.

I thought their decision made no sense in such a competitive news climate. I suspected they would relent. And they did. A week later, Keller and Abramson assigned me to two competitive national security stories: Saddam's use of the UN's oil-for-food program to buy banned technology and bribe diplomats and foreign officials, and back to the FBI's investigation into the anthrax letter attacks.

I had won the battle, but the victory felt hollow.

Chapter 20
Protecting Sources

I had setbacks at the paper before and had always bounced back. Bill Keller and Jill Abramson's edict in the fall of 2004 that I not cover national security was rescinded after a week. In addition to working on the Iraqi oil-for-food program and the anthrax attack probe, I was investigating with Will Rashbaum, a superb *Times* reporter, the New York Police Department's ambitious effort to prevent another 9/11-scale attack on the city, particularly involving WMD. Together Will and I were describing for the first time some of the NYPD's innovative programs.

I was also still gathering material for the book I hoped to write with Charles Duelfer about the Iraqi WMD intelligence failure. I was busy.

Richard Clarke, the former counter-terrorism czar who had turned on President Bush after the invasion of Iraq, urged me to leave the *Times.* "Why are you still working for people who don't value you?" he said as we sipped coffee on a cool fall day in 2004 on a bench outside the headquarters of ABC News, where he was a consultant. My bosses had tried to blame the government's bad WMD intelligence and the paper's ostensible institutional failings on me to save their jobs, he asserted. "You've got to get out of there."

I said nothing. Though I sensed he was right, I could not imagine quitting the paper that had been my home for twenty-seven years. Where would I go? Where would I work? Reporting for the *Times* was all I knew how to do.

There was a more compelling reason not to quit that I dared not share with Dick — or almost anyone else. I had begun confronting what I sensed might become the most grueling professional challenge of my life: I was waging two separate but concurrent efforts to protect my sources from a zealous prosecutor. Patrick J. Fitzgerald, the US attorney for the Northern District of Illinois, was demanding my home, office, and cell phone records — and those of Phil Shenon, another *Times* reporter — in a leak investigation involving two Islamic charities. Fitzgerald wanted to know who had told us about planned federal raids on the offices of the charities, which the government suspected of terrorist links. In 2002 we had written a story about a federal investigation of the charities. Our requests for comment had alerted them to the impending raids and damaged the government's inquiry, Fitzgerald said.

Now in a new incarnation as "special counsel," Fitzgerald was conducting a potentially more explosive leak inquiry into who had divulged the name and occupation of Valerie Plame, a CIA officer whose husband, former US ambassador Joseph C. Wilson IV, had infuriated White House officials by publicly accusing the administration of lying us into the Iraq War.

I feared that I might become ensnared in this investigation, too. I had spoken to many officials about Wilson's charges, and also about his marriage to the CIA official. It was a crime to disclose the identity of a covert agent. I feared that Fitzgerald might learn that I was one of the reporters who had been told about where Ms. Plame Wilson worked. He might want to know who had told me.

While I was determined not to disclose my confidential sources, I knew that I could never afford on my own — financially or professionally — to wage protracted legal battles to protect the confidentiality of my sources. I was stuck.

In July 2004, two months earlier, I had visited George Freeman, the *Times* lawyer, at our New York headquarters. Solidly built, in his fifties, with tortoise-rimmed glasses and a neatly clipped mustache, George was cheerful as usual. In his twenty-three years at the paper, he and his team had fended off an average of fifteen major cases a year: libel charges, government subpoenas for our telephone and email records in leak investigations, demands for our testimony before grand juries, and cooperation with government inquiries. George was a much-admired, popular advocate for the paper and its reporters.

What seemed to be the problem? Was it our phone records case?

No, I replied. I was worried about the government's criminal inquiry into who had compromised Valerie Plame's identity as a CIA agent. Special Counsel Fitzgerald had sent subpoenas to four journalists: Bob Woodward and Walter Pincus of the *Washington Post,* Tim Russert of NBC, and Matt Cooper of *Time* magazine. Judge Thomas F. Hogan in Washington had already found

Time and Matthew Cooper in contempt for refusing to identify their sources. He had ordered *Time* to pay $1,000 a day and Matt to be jailed until his sources were identified. The sanctions were suspended pending their appeal.

"What's that got to do with you?"

"I think I'm going to get a subpoena, too."

Suddenly I had George's undivided attention. "What makes you think that?" he asked me, closing his office door.

I told him that I had known for months that Valerie Plame Wilson was a CIA employee who worked on WMD. I had also been told that she had helped arrange her husband's trip to Africa to investigate whether Iraq had tried to buy uranium for its nuclear weapons program. And I was aware of the claim that White House officials had deliberately blown Plame's cover to punish her husband, former ambassador Wilson, for having challenged the administration's justification for the Iraq War.

George looked baffled. To a New York lawyer, the political firestorm in Washington over the leak of Plame's name sounded like a political game.

Describing the situation succinctly wasn't easy. The administration, I told George, had based its prewar claim that Saddam pos-

sessed WMD partly on intelligence assertions that Iraq had tried to buy yellowcake
(uranium ore) from Africa for its nuclear
weapons program. Some of the documents
about such an alleged sale had turned out
to be forged, but a year before the war, in
February 2002, Vice President Cheney had
asked the CIA about the accuracy of another intelligence report indicating that Iraq
was secretly trying to buy yellowcake from
Niger.

The CIA then asked Plame's husband, a
former ambassador to Gabon, to check it
out. Wilson went to Niger in February 2002
and concluded that the tip was not accurate.
But Iraq's alleged search for uranium, based
on other sources, including British intelligence, was included in the intelligence
community's secret National Intelligence
Estimate of October 2002. Meanwhile, the
CIA never told the White House that Wilson had been sent on such a trip.

The NIE's finding that Iraq was "vigorously trying to procure uranium ore and
yellowcake" from an African country helped
persuade some in Congress to support
military action against Iraq. President Bush
also mentioned the allegation in his 2003
State of the Union speech. Wilson was
dismayed. He thought the allegation was

false, and that Bush and his advisers must have known that. In July 2003 Wilson wrote an op-ed for the *Times* disclosing that he had investigated the tip in Niger and had concluded that no such attempt had occurred. He accused the White House of having twisted intelligence about the uranium purchase to help sell the war — an explosive charge.

On July 11, 2003, after a bitter internal battle, the CIA and the White House retracted "sixteen words" that Bush uttered in his State of the Union about the attempted uranium purchases.[1] The statement also asserted that no one at the White House had been aware of Wilson's trip or his conclusions.

The debate probably would have ended there, I told George, if *Chicago Sun-Times* columnist Robert Novak, a well-informed right-winger atypically opposed to the Iraq War, had not written a column a few days later about Wilson's trip. Quoting two "senior Administration sources," Novak wrote that Wilson's wife, "Valerie Plame," was an "Agency operative on weapons of mass destruction" who had "suggested" sending her husband to Niger.

The CIA spokesperson had confirmed Novak's story. Later the agency informed the Justice Department that Plame's cover had been blown. The agency routinely made such referrals when leaks of secret intelligence information appeared in the press. Barely a quarter of them were investigated by the FBI, and prosecutions were rare. But given the firestorm over whether America had gone to war under doctored intelligence, the Justice Department quickly launched a criminal investigation. The FBI was exploring not only who had blown Plame's cover but also whether doing so constituted a violation of the 1982 Intelligence Identities Protection Act, which bars the outing of covert agents.

To avoid the perception that the inquiry would be influenced by the White House, Attorney General John Ashcroft recused himself from the investigation, and in December 2003 Deputy Attorney General James Comey appointed Fitzgerald — whom he called his "friend and former colleague," and an "absolutely apolitical career prosecutor" with "impeccable judgment" — as special counsel. Bush ordered his staff to cooperate fully with the leak inquiry and promised that if the leaker was employed by his administration, he would be fired. Fitzgerald cast a wide net, interviewing dozens of officials and subpoenaing journalists.

George Freeman asked me whom I had talked to about Wilson and his wife, Plame. "Just about everyone," I told him. Initially, it had struck me as juicy gossip, a conversation opener, and possibly even a good story, since one official I interviewed described Wilson's trip as a boondoggle that his wife at the CIA had helped arrange. I hadn't been asked to investigate the tip further, I told George. But among the senior officials with whom I had spoken was I. Lewis "Scooter" Libby, Cheney's chief of staff. I didn't elaborate further, but I was worried about our discussion of the still-secret portions of the 2002 NIE on Iraqi WMD. I told George that I could not answer questions from a grand jury about my discussions of top-secret information without violating a pledge I had given Libby, who had given me sensitive information in confidence.

While most reporters, including me, do not like offering pledges of confidentiality, there is no way around them if the public is to learn how policies are developed and what the government wants (and, more often, does not want) Americans to know. The penalties for disclosing classified information are harsh. Many officials I interviewed took periodic polygraph tests that asked whether they had recently had unauthorized conversations with journalists. Preserving such contacts depends on awkward negotiations over how a source is to be identified, what can and cannot be published, and the development of trust, usually over years. Reporters who burned sources did not last long in national security reporting. Word got out; officials avoided them.

George asked me who at the paper knew about my conversations about Wilson and Plame.

"Only Jill Abramson," I replied, the Washington bureau chief at the time. I recalled my rushed meeting with Jill on a Friday afternoon a year earlier in July. She had seemed preoccupied, I remembered. Howell Raines and Gerald Boyd had recently been fired. Without warning, I had stepped into her office in July 2003 to tell her that Joe Wilson's wife worked at the CIA and had apparently helped send her husband on the trip to Africa before the war to investigate the uranium charge. If true, I said, the CIA was possibly guilty of nepotism and of covering up intelligence that disputed its prewar WMD claims. If the source was wrong, and Wilson's wife hadn't sent her husband to Africa, the White House might be trying to smear them. Either way, I told Abramson, the tip needed pursuing.

Had anyone followed up on the story? George asked.

Not to my knowledge. In fact, no one in the Washington bureau wrote about it until after Novak published his column outing Plame. I told George I was angry that the *Times* had been scooped on the tip I had passed along.

Had I written anything about any aspect of the allegation?

"No," I replied.

George smiled. "Then forget about it," he said.

"Why?"

"Because the paper never wrote about it until after Novak outed her. And you never wrote about it at all," he said. "Nobody is going to send you to jail for a story you never wrote."

My subpoena arrived in August 2004, a month later. After meeting with the paper's lawyers and me, Arthur Sulzberger announced that the *Times* would fight Fitzgerald's effort to force me to testify before a grand jury about my confidential sources. Nor would I share a month of interview notes with him.

"Journalists should not have to face the prospect of imprisonment for doing nothing more than aggressively seeking to report on the government's actions," Arthur said. "Such subpoenas make it less likely that sources will be willing to talk candidly with reporters, and ultimately it is the public that suffers."

George Freeman and Floyd Abrams, the celebrated First Amendment lawyer who had helped represent the paper on tough cases ever since the Pentagon Papers in 1971, expected that the *Times,* too, would be subpoenaed for its records, but it never was. Fitzgerald wanted only my notes between June and July, and my appearance before the grand jury.

By October 2004, most of the other subpoenaed reporters had cut deals with Fitzgerald.[2] Floyd and I had discussed whether I, too, should find a way to cooperate. Libby, after all, had signed a blanket waiver permitting reporters with whom he had spoken to cooperate with the inquiry. But I argued that he had done so only because the president had ordered him to: his waiver was not voluntary. A forced waiver would not free me from my pledge of confidentiality. Floyd agreed. But I authorized him to talk both to Libby's lawyer, Joseph A. Tate, about whether Libby would be willing to give me a personal waiver, and also to prosecutor Fitzgerald, to see whether he would narrow his demand for my notes, as well as the topics and sources to be covered before the grand jury.

In September Floyd and I met for breakfast in New York. Floyd, who was also representing Matt Cooper of *Time* magazine, told me that he and Tate had spoken on the phone, and that Tate pressed him about what I might say in my testimony. Floyd said that Tate declined to waive the pledge of confidentiality I had given Libby, though he had permitted other reporters with whom he had spoken to testify. Tate had also signaled, Floyd told me, that the blanket waiver that some other journalists had interpreted as permission to cooperate with the grand jury was not really voluntary.

The news from Fitzgerald was no better. He was insisting on examining my entire notebooks, not merely the notes of the discussions I had with various sources about Wilson's Africa trip. Nor was he willing to limit his questions to that topic. Finally, Floyd said, Fitzgerald was also unwilling to confine his questioning to a single source who had told me about Wilson's wife. That meant I would be unable to protect other confidential sources who had also given me sensitive information unrelated to Wilson or his wife. Fitzgerald was insisting on the right to ask me about all sources with whom I had discussed Valerie Plame. Floyd and I knew that Fitzgerald had called back Matt Cooper after his first appearance before the grand jury for additional testimony when he learned that Cooper had discussed Plame with a second official. I could not risk an open-ended prosecutorial fishing expedition into my sources.

I could not comply with the subpoena, even if it meant going to jail.

On a steamy, hot night in July 2004, days after I had told George Freeman that I feared being dragged into the Valerie Plame investigation and a month before my subpoena arrived, I was in my office, working late. The phone rang.

It was Adnan Saeed Haideri al-Haideri, the Iraqi chemical engineer who had described having worked on what he believed were sites for storing chemical and biological weapons. He sounded frantic. He told me that he was going to be arrested or deported; he wasn't sure which. I was his only "friend" in America, he pleaded. He needed my help.

I hadn't seen Haideri for over two years since I had flown to Thailand at Ahmad Chalabi's invitation to interview him about WMD. But I had never stopped looking for him.

Months earlier, a relative in Australia had given me his US cell phone number. I had left messages for him, but he had not called me back. Now, out of the blue, he had called.

One day later we were sitting together again, drinking tea, in a CIA safe house: a nondescript, two-story row house on Crystal Ford Lane in Centreville, Virginia. Haideri said the agency was renting it for him, a claim that his lawyer later confirmed and which the CIA did not deny.

Though Bill Keller had banned me from writing about Iraqi WMD (except for the competitive oil-for-food investigation for the *Times*), interviewing Haideri was crucial for the intelligence fiasco book I was researching and still hoped to write.

I had many questions for Haideri: First, above all, had he lied to me about having visited or worked at some twenty different Iraqi sites that he had been told were associated with Iraq's chemical or biological weapons programs? Had he exaggerated his claims? Had Saddam stored chemical or biological agents underneath the Saddam Hussein Hospital in Baghdad, as he had told me back in December 2001? Knight Ridder, the nation's second-largest newspaper publisher, had reported that when the CIA had taken Haideri back to Baghdad in February 2004 for a brief visit, he had been unable to identify any of the places where he claimed to have worked.[3] Was that true? Had he failed CIA polygraph tests, as journalists also alleged, and been labeled a fabricator?

Haideri, then forty-six, had aged considerably since our first meeting. Perspiring and breathing heavily, repeatedly rubbing his hand through his thinning, slicked-back brown hair, he was obviously nervous as I began questioning him. He swore that he had not lied to me or to the US government. Nor had Chalabi's people encouraged him to lie. Would the CIA, he asked, have hustled him out of Thailand to the island of Saipan, and then to Honolulu, and finally to Virginia if they thought he was lying? Would they still be paying for him, his wife and ex-wife, and their six, and later eight, children, if he had misled them? Would they have gotten him and his family I-94 entry cards, which he showed me, and a six-month visa, which had been renewed every six months since his arrival in the States two years earlier? Would they have given him a work permit, which he also showed me, and coached him on drafting a résumé? The agents had slipped him out of Thailand to protect him, he told me, after one of his wife's brothers had been shot at their home in Baghdad. His wife's sister, too, had been beaten.

In mid-2003 he had failed a second polygraph because, he claimed, the technician administering the three-day test made him nervous. But the CIA had continued paying his expenses since his arrival in Virginia over two years ago — more than $4,000 a month, he said, which his lawyer later confirmed. The agency was even paying for Selwa's English lessons, he told me.

I looked around at the drab décor — standard agency issue. Haideri was probably being truthful about the house, I thought; town houses in Virginia suburbs usually don't come equipped with cameras embedded in the living room and kitchen walls like the ones I noticed in this house.

Yes, intelligence agents had taken him back to Baghdad for a short stay in February 2004 to help the Iraq Survey Group identify places he claimed to have worked.

But they had taken him to only two sites, he insisted, the first of which he had located, but it had been badly looted, he said. He couldn't find the second; he had never driven there himself. But he had given the Americans the name of the manager in charge when he had worked there. What about the alleged secret rooms or laboratories at the Baghdad hospital? I asked. He reminded me that he had never entered the hospital. Instead, Iraqi officers had brought materials to his car from inside the hospital for him to inspect. I knew that while MET Alpha's and Bravo's WMD hunting teams had found secret rooms inside villas, mosques, and palaces, none had been found at the sites Haideri had identified.

As usual, CIA and DIA analysts disagreed about Haideri's value and veracity, even in late 2004. A CIA spokesman had told me that the agency considered Haideri "unreliable" after he failed a third polygraph in Baghdad. But DIA officials continued calling his information "useful," though not as "earth shattering" as the analysts initially thought. James Brooks, the DIA spokesman at the time, told me that the military had not walked away from Haideri. "He provided information for many reports on a lot of different topics," Brooks said. "There were frauds out there, but not this guy."

The CIA, however, apparently cooled toward him after his brief return to Baghdad. The day before my visit to Haideri's home, two immigration officials had come to the house and ordered him to prepare to leave the United States immediately. His visa was about to expire and would not be renewed this time. The officials had left, but for how long? Could I help him find a lawyer? he pleaded.

While I had intended to write about his saga in my book, Haideri's very presence in Washington was news. Two weeks earlier, Jim Dwyer, a New York–based *Times* investigative reporter, had reported that Chalabi's INC had coached Iraqi defectors he had steered to American journalists and US intelligence officials before the war. Dwyer had relied heavily on a former representative of the INC who had worked with several defectors, including Haideri. But the former INC official also acknowledged having had a bitter split with the group and having been arrested by the Americans, twice, after Saddam was defeated in April 2003. Dwyer based his claim largely on that embittered Iraqi. He also wrote that Haideri and the other defectors "could not be reached for comment." But here Haideri was, two weeks later, having tea with me in Virginia.

In May 2004, Keller's editor's note suggested that the paper had been "taken in" by Haideri's false claims. Okrent's public editor's note, too, suggested that American officials and Haideri invented their concern about the fate of his relatives back in Baghdad. Okrent clearly doubted that they were in jeopardy and that one of them may have been hurt or killed as a warning to other defectors. "Were they?" Okrent wrote. "Did anyone go back to ask? Did anything Haideri say have genuine value?"

The paper now had a chance to revisit Haideri's claims as its editors had urged: to publish the missing "follow-up" to my controversial front-page story. Haideri, the alleged fabricator, was hiding in plain sight. He even had a Facebook account.

I called Keller at home. Whatever our differences, the news came first. While Keller would not permit me to follow up on the story I had broken, another *Times* reporter could decide whether Haideri had lied or embellished — or, as his legion of critics charged, had misled our paper, its readers, and the country.

Keller was furious again. Why had I disregarded his order to stop reporting on Iraq and WMD? While I had no intention of writing about Haideri for the *Times,* I replied, I would continue trying to understand how and why the prewar WMD intelligence had failed. I was writing a book — on my own time, I reminded him. I had paid for my trip to Washington myself. This was purely a courtesy call to pass along a story that Keller had said the paper had an obligation to pursue.

In New York the next morning, Jim Risen, our intelligence reporter, called me. Keller had asked him to pursue the story. I gave him Haideri's address. Jim later told me that he had driven to Centreville, only to find Haideri gone. Selwa was unable to speak enough English to explain his disappearance. Jim did not tell me whether he or another reporter had pursued the matter further.

By 2014, Haideri had not been deported. John A. Rizzo, the CIA's former general counsel and an agency lawyer for over thirty years, told me in an interview in 2013 that while he did not recall the details of Haideri's case, defectors deemed to be fabricators were usually not compensated and were invariably forced to leave America. Soon after our 2004 meeting in Virginia, Haideri had hired a lawyer and applied for political asylum. In 2006 the CIA formally ended its relationship with him after negotiating what he and his lawyer claimed was a $400,000 payment in exchange for his pledge of silence.

The CIA refused to comment on him and other defectors. But in 2009 Charles Duelfer, who had led the search for WMD in Iraq in 2004, published *Hide and Seek: The Search for Truth in Iraq,* a book about his WMD hunt. His book confirmed my assertion that the intelligence community had debriefed Haideri at length and had issued many reports based on his reporting. "Sometimes what he said was correct; sometimes he was inferring too much," Duelfer concluded. He did not use the word *fabricator.*

By October 2004, I had gone from being a reporter who made headlines to becoming the headline myself.

It felt asphyxiating. I tried carrying on with my reporting, but I was increasingly preoccupied with legal meetings about how to avoid a confrontation with prosecutor Fitzgerald and jail. Though some critics wrote later that I was eager to go to jail as a First Amendment martyr, nothing was further from the truth.[4] Jason, my amazingly healthy husband who rarely even got colds, had been ill. In 2004 he had a stent placed in an artery near his heart. I was merely a good actress, putting up a stoic front. Deep down, I was scared stiff.

After several discouraging conversations with Floyd Abrams, I decided that I could not comply with Fitzgerald's demands, even if it meant going to jail.

It was ultimately my call, not the paper's. Unlike Matt Cooper, I had not discussed my sources in emails that belonged to the *Times.* George and Floyd, who were representing me as well as the paper, were content not to contest my view that my notebooks were not the paper's. If the paper did not own my notebooks, it, unlike *Time* magazine, could not be fined.

In October 2004 Judge Thomas F. Hogan of the federal district court ordered me jailed for as long as eighteen months to persuade me to change my mind. He suspended the sanction pending our appeal. "We have a classic confrontation between competing interests," he said from the bench. I was acting in "good faith," he allowed, doing my "duty as a respected and established reporter who believes reporters have a First Amendment privilege that trumps the right of the government to inquire into her sources." But I had no legal right to refuse to answer the government's questions.

Arthur Sulzberger, who had accompanied me to Washington, was supportive. The judge had said that I was a "great reporter doing a great job. And that's absolutely right," he told NBC. But journalists believed that we "have the law on our side," that the First Amendment "protects us from having to give this information." If we lost, I would be going to jail for something I never wrote and something we never published. "And that's just wrong," he said.

Arthur and I knew that the law was not on our side. While the *Times* is fond of recalling legal victories in the Pentagon Papers case, the dispositive decision on a journalist's right to protect a source was *Branzburg v. Hayes,* which Judge Hogan cited in holding Matt Cooper and me in contempt of court. In a 5-to-4 decision in 1972, the Supreme Court ruled that requiring reporters to appear and testify before grand juries does not abridge the freedom of the press that the First Amendment guarantees. A defendant has the right to "every man's testimony." A majority also ruled that the First Amendment does not give journalists the right to protect sources, especially if they have broken the law. James Goodale, then the general counsel of the *Times,* used opinions written by Justices Potter Stewart and Lewis Powell to carve out exceptions to the ruling.

Justice Stewart had proposed a three-part balancing test to weigh a grand jury's needs. The government had to demonstrate (1) "probable cause" to believe that the journalist has information relevant to the investigation; (2) that the information being sought cannot be gotten in another way; and (3) finally, that the government has a "compelling and overriding interest" in getting the information. Justice Powell gave journalists a bit more ammunition in his separate opinion. Though he had voted with the majority, he argued that the balancing test should be conducted on a "case-by-case" basis. In subsequent cases, the Supreme Court had usually sided with the government seeking the information. It would be an uphill battle, Floyd told me. Our chances were less than fifty-fifty.

Arthur predicted that we would win. Was I willing to stick with this? To the end?

I doubted I would have much choice, I replied. If I couldn't get a voluntary waiver of the confidentiality pledge I had given my source — and Floyd had told me that was most unlikely — I was prepared to go to jail. Given the *Branzburg* ruling, I would probably be spending some "quality time" there, I told him.

Arthur glanced away, reluctant to ponder the implications of losing such a high-profile case. I doubted that our fight would end as triumphantly as his father's victory in the Pentagon Papers case. In my case, the source being protected, I noted, was not a classic "whistle-blower": an obscure junior official trying to reveal wrongdoing in the public's interest. It was a senior official who may have leaked information to smear a subordinate or, best case, to protect his boss from an allegation of having lied the country to war. That would not resonate well with the public, or even journalists.

I wanted to set just a couple of ground rules. If I refused to cooperate, I wanted an open channel only to him. Arthur seemed pleased but puzzled by that request.

"But what about Keller?" he asked me, looking slightly alarmed.

I told Arthur that I no longer trusted Keller after he had nearly betrayed "Jim Preston," my DIA source.

I also told Arthur how wrongheaded I thought the decision to publish an editor's note had been. Knowing that he, as publisher, would surely have approved the note, and perhaps Dan Okrent's column as well, I said that neither the paper nor its reporters had been "taken in," as the note suggested. And I told him I felt I had been scapegoated. Though the editor's note had not mentioned my name, my journalistic integrity had been implicitly called into question. Since then, I told him, I had felt betrayed by the institution I had worked for for so long. For months, I had felt utterly alone.

Arthur leapt to his feet and wrapped his arms around me, hugging me tightly, something he had not done since our days as reporters together in Washington. "I know it's been rough on you," he said. I noticed that he did not contradict my assertion that he had approved Keller's note. "I know how stressful it's been," he added. "But that's all over now. You are not alone."

We stood together, motionless for a few seconds while I struggled to regain my composure. "I promise you," Arthur told me. "You will not be alone in this fight, Judy. I will never abandon you again."

CHAPTER 21
INMATE 45570083

"Praise Jesus! Push on through the pain! Do those squats! Feel that pull! *Praise* the *Lord!"*

It was late July 2005, *Gospelrobics* time at the Alexandria Detention Center, my home since Judge Hogan had jailed me until I agreed to discuss my confidential sources with a grand jury. Since the only exercise bicycle in Cell Block 2-E was broken, I was having fitness guru Reggie Thornton take me through his paces. I was punching the air to a Christian disco tune on the TV set in our lounge.

Because it was early on a Sunday, most of the twenty-two women in this unit were sleeping. Only a few were sitting on our threadbare couch or playing cards at the Formica tables. A couple were watching Reggie urge us to "give it up for Jesus."

"He's hot," declared Ricochet, a fellow inmate, eyes fixed on Reggie's pectorals and abs. "I wouldn't mind a piece of him."

Soon residents of 2-E would be eating breakfast. Then the unit's large steel door would be unlocked, and many would go next door to Bible class, one of the few places where male and female prisoners were permitted to mingle, which might account for its popularity. I would be able to switch from *Gospelrobics* or our usual BET channel to the Sunday news shows.

The choice of programming in 2-F, the second unit in which I spent time, was by consensus. 2-E, where I spent my first month at ADC, used a rotation system: each day an inmate chose the programming she preferred. Consensus meant there were few votes for Jim Lehrer's *NewsHour,* whereas hardly a day passed without Oprah and, on Sunday, Joel Osteen, the televangelist who filled stadiums throughout the country. We started our day with the TV serial *Charmed,* about a group of modern benign witches. Once a week at night, it was *Prison Break.*

It took fewer than twenty-four hours to go from being Judith Miller, investigative reporter, to Inmate 45570083 at ADC, a nondescript, eight-story brick building in Alexandria, Virginia.

On July 6, 2005, I was taken from a cell at the courtroom in which I had been sentenced, and "processed" through the system in record time (the prison director told me). I was photographed, fingerprinted, and given an olive green uniform with *Prisoner* embossed in faded white letters on the back of the jacket, along with two sets of underwear, one pair of sports shorts and a bra, two worn T-shirts, a sleeping gown, a beige plastic cup, one towel, two coarse brown sheets, a paper-thin mat and matching pillow, and one blanket. A see-through plastic bag held all my other worldly possessions: a comb, toothbrush, toothpaste, shampoo, deodorant, and soap.

I was not permitted to wear the gold stud earrings I had worn since my ears were pierced as a teenager. I could not keep any jewelry except my wedding ring, since it contained no precious stones. The goal was to separate inmates from their own world. Even wristwatches were banned. "Deputies," as we were told to call guards, had effectively abolished time.

My two-story cell block had six tiny cells per floor, which opened onto a large balcony on the top floor and a lounge on the lower level, the unit's only common space. Lit all day and dimmed only at night, the harsh fluorescent lights were not good for sustained reading. Fortunately, I am a sound sleeper, as I discovered in Iraq.

I learned gradually to estimate the time based on the amount and angle of light that shone through a slit in my cell's concrete wall, its only "window." The seventy-square-foot rectangular cell had no furniture — just an open toilet and sink that two women shared, plus a mirror made of polished metal that could not be shattered or used to slash a wrist or murder a cell mate.

Occasionally I had the cell to myself. But on busy summer weekends, I often had two cell mates, usually Hispanic illegal immigrants who spoke little English and were picked up in raids. The US Marshals Service rented space for them and other federal prisoners in this state facility.

The ADC was a maximum-security jail intended to house inmates awaiting trial or those sentenced to less than a year. Some had been here longer. Others were repeat offenders: men and women, even generations of families, who had spent much of their lives circulating in and out of this jail. For them, the deputies, counselors, and administrators were a second family.

Unlike prisons intended for longer-term confinement, ADC wasn't required to provide courtyards for exercise or access to fresh air. I envied Martha Stewart as I read about her jogs on the footpath that linked inmates' cottages and the afternoon volleyball games at minimum-security Camp Alderson, in West Virginia, known as "Camp Cupcake." Martha called the prison "Yale." Because males greatly outnumbered females at ADC, women were permitted on the basketball court, the jail's sole common recreational area, only at odd hours when our male counterparts weren't there. Sometimes an empathetic deputy would unlock a side door to the gym that opened onto an alcove with a wire-mesh roof, a giant birdcage. You could breathe fresh air there. In my eighty-five days at ADC, I had access to the alcove and fresh air five times.

The worst part of jail was not sleeping on a paper-thin yoga mat on the cold concrete ledges that had replaced more expensive cots; nor the vile food — mystery meats drenched in thick brown sauce that a fellow inmate dubbed "sloppy no's," accompanied by starches and carbohydrates in shades of brown and gray. Nor was it the constant din. (My jail notes are filled with unanswered requests for earplugs.) What unnerved me most was the unpredictability and loss of control. The jail had a theoretical schedule: cell doors were unlocked electronically on a buzzer system and an ear-shattering clang each morning between six thirty and seven, and slammed shut again sometime after eleven thirty at night. Though lockdowns in our claustrophobic cells were supposed to coincide with daily staff shifts, they were irregular. We were locked down during national security alerts or storm warnings, during the jail's frequent power failures, when a fight broke out among inmates anywhere in the jail, or sometimes to punish an entire unit when a few inmates became unruly or suicidal, the latter being the deputies' constant concern. There had never been a suicide at ADC, and the jail's staff intended to keep it that way.

"We are in control here," Mondre Kornegay, the jail's director of inmate services, told me soon after my admission. I would have an easier time when I accepted that.

I devised a plan to keep busy. I would consider jail a reporting assignment. The device would give me a mission beyond protecting my sources and restore some sense of control, however slender.

Jail was boring. It was also insanely bureaucratic. Run out of dental floss? Fill out a form. Want a new pair of socks? Sign a form, in triplicate. Need two aspirins for a splitting headache? Complete the form. I would eventually get the aspirin — if not the socks or dental floss — but days later, long after the headache. ADC often ran out of the forms.

The worst night was my first, July 7, in the jail's central booking facility. I had barely recovered from being surrounded by burly marshals and yanked out of the DC courtroom where Judge Hogan had ruled against me. I had just enough time to wave good-bye to Jason and hear my lawyers' protests. Judge Hogan had said that I would remain in jail until I agreed to testify, or at least until the end of the grand jury on October 28.

I was bundled out of the courtroom into an adjacent room and put in a holding cell just behind the judge's bench. The contrast was stark between the order and decorum of the proceedings (justice) and the lack of either on the other side of the door (punishment). After what seemed like an hour — my watch had been taken away — marshals slapped handcuffs on my wrists that were shackled to my ankles. I shuffled to a van that took me across the Potomac River to ADC.

During that first night in the cramped, airless holding cell in the booking area, one of the other three newcomers kept screaming. A wisdom tooth was killing her. She needed her Percocet. She wanted to see a doctor, a lawyer, her mother, a guard, *a-n-y-o-n-e*! There was a common toilet in the dank cell, which smelled of urine, sweat, and stale food, but there was no toilet paper. She wanted that, too.

Sometime in the early morning of that terrible first night, I was awakened by the distinctive wailing of British police car sirens; the sound of World War II movies. Disoriented by the incarceration and the blaring of British horns, I stepped over the other two sleeping women and inched toward the small, elevated rectangular window. Standing on tiptoes, I saw marshals huddled around a TV set.

There was a charred red double-decker bus on its side, scenes of evacuated tube stations, and video of the dazed victims stumbling through the streets. I had seen these images of carnage, chaos, and fear in Beirut and, twice, unforgettably, in New York. But this was London! More than thirty people were dead, the announcer said, a hundred more injured. Al Qaeda, I assumed, had struck again.

The women's units were clean and well run. There were some pleasant surprises — some of my fellow inmates, for instance. On my first night in Unit 2-E, a tall, attractive woman introduced — or, rather, reintroduced — herself to me. We had met before, she told me. She looked familiar, I replied hesitantly.

"We met in 1988 at the White House Correspondents' Dinner," Phyllis, I'll call her, reminded me. She had worked on Capitol Hill for Carol Moseley Braun, the first black woman elected to the Senate. She was a senior executive at the Black Caucus when we had met at the dinner.

She smiled at my obvious confusion. Though inmates were instructed not to discuss their cases, Phyllis gradually disclosed the details of hers. After working on Capitol Hill for several years, she had opened a boutique PR firm in Alexandria. One of her clients had paid with a large bad check. She had written checks to her suppliers that bounced. In Virginia, writing a bad check for over $200 is a felony. When creditors complained, she had tried to make restitution, borrowing money from relatives and friends. But "they still got me," she said. Claiming her prosecution was political, she had been fighting her conviction ever since.

How much of this saga was true, I did not know. I liked Phyllis, and so did other inmates, who tended to defer to her. Her survival tips were invaluable. I would be okay in jail, she predicted, because the other women knew I was in jail for refusing to snitch.

Apply to work in the laundry, Phyllis advised me. Although it paid only seven dollars a week, it would enable me to wash my clothes. She also urged me to volunteer to be a "trustee" who cleaned common areas, helped serve food, and did chores. Trustees were permitted to stay in the lounge during some lockdowns. They qualified for a contact visit with their spouse after working at a jail job for forty-five days. I would no longer be in jail by then, I told her. Phyllis smiled. "I know prosecutors," she said. "They are ambitious, vindictive SOBs. You'll be here." And so I was.

Ebony, a young black woman who hadn't gone to college, was a whiz at crossword puzzles. She knew the names of the presidents and vice presidents, the capitals of every state, their state birds, flowers, and songs. Her seventh-grade teacher had made her memorize them to music. This was her fourth time in ADC. Her mother and father had also been in jail. She had won a scholarship to Boston University. I read a few of her short stories. She was a natural writer.

The Hispanics were among the most heartbreaking. The few who spoke some English told horrific stories about their struggle to get to America. Two had been raped; some robbed. Unable to make bail, they were caught between the "coyotes" who threatened to kill their families back home if they talked, and immigration officials who vowed to keep them in jail forever if they didn't say who had smuggled them into the country.

Wanda haunts me still. A repeat inmate at ADC, she was in her early forties but looked older. Heavyset, with short, curly hair and coffee-colored skin, she had a low-pitched chuckle and a quick tongue. She talked nonstop about the things she was going to do when her six-month shoplifting sentence ended. As that day approached, she grew quiet. She told fewer funny stories about life "outside": about her favorite fried chicken restaurant and the local bar in DC where she used to hang out, smoking marijuana and nursing a beer while cheering the Redskins. The night before her release, she seemed despondent. There had been no reply at the number she had been calling for weeks, which supposedly belonged to a grandfather she barely knew. Her mother had died long ago. Wanda seemed to have no close relatives or friends willing to take her in for even a few days. She had nowhere to go.

The morning of her release, we gave Wanda the traditional round of applause before she distributed her few possessions. She barely spoke. She left jail with bus fare to get across the river to DC and almost no chance of finding the father of the father who had abandoned her. With no high school diploma and a repeat prison record, she had no job prospects. It seemed clear to us all that she would soon be back in jail, her only clean, safe, dependable home — a "safe place to detox and warm place to piss," as she had put it.

Several women in the two cell blocks where I spent eighty-five days never got a single telephone call, or letter, or visitor. They had no money to order from the canteen. Some of their public defenders had not shown up for their court dates. For some of these women, like Wanda, ADC was a step up in life. It was humbling.

Jail reminded me of how blessed I was. As the judge said and my lawyers reminded me, I was the only inmate with a key to the jail. If I agreed to testify, I could leave anytime. I was being incarcerated not for a crime but for a matter of conscience and principle.

Professionally, too, I was fortunate. I had gotten to the top of a demanding, rewarding profession; I was supported in jail not only by the *Times* but also by many journalists in America and abroad. Bernard-Henri Lévy, Günter Grass, Pedro Almodóvar, and other prominent European intellectuals signed a petition circulated by a Paris-based group called Reporters Without Borders that called my jailing a "miscarriage of justice." The editor in chief of the Russian newspaper *Izvestia* wrote me a letter, which hangs in my office, expressing his staff's sympathies for my incarceration and gratitude for defending freedom of speech and the press.

Harry Hurt III, who wrote a column for the *Times,* printed up "Free Judy" T-shirts. Fellow journalists Steve Byers and Robert Sam Anson plotted a jail breakout. I received letters and gifts and money (which went to a fund to provide free legal counsel to other journalists fighting government subpoenas), many from people I had never met, who praised me for standing on principle. Unlike so many inmates, I had a loving husband. My paper paid my hefty legal fees, with the cost of the lawyers and trials totaling more than $1 million, they told me.

I had a steady stream of well-wishers during the thirty-minute visiting period six evenings a week. I saw over a hundred of them, including soldiers from my embed in Iraq and First Amendment activists. My visitors held wide-ranging political views: from Richard Clarke, the former counter-terrorism chief whose book had assailed President Bush, to John Bolton, Bush's neoconservative ambassador to the UN.

The *Times* had encouraged me to meet with those who could not only help publicize my case — like Senators Bob Dole, Arlen Specter, and Chris Dodd — but also advocate for a media shield law that would protect journalists from being jailed or hauled before federal grand juries and forced to reveal sources. Senator Specter, a Republican, had an impressive ability to get quickly to the point.

"Tell me," he asked. "What is this investigation about?"

"I was hoping you could tell me, Senator."

Specter was aware that I had never written a word about Valerie Plame.

Was prosecutor Fitzgerald "political"? Specter asked. Did I think that his pursuit of key Bush officials was motivated by ideology?

"I suspect he wants to be attorney general or head the FBI," I told Specter.

"He would have to get confirmed first," the senator said dryly. Watching Specter's face, I somehow doubted that would happen if he was in the Senate.

Did I think Fitzgerald even had a case?

"Not really, Senator," I replied, unable to elaborate, since I had been warned that our phone chats through the glass partition window were monitored. In fact, I wasn't sure whether Plame, whom I had never heard of prior to Joe Wilson's charge against the White House, was covered by the 1982 Intelligence Identities Protection Act making it a crime to disclose a CIA agent's identity, whose violation Fitzgerald was investigating.[1] Fitzgerald himself had avoided asserting that Plame was covered by the law — the supposed cause of his investigation.

Specter asked whether I had been offered a waiver to testify, similar to what *Time*'s Matt Cooper had received from his source.

I recalled Matt's stunning statement in the courtroom the day I was sentenced. Neither Matt nor his lawyers, Floyd Abrams and Richard Sauber, another old friend, had warned us that they had just made a deal with Fitzgerald. Until Matt addressed the judge in the packed courtroom that day, I had thought that he and I were in this First Amendment fight together. After recounting how he had "kissed his six-year-old son good-bye" and told him he "didn't expect to see him for some time," Matt said that his source had just given him his "expressed personal consent" to testify, a waiver directly from his source to him.

Bob Bennett, my lawyer, grasped my hand as Matt sat down. He viewed Matt's last-minute deal with his confidential source skeptically, as did many journalists. But I was pleased for Matt. In an article he later wrote for *Time,* Matt disclosed that it was Karl Rove, President Bush's senior political adviser, who had first told him that Wilson's wife was a CIA officer who had helped send Wilson to Africa. Matt also said that when he asked Scooter Libby, the vice president's chief of staff, about Rove's assertion that Plame worked at the agency and had helped send him to Africa, Libby replied he had "heard that, too." At the *Times,* Libby's vague formulation would not have qualified as confirmation from a second source.

Shortly before Matt's courtroom appearance, *Time*'s editor in chief Norman Pearlstine had infuriated many journalists by turning Matt's emails and notebooks over to Fitzgerald. Pearlstine had called Fitzgerald a "modern Jimmy Stewart" and a "dedicated, brilliant public servant" who was "tall, imposing, unfailingly polite and laser-focused on the issues." He argued that given the *Branzburg* decision, the law required *Time* and its reporter to cooperate with the government's inquiry.[2] Pearlstine was of the view that *Time* owned its reporter's notes and emails. Without the backing of his magazine, and with both of his sources having specifically waived his pledge to them to keep their identities confidential, Matt's refusal to cooperate would have been pointless. Still, I suddenly felt very alone in this fight.

I did not have such a waiver, I told Senator Specter. If at any point my source had given me an explicit, voluntary waiver of my confidentiality pledge, and if prosecutor Fitzgerald had agreed not to ask me about other topics or my other sources, I would not be in jail.

I recalled that meeting with Floyd Abrams almost a year earlier, when he had briefed me on his discussion with Joe Tate, Scooter Libby's lawyer. Floyd had told me that once Tate grasped that my testimony might not exonerate Libby, he had refused to give me a waiver comparable to what Rove had given Matt. All members of my fractious legal team agreed that given what Floyd had told them, contacting Libby or Tate a second time to seek a waiver might be perceived as threatening on my part. Floyd's strategy was to argue after the grand jury ended on October 28 that nothing would be gained by keeping me in jail longer, since four months had proven I would not be coerced into testifying.

Bob Bennett, whom I hired in December 2004, had never bought that strategy. But he was stuck with it. We had settled on it months before he joined our legal team. Because Bob knew Judge Hogan well and had interacted with Fitzgerald, he was charged with handling the negotiations with Fitzgerald over what he would ask me if I ever got a voluntary waiver from my source and agreed to testify. Our goal was to persuade Fitzgerald to limit his questioning of me to what we called the three "ones": *one* source, *one* subject matter, *one* time. By the end of August, after almost two months in jail, we had not succeeded.

Though some critics would later blame Libby for putting me in jail, Fitzgerald's unwillingness to narrow the scope of his interrogation offered me little choice. Had I agreed to testify about my conversations with Libby about the Wilsons, I could not risk being questioned about other sources, or about whether Libby and I had discussed *other* top-secret information that would be potentially far more damaging to him. I could not tell a grand jury that we had discussed the highly classified version of the October National Intelligence Estimate on Iraqi WMD that the Bush White House had cited as justification for the Iraq War. Only later would I learn that by the time I interviewed Libby, Bush had already unilaterally declassified portions of the intelligence assessment so that Libby could disclose them to counter the claim that his administration had lied or exaggerated WMD-related intelligence.

Almost no one at the *Times* except my lawyers, Arthur Sulzberger and his top corporate executives, and, on the news side, Keller and Abramson, knew about these negotiations, much less my concerns about Libby's legal jeopardy. I had wanted to keep Keller and Abramson out of the loop, but Arthur had insisted they be kept informed. They managed the news, including stories about my case. I sensed that tension was building within the newsroom over the extent to which *Times* reporters were being permitted to investigate my case, our legal strategy, the identity of the sources I was protecting, and other competitive aspects of the story.

Most colleagues were enormously supportive of me while I was in jail, especially my closest friends at the paper — Jeff Gerth, Geri Fabrikant, David Barstow, and Claudia Payne — all of whom were early visitors. Jill came to see me. So did her close friend Maureen Dowd.

Keller visited. Having defended me in public as a "tenacious," "courageous" fighter for a free and independent press, he repeated his praise over the house phone in jail. On the day that Al Qaeda struck in London, he told me, he shared what must have been my intense frustration over languishing in jail in the wake of the attack. "I thought: if you weren't in jail, I'd have you on the first plane out to London."

I was thunderstruck. The executive editor who had tried to bar me from national security reporting for being too "passionate," as he put it, too much of a "lightning rod," was lamenting my absence from his staff. I was an "indispensable" part of the paper's investigative engine, he told me.

Dispirited by jail, I wanted to believe Keller.

Arthur Sulzberger visited shortly before

taking off to climb Machu Picchu. He would follow my case from Peru, he promised. He was "proud" of me. The paper would continue to write news stories and editorials about the First Amendment issues at stake. "We won't forget you in here," he pledged.

Bill Safire cheered me by holding up against the glass partition a copy of his testimony on Capitol Hill about the need for a federal shield law. "May the person monitoring this conversation get ear cancer," he boomed into the jail phone, a variation of the ancient Jewish curse.

Though he was ill and in great pain, Abe Rosenthal, too, came down from New York. Accompanied by Shirley Lord, his indefatigable wife, an author and editor at *Vogue,* he managed to balance himself on the small stool in the booth behind the partition and regale me with stories about Myron Farber, the first and only other *Times* reporter he had visited in jail. The New Jersey jail had permitted him to sit in the same room with Myron during his forty-day stint,[3] Abe complained. "I used to bring him steak!" he reminisced.

As my days in jail turned into weeks, and then months, I began to wonder why the news department had virtually stopped writing about my case. Though the editorial page ran about a dozen editorials on different aspects of the controversy, the news stories that Arthur and Keller promised did not appear. I was losing energy despite my effort to exercise, stay fit, and assume a cheerful front. Though I had stopped throwing up from the food, I was still losing weight: twenty pounds by early September. I hadn't been this thin since Iraq.

The low point were two lockdowns: the first a month after my arrival. I was awakened one night by deputies who seized all the notes I had written in jail. An inmate had complained that I was "snooping" on her and invading other inmates' privacy. Though jail officials were not supposed to read my memo pads, since they were clearly marked "Legal Notes," as my lawyers had instructed me to do, two deputies pored through them, hunting for evidence that I was secretly recording information about fellow inmates without their permission. Fortunately, years of note taking for the *Times* had trained me to mark the date, time, and place of my jailhouse interviews, and the terms under which people were speaking to me: "on the record," which meant I could identify them by name and tell their stories; on "background," which meant I could use their stories but not their names; or "off the record," which meant I could use neither their names nor the information they provided without corroborating it independently, which, of course, was impossible in jail. All the women whose stories I had recorded had spoken to me voluntarily. My notes were returned, but I became even more cautious.

Another low point came in late August when I was put in isolation for twenty-four hours for having hoarded food: apples. The jail forbade storing food in our cells, but I couldn't resist keeping three apples I had traded for packets of popcorn. I hadn't eaten fresh fruit in two months, so the mealy Delicious apples I once would have spurned were irresistible. The deputies found the contraband during an impromptu inspection one night.

Two lockdowns in less than sixty days — I was far from a model prisoner. Deputies warned me that if I continued pushing the rules, I might wind up in "administrative segregation": a permanent lockdown. I feared being confined for most of the day and night in my tiny cell.

The apple lockdown coincided with yet another downer: the arrival of dozens of angry postcards cursing me for protecting President Bush and the other "war criminals." The cards repeated a message suggested by a right-wing libertarian group: because I was "covering" for Bush's liars, I deserved to "rot in jail" for the rest of my "natural life." Not for the first or the last time, the Plame scandal enabled the left to find common ground with the radical right.

No paper or internet site was as consistently hostile as Arianna Huffington's *Huffington Post,* her relatively new website that was fixated on generating "buzz."

In late July 2005, as I sat in jail, Arianna, whom I knew socially since Washington, mocked the notion that I was a "First Amendment hero." I was trying to rehabilitate my reputation after "cheerleading for the invasion of Iraq" and "hyping the WMD threat," she wrote. She reported a "scenario" she claimed was making the rounds at the *Times:* I had refused to reveal my "source" at the White House because *I* was the source. Supposedly furious that Joe Wilson had challenged the administration's case for war and, by implication, my reporting, I had discovered that Wilson was married to a CIA agent and had "passed the info about Mrs. Wilson to Scooter Libby." Maybe I had told Karl Rove, too. I hadn't written about Plame because my goal "wasn't to write a story, but to get out the story that cast doubts on Wilson's motives."[4] When that "scenario" failed to catch fire, Huffington upped the ante. I had gone to jail not only to protect myself as the source of the Plame leak but also to get a lucrative book contract. Simon & Schuster had agreed to pay me an advance of $1.2 million, she wrote. She wondered if Alice Mayhew, my longtime editor, had visited me in jail to encourage me to enhance our book's sales by spending even longer in jail. Only after my agent, the *Times,* and S&S's president flatly denied the existence of such a contract (I couldn't respond from jail) did Huffington publish not a retraction or a correction but an "update" that repeated the book contract fabrication.

In truth, I had instructed Amanda Urban, my book agent, not to entertain offers to write about ADC or any aspect of the Plame investigation while I was in jail. She felt obliged to pass along news of only one proposal: a staggering offer of $100,000 from Graydon Carter's *Vanity Fair* for a single essay about life in jail and the case that brought me here. Though she knew I would say no, she thought it might cheer me up to know that my story was generating such interest. But I had decided against entertaining such offers precisely to avoid creating the impression that I was benefiting financially from what might be a protracted struggle. The second tough decision I made was to abandon my long-standing desire to collaborate with Charles Duelfer on a book about the Iraq WMD fiasco. Since I had no idea how long Fitzgerald's inquiry and my ordeal would last, Charles and I agreed that it would be better for him to proceed on his own. His book is essential reading for anyone seeking to understand the pitfalls of intelligence collection and the implications of what American weapons hunters found in Iraq.

Since I had no internet in jail, I usually learned about such attacks in the blogosphere from my lawyers. Saul Pilchen, Bob Bennett's partner, had broken the news to me about Arianna's scoops. "You are not going to like this," he said when he visited in July with a packet of such stories on her site, as well as the *Daily Kos, Slate, Editor & Publisher,* and other publications that had not asked for my comment on stories before and while I went to jail. "Don't get upset!" Saul counseled.

By September, life at ADC had become

semitolerable. In addition to my job in the laundry, the jail's director permitted me to organize the library. The jail did not permit visitors to bring prisoners books. So the *Times* was "donating" books to the jail's library so that I could read them. It seemed fitting that I would help catalogue and arrange the donations of over a hundred gifts from colleagues and other friends. The library had stacks of unread Bibles, but almost no books in Spanish, despite the many Hispanic inmates. The ADC had also banned categories of books: anything "pornographic," for instance, broadly defined. Books that encouraged violence or terrorism were out.

Reading was unpopular for other reasons, the lighting being just the most obvious. Because it is a solitary pastime, and we spent so much time in our cells, most of us craved companionship: sharing popcorn during a favorite TV show or playing cards. Many of the women were on medication for various psychological disorders. They rarely had the energy to read. A veteran counselor at the jail hinted at yet another reason: Did I not suspect that some of my fellow inmates might be unable to read? She suggested that when I picked out books for the book carts that circulated once a week through the units, I might include some fairy tales, children's books, and cartoon books. Her suggestion worked. Those offerings were a hit.

As weeks passed, I took comfort in small pleasures: hot dogs for lunch on Friday (a recognizable meat); a hard-boiled egg and real tea for breakfast on Sunday; the salad I was once given; and the quart of Coke I downed at the staff cafeteria to compensate me for the loss of several packages of trail mix an inmate was caught stealing from my cell. I learned a number of useful skills: how to make lipstick and rouge out of a paste of crushed red-colored Skittles and M&M's; how to use dental floss to tweeze my eyebrows; how to make a headband from the elastic portion of a sock. Ebony taught me how to do the electric slide, a line dance popular in her 'hood. Anna taught me the macarena, and Felicity the national anthem of Honduras. I learned five new yoga positions from Amy, and from Ricochet, the lyrics of "Just a Lil Bit" by rapper 50 Cent. I did not learn to crochet, despite the efforts of Ms. Denise Costley, the kind "empowerment" counselor.

I was not the ADC's most high-profile prisoner. That honor went to Zacarias Moussaoui, the alleged "twentieth hijacker," who eventually pleaded guilty to crimes in connection with the 9/11 attacks. "Moose," as the staff called him, was confined in what had once been the women's mental health unit on the fourth floor. He had six cells to himself. Though he was on twenty-two-hour lockdown, he had also been given a desk and office chair, a computer *with* internet, and even a hanging plant because he was defending himself at his trial. Moussaoui was clearly crazy, a deputy told me. But he was intelligent, surly, and mean. He refused to talk to most female guards. He signed some letters from jail "the 20th hijacker." The previous year, he had given himself a "birthday" party to celebrate 9/11. He often wrote "Death to America" on his laundry bag.

How could I interview him? I had already managed to meet the jail's other high-profile terrorism supporter: Taissir Rajab Al-Tamimi, a professor of Islamic law who was later given life for soliciting and providing material support for terrorism. I encountered him at the medical clinic early in my stay. I was having some stitches removed from my arm; he suffered from asthma. I recognized him immediately from his photos. He was pleased to meet me, he said agreeably. "I've read a lot about you."

"And I've written a lot about you," I replied noncommittally.

When he complained about the quality of the books on the circulating carts, I said that as the jail's newly appointed part-time librarian, I would try to include more interesting selections on the cart. I chose *The Federalist Papers,* attaching a sticky note to the book with his name on it, hoping he would spot it and would "read the arguments in favor of constitutionally enshrined freedom carefully." I was punished with a four-hour lockdown. Communicating without authorization with prisoners in another cell is strictly forbidden.

Despite the reprimand, I decided to add "Interviewing the Moose" to my list of "reporting" assignments in jail. But how would I get to the fourth floor to ask him whether he was, in fact, the twentieth hijacker? Like working in the laundry and organizing books in our library, plotting this unlikely encounter helped pass the time. After several weeks, I devised a plan. Women laundry workers distributed freshly washed sheets and towels on carts once a week to prisoners on other floors. I would trade some M&M's for a chance to distribute the laundry on the day it was sent to the fourth floor. When the deputy unlocked his cell unit's door, I would give Moussaoui his sheets and towels and pop the question: Was he a member of Al Qaeda and part of the 9/11 plot? My plan might have worked. But by the time I was assigned to distribution duty on Moussaoui's floor, Patrick Fitzgerald was en route to the jail to begin negotiating my release in exchange for my cooperation in the Plame case. I never got to meet the Moose, who is now serving a life sentence without parole in a maximum-security prison in Colorado.

Until mid-August 2005, our legal strategy had been fairly straightforward: I would stay in jail until the grand jury expired in late October. By then, Floyd Abrams predicted, Fitzgerald would either file charges against an alleged leaker or close his investigation and I would go home. Since the purpose of sending me to jail was to coerce my co-operation, we figured that I would have demonstrated by then that I could not be forced into testifying about a source.

Over time, Bob Bennett grew increasingly opposed to the strategy he had always disliked. It was his skepticism about almost everything that had attracted me to him when we had met in Washington the previous year. He was then representing a major bank involved in the government's Iraqi-related oil-for-food corruption investigation and had also represented Bill Clinton. For some time, Matt Mallow, a close friend and a senior partner at Skadden, Arps, had been urging me to expand my legal team. Floyd and Susan Buckley were brilliant First Amendment lawyers, he said. But I needed a lawyer with Washington and criminal expertise, someone who had no other client in this affair but me. For months I had resisted Matt's advice. The paper's goals and mine would always be the same, I told him. I could not imagine a situation in which our interests would diverge. But after Judge Hogan ruled me in contempt of court in October 2004, I wanted a second opinion. I asked Matt if he would arrange a meeting with Bennett.

"Protecting sources is the lifeblood of independent journalism," I told Bob one December night when we met at Matt's office. "For the paper and me, that cause is sacrosanct. The *Times* and I are inextricably bound by and committed to it." We would never disagree.

Bob frowned. "You don't know that," he warned. "Besides," he added, "I don't want to represent a 'cause.' I want to represent

Judy Miller." Keeping me out of jail, and if that was impossible, minimizing the time I spent there were the best ways to protect me and advance the cause. Bob told me there was a good chance I would be spending far more time in jail than I was being led to believe. He knew Fitzgerald. He was a dog with a bone. He would not give up. He had known Judge Hogan for years. He would *not* free me in October if Fitzgerald opposed it.

As summer turned to fall in jail, Bob's negotiations with Fitzgerald were not going well. Though Fitzgerald had not disclosed his intentions, Bob feared that he was preparing to empanel a new grand jury to force my testimony about all my possible sources. That might mean spending eighteen more months in jail, as Bob had initially predicted. He wanted my permission to call Joe Tate, Libby's lawyer, to see whether he had changed his mind about granting me a personal waiver of my confidentiality pledge now that I had spent so many weeks in jail.

George Freeman, the *Times* lawyer, visited me from New York a few days later to oppose contacting Tate. Calling Libby's lawyer would be seen as a sign of weakness. Fitzgerald was bluffing, he assured me. Though Floyd was less certain, George conceded, both he and Floyd were convinced that Judge Hogan would not let Fitzgerald keep me in jail after October. It would be too "controversial." The American press corps would rebel.

I felt unsure what to do. I doubted that I could count on the solidarity of the American press — half of which seemed to support Joe Wilson's stated desire to see Bush punished for the ill-fated Iraq War and Karl Rove "frog-marched out of the White House in handcuffs," as Wilson had demanded. Every other reporter who was subpoenaed had cooperated — all the "grandees" of our profession — several without even getting a subpoena.[6]

Despite this, I did not want to defy my paper's lawyers. I refused to let Bob call Libby's lawyer. Even if his assessment of my legal peril was correct, Fitzgerald had not agreed to limit his questioning of me to one source, as we insisted. If Fitzgerald would not agree to such restrictions, contacting Libby's lawyer was pointless, I argued. We needed more "reporting" about my ambitious prosecutor's intentions, I told Bob.

Without my knowing it, Bob had asked a mutual friend to help address my questions. On August 22, Stan Pottinger, who had been assistant attorney general for civil rights in the Nixon administration, brought me some disturbing news. His visit coincided with a dubious milestone: on that day, I had spent longer in jail to protect sources than any other American newspaper journalist.[7]

Stan delivered his dispiriting assessment in the cramped, airless cell as coolly as possible. Fitzgerald was no longer investigating criminal culpability for the leak of Plame's identity and was now focused on possible perjury by one of the president's men. He was determined not to end the inquiry without a scalp and would not close his investigation without my testimony. If I continued refusing to cooperate, he would extend the existing grand jury or empanel a new one. And he was prepared to increase the pressure by charging me with criminal contempt of court on top of civil contempt, which could keep me in jail for five years and result in a felony conviction. "Trust me," Stan concluded. "Fitzgerald is not bluffing."

The prospect of spending so much more time in jail made me rethink my options. It also made me think about Jason. I had assured him that I would be in jail for only a few months. When jail seemed unavoidable,

I had given him a puppy to keep him company: a willful black cockapoo he had named Hamlet. I encouraged him to take the Mediterranean cruise we had planned that summer.[8] But these were gestures. I had never really consulted him about my decision not to reveal my sources. Faced with the prospect of continuing confinement, I felt guilty about not having discussed such a crucial matter with him. That week, we fought on the phone after I had told him gently that I might be in jail after October. "We're in this together," he said. "You must get out of there. You cannot stay."

Despite my loyalty to the paper, I felt troubled and believed I owed it to Jason and myself at least to see whether Libby would now grant me the waiver he had given Matt Cooper. The decision was still tough. Until then, the paper and I had seen eye to eye on my case and our strategy. I had assured Arthur that I would never cooperate with Fitzgerald, since I couldn't imagine that Libby would ever really want me to testify. No waiver he gave would ever be truly voluntary, we had agreed. Now, for the first time, I considered the paper's stance unduly rigid. Perhaps Libby was no longer in legal jeopardy. Perhaps Fitzgerald was focusing on Rove or another of the president's men.

Faced with the prospect of many more months, possibly years, in jail, why should I not ask whether Libby had changed his mind about the waiver? Why should I stay in jail if I didn't have to?

After sleepless nights, I authorized Bob Bennett to call Joe Tate to see whether Libby had shifted his view on the waiver. After they spoke, Bob came to the jail. He seemed troubled. Tate had told him that not only was Libby willing to grant me a waiver, but he had *always* been willing to do so.

How could that be? Floyd had been adamant that Tate had said exactly the opposite the year before. I wasn't sure what to think. If Tate was telling the truth, then I had gone to jail based on a misunderstanding. But if he was now rewriting history to protect his client from being accused of obstructing justice by pressuring me not to testify — which is what Floyd believed — I could hardly call the waiver he was now willing to give me "voluntary."

Bob urged me not to dwell on the past. What Libby had authorized, or not, the previous year did not matter. He was now explicitly urging me to testify.

But how could I be sure that Libby's decision was voluntary? I wanted to hear directly from him.

"But you're in jail!" Bob exclaimed. "He can't exactly drop in for coffee!"

No, he couldn't, I agreed. But could he not write to me? Or could I not speak to him by phone? To be sure that Libby's waiver was voluntary, I needed to hear from him directly, I told my exasperated lawyer. I was adamant because Bob had told me that Fitzgerald had written to Libby, warning him against trying to persuade me not to testify. How could Libby possibly provide a voluntary waiver with Special Counsel Fitzgerald breathing down his neck?

On September 19, Libby telephoned me. Tate and Bob Bennett were on the conference call. In one of the most awkward conversations I have ever had with a source, Libby said he had always been willing to grant me a waiver. He wanted me to testify. He had written the letter I had insisted on to show me that his waiver was voluntary. The letter itself caused a stir. Libby had published a racy novel set in prewar Japan a few years earlier. His letter was filled with literary flourishes.

"Your reporting, and you, are missed," he began. While he admired my "principled stand," I had to get back to "what you do best, reporting." "Out West, where you vacation, the aspens will be turning. They turn in clusters, because their roots connect them. Come back to work — and life," he wrote. The allusion to the aspens was a reference to my having bumped into Libby with Jason at a rodeo in Jackson Hole, Wyoming. He had been wearing jeans, a cowboy hat, and sunglasses. I hadn't recognized him. In fact, I had interviewed Libby only three times, one of those on the phone.

His letter insisted that he had wanted me to testify all along. "I believed a year ago, as now, that testimony by all will benefit all," he wrote me, noting that "the public report of every other reporter's testimony makes clear that they did not discuss Ms. Plame's name or identity with me."

That was odd, I thought. Was Libby suggesting that my testimony would echo the reporters who had sworn that Libby had not discussed Plame's job with them? But my memory, as well as entries in my notebook, suggested that we had discussed her. What did Libby mean? Did he remember our conversation differently? Did he want me to lie?

Floyd and George were stunned by what they considered Libby's about-face on the waiver but acknowledged that it created an opening we had to pursue. Bob began speaking to Fitzgerald about our conditions for cooperating. I still refused to disclose conversations with sources other than Libby. I would not turn over my notebook or emails, Bob told him.

Bob and his team had been carefully reviewing the notebook containing my interview with Libby. While there were references galore to Valerie Plame, there were no other sources identified. And while I had written her name on several pages, even before my interview with Libby — including a joking reference to "Valerie Flame" — no entry was linked to any of the sources in the notebook. There were only free-floating references, verbal doodles. While I remembered having discussed the Plame-Wilson affair with many of the officials and experts I spoke to, I couldn't remember specifically when or with whom those conversations had occurred.

Given that, Bob said he thought he could make a deal with Fitzgerald and wanted my permission to try. Again the *Times* objected strenuously. But I saw no reason not to pursue what I considered a long shot.

Much to my surprise, Fitzgerald agreed to the deal he had rejected for so long. He would limit his questions and trust us to redact my notebooks and give him copies only of my conversations with Libby that pertained to the Plame-Wilson affair. He would not get the notebooks themselves.

We had won.

The *Times* had other ideas. In late September, all my lawyers met in the prison library to discuss whether I should accept Libby's waiver and Fitzgerald's agreement to limit his interrogation. Speaking for the *Times,* Floyd and George Freeman urged me not to testify. Libby's waiver was not truly voluntary, they argued. Testifying would mean that I had gone to jail for nothing. It would make us look weak. I had to continue to protect my source, even if he was rejecting my protection. George argued that people would not understand why I had changed my mind, even if my source had changed his. Whereas, if I served the full 120 days of my sentence and Fitzgerald then tried to extend my time in jail, it would look as if he were reneging on the judge's ruling and I would then be able to leave jail and testify "honorably." Anything short of that, he warned, would play badly from a professional "legacy" or "PR" standpoint. Bob Bennett thought this was nuts and told them so. When things got heated, I told the team I would think things over.

I was leaning heavily toward cooperating. Libby's view was key. My willingness to protect a source who had not lied to me depended on what he wanted me to do. Source protection was ultimately the source's call.

The next day, Arthur visited me. In Peru, he had bought me a lapis necklace, which he held up to show me through the window that separated us. He hoped I would wear it when I left jail — on October 28, he said. I shouldn't cooperate with the inquiry. I should stay in jail until the end of the grand jury as we had agreed, so that we could "win" this fight, despite Libby's waiver and despite Fitzgerald's agreement to limit his questioning. Fitzgerald had "caved" to our requests because the nation's press and public opinion were turning against him, Arthur said. Although the news side of the *Times* had done little reporting on my case since my confinement, he conceded, the editorial side had written fifteen editorials. Fitzgerald would have to let me go when the grand jury expired.

"Arthur, what if you're wrong?"

"Then we'll really open up on them, all guns blazing," he said.

My heart sank as Arthur, my friend and boss, left the visiting booth. I sensed that if I did not adhere to the course he favored, he would not forgive me.

CHAPTER 22
DEPARTURES

September 29, 2005

Before the prison van came to a stop, Arthur Sulzberger bounded out of his limo toward it. "Judy! Judy!" he hollered, pounding on the van's windows.

The marshal in front reached for his weapon. "Who's that?" he barked, as his colleague pulled into a parking lot near the Alexandria Detention Center, our release site.

"Don't shoot!" I said. "He's my boss."

The marshals ordered Arthur to "step back from the vehicle, sir," as my shackles were removed. When I stumbled out, Arthur threw his arms around me. Separated in jail from those I loved and other visitors by a pane of bulletproof glass, I hadn't hugged a friend other than my lawyers in almost eighty-five days. Then there were hugs all around: a bear hug from Bob

Bennett, a more restrained version from Bill Keller.

There was no sign that day of misgivings Arthur may have had about my decision to cooperate with Patrick Fitzgerald's inquiry. At the Ritz-Carlton Hotel in Georgetown, where Arthur had reserved a suite in advance of my grand jury testimony the following day, Jason was waiting for me, smiling. He brought my gold necklace with the tiny ruby pendant, which I had taken off and given him shortly before Judge Hogan accused me of "defying the law" and sent me to jail. He also had photos of Hamlet, the puppy I had given him. Now doubled in size, Hamlet was twenty-two pounds of energy, he said. I took a nap on the giant bed, wrapping myself in the beautiful cotton sheets — a welcome change from the concrete slab I had slept on in prison.

I learned later that Arthur and Bob Bennett had disagreed that afternoon about the celebratory dinner that Arthur had planned for me that night. Knowing how exhausted I was, Bob had wanted me to sleep and squeeze in a few more hours of grand jury preparation. Though Arthur had reluctantly scaled back his planned celebration, he refused to cancel it. After many champagne toasts, he told our small group that evening what he had told me in jail: he and the paper were proud of me; I was a credit to the *Times* and our profession; a "woman of true courage and principle," he was quoted as saying. Although he hoped I had enjoyed the massage and manicure he had arranged at the hotel, he joked that I shouldn't get used to such luxury: as soon as my testimony was over, it was back to my desk in New York. At the dinner's end, he gave me a medal that the paper had given only a few reporters — the last of a series of commemorative coins awarded for service to the paper.

Before my release, George Freeman had explained to Arthur diplomatically why I had heeded Bob Bennett rather than the *Times* legal team and agreed to testify. Floyd Abrams told me that Arthur had wanted my case to be what the Supreme Court's 1971 Pentagon Papers ruling had been for his father: a clear moral and legal victory for the *Times.* In that earlier confrontation, Pentagon contractor Daniel Ellsberg leaked the top-secret study of America's involvement in Vietnam to the paper. Nixon's Justice Department asked the federal court to restrain its publication. The Supreme Court decided against prior restraint and for the paper.

In my case, the *Times* was supporting an absolutist (or, as Bennett would later call it, "aggressive") stance regarding a reporter's privilege, an argument the court had rejected in its *Branzburg* ruling.[1]

George and Floyd, like Arthur, thought I should stay in jail until the grand jury expired a month later on October 28. But both told Arthur they understood my decision. Whether I cooperated with Fitzgerald had to be Libby's call, provided that his decision was made voluntarily.

In jail, I had jotted down what I considered the key features of a "voluntary" waiver and a source's rights and obligations. Oddly, our profession seemed not to have standards on this. First, I wrote, a reporter is honor bound to respect a promise not to reveal the identity of a "truthful" source: a source who hadn't attempted to deceive. Second, such a pledge should not be given casually. Third, a waiver is not voluntary if it is elicited from a source who was threatened with "dismissal from employment, harassment, prosecution, or other intimidation." (Blanket waivers elicited by those with "influence over or control of" the source's employment or benefits, such as the cooperation that Bush demanded his senior staff provide, automatically failed that test.)

Fourth, a waiver must be written and signed, addressed personally to the journalist who requested it, and specify what information could be shared. Fifth, the journalist must be able to interview the source "face-to-face or by telephone" to ascertain that the waiver was not coerced. Sixth, the source could not attempt to influence the journalist's testimony, either before or after the waiver is given. Finally, while journalists may show prosecutors notebooks, emails, and other communications with a source, they should insist on the right to redact "extraneous" information not relevant to the subpoena to prevent a "fishing expedition" into their sources.

Bill Safire said he hoped that journalists would debate what he insisted on calling the "Miller standard" for giving and waiving confidentiality pledges, whether or not Congress passed a media shield law. My jailing had enhanced the shield law's legislative prospects, he told Arthur.

That day, Arthur said he "fully supported" my decision to testify, just as he had backed my initial refusal to do so. "Judy has been unwavering in her commitment to protect the confidentiality of her source," he said. He was "very pleased" that I had finally received a "direct and uncoerced waiver."

Keller agreed. My "steadfastness in defense of principle," he said, had won "admiration from around the world, wherever people value a free, aggressive press."

At this point, Bob Bennett wrote later, the *Times*, Arthur, and I were clear "winners," getting "well-deserved credit for acting in a principled and responsible fashion."[2]

My three-hour grand jury testimony in late September 2005 recalling more than two-year-old discussions with Scooter Libby about Joe Wilson and Iraqi WMD went well, or so I thought. I had no inkling that some of the story I was writing about my conversations with Libby — or telling the grand jury — might turn out to be wrong.

I knew what was at stake. Patrick Fitzgerald's investigation was presumably focused on the narrow issue of whether White House officials had deliberately leaked classified information about Valerie Plame to columnist Robert Novak and other journalists in the summer of 2003 to punish Joe Wilson for challenging Bush's case for war. But bloggers and many in the mainstream media insisted that the inquiry was really about whether Wilson was right to charge that the Bush administration had "twisted" intelligence about Iraqi WMD to "lie" the country into war.

Much had been established by the time I appeared before the grand jury. Contrary to what Wilson claimed, neither Cheney nor anyone else at the White House had sent him to Africa or been briefed about his conclusions. The CIA had sent him without White House knowledge. And contrary to another initial claim, Valerie Plame had been involved in her husband's selection, as the Senate Intelligence Committee concluded in its 2004 report.[3] Wilson had returned from Niger with what the CIA interpreted to be a mixed message. On the one hand, it was "highly doubtful" a sale had occurred, he told CIA officials who informally debriefed him over Chinese takeout at his home. On the other hand, a former prime minister of Niger told him that Iraq had tried to acquire some uranium in the late nineties. Wilson had publicly shared the first part of his findings, which he and others cited as evidence that Bush lied about the WMD intelligence. But he did not write about or publicly disclose the former Niger official's view that Iraq had tried to buy uranium, which Bush supporters then stressed. The CIA analysts concluded — wrongly, it turned out — that Wilson's findings supported Britain's claim that

Iraq was still trying to acquire uranium for a weapons program. The agency's interpretation was cited as support for the now-infamous "sixteen words" President Bush spoke in his 2003 State of the Union address: "The British government has learned Saddam Hussein has recently sought significant quantities of uranium from Africa."

By the summer of 2004, the White House was trying to defuse the growing public furor over Wilson's charges by retracting that sixteen-word claim. Condi Rice said that it should not have been included in the speech because the evidence supporting it did not rise "to the level of certainty" required for a presidential speech. But rather than quell criticism, the retraction, which David Sanger and I wrote about, had inflamed it further.[4]

While the Senate committee disputed several of Wilson's assertions, it concluded that the intelligence community should not have included the uranium hunting claim in its NIE on Iraq's unconventional weapons. That claim, among so many others, the senators concluded, misrepresented and overstated what the intelligence community thought it knew about Iraqi WMD. The report did not blame the White House or assert that officials had "lied." The fault lay mainly with the CIA and its deplorable "tradecraft," its "group think," and other serious shortcomings the senators identified.

The sixteen words were part of this story — as were uranium in Niger, Iraqi WMD prewar intelligence, and Joe Wilson and the outing of his wife, Valerie Plame, in Robert Novak's column in mid-July 2003, eight days after her husband had accused the administration of twisting intelligence. I knew the grand jury might ask me about any or all of it.

I told my legal team in the fall of 2005 that I knew about Plame's job at the CIA before Novak "outed" her. While I couldn't recall who first told me, I remembered discussing her on several occasions — with those whom I talked to routinely. Libby was not among them. In my notebooks, Plame's name appeared in several places, but not as part of an interview — not even with Libby. I was fairly certain that Libby and I had talked in passing about her, based on my notes, but that he was focused on the situation in Iraq, the disputed WMD evidence, and what he called Wilson's "reckless" charges.

On September 30 I testified that I had not known Libby before the summer of 2003 and that we met on July 8, two days after the *Times* published Wilson's charge of intelligence manipulation. During our two-hour breakfast meeting at the St. Regis in Washington, Libby summarized the findings in the CIA's NIE, which I then believed were classified as secret.

When I reviewed my notes of our conversation, I told the grand jury, I found a reference in parentheses: "(wife works at WIN-PAC)" — the CIA's Weapons, Intelligence, Nonproliferation, and Arms Control Center. Based on where she worked, I assumed that she was an analyst, not a secret operator. I explained that I usually used parentheses when I was being told something I wanted to ask about, or to note something that I already knew but wanted to explore further. I thought I had heard about Plame's job at the CIA before that meeting with Libby, I told the jurors, but couldn't remember where or when. My recollection, I added, was "almost totally" note driven.

I stressed that Libby was angry mainly about suggestions that WMD intelligence had been "massaged," as Senator Jay Rockefeller charged. A year earlier, Rockefeller was among those warning that Saddam's WMD arsenals posed "real threats to America today, tomorrow." By the time of my grand jury testimony in 2005, he had accused Bush of having misled him with "good p.r. work."[5] Many who initially supported the invasion were now accusing Bush of deliberately distorting the evidence. When Libby and I met in the summer of 2003, all I knew for certain — all anyone seemed to know — was that no WMD were found in Iraq, and that the intelligence concerning Iraqi WMD which I and others wrote about before the war, was wrong.

I acknowledged talking to Libby by phone on July 12. Before that, I had most certainly talked to others about Wilson's wife. There were several references to her name in my notes, none connected to a specific interview. On one page are the words "Victoria Wilson" with a box around it. I told Fitzgerald that I was not sure Libby had actually used that name. One possibility was that I deliberately mentioned the name to him first, to see whether he would correct me or confirm her identity.

I assumed this would be my only grand jury appearance, as Fitzgerald and I had agreed. But a second was required. The fault was mine. After I testified, Fitzgerald asked whether I might have met with Libby earlier, sometime in June. It was possible, I said, since much of what he told me in July sounded familiar. Ten days later, after I returned to the *Times,* I found a second notebook that contained notes of an earlier Libby meeting. I was alarmed. How could I have forgotten that earlier conversation? What else had I forgotten?

These notes indicated that Libby and I had discussed Wilson's trip to Niger on June 23, 2003, nearly three weeks before the discussion on July 8 I first testified about. My notes of that meeting also contain a reference in parentheses to Wilson's wife.[6]

When I discovered the other notebook, Bob Bennett informed Fitzgerald. On October 12 I testified again.

My notes indicate that in our initial June meeting, Libby and I concentrated on the WMD intelligence failures in Iraq. Wanting to draw him out, I described the chaotic WMD search I had covered. I highlighted concerns, among them the often counterproductive competition between two military units hunting for WMD stockpiles and scientists: the army's XTF in which I was embedded, and a then-secret group called Task Force 20, whose existence was unknown to the XTF's senior officers until after the war had begun. Drawn from the Delta Force and the army's elite Special Forces units, Task Force 20 was inspecting some of the same sites the XTF was covering, and searching for some of the same scientists believed to be involved in Saddam's WMD programs.[7] I told Libby how the two groups, unaware of each other's movements, had once arrived at the same suspect site simultaneously, weapons drawn, and almost come to blows.

I told the grand jury that my notes of our June meeting show that Libby tried to insulate his boss from charges of intelligence manipulation. He insisted, for instance, that Cheney neither knew Joe Wilson nor that he had gone to Niger to verify the uranium hunting report. My notes, I told the grand jury, contain another reference to Wilson's wife: "(wife works in Bureau?)." While I was certain that Libby and I discussed Wilson's wife, I told jurors, I couldn't remember if that was the first time I had heard that she worked for the CIA.

Fitzgerald had repeatedly asked me before my testimony whether "Bureau" might not refer to the Federal Bureau of Investigation. Yes, I said: normally it would. But since I thought that Libby and I had been discussing the CIA, I couldn't be sure.

Only later did I grasp the significance of Fitzgerald's question.

When I returned to the paper after testifying in early October 2005, I asked Claudia Payne, my editor and friend, to meet me in the *Times*'s lobby. I was uncertain how my colleagues would react to my decision to cooperate with Fitzgerald. Howie Kurtz had reported in the *Washington Post* that some reporters and bloggers were criticizing me for leaving jail and testifying.[8] Arianna Huffington accused me of "grandstanding." "Effectively discredited" because of my WMD stories, Kurtz quoted her as saying, jail was merely "an opportunity to cleanse herself." The *Times* should insist that I provide readers with a "full accounting" of my grand jury testimony. Lucie Morillon, of Reporters Without Borders, told Kurtz that my decision to testify was a "setback" for journalism, a view apparently shared by many colleagues.

The Reporters Committee for Freedom of the Press, on the other hand, defended me. Lucy Dalglish, its executive director, had visited me in jail and later said she was struck by how "hostile" and "vicious" journalists were toward me, which she attributed to the weapons controversy and to my style. "She's not exactly a warm and fuzzy person," she told Kurtz, adding that I was "reserved." "She's not going to go out of her way to make lots of friends."

I was disappointed to hear that among those criticizing my decision was Myron Farber, the former *Times* reporter who had spent forty days in jail three decades earlier. Myron believed that a reporter should never testify about a source.[9]

A warning signal should have flashed as Claudia hugged me when I emerged in the lobby from the paper's heavy revolving door. Why had Keller or Abramson not escorted me back through the newsroom?

My apprehension subsided as we approached my cubicle. My desk was overflowing with flowers, handwritten notes, stuffed animals, and other small gifts; my computer was clogged with nearly one hundred thousand email messages. Most of the emails, said Walt Baranger, the paper's technology editor, were congratulatory.

Still, I sensed that many colleagues did not understand why I decided to cooperate with Fitzgerald; they shared Myron's view that a reporter should never testify about a source, even if the source granted a waiver. "Every day you're in, you win," was the slogan that David Barstow, my colleague and friend, created for me in jail. David had championed the absolutist stand I embraced before I was persuaded that Libby wanted me to testify.

I tried to explain my position in an impromptu speech to the newsroom. Flanked by Arthur and Bill Keller, I said that I felt I had upheld the principles I had gone to jail to protect. While I was sure that some of my decisions had annoyed both "First Amendment absolutists" and those who had urged me to "testify, testify" rather than "cover up for those people," my eighty-five days in jail had produced some victories for press freedom while respecting what I thought were the wishes of Scooter Libby, whom I identified publicly as the source I had been protecting since he had been authorized to do so.

Most reporters who had been subpoenaed had accepted blanket waivers of confidentiality, or they secured additional personal waivers from their sources. Since I had been unable to get a voluntary waiver from Libby, I explained, I felt that I had no choice but to go to jail.

Even after Libby offered me the waiver and encouraged me to testify, I refused to cooperate until Fitzgerald agreed to limit my testimony to my conversations with that one source (Libby), one subject (the Plame-Wilson affair), and to let me redact my interview notes. I had not allowed the government to search my notebooks and emails or ask about other sources. I spent an extra month in jail to extract these concessions and got most of what I wanted.

I had changed my mind about whether a waiver from a source under government investigation could be considered voluntary. Libby's telephone call and letter to me had persuaded me. In these tough calls, I "followed my conscience." In the end, I decided that my cooperation was Libby's call.

I could see that some colleagues were not convinced. I couldn't blame them. As I was speaking, Joe Tate, Libby's lawyer, was publicly contradicting Floyd Abrams's assertion that Libby had refused to give me a personal, voluntary waiver before I went to jail. In an exchange of angry letters, Tate and Abrams called each other liars.[10] Libby had been told that I was protecting other sources, not him, Tate claimed, defending his client. I did not know who was right. If I remained unsure, how could my colleagues know?

In an interview later that day by *Times* veteran Kit Seelye, I said I didn't know whether I would ever write an article, much less a book, about this episode. I hoped to take some time off, resume normal life, gain some weight, and lobby Congress to pass a federal shield law to protect reporters' confidential sources. She asked whether I had thought about what returning to the paper as a reporter would be like. I confessed that I hadn't. "This is my clan, this is my tribe," I said. "I belong here." [11]

Standing at my side in the newsroom that day, Keller said the paper would publish a "full account" of the episode as early as the following weekend. While the *Times* had been wary of revealing too much while I was in jail, for fear of compounding my legal jeopardy, he said that the staff and our readers had "a lot of questions about how this drama unfolded." Since I was now free, the paper would answer those questions in a "thoroughly reported piece." "We owe it to our readers, and we owe it to you, our staff."[12]

Bill Safire called me, alarmed. Why would the paper conduct such an inquiry? I would have to testify if Fitzgerald indicted Libby, he reminded me. The project implied that someone had done something wrong. Safire reminded me that the *Times* hadn't conducted such an investigation since the Jayson Blair affair, and we both knew how that had ended.

Bob Bennett was worried, too. He called Keller and Abramson when I told him they had assigned me to write a first-person account of my grand jury testimony and to cooperate with the paper's in-depth report. Grand jury testimony was supposed to be secret, Bob reminded them. While I had the legal right to disclose it, Fitzgerald had asked witnesses not to do so. I had not been permitted to take notes at the sessions, and since no lawyer had been allowed to accompany me, Bob and Saul Pilchen, the other lawyer on my case, had been able to debrief me only after hours of testimony about what I had said under oath. Would I omit key details? Get them wrong? Would my article irritate Judge Hogan, who had sent me to jail and could send me back if he thought I was still stonewalling the court? Would it anger Fitzgerald? Would the prosecutor think I was signaling to Libby what I had said under oath, so that he could work around it? The slightest variation between my testimony and the published story, no matter how trivial, Bob argued, could be exploited on cross-examination in a future trial to make it seem that I had lied or changed my story. Did Keller and Abramson realize they were putting me in legal jeopardy?

I was a *Times* employee, Keller and Abramson replied. I would do what they asked if I wanted to remain one. Bob described their tone as "very aggressive."

I was torn. Though I thought Bob was right, I felt loyal to the paper. Besides, I had done nothing wrong and had nothing to hide. I agreed with Keller and Abramson that our readers and my colleagues had a right to know why I had cooperated with Fitzgerald. I accepted the assignment and asked Bennett to cooperate with the four reporters writing the companion article.

He was not pleased. He sensed early on what I still did not see. With what must have been Arthur's approval, they seemed to be laying the groundwork to force me out, he warned me. But before they acted, he later wrote, they wanted my account of my grand jury testimony, a last Judy Miller exclusive.[13]

I was unaware of how exhausted I was by the seemingly endless battles at the paper and with the courts until I began reviewing what were by then almost three-year-old notes to comply with Keller's request for a firsthand account of my grand jury testimony about my conversations with Scooter Libby and my decision to testify. I was a wreck. I could barely write a sentence.

With Keller's okay, David Barstow helped me. Because we were friends, David had not participated in the paper's inquiry into my involvement in the Plame affair or its coverage of my jailing. Over two days and one long night, we wrote an account of what I had told the grand jury. After anonymous colleagues had leaked portions of my earlier emails and memos to the *Washington Post* and to bloggers, Barstow was one of the few I trusted to review the notebooks and the identity of sensitive sources. His byline did not appear over my story, but it should have. Bennett was right: I was in no condition to write such a sensitive account.

The team that Keller and Abramson assigned to the paper's reconstruction of my role in the Plame-Wilson affair was composed of four veteran reporters — Don Van Natta Jr., Adam Liptak, Clifford J. Levy, and Janny Scott. Only Van Natta had worked in Washington as an investigative reporter on national security. Although many colleagues considered Van Natta the paper's "attack dog" — a solid reporter whom senior editors could unleash — I feared that they would not place my legal battle in the politically charged context of the Plame-Wilson affair.[14] As I had struggled to respond to my colleagues' questions within the confines that Bennett had delineated for my legal protection, I became ever more concerned about their tone and focus.

I was stunned by their six-thousand-word piece on my role in the scandal and the blistering reaction to the first-person account David and I had written under my byline. Both stories were published on Sunday, October 16, four days after I testified before the grand jury for a second time.

The paper's account portrayed me as a "divisive" figure in the newsroom — an "intrepid" journalist, but one whom editors found "hard to control." It highlighted what it called my "unusual" sourcing arrangements, disputes within the paper about my reporting, and my alleged efforts to mislead the story's authors and my editors.

While the story noted that Arthur's editorial page had "crusaded on my behalf," the news department had chafed at having been scooped on aspects of my story. Keller and Abramson were quoted as saying they were shocked to learn that I had written "Valerie Flame" in my notebook. The story also quoted Roger Cohen, who had by then been reassigned as foreign editor.[15] He pointed to "concern" in the newsroom that I had been "convinced in an unwarranted way . . . of the possible existence of WMD" in Iraq. It quoted Doug Frantz, the paper's investigative editor, as claiming that I had boasted about being called "Miss Run Amok" and authorized to do "whatever I want."

The story reported my regret that my sources were wrong about the presumed existence of WMD in Iraq. It acknowledged that the paper's editor's note criticizing its prewar coverage had not blamed specific reporters and had called the prewar intelligence reporting failures "institutional." It implied that because I had written or cowritten "five of the six" articles singled out as "credulous," I was largely to blame. In fact, I had written two thirds of the articles discussed, some of them with others, and neither of the flawed, front-page exclusives about alleged connections between Al Qaeda and Saddam's ostensible training of jihadis at camps. The Van Natta story did not state that there had been a strong consensus within the intelligence community — and other countries' spy agencies as well — that Iraq was continuing to hide chemical and germ weapons and was ramping up efforts to acquire nuclear weapons.[16]

As I acknowledged in Van Natta's piece, I had gotten WMD "totally wrong." "If your sources were wrong," I told them, "you are wrong." I had done the best I could to verify the classified information I had often gotten first, the story quoted me as saying. But I was "wrong."

Officials I trusted had declined to share with me whatever doubts they may have had. State Department intelligence chief Carl Ford, for instance, whom I had covered for over a decade and was a key critic of the prewar intelligence, later told me he had not returned my calls or permitted his aides to meet with me because he had long refused on principle to discuss classified information with reporters. "Although my staff and I did not have to take polygraphs," he told me in 2013, "I believed then, and still do, that sharing classified intelligence with reporters would have been wrong."[17]

Richard Clarke, the counterterrorism adviser who had urged President Clinton to bomb Iraq and kill Bin Laden long before 9/11 and had fallen out with President Bush over the Iraq War and other issues, offered another explanation for his prewar silence. When I asked why he had said nothing to me about the thinness or quality of the WMD intelligence before the invasion, he replied: "Because I hoped it would work." In retrospect, I concluded, other doubters may also have remained silent in hopes of ridding the region of a tyrant whose ambitions were unlikely to have been contained. Or they may have kept quiet because they thought disclosing classified information about specific instances of weak or faulty intelligence would have risked their careers without affecting President Bush's determination to oust Saddam.

The *Times* article about my case implied that I misled Phil Taubman, a long-standing friend and Jill Abramson's successor as Washington bureau chief, by denying that I was one of six Washington journalists to whom White House officials had disclosed Plame's job. In fact, as the story noted, I told Phil that I had discussed Wilson and his wife with numerous sources. I also told him that I did not believe I had been targeted in a campaign to discredit Wilson.

When Van Natta asked why I hadn't written anything about Plame's job at the CIA, I answered that I tried to pass the tip along to the Washington bureau. I had stopped by Jill Abramson's office late one Friday afternoon in July to tell her about Plame's job and her alleged help in getting her husband sent to Africa. The tip needed pursuing, I told her.[18]

Asked by Van Natta what she regretted about the paper's handling of the Plame affair, Abramson replied: "The entire thing." Keller told the team that he wished the paper had been able to wage its First

Amendment fight for a reporter with less "baggage."

Bill Safire called. Though he said he was troubled by Keller's decision to run such a negative feature about me in the Sunday paper, he thought the crisis had peaked. I was out of jail; the Van Natta story was behind me. I was about to receive a First Amendment prize from the Society of Professional Journalists in Las Vegas. It was time to return to work.

I thought my speech to journalists on October 18 in Nevada went well. So, too, my appearance before the Senate Judiciary Committee. I argued that a federal shield law was needed to prevent reporters from being forced to reveal their sources. According to the Reporters Committee for Freedom of the Press and lawyers who handle First Amendment cases, as many as two dozen reporters were subpoenaed in the prior two years in cases involving confidential sources. Many of them faced the prospect of being jailed. Unless Congress passed a shield law to protect them and their sources, I said, Alexandria Detention Center might have to open "an entire new wing."

While the *Times* did not normally permit reporters to testify before Congress or lobby for legislation, the paper's management blessed my appearance, and our lawyers vetted my statement. Jail, I testified, had highlighted the need for congressional action. Anne Gordon, the managing editor of the *Philadelphia Inquirer* who supported shield legislation, said she thought the furor over my case may have "muddled the issue." I feared she was right. The source I had gone to jail to protect was not a whistleblower. The war had deeply polarized the country. Even many journalists thought Libby deserved to be punished for having promoted the war, never mind what he may or may not have said about Plame.

I was also still part of the news. Senator Arlen Specter joked at the hearing, wasn't I a "strong-willed person" who sometimes operated out of the control of editors, a proverbial "bull in the china closet"?

Investigative reporters needed to be "a little pushier than some sources or editors would like," I replied. But yes, I added, it sometimes created "tensions with editors."

Anne Gordon came to my defense. "Well-behaved women don't change the world," she told the panel.

When I returned from DC, David Barstow and I had coffee in the *Times* cafeteria. He seemed troubled. He had underestimated the hatred, jealousy, and resentment so many colleagues felt toward me, he told me. The slurs and slanders about me, my WMD reporting — by then over two years old — and the debate over whether I should have left jail a month early were drowning out issues my jailing had raised. A rebellion within the paper was brewing, he feared. As Lowell Bergman, my long-standing colleague and friend at the journalism school at UC Berkeley also warned me, I was becoming a "surrogate" for what so many Iraq War critics wanted to do to the Bush administration.[19] That was a dangerous place to be, he told me.

I stopped by Keller's office to talk about my next assignment. He was huddled with Arthur Sulzberger. Though they seemed to be having an intense conversation, Keller waved me in. Arthur congratulated me on my testimony and the SPJ award. I had done well, he said.

"If we all hang in there together, we shall weather this storm," I said.

They exchanged a glance that I couldn't read. "Hang in there," Arthur said. "Well, that's one way of putting it."

The following day, Friday, October 21, I took an early bus home to Sag Harbor. By the time I arrived, the cell phone I had turned off for the ride showed over twenty messages. What was happening? Jason asked when I got home. The phone, which he had stopped answering, had been ringing nonstop. I found a lengthy "message to the staff" in my email in-box from Keller. He said that he wished he had dealt with the controversy over our coverage of WMD as soon as he had become executive editor. "In this case," he said, referring to the Valerie Plame saga, he had missed what should have been "significant alarm bells." For instance, I had "misled" Washington bureau chief Phil Taubman about the extent of my involvement in the leak case, something that Phil had not claimed.

Until Fitzgerald came after me, Keller wrote, he said he had not known that I was "one of the reporters on the receiving end of the anti-Wilson whisper campaign." "I should have wondered why I was learning this from the special counsel, a year after the fact," he added.

If he had known the details of my "entanglement" with Libby earlier, he would have been more careful about how the paper had articulated its defense, and "perhaps more willing than I had been to support efforts aimed at exploring compromises."

I couldn't believe what I was reading. Arthur had insisted on keeping Keller informed of all key developments in my case. Neither Arthur nor he had asked to see the notebooks that Bob Bennett and others on my legal team had examined. And what was he implying by asserting I had an "entanglement" with Libby?

"I'm a publisher, not a lawyer," Jason said coolly, reading the memo over my shoulder. "But he has just libeled you. Call Bob Bennett and tell him to get you the hell out of that snake pit now."

Keller was in China, Diane, his assistant, told me, part of a long-scheduled tour of the paper's bureaus in the Far East. I called George Freeman, who said that he had not seen Keller's memo before its distribution. He would not have approved such a message, he assured me. I called Arthur's cell phone. An hour later, he returned my call. He knew I must be upset, he told me. We would talk in his office — Monday.

On Saturday, Maureen Dowd called me a "woman of mass destruction" who gravitated toward powerful men. She accused me of "stenography." I was imperious. I lacked skepticism. A decade ago, I had taken her seat at a White House press briefing. I had challenged Jill Abramson.[20]

In describing my grand jury testimony,

Dowd wrote, I had "casually revealed" that I had agreed to identify Libby as a "former Hill staffer" because he had once worked on Capitol Hill, and that I was implying that "this bit of deception" was a common practice for reporters. It wasn't, she asserted. She did not note that I had not identified Libby at all or written about his allegations. I would never have tried, or have been permitted, to identify Libby in print as a "former Hill staffer."

In twenty-eight years at the paper, I had never once been accused of misrepresenting a source.[21] I had agreed to Libby's terms to hear his version of events. If his claims could be verified, I would have insisted on a more accurate description of him or refused to publish his account. This was a fairly common technique among investigative reporters. The *Times* style and standards book permits such intricate negotiations between reporters and their sources. As the paper's policy on confidential sources states, there are occasions when "we may use an offer of anonymity as a wedge to make telephone contact, get an interview or learn a fact."

Dowd concluded by saying that I had hoped to continue reporting on "threats to the nation." If I were permitted to do so, she wrote, "the institution most in danger would be the newspaper in your hands."

Because she worked for the publisher, not the news division, Arthur had to have known in advance about her column.

Public editor Byron Calame opened the third front of the paper's campaign the next day. He concluded that it would be "difficult" for me "to return to the paper as a reporter."

Bob Bennett, Saul Pilchen, Floyd Abrams, and my entire legal team shared my astonishment. What was the paper doing? Bennett exclaimed over the phone that weekend. Why had Arthur sanctioned what he called a paperwide "war on Judy"? Why had the *Times* suddenly decided to destroy the reputation of a reporter it had just spent over a year defending?

On my way to my meeting on the fourteenth floor with Arthur, I read what my old friend the publisher had told the *Wall Street Journal* over the weekend. While Keller had spoken for the newsroom, "I concur with his position," he said. "Some of Bill's 'culpas' were my 'culpas,' too."

Already under fire for his stewardship of the paper, he, too, was now scrambling for political cover. Bob Bennett and Bill Safire had seen this drama play out before, they told me. Just as the White House and intelligence community were now blaming each other for the prewar intelligence fiasco, as politicians who had once championed the war were now claiming to have been lied to, as the analysts who had remained silent or signed off on flawed estimates now asserted they had doubted such assessments all along, Arthur, too, was trying to find someone to blame to avoid a second blogger-fueled newsroom rebellion in less than two years, Bill Safire said. He did not want to be the target of critics assailing the paper for its Iraq War coverage, or challenged from within, as were Howell Raines and Gerald Boyd.

Times reporters were now angry and fearful. Another round of layoffs and "voluntary" buyouts was about to begin. The staff had traditionally taken pride and refuge in the paper's reputation for probity — its authority, credibility, its influence. But that, too, was under assault because of the paper's declining financial fortunes and the explosion of gossip-filled social media whose members mocked the paper's self-regard.

The impassioned pro–Iraq War editorials that Bill Keller had written before becoming executive editor were now an embarrassment; Jill Abramson's management of the Washington bureau was under assault for her alleged lack of skepticism about her reporters' "credulous" pre–Iraq War stories. Neither of them, Safire told me, wanted to become the next Raines and Boyd.

Arthur had not yet arrived when I was ushered into his inner office. In sharp contrast to the din of the newsroom, Arthur's room was a tomb. No phones rang. No computers hummed. No assistants barged in with questions that couldn't wait. The only sound I heard was the ticking of his antique grandfather clock. A few minutes later, he arrived, apologizing for having been delayed by a call. Arthur hated being late.

What the hell is going on? I asked him bluntly. Why had he permitted Keller to libel me in our paper? Was this the same Bill Keller who only six months earlier had awarded me a $21,000 bonus for my work in 2004 as a senior writer and my "efforts and energy over the years"? And why had he let Maureen Dowd write such a vituperative column?

Arthur launched into a decision "the paper" had made. I had become too controversial. I had lost Keller's confidence and the newsroom's. Given my long-standing service to the paper, however, I would be permitted to stay at the *Times* as long as I liked. A "satisfactory" job would be found for me.

I made a quick mental note: I was not being fired. I had committed no fireable offense. However, I would no longer be permitted to edit or write for the paper.

I had almost lost my capacity for surprise. What job did he have in mind? I asked.

Arthur seemed stumped. He didn't really know yet, he said, hesitating to go beyond what I assumed were his lawyers' instructions.

"If you want me to quit, Arthur, just say so," I told him.

No, he said. He didn't want that. He repeated the offer.

I told him I would consider my options, but added that his lawyers would almost certainly be hearing from mine — the ones whose legal fees he had been paying. I didn't volunteer that Bob Bennett was so angry about the paper's attacks on me that he had volunteered to represent me for free if necessary in whatever negotiations with the paper ensued. "Pro bono publico." And perhaps, I added, his attorneys would also be hearing from the *Times* Guild.

Arthur's face darkened at the mention of the paper's union. Recalling the family's protracted fights with the guild, a visit from its officers was the last thing he wanted.

I didn't tell Arthur that I had more or less made my decision. After such attacks on my professional integrity, I no longer wanted to remain at the paper.

I looked at him carefully. After the *Times*'s board had forced him to fire Howell Raines and Gerald Boyd two years earlier, I had seen that same look: fear.

As I stood up, I asked Arthur once more what he thought he was doing. We had started at the paper together in Washington. We had shared professional and personal highs and lows. I had written literally thousands of articles over the course of twenty-eight years, many on the front page. I had nearly been killed in Afghanistan researching the Al Qaeda story, nearly shot in Beirut, and nearly trampled by a mob at a hanging in Khartoum. I had worked extraordinary hours after 9/11 and helped win the paper a Pulitzer, a duPont, and an Emmy. I had devised new beats and talked my way into places that were off-limits to reporters. And I had gone to jail to defend the journalistic principles I thought he shared. We had been friends for years, I said. I was entitled to an explanation. What on earth had I done to offend him or betray the paper?

I hadn't stayed in jail as I had promised, he mumbled.

Was that it? I wondered. I had embarrassed him and the paper by changing my mind? "The situation changed, Arthur," I replied. "Libby gave me a waiver that I hadn't thought possible, and Fitzgerald had agreed to our terms."

"But that's not what you *said* you would do," he replied. "That wasn't what you told us when this started."

I stared at him, suddenly speechless. There was nothing more to say. Seconds later, I left the room. This time there was no hug or promise of eternal loyalty. We did not even say good-bye.

EPILOGUE

I resigned from the *Times* on November 8, 2005. My departure was announced in orchestrated statements by the paper and me, the result of negotiations between our lawyers.

Bill Safire asked my permission to approach Punch, Arthur's father. Bill had tried to intervene with Punch once before, when Arthur dismissed Abe Rosenthal as a columnist and denied him continued access to an office, secretary, and identification with the paper. Arthur had already reduced his columns from twice to once a week, humiliating for a man who had dedicated his life to the paper and whose tombstone bears only his name and proudest achievement: "He kept the paper straight."[1]

I declined Bill's offer. I had no idea what the elder Sulzberger thought about how Arthur had handled the "Miller Mess," as the public editor called my First Amendment stand. The masthead had forced Arthur to fire Howell and Gerald. I doubted he would have risked another confrontation with senior executives without first having checked with them.

While I could no longer imagine continuing to work for the *Times,* I was determined not to leave until Keller retracted his defamatory statements about me and the false claims about my reporting were rebutted.[2]

In a letter to both Arthur and me, dated November 1, 2005, Bill said he was writing as a self-appointed "counsel for the situation." His goal was to help avert a "train wreck." He cautioned Arthur against trying to "threaten Judy with bondage" or let me "storm out" with "legal and union support" in "unrelenting hostility." Severance and legal fees, retirement benefits, and the like were not the issue, he wrote, citing what I had often jokingly told him: had I cared about money, I would have become an investment banker or married one.

The core issue, he wrote, was "reputational." The paper had not only damaged my "professional reputation" as well as its own but risked undermining my "credibility as a witness" in the impending Libby trial. Both the paper's standing and mine would take an "extended beating from gleeful critics" unless this crisis was fairly and promptly resolved. The damage was far from irreparable, provided that Keller retracted the "memo to the staff" that *Times* reporters and editors — then over 1,200 employees — had found in their email in-boxes accusing me of an "entanglement" with Libby. "That word," he wrote, "highly charged with insinuation in the context of salacious gossip spread by bloggers," was "laced with wrongdoing in light of accusations of felonies by the source," by which he meant Libby. "Surely Keller, normally a careful writer, did not intend any such meaning and realized too late that he made a terrible mistake," Bill wrote. A later version of the memo had changed "entanglement" to "engagement (hardly any better)," Bill continued. Nor could Keller turn to the word *relationship* with its "Clintonian connotation." "Entanglement" was now "hanging around Judy's neck and won't go away." The previous day, the *Washington Post* had quoted it on its front page, "magnified by the sly 'enigmatically,' imputing a mystery to what the *Times* editor apparently thought was going on between reporter and source."

Maureen Dowd's column, Bill wrote, was "the most savage denunciation" of "character and professionalism" that he had ever read at the paper. Though he had written over 1.25 million words on the op-ed page over three decades, many of which had differed sharply with editorial policy, he had never written "one word personally criticizing a colleague."

Safire proposed that Keller "admit error" and "express regret and move on." He also had to "revisit" his memo's charge that I seemed to have misled Phil Taubman, the Washington bureau chief, a "stinging accusation of professional deception that does not belong in the news columns (or even in an op-ed column)." As for Judy, he wrote, once I "cooled down" over Keller's email, Maureen's op-ed, and public editor Byron Calame's column, which had falsely accused me of taking ethical "short-cuts" and not mentioned that I had just spent eighty-five days in jail, we could attempt to resolve the dispute with Jill Abramson over whether I had told her that Valerie Plame worked for the CIA. He urged Arthur to let me post a dignified "Reporter's Farewell" column on the op-ed page on Sunday.

Our agreement resembled Safire's proposal. Arthur said that he respected my decision to retire from the *Times,* and expressed gratitude for my "significant personal sacrifice to defend an important journalistic principle." Keller praised me for having "participated in some great prize-winning journalism." He also made public a letter he had written me retracting his October 21 email. In using the words *entanglement* and *engagement* in reference to my relationship with Libby, he wrote, he had not intended to suggest an "improper relationship." While noting that he remained "troubled" by whatever had happened in the Washington bureau, he withdrew his claim that I had misled the bureau chief. The *Times* quoted me as "gratified" that Keller had "clarified" remarks that were "unsupported by fact and personally distressing to me." The news story quoted my denial that I had been insubordinate. "I have always written the articles assigned to me, adhered to the paper's sourcing and ethical guidelines and cooperated with editorial decisions, even those with which I disagreed." The article about my resignation noted that I had been "locked up longer than any other reporter in American history" for refusing to testify or reveal my sources in a leak case. Although some colleagues had disagreed with my decision to testify, the story presented my explanation: "For me to have stayed in jail after achieving my conditions would have seemed self-aggrandizing martyrdom, or worse." In addition, the paper published my "Reporter's Farewell," though it ran as a letter to the editor, not on the op-ed page, my sole concession.

My lawyers insisted on another demand, one that had not occurred to me but should have: in addition to remaining silent about the content of my severance package, no *Times* "executive" and "senior editorial management" could make statements that were "inconsistent with, or contradictory to" those made in the paper by Arthur or Keller, the paper's press release about my resignation, or any other statement related to my "departure from the *Times*" and "dealings with Scooter Libby." I was free to say what I liked, but the *Times* had to stick to our agreed-upon language.

My lawyers were pleased with this provision, but we would soon be disappointed, for the ink had barely dried when anonymous *Times* sources began leaking false and unflattering versions of what had occurred. In the beginning, I ignored such lapses, but perhaps I shouldn't have. I failed to appreciate early on that the planted gossip about my fierce temper, imperious ways, rogue reporting, and overall pushiness — the way in which aggressive female journalists were then and continue to be characterized — were part of a narrative the paper would use to blame me for what the editor's note itself had called institutional failings. But since I had achieved my major demands, I was eager to move on with my life.

I spent the next year redefining my identity. Having introduced myself professionally for almost three decades in English, French, and Arabic as "Judith Miller of the *New York Times,*" I felt stateless. I discovered slowly that I had become my own brand — for better or worse. For many readers, the paper is their secular bible; what it writes is gospel — "all the news that's fit to print." Some seemed unsure what to think: Had the paper coddled me for too long, or had it panicked and betrayed me?

In interviews about what jail was like and why I had left the paper, I repeated my initial story, which was true enough: that I had left partly because "I had become the news, something no reporter wanted to be."[3] In my letter to the paper, I had acknowledged that even before I went to jail, I had become a "lightning rod for public fury over the intelligence failures that helped lead our country to war." But mostly I remained silent. A criminal trial lay ahead.

Whatever I said about my quarrels with the paper could impact the credibility of my testimony and possibly the trial's outcome.

In the summer of 2006, Fitzgerald won another round. In a 2-to-1 decision in August, a federal appeals court in New York ruled that he could inspect my home, office, and cell phone records and those of Phil Shenon to determine who had told us about raids and asset seizures the government was planning against two Islamic charities suspected of supporting terrorism: the Holy Land Foundation for Relief and Development in Texas and the Global Relief Foundation in Illinois. With Floyd Abrams and George Freeman representing us, Phil and I had vigorously resisted subpoenas to the telephone companies for our phone records, to prevent Fitzgerald from identifying our sources. The verdict from a court that had been historically sympathetic to claims that journalists were entitled to protect their sources was a blow and, we argued, an intrusion on the First Amendment. It had also reversed a lower court ruling and, as the *Times* wrote, "dealt a further setback to news organizations, which have lately been on a losing streak in the federal courts."

I was appalled as I watched copies of page

after page of calls that I had made or received turned over to Fitzgerald. The logs contained hundreds of calls that Phil and I had made before our story ran. The media paid little attention to this case compared with the ink and airtime they devoted to the Plame investigation and Scooter Libby. That was unfortunate. For Fitzgerald's seizure of our telephone records turned out to be a far more important bellwether of the challenge that journalists would soon face from a cyber-wise, techno-savvy government intent on plugging national security leaks.

Despite access to our phone logs, Fitzgerald was apparently unable to identify our sources. Perhaps he did so, but no one was ever charged with disclosing classified information in his inquiry, and none of our sources told us that they had been asked about their discussions with us. Phil and I managed to protect our sources because Jeff Gerth, my friend and colleague with whom I had collaborated on sensitive investigative stories, had drilled into his friends the importance of taking defensive measures to protect our sources. While I initially felt silly, and even a bit paranoid, using unregistered cell phones to call sensitive sources and acting like an amateur drug dealer, Jeff was right. With the government ever more able and willing to inspect journalists' phone calls and emails to identify their sources, such precautions were becoming essential tradecraft.

Nor did the story we wrote in the summer of 2001 cripple the government's effort to move against the charities or thwart terrorism, as Fitzgerald claimed. The Holy Land Foundation and several of its officers were eventually convicted of having provided material support for terrorism. The Global Relief Foundation remained closed, and the Treasury Department's seizure of its assets stuck, despite a libel suit it filed against the *Times* and other papers for having published the government's charges, as well as a lawsuit challenging the government's designation of the charity as linked to terrorism.

In January 2007 the long-awaited trial of Scooter Libby began. Antiwar activists and other administration critics confidently predicted that the trial would prove that there had been a White House conspiracy to expose Plame's CIA job. The public disclosure in 2006 that the original source of the leak was Richard Armitage, the deputy secretary of state, Colin Powell's alter ego, and a skeptic of the war, had jolted antiwar critics. By the time the trial began, so much was known about intelligence failures and the Plame case that the trial was an anticlimax.

Fitzgerald had known since his appointment in December 2003 that Armitage was the source of the Plame leak to Bob Novak. He had also known that the leak — apparently aimed at protecting the State Department from blame for the Wilson mess and the faulty WMD estimates — had been confirmed by Bill Harlow, the CIA's spokesman. Neither was a neocon. The only senior official involved in this supposedly White House — orchestrated plot was Karl Rove, Bush's political adviser. But since he had acknowledged having done little but confirm what Novak had heard from Armitage and Harlow, he had not been indicted. So the alleged White House scheme was a conspiracy of one: Scooter Libby, who was charged not with leaking Plame's identity, but with lying to federal officials about what he had said to two other reporters and me. No one was ever charged with the leak.

I was one of ten journalists among nineteen witnesses to testify at the trial. Most of the other journalists — Bob Woodward, Glenn Kessler, and Walter Pincus from the *Washington Post;* David Sanger of the *Times;* and Bob Novak — swore that Libby had never mentioned Plame or her CIA job. I was the only reporter to state that Libby had discussed Wilson's wife. So my testimony, Fitzgerald said in his closing arguments, was crucial to the case against Libby. It was also crucial to Fitzgerald's assertion that the vice president had been involved, since Libby had told the grand jury that Cheney had approved his suggestion that he discuss the intelligence estimate about Iraq and WMD with me.

At the same time, I testified that I did not recall Libby's having mentioned Plame's name, the fact that her job was secret, or that she had helped send her husband to Niger for the CIA. Although I testified that my notes and memories of our conversations were often sketchy, Fitzgerald endorsed my memory of our conversations over Libby's.

Two other journalists were key to Fitzgerald's case. Matt Cooper, who by then had left *Time,* testified that Karl Rove had first told him that Wilson's wife worked at the CIA and may have helped send him to Niger. When Cooper had asked Libby whether he, too, had heard that, Libby had responded, "Yeah, I've heard that, too," Cooper quoted Libby as saying.[4] Tim Russert, NBC's Washington bureau chief, said that Plame had not come up in his conversation with Libby, and that he had not told Libby about Plame's job and role in Wilson's trip, as Libby recalled.

Both Fitzgerald and my lawyers instructed me not to follow news accounts of the trial or what other witnesses were saying, lest it influence my testimony. I complied. Only later did my lawyers tell me that Judge Reggie B. Walton ruled there was no evidence that Libby had lied about the last of our three discussions and dismissed the prosecution's charges that we had discussed Plame in a telephone conversation on July 12, 2003.

In March 2007, after deliberating for ten days, the eleven jury members convicted Libby on four counts of making false statements to the FBI, lying to a grand jury, and obstructing justice. They acquitted him on one count: lying to the FBI about his conversation with Matt Cooper.

In June, Judge Walton sentenced Libby, the most senior White House official to be convicted of a felony since the Iran-contra scandal twenty years earlier, to thirty months in prison and a fine of $250,000. He was spared jail when President Bush, at the last possible minute, voided his prison term and commuted his sentence.[5] But to

Dick Cheney's enduring fury, Libby did not receive one of the twenty-nine pardons that the president issued shortly before leaving office, in December 2008. I had expected Bush to pardon Libby. If he didn't, I had expected Libby to appeal the verdict. But Libby had told friends that an appeal would be too hard on his family, financially onerous, and would prevent him from moving on with his life.

The day after Libby's lawyers announced that he was dropping his appeal, Bill Safire called me. I had to write my own account of the ordeal — *"Now!"* he ordered. Bill knew that I was determined not to write anything that could be subpoenaed for another trial. Still, I hesitated. Reviewing my emails, memos, and notes about the *Times,* my months in jail, and my trial testimony was painful. I might have abandoned the project had it not been for a chance encounter with Libby at a national security conference in Israel in 2010.

We had not spoken since 2003, and when he saw me enter the hall, he gave me a decidedly chilly look and did not approach me. I couldn't blame him. We had barely known each other before our meetings in the summer of 2003 became the talk of Washington and ammunition in Fitzgerald's hands. Our "entanglement," as Keller had first called it, had consisted of two interviews, one telephone call, and a chance two-minute encounter with my husband and me at a rodeo in Jackson, Wyoming.

After most guests had left the hall, I asked Libby how he was doing. I told him, neutrally, that I regretted how things had turned out. We spoke briefly about our lives since the trial. I did not mention jail. He seemed cautious. Before leaving, he asked whether I had read Valerie Plame's memoir, which had been published soon after his trial in 2007. No, I hadn't, I confessed. In fact, I had read little about those troubled times; I had no wish to do so.

He suggested that I might find something of interest.

A few months later, I read *Fair Game.* Though I had occasionally encountered Joe Wilson at social events before the trial, I had never met his wife.

Libby was right. The book was certainly of interest. In addition to Bush, Cheney, and Libby, Plame was also furious at the CIA, which she accused of having failed to protect her family after her "outing."[6] Her account of how the Bush administration's campaign had ended her career and nearly ruined her marriage sold well and became a

Hollywood movie starring Sean Penn as Wilson and Naomi Watts as Plame. She expressed regret about letting *Vanity Fair* photograph her in secret spy gear — a Hermès head scarf and large, dark sunglasses — seated alongside her husband in his Jaguar convertible. When the photo spread hit newsstands in January 2004, she complained that the right had denounced her "publicity stunt" and "self-promotion" and what Rove called the Wilsons' unmasking as "vain, arrogant celebrity wannabes." She attributed her lapse in judgment, which she acknowledged had embarrassed the CIA and even her supporters, to one of those "what the hell" moments after having been "beaten down."

Of most interest to me in Plame's book was the revelation that while working overseas for the CIA, Plame's cover were jobs at the State Department. The CIA is organized by offices within divisions — such as the counterproliferation division of the Directorate of Operations, in which Agent Plame worked. But the State Department is divided into functional offices and regional and other "bureaus": the Bureau of European Affairs, the Bureau of Consular Affairs. Both, I was learning, had served as her cover.

That Plame had worked for a State Department bureau as cover stopped me cold. I found the notebook in which I had recorded my initial conversation with Libby on June 23, 2003. On page 1, I had written "Scooter Libby — uranium." On page 26, well before my interview with Libby, I had written Joe Wilson's name and phone number. It was underlined four times. My notes with Libby did not begin until page 33. My first question to Libby involved the NIE: "Was the intell slanted?" A page and a half later, in the midst of our discussion of the NIE and Iraq's reported efforts to acquire uranium, was a note in parentheses: "(wife works in Bureau?)."

I remembered what I had learned after the trial: that Libby had consistently told the FBI in October and September 2003, and a grand jury in March 2004, that Cheney had told him sometime before June 11, 2003, that Plame worked at the CIA. If Libby, a seasoned bureaucrat, had been trying to plant her employer with me at our first meeting in June, he would not have used the word *Bureau* to describe where Plame worked. But a source who thought that she *really* worked at the State Department might have described her job that way. A terrible thought raced through me: Contrary to my testimony, had someone *else* told me that Plame worked at the State Department before my meeting with Libby? Someone who may have given me Wilson's telephone number? Had I written *Bureau* between parentheses to ask Libby about her job that day?

I searched for the notes of my conversations with Fitzgerald before my testimony. He had asked me several times: What did Libby mean when he said "Bureau"? Did he mean the FBI? No, I had replied. While I normally used the word *Bureau* to refer to the FBI, Libby and I had been discussing the CIA and its faulty intelligence estimates.

I called William Jeffress, Libby's lawyer. Had Libby known that Plame had used the State Department as official cover? I asked him. No, Jeffress replied. Although Libby's lawyers had requested information about Plame's status and job, including the nature of her cover, Fitzgerald had refused to provide it. Her status wasn't relevant, the prosecutor claimed, which Judge Walton had upheld. So no one on Libby's defense team had learned about Plame's State Department cover until they, too, had read her memoir after Libby's conviction.[7] "But Fitzgerald clearly knew," Jeffress said. "I could have made good use of that."

Prosecutors are required to provide potentially exculpatory information to defendants and witnesses who testify against them. Fitzgerald surely knew about Plame's cover at a State Department bureau when we discussed and rehearsed my testimony about that word before the trial.

Reading Plame's book had put my reference to that word — in parentheses and with a question mark — in a new light. Libby probably hadn't used it, or talked about Plame with me that day. But someone else had, perhaps one of the twenty or more nonproliferation experts I routinely spoke to at the State Department, the Pentagon, and other government agencies who dealt with Foggy Bottom's many bureaus. I thought hard. I still could not remember when and from whom I had first learned that Wilson had a wife at the CIA. But since Cheney had already told Libby that Plame worked in the CIA's nonproliferation office that had sent Wilson to Africa by the time Libby and I first met, Libby had probably not been the source of my reference to his wife's work for a bureau.

My testimony, though sworn honestly, might have been wrong.

I had always been troubled, as I had warned Fitzgerald, about my having surrounded that phrase with parentheses and a question mark. The format itself — my use of parentheses or, more often, brackets to reflect information I had already learned — suggested that I had intended to pursue the issue with Libby that day, rather than a reference to something that Libby and I had discussed. It may not even have struck me initially as all that important. I hadn't said anything about what would have been an intriguing tip to Jill Abramson the day after my initial meeting with Libby. If we had discussed Plame or her work, wouldn't I have mentioned it to her in June rather than July? Perhaps, like Bob Woodward, I had intended to ask Libby about Wilson's "wife," but neglected to do so. Woodward had testified that Libby had not told him anything about Plame when they spoke. Novak had told the jury the same thing. I was the only journalist who testified that Libby had talked about Plame.

I reread the notebook containing the notes of my second interview with Libby on July 8. While there were ten notations of Plame's name, or versions of it, scattered throughout the notebook, none was part of my conversation with Libby. Nor, for that matter, was her name linked to any other source identified in the notebook. Given the placement of the doodles, however, I had clearly learned by then that Wilson's wife had worked at the CIA. Precisely when and from whom, I still could not recall.

The notes of that second interview with Libby also contained a comment inside parentheses: "(wife works at WINPAC)." The acronym stood for Weapons, Intelligence, Nonproliferation, and Arms Control Center, the unit within the CIA that, among other things, tracks the spread of unconventional weapons. I believed this was the first time, I had testified, that I had heard — I said from Libby — that Wilson's wife worked in that office. I said that the notation had led me to conclude that Plame was an analyst, not a secret undercover operative. But while there were several additional references to WINPAC in my two-hour-long interview with Libby, there was no other reference to Wilson's wife.

Again, I was seized with doubt. Had I been told, incorrectly, that Plame worked at WINPAC before my meeting with Libby? Or if I had already been told that Plame worked at the CIA, and since Libby and I had been discussing the WMD intelligence estimates that WINPAC had helped prepare, had I put two and two together and gotten five? Had someone else told me, or had I concluded on my own that Plame worked at WINPAC?

Only after the trial did I learn that Cheney had told Libby by phone in early June that Plame worked in the CIA's counterproliferation division. So why would Libby have told me that she worked at WINPAC? Suddenly the explanation I had given under oath — that Libby had identified her as a CIA weapons analyst in WINPAC — made no sense. No other witness had heard Libby associate Plame with that office.

My heart sank as I closed the notebooks. What if my testimony about events four years earlier had been wrong? Had I misconstrued my notes? Had Fitzgerald's questions about whether my use of the word *Bureau* meant the FBI steered me in the wrong direction?

Though I felt certain before the trial that Libby and I had discussed "the wife," if only in passing, my memory may have failed me. Rereading those elliptical references and integrating them with what I had learned since the trial and with the information about Plame's cover that Fitzgerald had withheld, it was hard not to conclude that my testimony had been wrong. Had I helped convict an innocent man?

■ ■ ■ ■

Memory can be treacherous. Daniel L. Schacter, the chairman of Harvard's psychology department, with whom Libby had consulted before his trial, told me when I called him years later that such memory "transgression" was common. Scientific research had shown time and again that "misattribution" — falsely remembering how or where we had heard or learned things — was normal, and far more common than people understood. But the judge had not permitted the jury to hear such evidence.

Schacter told me he was convinced that the jury lacked the information it needed about memory failure to make a reasoned opinion about Libby's guilt or innocence. Based on what the jury saw, he said, "I could not have rendered a fair decision based on the evidence. I do not believe that they could either."[8]

In my *Times* story about my grand jury testimony in October 2005, I described my chance meeting with Libby in August 2003 at that Jackson rodeo. The point of the story was that I hadn't recognized Libby when he had said hello to Jason and me partly because I had met him only twice before and because he was not wearing a suit, Washington's uniform, but jeans, sunglasses, and a cowboy hat. Jason, too, recalled our encounter and my embarrassment about not having recognized the senior official he called the "guy in a cowboy hat." But those clear memories were wrong. Libby had not worn a cowboy hat that day. He did not own a cowboy hat, he told me when we later discussed our respective memory lapses and impressions of an episode that neither of us thought we would ever forget.

But I was sure about the hat, I told him. Libby permitted himself a tight smile. "Are you more or less certain about the cowboy hat than you were about our having discussed Valerie Wilson's CIA job?" he asked me.

I called Steve Sestanovich, a professor at Columbia and Bill Clinton's expert on Russia, and Jenny Mayfield, who had worked on Cheney's staff as what she called "Scooter's memory bank." Both had been at the rodeo with Libby that day and told me that he hadn't worn a cowboy hat. "If he had," Sestanovich told me, "I would have been talking about it for years." In their six years working together, Mayfield told me, Libby had never worn a cowboy hat. "Scooter thought it was fine for cowboys to wear them," she said, but "he was definitely not a cowboy hat kind of guy."

The Libby trial and growing public furor over the Iraq War were interwoven. Jury selection began the week after the president enraged war critics by unveiling a new strategy for Iraq over the objections of most of his own senior staff, except Cheney, who had vigorously promoted a counterinsurgency approach for months. Rather than withdraw American forces, as an all-star bipartisan commission headed by Republican guru James Baker and Democrat Lee Hamilton recommended, America would "surge" its forces in Iraq. At the trial, antiwar protesters in front of the Capitol denouncing the "surge" and Bush's "lies" could be heard at the courthouse from blocks away.

At a press conference in October 2005, Fitzgerald said the trial would not be about the war in Iraq but about whether one man had lied and obstructed justice. His closing remarks to the jury framed the issue more broadly. "What is this case about?" he asked them. Wasn't it about "something bigger" than perjury and obstruction of justice charges against Libby? "There is a cloud over the vice president," Fitzgerald intoned, referring to Libby's assertion that Cheney had authorized him to discuss with me the Iraqi WMD estimates, which the president had declassified. "And that cloud remains because this defendant obstructed justice," Fitzgerald claimed.

Apart from conservatives, few reporters protested Fitzgerald's expansion of an alleged conspiracy to Cheney. Fitzgerald, in fact, had placed Iraq at the center of the proceedings. The media elaborated. What was really on trial, wrote Michael Duffy of *Time,* was "the whole culture of an Administration that treated the truth as a relative virtue."

The outing of Plame, a CIA officer with classified status, Fitzgerald declared at the press conference, was "not widely known outside the intelligence community." He also painted a specter of grave, if unspecified, harm to America's national security.

John Rizzo, the CIA's general counsel and a lawyer there for over thirty years, challenged both. In a memoir published in 2014, he wrote that "dozens, if not hundreds of people in Washington" knew that Plame worked for the CIA. By all accounts, he noted, Plame was a "dedicated, capable" employee who hadn't sought the limelight, unlike her "publicity-seeking, preening blowhard of a husband." But she was hardly a female James Bond whom the Hollywood movie version of her book had portrayed running Iraqi agents and tracking down endangered WMD scientists before Israel's Mossad could kill them. Plame, Rizzo wrote, was an "obscure . . . mid-level agent" whom he had never heard of or met. He added that a CIA damage assessment of the leak, completed in late 2003 or early 2004, before I went to jail and Libby was indicted, had produced "no evidence" of harm to any CIA operation, agent in the field, or anyone else, including "Plame herself."[9] But this crucial CIA finding was disclosed only when Rizzo's book was published.

Given the CIA's internal assessment, Rizzo had predicted to colleagues there was "no way" that the Justice Department would pursue it. Because the impact of Plame's outing was "negligible," "I fully expected Justice to treat it the way it treated 99 percent of our crimes reports, which is to say, to do little or nothing." George Tenet told Cheney that he estimated there were close to four hundred reports of possible criminal violations involving leaks of classified information that Justice had seldom if ever pursued.[10]

Rizzo's conclusion was that the department's pursuit of Libby could be explained only by "partisan political pressure being applied . . . by opponents of Bush administration policies in Iraq." His view of that decision is harsh: "The crimes reporting process had never been trivialized and distorted like that in all my years at the CIA," and the leak investigation was "a seemingly interminable distraction and a colossal waste of time and money."

After reading his book and talking to Rizzo, I was glad that he had finally made public what my CIA sources had been telling me on background for years. The CIA had cleared Rizzo's book. But I couldn't help but wonder: Where was anyone from the CIA, when Americans were debating whether the leak had caused great harm?

Cheney and other former senior officials assert that the Libby investigation may have had consequences for American policy and, arguably, the course of the Iraq War. In an interview, Cheney said that Fitzgerald's four-year inquiry distracted and undermined the effectiveness of his chief of staff and adviser to the president, a skilled political infighter who recognized — long before other White House officials — the mistakes being made in Iraq and the need for a new war-fighting strategy there. Known in political shorthand as the "surge," the crucial shift to a counterinsurgency strategy and the troop increase to implement it allowed the United States to stabilize Baghdad, curtail violence in most of the country, at least temporarily, and, under Obama, to leave Iraq with tattered dignity.

Meghan O'Sullivan, a former deputy national security adviser on Iraq and Afghanistan who worked in Baghdad and Washington between 2003 and 2007, said she doubted that the strategy shift could have occurred much earlier, given what she called the "facts on the ground" in Iraq and Washington, a view echoed by several others who worked intensively on Iraq.[11]

Some experts disagree. Gary J. Schmitt, now a scholar at the American Enterprise Institute who was Senator Daniel Patrick Moynihan's aide and staff director on the Senate Intelligence Committee, said that in the summer of 2003, Libby invited him and a few other experts to a small meeting to discuss the deteriorating security situation in Iraq. Having encountered resistance to a course correction from the Joint Chiefs of Staff and Secretary Rumsfeld, Libby appeared quietly frustrated by Bush's passive response to the growing insurgency and his decision to let L. Paul (Jerry) Bremer preside over a two-year occupation. Schmitt said that Libby encouraged him to write an essay urging that a new strategy be adopted, and US troops surged, to restore stability against an insurgency. "Libby was discreet," Schmitt said in an interview, "but he wouldn't have encouraged me to write unless he felt that the administration was on the wrong path in Iraq." "The Right Fight Now: Counterinsurgency, Not Caution, Is the Answer in Iraq" was published in the *Washington Post* in October 2003.[12]

In an interview in 2013, Paul Wolfowitz, the former deputy secretary of defense and among the most ardent neocon advocates of invading Iraq, described Libby as his "principal ally" in several early battles over the conduct of the war. Libby's "strong voice" was most badly missed, Wolfowitz said, on the issue of military requirements for Iraq. Having grasped that early post-invasion planning for a very small Iraqi army for external defense "made no sense," Libby kept pressing as early as June 2003 for what military planners call a "requirements analysis." Wolfowitz said that such a review might have led to a new strategy and to the formation of Iraqi security forces capable of countering the insurgency years before the 2007 surge.

In 2013 Gen. Jack Keane, the Iraq surge's key promoter, told me that Libby had been among the first White House officials to grasp that America might well lose the war in Iraq if Washington did not stop the Sunni insurgents and Al Qaeda from gaining ground. Libby had worked closely with one of Keane's top allies, Col. Derek Harvey, an expert on Iraq and its ruling Ba'ath Party, to arrange briefings on what Harvey argued was a Ba'athist-led insurgency and on the numbers of US forces that would be required to implement a counterinsurgency strategy. "Until he was distracted and ultimately taken out by the investigation," Keane told me, Libby had worked hard to convince skeptical officials to revisit America's failing war-fighting strategy. "Without Scooter's relentless early efforts," Keane said, "I'm not sure the White House would have admitted failure and changed the military strategy."

"It took enormous courage to walk into a crowded interagency meeting and say that you are all wrong," Cheney asserted in an interview in 2013. "And then to stick to your guns when they all gather around the conventional wisdom and dispute or dismiss you." Libby had done that, repeatedly.

Fitzgerald, a forty-seven-year-old prosecutor in Chicago when the Plame investigation began, had made a name for himself in the 1990s in New York for his tenacious prosecution of terrorists in the first World Trade Center bombing. Our meetings during the Plame investigation had always been professional, his manner gracious and polite. Even after he had put me in jail and got access to my telephone records, I agreed to testify as a prosecution witness in 2008 against militant Islamists in Chicago whom he accused of having provided material support for terrorism. But as we talked at the trial preparation sessions in Washington and Chicago, I thought that Fitzgerald had put his Plame inquiry — with no time constraints, budgetary limits, or oversight — foremost.[13]

To learn the source of a story I had never written, Fitzgerald had put me in jail. In so doing, argued James Goodale, the former vice chairman of the *Times,* he had destroyed the long-standing delicate balance between reporters and editors, courts and the government. "For a generation," Jim wrote, "the press, the courts, and prosecutors" had avoided precisely such a confrontation. Fitzgerald, he concluded, had no understanding of the press's role in a democracy.

Libby's colleagues and friends saw in Fitzgerald's pursuit self-righteousness and moral indignation. They suspected that what motivated him was a desire, as Karl Rove charged, to make a name for himself by hooking a really big fish.

As Peter Baker, the *Times* reporter, would report in his 2014 book on the relationship between Bush and Cheney, the vice president believed that he, not Libby, had been Fitzgerald's real target, a view that Cheney confirmed to me in 2013. Libby, Cheney said, was the instrument the prosecutor had used to acquire a more prominent, career-making scalp.

Fitzgerald declined to discuss the case with me — though he was now working at the Chicago office of Skadden, Arps, the law firm that represented me. But Joe Tate, the lawyer who represented Libby until his criminal trial, and who was Libby's law partner and long-standing friend, told me in an interview in 2014 that Fitzgerald had twice offered to drop all charges against Libby if his client would "deliver" Cheney to him.

Fitzgerald had hinted at a deal even before Tate had flown to Chicago to discuss Libby's case before his indictment, Tate said. When they spoke by phone before his trip, Fitzgerald warned him not to "waste" his time coming to Chicago unless he could "deliver something beyond what we've heard," Tate said. "I went out there anyway."

By that time, Tate said, Fitzgerald was no longer looking at who had released Plame's name. "They needed a scalp and were flyspecking Libby's FBI interviews and grand jury appearances." Arguing that such inconsistencies were immaterial, he asked Fitzgerald, "Why are you doing this?"

He reported that Fitzgerald replied, "Unless you can deliver someone higher up — the vice president — I'm going forth with the indictment." "I knew then he was out of control," Tate said.

Bound by the legal agreement limiting what *Times* editors could say about me, they usually said nothing at all. My name rarely appeared in the paper, even in news stories about First Amendment battles or the struggle to pass a media shield law in Congress.

Two years after my resignation, David Barstow, my former colleague, still had no explanation for the press's almost uniformly hostile coverage of me and my role in the

WMD intelligence failures and the Libby case. "Why it is that Judith Miller somehow became the embodiment of all those failures," he wrote, remained "simply unfathomable to me." It was both inaccurate and unfair, he insisted. But as Barstow himself noted, I was a pushy, high-profile reporter at the nation's highest-profile newspaper. Other news outlets had followed my lead. That made me Azazel, the biblical goat upon which the community heaped its many sins.

The blogosphere, which had been granted credentials to cover the Libby trial and had grown increasingly influential, filled in whatever blanks the paper left. The attacks were relentless, sexist, and ugly — the pernicious side of a technology whose ability to spread knowledge widely and instantly has transformed journalism and global communications.

Occasionally, an independent thinker such as Niall Stanage, a young Irish journalist writing for the *New York Observer,* would read my WMD stories and challenge the conventional wisdom. He noted that my articles were filled with qualifiers; they were not based largely on Chalabi or anonymous sources, but quoted officials and experts by name. "Judith Miller: Was She Really So

Bad?" the title of his essay asked. But such were minority voices. In the blogosphere, a cyber Roman Forum, and even in publications that should have known better, my name was increasingly linked with the "disgraced" plagiarist and fabulist, Jayson Blair, whom the paper had fired in another of those "scandals" that had "bloodied the profession," as the *New Republic* wrote.

More than the prospect of a second newsroom revolt, the steady rise of the blogosphere preoccupied Arthur and other senior *Times* executives. Arthur and I had spoken often of the blogs' growing, in his view, often pernicious impact on mainstream journalism. When the war began in Iraq, there were roughly one hundred thousand bloggers. By the time of Valerie Plame's outing, there were an estimated twenty-seven million of them.

The *Times* circulation numbers, along with paid advertising, revenues, and stock price, continued to plummet through 2013. The paper's efforts to boost its digital profile faltered. In the spring of 2014, an internal report by Arthur Gregg Sulzberger, Arthur's son, warned that in the past year, readership had fallen "significantly" not only on the website but also on smartphones and other mobile platforms.[14]

Rounds of layoffs and buyouts of some of the paper's most experienced talent and the departure of younger, digitally savvy stars fueled gloom. Among the veterans pushed out in the spring of 2012 was George Freeman. The *Wall Street Journal* had quoted him in late 2005 defending me against the paper's attacks, implicitly criticizing the *Times*'s leaders. Though sixty reporters wrote to Arthur Sulzberger protesting the decision to dismiss the lawyer who had defended so many of us for so long in libel and source protection cases, there was no reprieve. Freeman told me he did not think that his defense of me might have played a role in his termination. But the paper did dock his pay a bit because he had talked to the *Wall Street Journal* without authorization.

After Keller resigned as executive editor in 2011, he told *Editor & Publisher,* a magazine and online industry site, and Media Matters for America, a liberal, pro-Democratic online group created to criticize Fox News, that the "whole Judy Miller WMD experience" was "one of the low points" of his eight years. He had decided to review the paper's prewar reporting, he told Media Matters, after "a lot of people, particularly people on the left, became disenchanted with the *Times* because they saw it as having been cheerleaders for the war." He told *Esquire* that he had erred in not having acted sooner to put me "on a leash."

Lawyers from Skadden, Arps, and I wrote to Arthur Sulzberger, reminding him that such comments violated our agreement. Arthur, who declined to be interviewed for this book, replied that he had forwarded our complaints to Keller, who wrote that he saw nothing pejorative in them. In May 2013 my lawyers complained again when the paper's "public editor" described me in print as the "disgraced" reporter. By then, I had written major stories for the *Wall Street Journal,* the *Los Angeles Times,* and a dozen other prominent newspapers and magazines, and was appearing regularly on Fox News as a national security and First Amendment commentator. Margaret Sullivan, the public editor, had never called me for comment. But the paper's general counsel wrote back that because Sullivan was "neither an 'executive' of the *Times* nor a part of the senior editorial management" and because her observation was unrelated to my "departure from the *Times* and her dealings with Scooter Libby," her characterization was not "inconsistent with or contradictory to the references statements."

The nature and focus of my reporting changed after leaving the *Times*. Though I reported in cities throughout the nation and in a dozen different countries, I was no longer able to hop on a plane and travel anywhere to pursue a story without advance planning and financial commitments from news outlets to offset the cost. But soaring travel costs and plummeting circulations and advertising were forcing many publications, even wealthier TV networks, to reduce international coverage as well.

Political changes in the Middle East, too, affected my reporting. In 2012 some 119 journalists — a record in modern times — were killed in the field, most of them in Syria and the Middle East. While I continued returning to Iraq to report on the state of the war and its impact on Iraqis and American forces, I, too, became increasingly focused on security. After Marie Colvin was killed in Syria in early 2012, I reevaluated the risks I had once downplayed. Marie, my friend since our days as young correspondents in Paris, had been among journalism's most courageous, relentless reporters. When we reported together in Tahrir Square during the eruption of the Arab Spring in Egypt in 2011, I told her that I feared she had become cavalier about the dangers of reporting in war zones. Other friends had pleaded with her not to take so many chances. No story was worth it, we said. The night before she was killed, her editor ordered her to leave the besieged part of Homs, which was being shelled by government forces. But Marie could not bring herself to abandon the story.

After Scooter Libby's conviction, some media critics called the testimony of a parade of reporters, including mine, a catastrophe for journalism. Several predicted that sources would dry up, that there would be a permanent chill between reporters and officials. Confidentiality pledges would be disregarded; waivers would routinely be required. Prosecutors like Fitzgerald would have little reason not to subpoena reporters with impunity.

Some concerns proved warranted. Under President Obama, who had promised to run the most open and "transparent" government possible, access to senior officials declined sharply and the number of leak investigations soared. As of June 2014, six government employees, plus two government contractors, had been the subjects of felony criminal prosecutions under the 1917 Espionage Act for alleged leaks of classified information to the press — compared with a total of three such prosecutions in previous administrations. In two of these cases, the Justice Department had secretly subpoenaed and seized reporters' phone logs and emails.

Many officials became more fearful of even talking to the press, much less leaking to us, according to a forty-page report by the Committee to Protect Journalists in 2013.[15] Those suspected of doing so were given lie detector tests and had their telephone and email records scrutinized. An "Insider Threat Program" throughout agencies instructed federal workers to help prevent unauthorized disclosures by monitoring their colleagues' behavior. By June 2012, the report notes, the director of intelligence's inspector general was reviewing 375 unresolved investigations of employees of the nation's sixteen intelligence agencies. Moreover, President Obama's political advisers increasingly used social media — their own videos, sophisticated websites, even their own official photographer — to give Americans the information they wanted them to know.

Though many reporters at mainstream

news outlets initially voiced little protest, criticism of the administration's secretive style and policies increased in Obama's second term. David Sanger, my former colleague and a veteran Washington correspondent, called Obama's White House the "most closed, control freak administration I've ever covered." Jill Abramson, before Arthur Sulzberger unceremoniously fired her in May 2014 for having lost the newsroom's "confidence," called Obama's White House the "most secretive" she had covered in twenty-two years of political reporting.[16]

Despite the administration's passion for secrecy, however, reporters continued getting world-class scoops. While the internet and cybertechnology made it simpler for the government to spy on its citizens without warrants or cause, they also made it easier for a Private Manning to download over 750,000 classified documents from a workstation in Iraq and post them on WikiLeaks or an Edward J. Snowden to steal tens of thousands of sensitive documents outlining the NSA's secret surveillance methods. But leaks involving discussions of what those documents mean, and how policies are made — information citizens need to evaluate government decisions and the damage of a leak — have become rarer.

Since my stint in jail, although the number of leak investigations has increased sharply, subpoenas to reporters have declined. The surveillance technology that enables Washington to collect, store, and access trillions of telephone calls and emails a day means that the government no longer needs to force reporters to divulge our sources, or in most cases, to testify at criminal proceedings. It was enough for prosecutors to see that the *Times*'s Jim Risen had contacted former CIA official Jeffrey Sterling over a dozen times in less than a year to identify him as the probable source for a book chapter that Risen wrote in 2004 about a failed CIA effort to stop Iran from getting a nuclear weapon. It was sufficient for a prosecutor to know that James Rosen, of Fox News, had sent numerous emails and made numerous calls to a nuclear expert at the State Department to charge and eventually convict him of leaking a story on North Korea's nuclear program. For months, some of the warrants judges issued authorizing the transfer of such records to the government were themselves secret.

Lucy Dalglish, the former head of the Reporters Committee for Freedom of the Press, who defended me when I went to jail, says that the government now uses technology instead of subpoenas to identify the sources of leaks. "Prosecutors have figured out how to build cases simply by seeing whom we have been talking to," she said. As one government prosecutor told her at a meeting in 2011: "We don't need you anymore." George Freeman recently worried that given the government's surveillance capabilities, journalists might well have to resort once more to meeting sources "in parks and garages so that their emails and phone numbers can't be traced."

In 2014 Congress moved to restore some balance by taking up a version of the federal shield legislation that I lobbied for after leaving jail nine years ago. The earlier effort to protect reporters from being forced to reveal sources in federal cases was doomed by several factors — WikiLeaks, for one. But Bob Bennett, among others, argued that the *Times*'s abandonment of me and some of its own core principles undermined the credibility of the reporter who was, for better or for worse, then the campaign's most visible spokesperson.

"Your case was a political nightmare," Lucy Dalglish said. "Media people were eating one another alive." Journalists were as polarized by the war and Bush as the nation itself. "The lack of professional solidarity —

our inability to convince even some journalists that there were broader principles called source protection and press freedom at stake here — was crippling." The passions may have subsided, but the polarization within American journalism and politics has intensified. I try to ignore it and focus on doing my job: asking questions, seeking answers, knowing that, like most journalists who cover the secretive intelligence and national security agencies, I will continue getting some stories right and others wrong.

I have continued covering First Amendment issues, militant Islam and its terrorism, WMD and other unconventional weapons, and the Middle East, where the "tide of war" has not receded, despite President Obama's desire that it be so. In 2014 the Islamic State in Iraq and Syria (ISIS), a pernicious offshoot of Al Qaeda too radical even for that extremist group, declared itself a caliphate and the hub of a new Islamic state encompassing land seized from Iraq and Syria. The spread of Al Qaeda branches and likeminded Islamic extremist groups throughout the Middle East, Africa, and even Asia means that America and its allies will remain targets for years to come, notwithstanding Washington's wars on terror, Bin Laden's killing, and the decimation of Al Qaeda's original leadership. The extremists' search for unconventional weapons with which to strike America and its allies also continues.

The bloodshed, sectarian strife, and terror in Iraq and Syria are the result of decisions by two presidents. George Bush, whose invasion of Iraq was justified by bad intelligence, ran the war badly. After six years, his shift in strategy and troop surge, a move opposed by most of his close advisers, stabilized Iraq militarily, if not politically. But by then, America's patience with the war in Iraq was exhausted. Barack Obama, having vowed to withdraw American forces, did so in late 2011 according to the schedule and on terms negotiated by his predecessor. But in honoring his campaign pledge, disregarding advice from his military, and downplaying Prime Minister Maliki's ruinous suppression of the Sunnis, Obama sacrificed Iraq's stability and other gains of the surge secured at a cost of over 4,400 American soldiers' lives. This president, too, blamed his actions on bad intelligence. But his decision to downplay the danger of the civil war in neighboring Syria enabled ISIS and other groups with similar convictions to sink roots.

The war in Iraq undermined the public's

faith in the press and government and strengthened long-standing isolationist impulses.[17] Only after ISIS's beheading of two American journalists in August 2014 did the percentage of Americans who said the government was doing too little to counter global threats double, from 17 percent to 31 percent, according to a Pew Research Center poll that summer.[18] A majority continued opposing sending US forces to the region.

I remain a reporter in New York, where terrorism has struck three times in twenty years: twice at the World Trade Center near my apartment where the Freedom Tower now stands, and once invisibly, in the form of a powdered germ in our mail. Having witnessed the first bombing and 9/11, I saw the price of ignoring or underestimating such threats, our intelligence community's most consistent failing. After 9/11, I became increasingly convinced that the United States must reserve the right to use force, in concert with others but unilaterally if necessary, to prevent the worst people from acquiring the worst weapons. In a world in which ISIS and the like-minded seek unconventional weapons, as a former president said, "If we wait for threats to fully materialize, we will have waited too long."

The WMD failures in Iraq, however, taught me that overestimating a threat can also be costly — for individuals, families, communities, and the nation. Relying on the conclusions of American and foreign intelligence analysts and other experts I trusted, I, too, got WMD in Iraq wrong. But not because I lacked skepticism or because senior officials spoon-fed me a line. Having covered Iraq and the region for decades, I simply could not imagine that Saddam would give up such devastating weapons or the ability to make them again quickly once international pressure subsided. The first half of that assumption was wrong: the second all too accurate but forgotten in the bitter recriminations about how and why America went to war.

I remain committed to journalism's missions: exposing both wrongdoing and all-too-quiet successes, debating the delicate balance between preserving security and freedom, and disclosing what government is doing, or failing to do, to keep us both safe and true to the nation's laws and values. I have tried to review my mistakes, to correct errors, add new facts, and update them in the fullness of time. I continue trying to tell the story.

ACKNOWLEDGMENTS

Journalists are magpies. We steal, reinterpret, and regurgitate the insights and assessments of others. Occasionally we have an original idea or formulation. But mostly our job is publicizing the thoughts of others. At our most scrupulous, we identify and acknowledge those whose best lines we steal. That is why I found writing a memoir about reporting so difficult. The words *I, we,* and *me* do not come naturally to most journalists; they run counter to a lifetime of training and habit.

Some of the stories in this book are drawn from accounts of experiences initially reported in the *Times* or my earlier books. Still, this book, too, has been shaped by the ideas and insights of others. The mistakes are all mine, to be sure. But many friends, sources, and experts kept me from making more of them.

Some of those who helped shape my views

about foreign policy, national security, and journalism never realized their impact. Norman Mailer, whom my husband, Jason Epstein, edited for many years, was among them. Happily, I met him after he had finally found the perfect soul mate, Norris Church, who died in 2010 three years after his death, and long after he had tamed his more aggressive impulses. When I began questioning my skepticism about the democratic experiments under way in several Arab countries and the conviction of my leftist and neoconservative friends that democracy was the "solution" to ending centuries of mostly authoritarian oppression in that unhappy region, Norman supported my skepticism. Over dinner one night at his home in Provincetown, he asserted that democracy was likely to flourish only in countries in which its institutional pillars and cultural requisites were firmly in place — namely, an independent judiciary to guarantee the rule of law; traditions of respect for different ethnic, religious, and ideological minorities and minority views; equal rights and opportunities for all citizens, regardless of race, creed, religion, or gender; political transparency; and accountable power. Democratic experiments in countries lacking such traditions were likely to end in tears — or as I once argued in print, "one man, one vote, one time." Democracy, Mailer concluded, was truly a "grace note."

Bill Safire was crucial to this book. Until shortly before his death from cancer in September 2009, he often badgered me about my obligation as a journalist to tell my version of this story. I deeply regret that he did not live to see the result. After Bill died, Doug Schoen, Bill Clinton's former pollster, an author, and fellow commentator at Fox, took his place. Doug can be very persistent. I'm deeply grateful for his encouragement, advice, and, above all, friendship.

Jail was an unusual ordeal. So, too, was leaving the *Times.* I was fortunate to have the support of friends and sometime anonymous fans who called, wrote, and helped me through both. Among the staunchest were members of my legal team: Bob Bennett, Saul Pilchen, Nathan Dimmock, and Jackie Pearo. At Cahill Gordon, I want to thank Susan Buckley, in addition to Floyd Abrams, for support and legal guidance. George Freeman, my lawyer at the *Times,* was calm and steadfast through several lengthy legal and professional battles.

Friends from Sag Harbor visited me in

jail or called repeatedly to boost my spirits after I left the paper — among them, Steve Byers and Robert Sam Anson, fellow writers who share my passion for inhospitable places and stories; and Susan Penzner, my neighbor as a well as a friend. Thanks, too, to the friends who read portions of the manuscript and challenged my assertions and memory — the incomparable journalists David Samuels and Alana Newhouse, who edit *Tablet* magazine. Both of them, as well as Tunku Varadarajan, a talented writer and editor, give me faith that journalism has a future.

I owe more than I can say to Matt Mallow, then of Skadden, Arps and now general counsel of Blackrock, and Ellen Chesler, whose own biography of Margaret Sanger remains a model of the genre. They not only made invaluable suggestions about the manuscript but provided other vital support and guidance. So, too, did Carolyn Seeley Wiener and Karin Lissakers, my close friends since our days in Washington; Karin's husband, Martin Mayer, a prolific writer and fellow opera fan; Marilyn Melkonian; Janice O'Connell; Frances Cook; Walter Shapiro (whose best line got deleted); Meryl Gordon; and Larry and Susan Grant Maisel, friends since Paris and the parents of my amazing godson Nicholas. Shirley Lord Rosenthal has remained dear to me, before and after the death of her husband, Abe Rosenthal, to whom I will always be indebted. An Israeli journalist, Smadar Perry, who covers Arab affairs for *Yedioth Ahronoth,* has been among my closest friends for many years. She traveled to Virginia to see me in jail and has kept me grounded in Middle Eastern realities. She has never abandoned the vision of a world in which Jews and Arabs can coexist in peace, if not harmony. Tammy Bruce, a newer friend whom I met through our on-air debates on Fox, bucked me up during periods of doubt and reinforced my view that friendship almost always trumps political differences. My aunt, Eileen Connolly, read an early version of the book and told me that she would buy a copy if it were published. Jacob and Helen Epstein kept asking tough questions.

Since 2007, Larry Mone, president of the Manhattan Institute, has given me an office, title, and talented colleagues who take pride in challenging conventional wisdom. I am especially indebted to Brian Anderson, a fellow author and the inspired editor of MI's quarterly, *City Journal,* not only for reading the manuscript but for his patience at my prolonged absence from his pages. Howard Husock, another MI colleague who is on the board of the Corporation for Public Broadcasting, told me I needed a prologue. I did.

Military veterans of the ill-fated hunt for WMD in Iraq and other soldiers whom I met during my embeds in Iraq and Afghanistan have been among my most steadfast supporters. I owe special thanks to retired Generals Richard McPhee and David Petraeus, Ret. Chief Warrant Officer Richard Gonzales, Major Ryan Cutchin, David Temby, Tewfik Boulenouar, Drew Pache, and Rich Corner. Col. Michael Endres died too soon of a heart attack after leaving the army; he loved to help veterans at George W. Bush's foundation. No one made me laugh harder or taught me more about the army and its traditions than Mike. Hooah.

Roger Ailes offered me a job as a commentator at Fox News in 2008, opening a new world of broadcast journalism. I cannot thank him enough — along with Bill Shine and John Moody — for taking a chance on a print journalist, a brunette with little prior TV experience, and allowing me to learn from Fox's talented news professionals. When Jason and many of my liberal friends who consider the network the Antichrist wonder why I joined Fox, I tell them that I enjoy the challenge of a contrary point of view and that there is a greater diversity of opinion at Fox than there was at the *Times.* I'm a reporter and therefore allergic to ideology. Before and after joining Fox, I've steadfastly been inspired by curiosity about the world in all its manifestations. There are too many colleagues to thank at Fox. But Lynne Jordal Martin, the editor of Fox's opinion pages, published some of my first columns for the network's website and became an early friend. Her husband, Terry Martin, coached me on the strange new medium of TV, where less is often more. Gwen Marder encouraged me to wear colors. Jim Pinkerton challenged many of my views and helped me master articulating them in sound bites. Through Fox, I have benefited from great medical assistance. Dr. Mark Siegel, a fellow commentator, became my doctor after the incomparable Stanley Mirsky died. I have marveled at Dianne Brandi's wise counsel not only on legal matters but also on ethical issues in journalism. I'm proud to be associated with a network that has so staunchly defended its journalists in clashes with the government on First Amendment and other transparency challenges.

595

I am indebted to several former colleagues at the *Times* — Jeff Gerth, Geri Fabrikant, Claudia Payne, Richard Bernstein, Steve Engelberg, Dave Jones, Bill Broad, Craig Whitney, Marty Arnold, and David Barstow. Only Broad and Barstow remain at the paper. Others took buyouts or pursued other options. Thanks, too, to those who asked not to be named for keeping me abreast of developments at the paper.

For research on WMD and other topics at the heart of this book and for so much more, I am grateful to Pratik Chougule, a former speechwriter at the State Department in the Office of the Under Secretary for Arms Control and International Security, who has helped several former officials write memoirs. Once day he will write his own superb book.

Amanda "Binky" Urban, at ICM, has been my book agent and early reader for many years. Her calm, firm, candid advice has been indispensable. Thanks, too, to Gary Press, my accountant, friend, and fellow Florida fan.

Simon & Schuster has published all my books except my instant paperback on the Gulf war. The hardworking editorial team — Stuart Roberts; Martha Schwartz, a superb production editor; Cary Goldstein, executive director of publicity; Leah Johanson, publicist for the adult publishing group; and Stephen Bedford, a marketing specialist — have worked very hard on this book. Thank you so much. But above all, I thank Alice Mayhew, my friend, chief editor, and the publisher of all my hardback books. Alice is a legend in her profession. Deservedly. This book would not exist without her advice, patience, faith in me, and fearsome red pencil.

Ditto my other informal editor, the wisest man I know, my best friend and partner, Jason Epstein, who made me realize, finally, that there is far more to life than the story.

NOTES

Prologue

1. Howard Gardner, ed., *Responsibility at Work: How Leading Professionals Act (or Don't Act) Responsibly* (San Francisco: Jossey-Bass, 2007). Gardner, the editor of that volume, wrote the chapter about me entitled "Irresponsible Work." While he quotes from my website and thanks eleven people for having provided "useful feedback on earlier drafts of this chapter," five of whom worked at one time for the *Times,* there is no indication that he ever tried to contact me for comment, a basic pillar of the craft. Quoting "many observers," all of them anonymous, he describes me as a " 'piece of work,' " a "middle-aged" reporter who "consistently behaved in a high-handed manner," pursued stories "at all costs," and ignored the "directives of her immediate supervisors." He echoes

anonymous claims that I was "too close to her sources" who helped me "spread a narrative for which there was little, if any, solid evidence." He offers no examples of my supposedly egregious reporting and makes no mention of my Pulitzer. At the time of publication, he had still not responded to my request for a retraction and an apology.

Chapter 1. Anbar Province, Iraq

1. "Statement of Hon. Richard L. Armitage, Deputy Secretary of State, Department of State, Washington, DC," *The January 27 UNMOVIC and IAEA Reports to the U.N. Security Council on Inspections in Iraq: Hearing Before the Committee on Foreign Relations, United States Senate, One Hundred Eighth Congress, First Session, January 30, 2003* (Washington, DC: US Government Printing Office, 2003), pp. 12–16, www.gpo.gov/fdsys/pkg/CHRG-108 shrg85796/pdf/CHRG-108shrg85796 .pdf.
2. Judith Miller, "After the War: Unconventional Arms; A Chronicle of Confusion in the U.S. Hunt for Hussein's Chemical and Germ Weapons," *New York Times,* July 20, 2003, www.nytimes.com/2003/07/20/

world/after-war-unconventional-arms-
chronicle-confusion-us-hunt-for-hussein-s
-chemical.html.

3. Charles Duelfer, "No Books Were Cooked," *Foreign Policy,* March 18, 2013, www.foreignpolicy.com/articles/2013/03/18/no_books_were_cooked_bush_iraq_wmd_intelligence.

4. Michael Rubin, *Dancing with the Devil: The Perils of Engaging Rogue Regimes* (New York: Encounter, 2014), p. 203.

5. Judith Miller and Laurie Mylroie, *Saddam Hussein and the Crisis in the Gulf* (New York: Times Books, 1990).

6. Rubin, *Dancing with the Devil,* p. 207; Bruce W. Jentleson, *With Friends Like These: Reagan, Bush, and Saddam, 1982–1990* (New York: W. W. Norton, 1994), pp. 33, 42.

7. Con Coughlin, *Saddam, King of Terror* (New York: Ecco Press, 2002), p. 174.

8. Samir al-Khalil (Kanan Makiya), *Republic of Fear: The Politics of Modern Iraq* (Oakland: University of California Press, 1989), p. 110.

9. Ibid.

10. Ibid., p. 120.

11. Dick Cheney with Liz Cheney, *In My Time: A Personal and Political Memoir*

(New York: Threshold Editions, 2011), p. 191.

12. Judith Miller, "Saudi King Says He Expects Iraq to Yield," *New York Times,* January 7, 1991, www.nytimes.com/1991/01/07/world/ confrontation-in-the-gulf-saudi-king-says-he-expects-iraq-to-yield.html.

13. Judith Miller, "Egypt's President Calls for a Delay in Attacking Iraq," *New York Times,* November 8, 1990, www.nytimes.com/1990/11/08/world/mideast-tensions-egypt-s-president-calls-for-a-delay-in-attacking-iraq.html.

14. Dick Cheney, interview, January 2014.

15. Another prime mover of the effort to expose Saddam's brutality and war crimes against the Kurds was Peter Galbraith, who, first as a staff member of the Senate Foreign Relations Committee and later as an adviser to the Kurdish government, worked tirelessly toward this end.

16. Judith Miller, "Iraq Accused: A Case of Genocide," *New York Times Magazine,* January 3, 1993, www.nytimes.com/1993/01/03/magazine/iraq-accused-a-case-of-genocide.html.

17. That year, the Abu Mahal tribe in Al Qaim had rallied briefly to America's side. But undermanned, hamstrung by tribal

vendettas, and supported by too few American forces, this first, mini–Anbar Awakening was quickly overwhelmed by Al Qaeda. The next year, when Abdul Sattar Abu Risha, a dynamic younger sheikh with excellent smuggling and insurgent credentials from Anbar's largest tribe, the Dulaimi, sided with the Americans, Al Qaeda began losing ground.

18. A debate has long raged in academic and policy circles over whether it was the increase in US troops in Iraq or the Awakening that enabled the new counter-insurgency doctrine to succeed in Iraq. My own view is that they reinforced each other. The strategy shift and the surge, which the military called COIN, would never have worked without the Awakening, and vice versa. But it was the indigenous political shift among Iraqis a full year before the thirty thousand extra American forces started flowing into Iraq in February and March 2007 that initially prevented an American rout.

19. Chief Warrant Officer-4 Timothy S. McWilliams and Lieutenant Colonel Kurtis P. Wheeler, eds., *Al-Anbar Awakening*, vol. 1, *American Perspectives* (Quantico, VA: Marine Corps University Press, 2009), p. 33.

20. In its final report to Congress in 2010, the independent Commission on Wartime Contracting concluded that nearly $60 billion had been lost over the decade to waste and financial fraud, mostly in Iraq but also in Afghanistan, due to poor government oversight of contractors, even poorer planning, and gargantuan payoffs to warlords or insurgents.

21. Charles Duelfer, *Hide and Seek: The Search for Truth in Iraq* (New York: Public Affairs, 2008), p. 408.

22. In 2004 Galbraith was instrumental in arranging for DNO, a Norwegian oil company, to become the first foreign oil company to operate in Kurdistan. This became controversial in October 2009, when *Dargens Nœringsliv,* a Norwegian tabloid, published documents linking Galbraith financially to DNO. In November 2009 the *New York Times* wrote that Galbraith's role as adviser to the Kurds on the constitutional negotiations with Baghdad and his undisclosed financial ties to DNO could raise "serious questions about the integrity of the constitutional negotiations themselves" and fuel suspicions that the "true reason for the American invasion of their country was to take its oil." Galbraith denied any conflict of

interest, since the Kurds knew of his role with DNO when they asked for advice on the constitution, and there was a congruence of interest between the Kurds' desire to control their own oil and encourage foreign investment in the oil sector. He noted that he had also disclosed his compensation in a book about Iraq's future, *The End of Iraq: How American Incompetence Created a War Without End* (New York: Simon & Schuster, New York, 2006). In 2010 the *Times* reported that a British court had ordered DNO to pay Galbraith and a Yemeni investor between $55 million and $75 million for their stake in the oil deal.

In an interview in July 2014, Galbraith said that although he continues to advise the Kurds informally, he has no ongoing financial stake in Kurdistan or any company doing business there, and remains "proud" of his role in helping create "the financial basis for independence" for the Kurds, whose suffering under Saddam he did much to document. The website for the Kurdistan Regional Government says that Galbraith's work on Iraq's murderous campaign against the Kurds "led the US Senate to pass comprehensive sanctions on Iraq in 1988."

23. McWilliams and Wheeler, *Al-Anbar Awakening,* p. vii.

24. Ali Khedery, "Why We Stuck with Maliki — and Lost Iraq," *Washington Post,* July 3, 2014, www.washingtonpost.com/ opinions/ why-we-stuck-with-maliki–and-lost-iraq/2014/07/03/0dd6a8a4-f7ec-11e3-a606-946fd632f9f1_story.html. Khedery, an Iraqi-American who heads Dubai-based Dragoman Partners, was from 2003 to 2009 a special assistant to five U.S. ambassadors and an adviser to three heads of US Central Command. In 2011, as a private oil company adviser, he negotiated Exxon-Mobil's entry into Kurdistan.

Chapter 2. Nightclub Royalty in the Shadow of the Bomb

1. Franklin Foer, "The Source of the Trouble," *New York,* June 7, 2004, http:// nymag.com/nymetro/news/media/features/ 9226.

2. The quotes from Hank Greenspun's "Where I Stand" columns are from the archives of the Atomic Testing Museum, Las Vegas, Nevada; Judith Miller, "The Melted Dog: Memories of an Atomic Childhood," *New York Times,* March 20, 2005, http://www.nytimes.com/2005/03/

30/arts/artsspecial/30atom.html?_r=0&
pagewanted=all&position=.

3. Howard Ball, "Downwind from the
Bomb," *New York Times Magazine,* February 9, 1986, www.nytimes.com/1986/02/
09/magazine/downwind-from-the-bomb
.html, adapted from *Justice Downwind:
America's Atomic Testing Program in the
1950s* (New York: Oxford University
Press, 1986).

4. Derek S. Scammell, ed., *Nevada Test Site
Guide* (DOE/NV–715) (Las Vegas: National Nuclear Security Administration,
Department of Energy, 2005, p. 45, http://
www.nv.doe.gov/library/publications/
historical/DOENV_715_Rev1.pdf).

5. Harvey Wasserman and Norman Sol-
omon, *Killing Our Own: The Disaster of
America's Experience with Atomic Radiation*
(New York: Delta Books, 1982), p. 49.

6. Ball, "Downwind from the Bomb."

7. Wasserman and Solomon, *Killing Our Own,*
pp. 43–44.

8. Howard L. Rosenberg, *Atomic Soldiers:
American Victims of Nuclear Experiments*
(Boston: Beacon Press, 1980), pp. 64–65.

9. Among them was a young Corporal Max
Frankel, a budding reporter then in the
army. In 1955 he wrote about the classi-

fied test of a tactical nuclear weapon at the Nevada Test Site with the military's blessing to help boost the weapons' budget. The incident helped shape Frankel's attitude toward government secrecy and nuclear security. Frankel, a Pulitzer Prize–winning reporter, was the *Times*'s executive editor from 1986 to 1994.

10. Wasserman and Solomon, *Killing Our Own*, p. 47.

Chapter 3. The *New York Times*, the Token

1. Nan Robertson, *The Girls in the Balcony: Women, Men, and The New York Times* (New York: Ballantine Books, 1992).

2. Ibid. p. 182.

3. "Women and the *New York Times*," *Media Report to Women* 6 (December 31, 1978): 7.

4. Blair Jackson, "Traffic's 'Dear Mr. Fantasy,' " Mix Online, February 1, 2003, http://mixonline.com/recording/interviews /audio_traffics_dear_mr/.

5. The project was known for the hill on which it was to be situated: Nebi Samuel. My paper on the successful campaign to reduce its scale and design — which succeeded with US government assistance —

was well received by my adviser at the Woodrow Wilson School, Richard Ullman, a professor and eminent scholar who greatly influenced my early thinking about the Middle East and US foreign policy. Ullman died at age eighty in March 2014 after a long battle with Parkinson's disease.

Chapter 4. The Washington Bureau

1. Robertson, *The Girls in the Balcony.* Nan's book contained examples of sexism at the *Times,* of which most young women at the paper today are probably not aware. Dan Schwarz, the Sunday editor, had responded to the London bureau's recommendation that a young woman be hired by asking "What does she look like? Twiggy? Lynn Redgrave? Perhaps you ought to send over her vital statistics, or a picture in a bikini?" Another file quoted by Nan contained an assessment of a woman in the circulation department: "Good at short-hand and typing," wrote Robert MacDougall. "Her chief ambition is probably to get married. Has a good figure and is not restrained about dressing it to advantage."
2. Ibid., p. 195.

3. Edwin Diamond, "Crashing the Boys' Club at *The New York Times*," *American Journalism Review* (April 1992). Diamond's own book about the paper, *Behind the Times* (New York: Villard Books, 1994), contains insightful accounts of discrimination toward women and minorities and other internal sources of dissension.

4. Max Frankel, *The Times of My Life and My Life with "The Times"* (New York: Random House, 1999).

5. Arthur Gelb, *City Room* (New York: G. P. Putnam's Sons, 2003), p. 573.

6. Jeff would later be criticized — unfairly, I thought — by some colleagues and liberal Democrats for having broken the story on President Clinton's Whitewater property, in which the Clintons had invested and lost money.

7. After leaving the *Times* to make a fortune, Rattner became a major fund-raiser for the Democrats, became President Obama's "car czar," and rescued ailing General Motors. But he was punished for his alleged role in a "pay-to-play" scandal involving his former investment banking firm, Quadrangle. Without admitting or denying SEC charges of wrongdoing, he paid a multimillion-dollar fine. He was

also banned from appearing "in any capacity before any public pension fund within the State of New York for five years," *New York* magazine reported, and from "associating with any investment adviser or broker dealer" for two years. Despite Rattner's long association with the *Times,* the paper gave front-page coverage to the scandal. He considered the coverage pejorative, slanted against him, and unfair. But he has remained close to Arthur Sulzberger, the publisher and his long-standing friend.

8. Susan E. Tifft and Alex S. Jones, *The Trust: The Private and Powerful Family Behind "The New York Times"* (Boston: Little, Brown, 1999), p. 560.

Chapter 5. Becoming a "Timesman"

1. Les and I remained close friends until his death in 1995. When Jason Epstein and I finally decided in 1993 to marry, Les was President Bill Clinton's secretary of defense. I told Les about my decision over breakfast in his conference room at the Pentagon. Three months later, President Clinton asked for his resignation following the death of American soldiers in Somalia. Suffering from a congenital heart problem,

Les never really recovered. After Les's death, Dick Holbrooke badgered the White House into hosting a memorial service for him, which it did reluctantly.

Chapter 6. Egypt: Foreign Correspondent

1. Eric M. Hammel, *The Root: The Marines in Beirut, August 1982–February 1984* (New York: Harcourt Brace Jovanovich, 1985), p. 303.
2. Judith Miller, "Reagan Declares Marines' Role in 'Vital' to Counter Soviet in Lebanon: Toll at 192," *New York Times,* October 25, 1983, www.nytimes.com/1983/10/25/world/reagan-declares-marines-role-in-vital-to-counter-soviet-in-lebanon-toll-at-192.html.
3. American intelligence would eventually identify the suicide bomber as Ismail Ascari, an Iranian national. But this information, along with the extent of Iranian complicity in the attack, would not be known to the public until 2003, when a victim of the attack sued the Islamic Republic of Iran in a US District Court in the District of Columbia. See *Peterson, et al. v. Islamic Republic, et al.*
4. A more detailed account of my trip through southern Lebanon is contained in

God Has Ninety-nine Names: Reporting from a Militant Middle East (New York: Simon & Schuster, 2006), pp. 253–58, my book describing the growth of militant Islamic movements in ten Middle Eastern countries.

5. *Report of the DOD Commission on Beirut International Airport Terrorist Act, October 23, 1983* (Washington, DC: US Government Printing Office, 1984), http://fas.org/irp/threat/beirut-1983.pdf.

Chapter 7. From the Nile to the Seine

1. Judith Miller, "Economy Gives Saudis Growing Pains," *New York Times,* November 2, 1983, www.nytimes.com/1983/11/27/weekinreview/economy-gives-saudis-growing-pains.html.
2. Judith Miller, "A Saudi Amnesty Frees Half of Jailed Americans," *New York Times,* August 4, 1984, www.nytimes.com/1984/08/04/world/ a-saudi-amnesty-frees-half-of-jailed-americans.html.
3. This description of my life in and love for Egypt can be found in *God Has Ninety-nine Names,* pp. 19–83.
4. Judith Miller, "Refugees Are Hostages of Lebanon Talks," *New York Times,* November 2, 1983, www.nytimes.com/1983/11/

02/world/refugees-are-hostages-of-lebanon-talks-1.html.

5. Judith Miller, "A Mideast Odyssey," *New York Times Magazine,* August 13, 1984, www.nytimes.com/1984/08/13/magazine/a-mideast-odyssey.html.

6. Judith Miller, "Erasing the Past: Europe's Amnesia About the Holocaust," *New York Times Magazine,* November 16, 1986, www.nytimes.com/1986/11/16/magazine/erasing-the-past-europe-s-amnesia-about-the-holocaust.html.

Chapter 8. "Be Careful What You Wish For": Washington News Editor

1. Frankel, *The Times of My Life.*

2. Howell Raines, *The One That Got Away: A Memoir* (New York: Lisa Drew/Scribner, 2006), p. 33.

3. Gerald M. Boyd, *My Times in Black and White: Race and Power at the "New York Times"* (Chicago: Lawrence Hill Books, 2010), p. 138.

Chapter 9. The Gulf War

1. Miller, *God Has Ninety-nine Names,* p. 118.

2. More detailed descriptions of Bin Laden's

conduct and state of mind in his meetings with Saudi princes would later be reported by Douglas Jehl in the *New York Times,* December 27, 2001, and by Steve Coll in his book on Bin Laden and the CIA's involvement in Afghanistan, *Ghost Wars: The Secret History of the CIA, Afghanistan, and Bin Laden, from the Soviet Invasion to September 10, 2001* (New York: Penguin, 2004), pp. 222–23.

3. Coll, *Ghost Wars,* p. 528.

4. Judith Miller, "Israel Says That a Prisoner's Tale Links Arabs in U.S. to Terrorism," *New York Times,* February 17, 1993, www.nytimes.com/1993/02/17/world/israel-says-that-a-prisoner-s-tale-links-arabs-in-us-to-terrorism.html.

Chapter 10. Terror in Tiny Packages

1. Ken Alibek with Stephen Handelman, *Biohazard: The Chilling True Story of the Largest Covert Biological Weapons Program in the World — Told from Inside by the Man Who Ran It* (New York: Delta Books, 1999). This book was one of the first insider accounts of the Soviet program. Alibek said he had written it to counter what he called the "alarming level of ignorance about biological weapons" that

he had encountered since his defection from Moscow.

2. The same conclusion would be reached by Amy E. Smithson, a biological weapons expert at the Washington, DC, office of the James Martin Center for Nonproliferation Studies, whom Bill and I quoted often. Her book, *Germ Gambits: The Bioweapons Dilemma, Iraq and Beyond* (Stanford, CA: Stanford University Press, 2011), a study of UNSCOM's activities in Iraq, was published thirteen years after our article.

3. William J. Broad and Judith Miller, "The Deal on Iraq: Secret Arsenal: The Hunt for the Germs of War — A Special Report; Iraq's Deadliest Arms: Puzzles Breed Fears," *New York Times,* February 26, 1998, www.nytimes.com/1998/02/26/world/deal-iraq-secret-arsenal-hunt-for-germs-war-special-report-iraq-s-deadliest-arms.html. A similar account is contained in Judith Miller, Stephen Engelberg, William Broad, *Germs: Biological Weapons and America's Secret War* (New York: Simon & Schuster, 2001), p. 183.

4. Judith Miller with William J. Broad, "The Germ Warriors: A Special Report; Iranians, Bioweapons in Mind, Lure Needy Ex-Soviet Scientists," *New York Times,*

December 8, 1998, www.nytimes.com/ 1998/12/08/world/ germ-warriors-special-report-iranians-bioweapons-mind-lure-needy-ex-soviet.html.

5. Judith Miller, "Poison Island: A Special Report; At Bleak Asian Site, Killer Germs Survive," *New York Times,* June 2, 1999, www.nytimes.com/1999/06/02/world/ poison-island-a-special-report-at-bleak-asian-site-killer-germs-survive.html.

Chapter 11. Al Qaeda

1. Judith Miller and William J. Broad, "Clinton Describes Terrorism Threat for 21st Century," *New York Times,* January 22, 1999, www.nytimes.com/1999/01/22/ world/ clinton-describes-terrorism-threat-for-21st-century.html.

2. Bill Clinton, *My Life* (New York: Knopf, 2004), pp. 833–34.

3. *Wag the Dog* is a 1997 black comedy film starring Robert De Niro as a Washington spin doctor who distracts the electorate from a presidential sex scandal shortly before an election by teaming with a Hollywood producer (played by Dustin Hoffman) to start a fake war with Albania, complete with fabricated film footage. The film, an enormous hit whose title quickly

became part of the nation's political lexicon, came out just before the Monica Lewinsky scandal erupted and Clinton bombed the Al Shifa pharmaceutical factory in Sudan. Clinton's critics lost no time in calling the controversial military strike a "wag the dog" action.

4. William J. Broad and Judith Miller, "Attack on Iraq: The Arms Monitors; Iraq Said to Hide Deadly Germ Agents," *New York Times,* December 17, 1998, www.ny times.com/1998/12/17/world/attack-on-iraq-the-arms-monitors-iraq-said-to-hide-deadly-germ-agents.html.

5. Barbara Crossette, Judith Miller, Steven Lee Myers, and Tim Weiner, "After the Attacks: The Overview; U.S. Says Iraq Aided the Production of Chemical Weapons in Sudan," *New York Times,* August 25, 1998, www.nytimes.com/1998/08/25/world/after-attacks-overview-us-says-iraq-aided-production-chemical-weapons-sudan.html. Precisely what was being done at the Al Shifa plant remains in dispute. Sudan and the plant owner denied that any illicit chemicals were being produced there. And US officials acknowledged later that the evidence that prompted the strike was not as credible as first claimed. But Washington never of-

ficially rejected the possibility that Al Shifa was linked in some way to chemical weapons.

6. Charles Duelfer's report revealed later that several senior French and Russian officials had taken bribes from Saddam's regime, which may have accounted in part for their opposition to stronger UN sanctions and other measures against him. *Comprehensive Report of the Special Advisor to the DCI on Iraq's WMD* (Washington, DC: Central Intelligence Agency, September 30, 2004), https://www.cia.gov/library/reports/general-reports-1/iraq_wmd_2004/.

7. Peter Bergen, "My 18 Year Odyssey on the Trail of Osama bin Laden," *New Republic,* August 24, 2011, www.tnr.com/article/world/magazine/94159/ september-11-chasing-al-qaeda#.

8. Ahmed Rashid, *Taliban: Militant Islam, Oil, and Fundamentalism in Central Asia* (New Haven, CT: Yale University Press, 2001).

9. Camelia Fard and James Ridgeway, "The Accidental Operative: Richard Helms's Afghani Niece Leads Corps of Taliban Reps," *Village Voice,* June 12, 2001, www.villagevoice.com/content/printVersion/164992.

Chapter 12. Ashes and Anthrax: The Shadow of 9/11

1. Jason Epstein played a role in helping Philip Zelikow secure the broadest possible readership for what all three of us sensed early on would be a historic report. Over one of our occasional dinners with him when he was visiting New York and just starting his investigation, Jason encouraged Philip to contract with a commercial publisher to produce an instant version of the final report rather than rely on the US Government Printing Office, which had limited ability to publish complex documents quickly and widely and disseminate them cheaply. Jason recommended W. W. Norton and introduced Philip to Drake McFeely, the head of Norton. Philip wound up selecting Norton to publish the 567-page report. It was an inspired choice. The 9/11 Commission report was a huge bestseller.

2. Paul R. Pillar, *Terrorism and U.S. Foreign Policy* Washington, DC: Brookings Institution, 2001). Bound galleys of the book, which was published in April, before 9/11, argue that terrorism, though likely to remain a significant challenge for the United States, must be managed rather

than defeated. He argues that assassination "should not be relied on as a counter-terrorist instrument" and belittles the danger of WMD terrorism (which he calls CBRN, for "chemical, biological, radiological, or nuclear) as overrated or "much-ballyhooed." A later book *Intelligence and U.S. Foreign Policy* (New York: Columbia University Press, 2011) accuses the Bush administration of deciding on war in Iraq without an orderly decision-making process, successfully pressuring analysts to distort their estimates and, in general, of politicizing intelligence. In a review of the book, Carl W. Ford, Jr., the former director of the State Department's intelligence unit, whose Iraqi WMD estimates proved most accurate of all the agencies, strongly disputes Pillar's thesis. With respect to the WMD estimates, he argues, the problem was not pressure but poor quality. "I believe that the image depicted in the book of intelligence officers bending to pressure applied by hard headed, opinionated policy-makers is highly exaggerated," he writes in a review for H-Diplo/ISSF, *Roundtable* 3, No. 15 (June 2012), http://h-diplo.org/ISSF/PDF/ISSF-Roundtable-3-15 pdf.

3. The unusual CIA office was called the

"Alec" station after the son of its first chief, Michael Scheuer.

4. Seth Mnookin, *Hard News: Twenty-one Brutal Months at "The New York Times" and How They Changed the American Media* (New York: Random House, 2005), p. 61. He quotes the *New Yorker* story on the paper's September 12, 2001, coverage as having devoted 82,500 words to its coverage of the attack.

5. Murray Weiss, *The Man Who Warned America: The Life and Death of John O'Neill, the FBI's Embattled Counterterror Warrior* (New York: ReganBooks, 2003). Weiss's book was among the first to examine the life of a man whose professional life was defined by his effort to persuade the US government that Bin Laden posed a grave threat to the American homeland and to take his warnings and growing capabilities seriously. Weiss pays tribute to this admittedly complex man, warts and all, in a book that is dedicated to O'Neill, a man he described as a friend, and to the other victims of 9/11.

6. Condoleezza Rice, *No Higher Honor: A Memoir of My Years in Washington* (New York: Crown, 2011), p. 98.

7. Condoleezza Rice, interview, December 19, 2001.

8. Ibid.; *No Higher Honor,* pp. 101–3.

9. Ibid., p. 101.

10. William J. Broad and Judith Miller, "A Nation Challenged: The Bacteria; Officials, Expanding Search, Warn Against Drawing Conclusions on Anthrax Source," *New York Times,* October 26, 2001, www.nytimes.com/2001/10/26/us/nation-challenged-bacteria-officials-expanding-search-warn-against-drawing.html; William J. Broad and Judith Miller, "A Nation Challenged: The Germ Attacks; Inquiry Includes Possibility of Killer from a U.S. Lab," *New York Times,* December 2, 2001, www.nytimes.com/2001/12/02/us/nation-challenged-germ-attacks-inquiry-includes-possibility-killer-us-lab.html.

Chapter 13. The Defector

1. Richard Bonin, *Arrows of the Night: Ahmad Chalabi's Long Journey to Triumph in Iraq* (New York: Doubleday, 2011), pp. 2–5. According to Bonin's well-sourced, highly readable account, with which Chalabi cooperated, the informal meeting at Richard Perle's house was attended by Paul Wolfowitz, who would become deputy defense secretary; Doug Feith, who would get the third-most senior Pentagon post;

Zalmay Khalilzad, who would be a special assistant to Bush and ambassador at large for Iraqi exiles; and John P. Hannah, Vice President Dick Cheney's national security adviser. I verified his account in subsequent interviews with Chalabi, Perle, Feith, Hannah, and others who'd attended the brunch.

2. Ibid., p. 106.

3. Ibid., pp. 100–16. Chalabi confirmed Bonin's detailed account of the events of 1995 and 1996 in interviews after 2003. A similar account of Chalabi's 1995 planned insurrection appeared a decade earlier in Robert Baer's *See No Evil: The True Story of a Ground Soldier in the CIA's War Against Terrorism* (New York: Random House, 2002), pp. 191–205.

4. Judith Miller and James Risen, "Tracking Baghdad's Arsenal: Inside the Arsenal: A Special Report; Defector Describes Iraq's Atom Bomb Push," *New York Times,* August 15, 1998, www.nytimes.com/1998/08/15/world/ tracking-baghdad-s-arsenal-inside-arsenal-special-report-defector-describes-iraq.html and http://www.nytimes.com/1998/08/15/world/tracking-baghdad-s-arsenal-defection-cia-almost-bungled-intelligence-coup-with.html.

5. Haideri was about to be named by Paul

Moran, an Australian freelance photojournalist, in a broadcast about his WMD claims for the Australian Broadcasting Corporation. Moran, who worked occasionally for the Rendon Group, a consulting firm that the CIA had retained to help promote Chalabi's INC, had also interviewed Haideri — though I learned that only after returning to the United States from Bangkok. According to Wikipedia, Moran was the first "international media casualty of the Iraq war." He was killed in a car bomb attack in northeastern Iraq near the border with Iran on March 22, 2003. We never met.

6. Judith Miller, "Secret Sites: An Iraqi Defector Tells of Work on At Least 20 Hidden Weapons Sites," *New York Times,* December 20, 2001, www.nytimes.com/2001/12/20/international/middleeast/20DEFE.html.

Chapter 14. Phase 2: Iraq

1. In 2002 alone, I shared bylines with nineteen reporters — most often with William Broad, my coauthor for *Germs,* as well as intelligence correspondent James Risen and David Sanger, the White House reporter.

2. Ron Suskind, *The One Percent Doctrine: Deep Inside America's Pursuit of Its Enemies Since 9/11* (New York: Simon & Schuster, 2006), pp. 61–62; George Tenet with Bill Harlow, *At the Center of the Storm: My Years at the CIA* (New York: HarperCollins, 2007), pp. 264–65; Peter Baker, *Days of Fire: Bush and Cheney in the White House* (New York: Doubleday, 2013), p. 178; Dick Cheney, interview, January 2013.

3. George W. Bush, *Decision Points* (New York: Crown, 2010), pp. 153–54.

4. Jacob Weisberg, *The Bush Tragedy* (New York: Random House, 2008), pp. 189–94. Almost a decade would pass before the FBI finally named Bruce Ivins, a US military scientist, as the likely anthrax letter culprit, and only after years of arguing, wrongly, that Steve Hatfill, a scientist and military contractor whom I had interviewed for our book *Germs,* was to blame.

5. Tenet, *At the Center of the Storm,* p. 370.

6. Explaining his own vote in October 2002 to support the use of force in Iraq, John Kerry said he believed that "a deadly arsenal of weapons of mass destruction in his hands is a real and grave threat to our security." Hillary Clinton, too, who had not read the classified version of the NIE,

echoed the Bush administration's claims. She asserted repeatedly that Saddam "had given aid, comfort, and sanctuary to terrorists, including Al Qaeda members," and that he was determined to increase his stockpile of germ and chemical weapons and "keep trying to develop nuclear weapons."

7. One of the many paradoxes of this saga is Scooter Libby's opposition to issuing the National Security Study Directives (NSSD) in the fall of 2002. Libby argued at interagency meetings — futilely, it seems — that the national security doctrine would be interpreted by Bush's critics as justification for the war in Iraq. Libby, speaking on behalf of the vice president's office, argued that the rationale for the war was not preventive war but Iraq's failure to adhere to its UN WMD and antiterror commitments, as illustrated by sixteen UN resolutions criticizing Iraq.

8. Baker, *Days of Fire,* p. 213.

9. President Bush and others have discussed what he called Powell's "passionate" warning about the potential consequences of an Iraq discussion in their one-on-one White House meeting. One of the best third-party accounts of the so-called Pottery Barn meeting is in Peter Baker's book

Days of Fire, pp. 207–8, in which Powell lists the possible adverse effects as the "cost to international unity, the possibility of oil price spikes, the potential destabilization of Saudi Arabia, and other allies in the region." An invasion, he warned, would "suck all the oxygen out of Bush's term . . . and would mean Bush would effectively be responsible for a shattered country, for twenty-five million people and all their hopes and aspirations."

10. Ronald I. Christie, interview, February 2014.

11. Frank P. Harvey, *Explaining the Iraq War: Counterfactual Theory, Logic and Evidence* (Cambridge: Cambridge University Press, 2012), pp. 70–76; Stephen F. Knott, *Rush to Judgment: George W. Bush, the War on Terror, and His Critics* (Lawrence: University Press of Kansas, 2012), pp. 138–40. The books contain numerous prowar quotes from leading Democrats who would later backpedal their support for the Iraq War.

12. Rand Beers was the only senior White House official I knew who quit his National Security Council staff job over Iraq, though Condi Rice later told several top aides that Beers, who then began working for Kerry's 2004 presidential campaign,

had denied in his exit interview with her that Iraq was the cause. Richard A. Clarke, in his book *Against All Enemies: Inside America's War on Terror* (New York: Free Press, 2004, p. 241), says Beers quit over Iraq.

13. Jack S. Levy, "Preventive War and Democratic Politics," *International Studies Quarterly* 52, no. 1 (March 2008): 1–24. Levy clearly articulates a distinction that is widely agreed upon by legal scholars and academics but less so by White House speechwriters and journalists between "preemptive war," in which the initiator acts against imminent aggression, and "preventive war," which he defines as a "strategy designed to forestall an adverse shift in the balance of power and driven by better-now-than-later logic." While many who wrote about the Bush doctrine asserted that Bush had endorsed preemptive war, he was, in fact, embracing the legitimacy of unilateral, aggressive prevention. I'm indebted to Philip Zelikow for my initial tutorial on this and other subjects.

14. Harvey, *Explaining the Iraq War,* p. 7.

15. Baker, *Days of Fire,* p. 210. In an interview, James Baker III makes clear to the author, who is no relation, that he was

opposed to Cheney's alleged preference for going to war alone, but not to the war itself, unlike his former fellow Bush Sr. colleague, Brent Scowcroft, who blindsided Bush '43 by opposing an invasion in an op-ed in the *New York Times* in the summer of 2002.

16. Former deputy UNSCOM inspector Charles Duelfer initially made this argument.

17. Judith Miller, "A Nation Challenged: Diplomacy; In Visit to U.S., Kuwaitis Support Action on Iraq," *New York Times,* February 3, 2002, www.nytimes.com/ 2002/02/03/world/a-nation-challenged- diplomacy-in-visit-to-us-kuwaitis-support- action-on-iraq.html.

Chapter 15. "Where's Waldo?" The Hunt for WMD in Iraq

1. These restrictions applied to all reporters embedded in units or headquarters that dealt routinely with classified information, but critics would later write, inaccurately, that I had accepted unusual military censorship of my stories in exchange for access. No one who printed or broadcast that allegation ever spoke to me for comment — a basic rule of fair-minded, objec-

tive journalism. Unlike many of my colleagues, I refused to sign a standard embed agreement for reporters with access to classified information that would have enabled a commander to review my notes. I scratched out that portion of the agreement before signing it. I do not know if other reporters did the same.

2. Coalition Forces Land Component Command (CFLCC) OPLAN COBRA II, ORCON Rel MCFT//X4, Camp Doha, Kuwait, February, 1, 2003.

3. Deeply religious and allied with an Iranian-linked political party, Shahristani would later be tasked with restoring his country's oil sector.

4. A year later, I would learn that, if anything, my story, which several critics had cited as an example of my stories that had exaggerated the risk of WMD, had underestimated Iraq's quest for atropine. In 2004, Charles Duelfer, the former weapons inspector and leader of the Iraq Survey Group's hunt for WMD in Iraq, reported in his landmark study that by September 2002, Iraq had bought over nine hundred thousand of the antidote auto-injectors. See Charles Duelfer, "Table, Regime Strategy and WMD Timeline Events," in *Comprehensive Report of*

the Special Advisor to the DCI on Iraq's WMD, September 30, 2004, www.cia.gov/library/reports/general-reports-1/iraq_wmd_2004/WMD_Timeline_Events.html.

5. I never learned whether Abbas's charges or the report that MET Alpha filed on it had played a role in the substance or timing of the president's statement. In interviews years after the war, senior White House officials involved in nonproliferation told me they could not recall what specifically had triggered Bush's warning. Robert Joseph, the NSC point man on nonproliferation, said that the White House had been receiving myriad reports around that time expressing concern that WMD stockpiles might not be found. He said he did not remember reading a report from the XTF from Abbas. "There was a ton of material flowing in at that time," Joseph said in an interview in mid-2013.

Chapter 16. The Revolt

1. Gellman's brief embed did not end happily. The XTF's senior officers wrote an angry letter to the *Washington Post* complaining about alleged errors in his stories. Col. Michael Endres, who died of natural causes in 2012, shared the letter with me.

2. Judith Miller, Michael Moss, and Lowell Bergman, "Leading Exile Figure Draws Mixed Reviews," *New York Times,* April 10, 2003, www.nytimes.com/2003/04/10/international/worldspecial/10OPPO.html.

3. Shortly before I left New York, Rick Bragg, a national correspondent who had been one of Howell's favorites, was suspended for two weeks for having failed to disclose that a year-old story carrying his byline had been reported mainly by a stringer. Rick had blasted the paper's decision in an interview with Howard Kurtz of the *Post.* Most *Times* correspondents, he asserted, relied on stringers, researchers, interns, and others. My colleagues erupted in indignant fury, demanding Bragg's ouster. Instead, he quit. Howell issued a terse notice to the staff saying that Rick Bragg had "offered his resignation, and I have accepted it."

Chapter 17. The War Within

1. Boyd, *My Times in Black and White.*
2. Ibid., p. 280.
3. Rod Barton, *The Weapons Detective: The Inside Story of Australia's Top Weapons Inspector* (Melbourne, Australia: Black Inc. Agenda, 2006), p. 145; Tom Mangold and

Jeff Goldberg, *Plague Wars: A True Story of Biological Weapons* (London: Macmillan, 1999), p. 307.

4. Mangold and Goldberg, *Plague Wars,* p. 288.

5. Judith Miller, "Threats and Responses: Germ Weapons; C.I.A. Hunts Iraq Ties to Soviet Smallpox," *New York Times,* December 3, 2002, www.nytimes.com/2002/12/03/world/threats-and-responses-germ-weapons-cia-hunts-iraq-tie-to-soviet-smallpox.html.

6. See, among others, Jack Shafer, "Reassessing Miller," *Slate,* May 29, 2003, www.slate10.com/articles/news_and_politics/press_box/2003/05; shreassessing_miller.html. See also Herbert L. Abrams, "Weapons of Miller's Descriptions," *Bulletin of the Atomic Scientists* 60, no. 4 (July 2004): 56–64.

7. By then, I had told Gerald that another group — Task Force 20, an intelligence-driven unit — was also scouring the country for WMD-related scientists and programs. Perhaps I could find a way to follow them, Gerald suggested, though so far the military had not even permitted reporters to mention the existence of such a group.

8. Judith Miller, "After the War: Unconven-

tional Arms; A Chronicle of Confusion in the U.S. Hunt for Hussein's Chemical and Germ Weapons," *New York Times,* July 20, 2003, www.nytimes.com/2003/07/20/ world/ after-war-unconventional-arms-chronicle-confusion-us-hunt-for-hussein-s-chemical.html. See also Barton, *The Weapons Detective.* In 2006, Rod Barton, an Australian biologist and weapons inspector who had worked for UNSCOM and the Iraq Survey Group under David Kay and Charles Duelfer, summarized what he thought were the principal weaknesses of the XTF, in which I was embedded. First, he noted, the task force was comprised of "U.S. military personnel with little knowledge of WMD" and only "a few technical specialists" from the Pentagon. But the root cause was a faulty assumption, he writes: "Everyone in the U.S. Administration was so certain that weapons were there that the 75th ETF's [*sic*] instructions were simply to 'search and find.' No one saw any need to conduct a more systematic investigation" (Barton, p. 230).

9. In an interview in July 2014, Howard Kurtz, who now works at Fox News, where I also work part-time as a contributor, said that he stood by his sources.

10. The rest of Petraeus's email states as follows: "I did what I thought was the right thing at the time to help facilitate the search for possible WMD at a critical time in that effort. MET-Alpha had leads to run down, as you well know; some of them were potentially perishable, and they sure couldn't have pursued them in Kuwait."

11. "Iraq's Weapons of Mass Destruction: The Assessment of the British Government," September 24, 2002, http://www.publications.parliament.uk/pa/cm200102/cmhansrd/vo020924/debtext/20924-07.htm.

Chapter 18. Correcting the Record

1. Juan Cole, "Judy Miller and the Neocons," *Salon,* October 14, 2005, www.salon.com/2005/10/14/neocon_4.

2. Robert Jervis, *Why Intelligence Fails: Lessons from the Iranian Revolution and the Iraq War* (Ithaca, NY: Cornell University Press), p. 150. Jervis, who was part of a small group that the CIA asked to explore the WMD failure in Iraq and to recommend steps to avoid repetitions, shared this and other insights with me in an interview at Columbia University in 2012,

where he teaches international politics. His book is the most balanced analysis about the WMD intelligence disaster.

3. Patrick E. Tyler and John Tagliabue, "Czechs Confirm Iraqi Agent Met with Terror Ringleader," *New York Times,* October 27, 2001, www.nytimes.com/2001/10/27/international/europe/27IRAQ.html.

4. For one of several efforts by fellow journalists to push me into expressing a personal view about the war, see Richard D. Heffner, on *Open Mind,* a conversation aired by PBS about *Germs: Biological Weapons and America's Secret War,* November 6, 2002, http://video.pbs.org/video/2047213129.

5. Bill Keller, "The I-Can't-Believe-I'm-a-Hawk Club," *New York Times,* February 8, 2003, www.nytimes.com/2003/02/08/opinion/the-i-can-t-believe-i-m-a-hawk-club.html.

6. *Times* rules are strict with respect to what reporters can say publicly about the subjects they cover, and even topics they don't cover. As a columnist, he had been entitled to express that view, but he had not yet retracted or apologized for that stance, either. As a reporter, I was barred only from expressing a view publicly.

7. There was no investigations editor for much of the prewar period. Investigations chief Steve Engelberg, my *Germs* coauthor, who had edited my article on engineer Haideri with his usual skepticism and thoroughness, had left the paper in June 2002. Doug Frantz, his successor, had taken over in October 2002 and resigned after a six-month stint to join the *L.A. Times*. Matt Purdy, whom I liked and respected, became editor only in January 2004, long after the articles had run. In any event, an investigative "exclusive" from Washington would rarely be sent to New York without a light edit by the bureau and its approval.

8. Judith Miller and William J. Broad, "Some Analysts of Iraq Trailers Reject Germ Use," *New York Times*, June 7, 2003, www.nytimes.com/2003/06/07/world/some-analysts-of-iraq-trailers-reject-germ-use.html?scp=22&sq=&st=nyt.

9. Judith Miller, "U.S. Aides Say Iraqi Truck Could Be a Germ-War Lab," *New York Times*, May 8, 2003, www.nytimes.com/2003/05/08/international/worldspecial/08WEAP.html; Judith Miller and William J. Broad, "Aftereffects: Germ Weapons; U.S. Analysts Link Iraq Labs to

Germ Arms," *New York Times,* May 21, 2003, www.nytimes.com/2003/05/21/world/aftereffects-germ-weapons-us-analysts-link-iraq-labs-to-germ-arms.html; Miller and Broad, "Some Analysts of Iraq Trailers Reject Germ Use."

10. Three of Jim Risen's seven prewar articles on the administration's handling of intelligence on Iraq refer to debates about whether Iraq intended to use aluminum tubes it bought in a nuclear program or for other purposes. But Risen also wrote (with David Johnston) on February 2, 2003, that unidentified "officials" were saying that the United States had obtained "communications intercepts that show Iraqi officials coaching scientists in how to avoid providing valuable information about Iraq's weapons programs to inspectors." See James Risen and David Johnston, "Split at C.I.A. and F.B.I. on Iraqi Ties to Al Qaeda," *New York Times,* February 2, 2003, www.nytimes.com/2003/02/02/international/middleeast/02INTE.html. Long after the war, I learned that Jill Abramson had refused to run the one prewar story Jim wrote that cast doubt on the WMD estimates, a decision for which she later apologized in print. Jill Abramson, "The Final Days," *New York Times,*

September 26, 2008, www.nytimes.com/ 2008/09/28/books/review/ Abramson-t.html?pagewanted=all&_r=0.

11. Al Gore, September 23, 2002, speech before the Commonwealth Club of San Francisco, http://www.washingtonpost .com/wp-srv/politics/transcripts/gore_text 092302.html.

12. John Lott, "What Democrats Said Early on About the Threat that Saddam Hussein Posed," Johnrlott.tripod.com/other/ WhatDemsSaidEarlyOnIraq.html.

13. Hans Blix, *Disarming Iraq* (London: Bloomsbury, 2004).

14. Paradoxically, Pentagon Secretary Donald Rumsfeld struck one of the few official cautionary notes about WMD intelligence in a memo famously titled the "Parade of Horribles." In mid-October 2002, he highlighted the risk that WMD might not be found in the event of war in Iraq. See Douglas J. Feith, *War and Decision: Inside the Pentagon at the Dawn of the War on Terrorism* (New York: HarperCollins, 2008), p. 352.

15. Will Tobey, interview, March 2012; Colin Powell with Tony Kolitz, *It Worked for Me: In Life and Leadership* (New York: Harper, 2012), p. 223.

16. Though INR proved correct in its

doubts about Saddam's nuclear intentions and capabilities, the State Department's intelligence unit has traditionally been the smallest of the intelligence agencies and the least influential, given its record of having underestimated the capabilities and intentions of several WMD aspiring states.

17. The memoirs of Bush, Cheney, Condi Rice, and other key players in the Bush White House contain no suggestion that CIA director George Tenet doubted that Saddam had chemical and biological weapons and an active nuclear program. In an interview, Dick Cheney said that Tenet had never given him any reason to doubt the accuracy of the NIE and its other reporting on Iraqi WMD. But Les Gelb, a former State Department official and *New York Times* columnist, who headed the Council on Foreign Relations during the Iraq War, said that he believed Tenet had doubts about the WMD estimates. In an interview in March 2014, Gelb said that several months before the invasion, he had met privately with Tenet, whom he had known for many years, and asked him whether he had "smoking gun" evidence that Saddam Hussein had retained chem-bio weapons and was continuing work on an atomic bomb. Tenet

said no. Gelb told me that he interpreted Tenet's statement as confirmation that the evidence underlying the NIE's WMD claims was shakier than the CIA and other intelligence agencies had led the White House and American citizens to believe.

18. Jervis, *Why Intelligence Fails,* p. 143. Jervis, moreover, points out that the CIA and the Energy Department had a "history of strong disagreement" about centrifuges in general dating back a decade or more, which would also explain, at least in part, why an interagency group charged with resolving technical disputes never did so.
19. The Commission on the Intelligence Capabilities of the United States Regarding Weapons of Mass Destruction, *Report to the President of the United States, March 31, 2005,* pp. 55–56, http://govinfo.library .unt.edu/wmd/report/report.html#chapter 1.
20. Bob Woodward, *State of Denial: Bush at War,* part 3 (New York: Simon & Schuster, 2006), p. 278.
21. Robert G. Kaiser, " 'Now They Tell Us': An Exchange," *New York Review of Books,* March 25, 2004, www.nybooks.com/ articles/archives/2004/mar/25/now-they-tell-us-an-exchange.
22. Though Massing accused us of having

fingered Iraq as the bio attack's likely culprit, the record shows that Steve, Bill, and I were among the first to cast doubt on Iraq as the likely perpetrator. There was little substantial evidence "linking Iraq to the Sept. 11 attacks or to anthrax bioterrorism," we wrote in October 2001. See William J. Broad and Judith Miller, "A Nation Challenged: The Investigation; Anthrax Itself May Point to Origin of Letter Sent to Daschle," *New York Times,* October 18, 2001, www.nytimes.com/2001/10/18/us/nation-challenged-investigation-anthrax-itself-may-point-origin-letter-sent.html.

23. Michael Gordon, " 'Iraq: Now They Tell Us': An Exchange," *New York Review of Books,* April 8, 2004, www.nybooks.com/articles/archives/2004/apr/08/iraq-now-they-tell-us-an-exchange/?pagination=false.

Chapter 19. Scapegoat

1. Howell Raines, email message to author, March 5, 2013.
2. In my meeting with Keller and Jill Abramson the week before the editor's note was published, I had warned them against getting out ahead of the experts who were

still trying to determine the fate of the Iraqi unconventional weapons for which Saddam had not yet accounted. My warning was based on conversations with David Kay and Charles Duelfer, the respective former and current chiefs of the American WMD hunt in Iraq. Both were widely regarded as independent experts, given their earlier work for UNSCOM, the international inspectors initially charged with monitoring Iraq's disarmament pledges.

3. Sonya Moore, "Sulzberger on Blair, Miller, Getting a Job at the 'Times,' " *Editor & Publisher,* March 22, 2004, www.editor andpublisher.com/Article/Sulzberger-on-Blair-Miller-Getting-a-Job-at-the-Times-.
4. Jack Shafer, "Press Secretary Sulzberger," *Slate,* November 11, 2005, www.slate .com/articles/news_and_politics/press_box/2005/11/press_secretary_sulzb erger.html. In one of his many assaults on me, Jack Shafer reported erroneously both the number of articles the editor's note had featured as well as the number I had written or coauthored. "Nine of the 11 flawed stories highlighted in the 'From the Editors' note are by Miller or co-bylined by her," Shafer wrote. Nor was he the only media critic who had had apparent dif-

ficulty counting. Yet another example, one of several, was an article published on October 21, 2005, in a magazine called *In These Times*. Entitled "Lies Judith Miller Told Us," Joel Bleifuss, a former director of the Peace Studies Program at the University of Missouri-Columbia, and the publication's editor and publisher, wrote that Keller had cited "six faulty stories about the threat posed by Iraq, all but one of which was written or cowritten" by me.

5. Okrent was the first journalist to occupy a post that the paper had created under pressure in response to the Jayson Blair fiasco. Billing himself as the "readers' representative," Okrent described himself as an outsider. *Times* reporters did not discuss our sources or reporting techniques with outsiders.

6. In an email, Howell Raines told me that Okrent had never contacted him — or Gerald Boyd, he believed — to discuss the editing of my stories, my many wrangles with the military during my embed, and about what the paper had done at the government's request to protect al-Husayni and other Iraqi informants, credible or not, whose lives were then in jeopardy because of their cooperation with Washington.

7. In an interview in the spring of 2013, Ford told me that the CIA had deliberately suppressed information contradicting its conclusions that should have been shared with his Bureau of Intelligence and Research analysts and with other intelligence agencies. He had not learned until he read the Senate Intelligence Committee and Robb-Silberman commission reports years after the invasion, he told me, that a centrifuge model that a CIA contractor had built to show that the tubes could spin efficiently had broken down after only a few hours of operation and could not be made to work again. Nor had the CIA shared with him and his analysts the results of interviews with Iraqi-Americans it had sent back home to Iraq to visit relatives who were believed to have worked in Saddam's WMD programs. After their return, virtually all of them had told the CIA that their relatives claimed to no longer be involved in such work. Such information would normally have forced the CIA to include the missing qualifiers in the intelligence estimates, he told me. "Instead, they kept telling us: 'This is rock solid,' " Ford recalled. "They lied," he told me.

8. In an email to me almost a decade later,

Howell Raines criticized Okrent for having joined Keller in accusing him and Gerald Boyd of having relaxed standards for favored reporters such as me, which he called "categorically untrue." Moreover, Raines complained, Okrent had never contacted him or Gerald for comment before he wrote his essay. Nor had Keller before publishing his own editor's note, Raines said. As a result, neither the editor's note nor Okrent's column gave readers any insight into the difficult judgment calls he and Boyd had made about what to publish or not publish — often to protect American or Iraqi HUMINT, the Iraqi weapons scientists whose cooperation with Washington had put them in jeopardy once the *Times* disclosed it.

"My old newspaper used to believe that a person had to be contacted in advance every time he or she was named as an actor in a news story," Howell wrote. Okrent's failure was a "violation of basic reporting principles." Only a handful of the dozens of journalists who had written blogs or articles had contacted me, either, for comment in advance of publishing their stories. Jack Shafer, for instance, who had written six personal attacks for the online *Slate* on what he had called my "wretched" Iraq reporting, had never once sought a response from me. For Shafer and others like him, buzz and internet clicks were what mattered, not truth or journalistic principle. This was the "new journalism."

9. The most detailed description of the allegations against Chalabi are in Bonin, *Arrows of the Night,* pp. 234–44.

Chapter 20. Protecting Sources

1. Several officials in the Bush White House opposed the retraction vehemently, arguing, presciently, that it would provide fodder to critics who claimed that senior officials had lied the country to war. This minority argued that the president's statement was accurate, especially because it attributed the claim that Iraq had sought uranium in Niger to Britain, which continued to stand by the claim. So retracting the statement risked antagonizing Britain, America's closest ally in the Iraq War. In a telephone interview as late as October 2013, Richard Dearlove, the former head of MI6, Britain's chief spy agency, continued to stand by the claim but refused to reveal why British intelligence officials continued to believe it. Two independent

British inquiries have also stood by the claim.

2. Walter Pincus, a veteran national security reporter who had gone to law school in his spare time, disclosed eventually that he had agreed to testify about what his source had said without specifically identifying the source, who testified separately before the grand jury. Robert Novak, who had outed Plame, would later write a book in which he reiterated the reasons for his decision to cooperate with the prosecution: the *Sun-Times* would not cover his legal expenses, and he could not afford to fight Fitzgerald on his own. Tim Russert of NBC, whose news organization could afford to wage the fight, agreed to cooperate immediately in the inquiry and disclosed his confidential conversations with Libby and other sources. Norman Pearlstine, the editor in chief of *Time,* agreed to turn over to Fitzgerald Matt Cooper's emails despite the objections of many reporters and members of the magazine's legal team. His emails compromised, Cooper's testimony became less crucial. Nonetheless, he received a personal written waiver from Scooter Libby, his source, whom he identified subsequently. I did not until I had spent almost

three months in jail.

3. Jonathan S. Landay, "White House Released Claims of Defector Deemed Unreliable by CIA," Knight Ridder Newspapers, May 17, 2004, www.mcclatchyde .com/2004/05/17/16331/white-house-released-claims-of.html.

4. Arianna Huffington, "Judy Miller: Do We Want to Know Everything or Don't We?," *Huffington Post,* July 27, 2005, www.huff ingtonpost.com/arianna-huffington/judy-miller-do-we-want-to_b_4791.html. Among others, Arianna Huffington, writing repeated attacks on her fledgling eponymous site while I was in jail, challenged my motivation for going to jail.

Chapter 21. Inmate 45570083

1. The act, which makes it a crime for those with access to classified information to disclose the name of a "covert" agent intentionally to damage national security, was enacted in the wake of the outing of scores of covert operatives by Philip Agee, Lewis Wolf, and Aldrich Ames. All three had sought to cripple the CIA's clandestine services by outing its agents. Several legal analysts said they doubted that the outing of Plame, though reprehensible if

intended as payback for Wilson's criticism of the White House, would have been covered by the law. Among the most articulate advocates of this position was Victoria Toensing, a Republican who had been chief counsel to the Senate Intelligence Committee. A key drafter of the act, Toensing insisted that Plame did not meet its definition of "covert," and, hence, that Fitzgerald's inquiry was "flawed from the get-go." Victoria Toensing and Bruce W. Sanford, "The Plame Game: Was This a Crime?," *Washington Post,* January 12, 2005, www.washingtonpost.com/wp-dyn/articles/A2305-2005Jan11.html.

2. Norman Pearlstine, *Off the Record: The Press, the Government, and the War Over Anonymous Sources* (New York: Farrar, Straus and Giroux, 2007), pp. 112–14.

3. Farber, a dogged reporter, had served forty days in Bergen County Jail in 1978 for contempt of court, and the paper was fined $286,000 for having refused to turn over his notes about a murder case he had investigated. The case was complicated and, like mine, had aroused intense debate. Although Myron had testified before a grand jury, he refused to give anyone notes that would betray his confidential sources. Determined to fight the growing

number of subpoenas for reporters' notes and sources, Abe Rosenthal and publisher "Punch" Sulzberger, Arthur's father, had strongly supported Myron. After Myron was freed, New Jersey governor Brendan T. Byrne returned $101,000 of the $286,000 that the *Times* had paid in fines and pardoned both him and the paper. Myron's case prompted New Jersey to toughen further its state shield law, making it one of the nation's best. Though his ordeal had coincided with New York's devastating newspaper strike, when the paper was under tremendous financial pressure, Abe's support for him never wavered, during and after jail.

4. Huffington, "Judy Miller: Do We Want to Know Everything or Don't We?"

5. Since I had already written two number one bestselling books, I was never worried about getting a book contract. But I sensed that if ever I got a waiver and had to testify, it would be impossible to write honestly about the case until the fate of the accused had been decided.

6. Bob Novak had voluntarily testified that Karl Rove had told him about Valerie Plame's identity. Matt Cooper had testified without going to jail about two of his sources. His boss, Norm Pearlstine, had

turned over to Fitzgerald all of Matt's emails and notes. Walter Pincus negotiated a deal with Fitzgerald to appear before the grand jury without disclosing the identity of his source, who testified separately before the panel. Tim Russert had spoken to the FBI about his conversations with Libby before he received a subpoena. NBC White House correspondent Andrea Mitchell had also been questioned. It was eventually revealed that Bob Woodward, who had volunteered in a TV interview to take my place in jail if he could, had learned of Plame's identity from Richard Armitage five days before I had even met with Scooter Libby. Armitage turned out to have been the initial leaker, which the State Department's top lawyer knew. They offered to discuss Armitage's leak with the White House but said nothing when told that senior administration officials had no need for this information.

7. In 2001 Vanessa Leggett, a former private investigator, spent 168 days in jail for refusing to compromise her sources in an investigation into the 1997 murder of a Houston socialite. But this brave, principled woman had been doing research for a book, not working for a newspaper.

8. The tabs and other gossipmongers made much of my husband's luxury cruise with friends while I languished in jail. But Jason, under enormous pressure, needed the rest. I had encouraged him to go.

Chapter 22. Departures

1. The paper's coverage of my situation was also being criticized. While the editorial page had crusaded on my behalf, the news department had been scooped repeatedly, even on my release from jail, which was reported first by the *Philadelphia Inquirer.*
2. Robert S. Bennett, *In the Ring: The Trials of a Washington Lawyer* (New York: Three Rivers Press, 2008), p. 357.
3. The committee had released portions of an email from Plame to a senior CIA official noting that her husband had "good relations with both the PM [prime minister] and the former Minister of Mines (not to mention lots of French contacts), both of whom could possibly shed light on this sort of activity." She said that she had approached her husband only after her bosses had selected him for the mission, but the committee noted that she had mentioned that her husband was planning a business trip to Niger and "might be

willing to use his contacts in the region."

4. As several in the White House had warned, the retraction seemed to validate rather than undercut Wilson's charges. Once reporters smelled what Anna Perez, Condi Rice's press adviser, had called "blood in the water," they had used the retraction to challenge all of the White House's intelligence claims. Several officials, including Dick Cheney, who had never made the Niger claim, had warned that retracting the sixteen words was "intellectually dishonest," as Karl Rove would later assert in his memoir. (Britain, America's closest ally in the war and a main source of the intelligence, continued to stand by the claim.) It was also, they argued, a catastrophic political error that would reinforce, not rebut, Wilson's charges about the White House having lied the country into war.

5. Harvey, *Explaining the Iraq War,* pp. 168–69.

6. I had found the notebook under my desk in a Bloomingdale's shopping bag filled with notebooks stacked in chronological order. When, in October, the paper posted twin stories about my jailing and the paper's handling of the Wilson-Plame scandal, a blogger named Tim Porter,

whose story was featured as an online link to the *Times*'s account of my grand jury testimony, concluded that my failure to remember my earlier meeting with Libby and belated discovery of crucial notes in a shopping bag reflected "sloppy" and "disorganized" reporting. Tim Porter, "Judy Miller: What a Horribly Ordinary Affair," *First Draft,* October, 17, 2005, www.tim porter.com/firstdraft/archives/000507 .html.

This is typical of the venomous reactions to my account of my grand jury testimony and a lengthy companion piece written by several colleagues on October 16 about my role in the Valerie Plame affair. Described by its author as a blog about "Newspapering, Readership & Relevance in a Digital Age," Porter's attack is still featured by the *Times* as a link to our stories in its web editions, the second offering in a column entitled Bloggers Discuss the Miller Case. While Porter called my notebook storage system and memory lapses evidence of "sloppy" reporting, how many bloggers would have been able to retrieve two-year-old notes about a subject that, prior to an unforeseeable grand jury, had seemed to be little more than Beltway gossip?

7. I had not written about the secret group because the embed agreements signed by most reporters banned stories about such still-secret groups and operations. But Barton Gellman of the *Washington Post,* who was permitted to cover the XTF in action during a brief period in May, disclosed the existence of Task Force 20, as well as its composition and mission, in his paper. His exclusive, "Covert Unit Hunted for Iraqi Arms," was published on June 13, 2003, www.washingtonpost.com/wp-dyn/content/article/2006/06/12/AR2006061200926.html. Asked by editors in New York why I had not written the story, I said it would have violated the terms of my embed agreement — a disadvantage of privileged access to sensitive military operations on the military's terms.

8. Howard Kurtz, "Miller and Her Stand Draw Strong Reactions," *Washington Post,* October 1, 2005, www.washingtonpost.com/wp-dyn/content/article/2005/09/30/AR2005093001553.html.

9. Myron Farber would later go public with his disdain for my decision. In an interview with Seth Mnookin in *Vanity Fair* (December, 2005) about my role in the Plame affair and dispute with the paper, Farber, who had been jailed three decades earlier,

was quoted as opposing my decision to accept the waiver and narrow my testimony. "I just can't imagine doing it," he told *Editor & Publisher.* "I am just against the notion of waivers. When I was in jail, the thought of accepting one never crossed my mind."

10. "Lawyers' Correspondence in Miller Case" (letters from I. Lewis Libby to Judith Miller; Joseph A. Tate to Patrick Fitzgerald; Floyd Abrams to Joseph A. Tate), *New York Times,* October 4, 2005, www.nytimes.com/packages/pdf/national/nat_MILLER_051001.pdf.

11. Katharine Q. Seelye, "Freed Reporter Says She Upheld Principles," *New York Times,* October 4, 2005, www.nytimes.com/2005/10/04/national/04reporter.html.

12. Ibid.

13. Bennett, *In the Ring,* p. 358.

14. In 2010, for instance, the *New York Times* assigned Don Van Natta Jr. to investigate alleged wrongdoing at the *News of the World.* On September 5, 2010, the paper published the results of his six-month investigation of the British tabloid, owned by Rupert Murdoch's News Corporation. The British paper called the allegations unsubstantiated and accused the *Times* of flawed reporting and of being

motivated by commercial rivalry. Specifically, the Murdoch paper charged the *Times* with "seven breaches" of its own "ethical guidelines" involving accuracy, the use of anonymous sources, bias, impartiality, honest treatment of competitors, reader benefit, and conflict of interest. The paper also challenged Van Natta's "professional detachment," claiming that he had sent a Twitter message linking to a personal attack on Murdoch alongside a message that stated: "The Last Great Newspaper War." In his blog, Michael Wolff, the media commentator, called Van Natta Jr. a *Times* "enforcer" and "insider, loyalist, and gun." In his response, Arthur Brisbane, then the *Times*'s public editor, supported the paper's reporting but agreed that Van Natta had relied heavily on anonymous sources. He also said that the paper's presentation of the story and gratuitous references to Murdoch could leave room for suspicions of a "hidden agenda."

15. Many reporters and fellow editors had complained about Cohen's stewardship of the foreign desk. Cohen and I had clashed ever since he joined the *Times* in 1990, when he worked as a reporter in what was then a newly created desk to cover media

news. Martin Arnold, the paper's former media editor, and I, his deputy, had edited Cohen's stories; we'd refused to run at least one major feature he'd written about two *Time* magazine reporters unless he made major changes. As time passed, both of us grew increasingly skeptical about the neutrality and thoroughness of Cohen's reporting.

16. Even the State Department's INR — the smallest intelligence unit, with the fewest people and smallest budget, and a historic tendency to miss or downplay significant potential threats to the nation — did not dispute the NIE's key finding that Iraq "has chemical and biological weapons" or that if it got fissile material from abroad, it "could make a nuclear weapon within several months to a year," judgments to which the intelligence community had assigned a "90 percent" level of confidence.

17. The Van Natta article had many other ill-founded complaints. It said, for instance, that although I had given the paper's reporting team two (lengthy) interviews about my role in the Plame affair, I had refused to elaborate on my grand jury testimony or my sources, or allow my colleagues to review the notes I

had gone to jail to protect. The article did not say that my lawyer had explicitly warned me not to comment on such issues in light of the ongoing criminal investigation. After I left jail, Bob Bennett had permitted me to give only two broadcast interviews. I decided to talk to Barbara Walters and Lou Dobbs, reporters I respected and trusted, and whose medium, television, more or less prevented in-depth probing of issues that could prove problematic if I were to be a witness in a future criminal trial.

18. If Jill told Van Natta that she didn't recall discussing Plame with me, I would understand. Who could blame her for having forgotten one of what had probably been a dozen such tips a week from her thirty-five-person bureau. I recall that she had seemed tense that day, which was understandable, since Howell Raines, her nemesis, had just been fired, but her own future was at that point undetermined. But she denied that I had told her anything at all about Plame. Van Natta did not report that I had told George Freeman, the paper's lawyer, about having passed along the tip to Jill. The dispute between us was never resolved, but when she testified at the Libby trial two years later, she

did not deny that I had told her about it. Asked whether she and I had discussed Wilson's wife, she replied that she did not recall. Perhaps I remembered our conversation because I knew that, given my strained relations with Keller, she was unlikely to let me pursue the Plame tip, even though David Sanger and I had coauthored the paper's account of Steve Hadley's apology for having permitted "faulty intelligence" — the infamous sixteen words about hunting for uranium in Africa — to appear in Bush's State of the Union address. See David E. Sanger with Judith Miller, "After the War: Intelligence; National Security Aide Says He's to Blame for Speech Error," *New York Times,* July 23, 2003, www.nytimes.com/ 2003/07/23/us/after-war-intelligence-national-security-aide-says-he-s-blame-for-speech-error.html?scp=28&sq=&st= nyt.

19. Barstow and Bergman would relay similar concerns and observations about my case to Marie Brenner, a friend and journalist whose articles I long admired, and who wrote about the impact of the Valerie Plame affair for *Vanity Fair.* See Marie Brenner, "Lies and Consequences: Sixteen Words That Changed the World,"

Vanity Fair, April 2006, www.vanityfair
.com/politics/features/2006/04/brenner
200604?currentPage=1.

20. Dowd's column did not identify Jill
Abramson as one of her closest friends.

21. In May 2009, Dowd was accused of
having lifted without attribution a forty-
plus-word paragraph from a posting by
Josh Marshall on the online site Talking
Points Memo. Dowd admitted making a
mistake and ran an update that attributed
the paragraph to Marshall. The paper ran
a correction. Her explanation — that she
had not read the TPM column but solic-
ited input from a friend and then cut and
pasted that response into one of her
columns — was criticized by several media
critics and bloggers.

Epilogue

1. Before Bill Safire could talk to Punch,
Abe, spurned and humiliated, accepted an
offer to write a column for the New York
Daily News. According to numerous accounts, Arthur had long resented Abe
Rosenthal for having challenged his conduct and judgment in front of his father
and other perceived slights. See Mnookin,
Hard News, and Tifft and Jones, *The Trust.*

2. At one point in our talks, the paper announced publicly that I would be reporting back to work in the newsroom by November 2. One of my lawyers interpreted this as an indication that Arthur was having second thoughts about whether an amicable settlement of our dispute was preferable to a dignified separation. But Matt Mallow, then a senior Skadden, Arps, partner and a friend, asked me a clarifying question: Even if I got a public apology from the paper, would I feel comfortable working again for the *Times*? Did I want to continue working for a paper that had "turned so quickly and easily on one of its own"? Would I ever again trust journalists who had, as Bob Bennett wrote in his memoir, "snatched defeat out of the jaws of victory" by assailing me after my almost three months in jail?

3. I gave two interviews soon after I came out of jail: one to ABC's Barbara Walters, whose father, a nightclub owner, had introduced my parents; and the other to Lou Dobbs, who was then at CNN and had run a clock at the top of the screen counting each day of my incarceration. I rejected numerous offers to write tell-all articles about jail and my fight with the paper and inquiries from filmmakers seek-

ing my cooperation with a movie based on about my experience. In 2006 at the request of my lawyer, Floyd Abrams, who was involved in the project, I had lunch with Kate Beckinsale, the gifted actress who was preparing to play a reporter in a film about a court battle similar to mine. The film, *Nothing But the Truth,* written and directed by Rod Lurie, opened in the fall of 2007 went quickly to video distribution. Floyd was compensated. I did not participate.

4. Libby's version of their conversation is different. Libby told the grand jury that in response to Cooper, he had said that he did not know whether Cooper's claim that Plame worked at the CIA was true. Cooper's contemporaneous notes of their conversation support Libby's description.

5. Although Bush commuted Libby's sentence, he still paid the hefty fine, served four hundred hours of community service, and had his law license revoked.

6. John Rizzo, *Company Man: Thirty Years of Controversy and Crisis in the CIA* (New York: Scribner, 2014), p. 208. In his book, the former CIA general counsel challenged another of Plame's complaints: she had not been forced out of the CIA by its indifference to her family's personal

safety, he asserted. In her memoir, Plame said that she was forced to leave Langley partly because her bosses had denied her pleas for added security for her and her young twins after her family had been explicitly threatened. But Rizzo, who had investigated her request for "round-the-clock security protection," determined that neither she nor her family was in "any sort of danger." As a result, he wrote, he had "reluctantly" concluded that the CIA "could not lawfully expend the considerable amount of taxpayer money that would be required to shield her from a nonexistent threat." Plame's book also revealed, among other things, that the CIA had recalled her from her first covert overseas assignment in 1997 because the agency feared that she "might be among the officers betrayed to the Russians by traitor Aldrich Ames," the CIA official who spied for Russia for nine years before being caught in 1994. While the agency never determined whether Plame was among the compromised spies, the disclosure meant that it was not senior Bush officials who had ended Plame's career overseas as a full-time undercover operative but a traitor within the CIA.

7. My belated discovery of the importance

of my notation of "Bureau" explained something that puzzled me during the defense's cross-examination of me on the stand in 2007. Libby's lawyers kept asking me whether other agencies, such as the State Department, had "bureaus" rather than "offices" or "divisions" or "directorates." But since neither they nor I knew that Plame had used the State Department as cover for her CIA work, the questions seemed odd, and their intention, at least to me, unclear.

8. Stan Crock, "*Fair Game* Glamorizes Distortions and Perpetuates Myths," *World Affairs,* November 8, 2010, p. 4; http://www.worldaffairsjournal.org/article/fair-game-glamorizes-distortions-and-perpetuates-myths.

9. Rizzo, *Company Man,* pp. 206–7.

10. Dick Cheney, interview, January 2014.

11. O'Sullivan, who worked at the State Department before being sent to Iraq soon after the invasion in 2003, argues that "there was no Sunni partner" willing to work with US forces to oppose Al Qaeda until 2006. Until then, she said, the US military's top brass was convinced that the occupation of Iraq by US forces was the root cause of the insurgency, rather than Sunni bitterness over having

lost control of the state they had controlled until Saddam's ouster.

12. Thomas Donnelly and Gary J. Schmitt, "The Right Fight Now: Counterinsurgency, Not Caution, Is the Answer in Iraq," *Washington Post,* October 26, 2003, http://pqasb.pqarchiver.com/washington post/doc/409635877.html?FMT=ABS& FMTS=A BS:FT&date=Oct+26%2C+ 2003&author=Tom+Donnelly+and+ Gary+Schmitt&pub=The+Washington +Post&edition=&startpage=&dese= The+Right+Fight+Now%3B+Counter insurgency%2C+Not+Caution%2C+Is +the+Answer+in+Iraq.

13. Judith Miller, "A Witness Against Al Qaeda Says the U.S. Let Him Down," *New York Times,* June 3, 2002, www.nytimes .com/2002/06/03/us/a-witness-against-al-qaeda-says-the-us-let-him-down.html. Despite my admiration of Fitzgerald's vigorous prosecution of terrorists in the first World Trade Center bombing, I was one of the few journalists to write critically about his mistreatment of Essam Al Ridi, an Egyptian pilot who helped him convict Bin Laden's personal secretary. Al Ridi told me, and an FBI agent quoted in my article agreed, that once Al Ridi's usefulness as a witness ended, Fitzgerald

did not honor promises he had made that he would not be penalized in the United States or mistreated in his native Egypt.

14. "Innovation, A *New York Times* internal report," March 24, 2004, http://www .scribd.com/doc/224332847/NYT-Innovation-Report-2014.

15. Leonard Downie, Jr., *The Obama Administration and the Press* (New York: Committee to Protect Journalists, October 10, 2013), http://cpj.org/reports/2013/10/ obama-and-the-press-us-leaks-surveill ance-post-911.php.

16. The news of Abramson's firing stunned the media but generated little interest among readers, even at the *Times.* The front-page article about the dismissal of the first female head of the nation's leading newspaper was only the tenth most emailed story of the day — behind a story entitled "Steak That Sizzles on the Stovetop" and Frank Bruni's column, "Read, Kids, Read." BuzzFeed's Kate Aurthur, a former *Times* employee, wrote that Abramson "got fired with less dignity than Judith Miller, who practically started the Iraq War."

17. By late 2005, according to a Pew poll, 43 percent of Americans thought that America's and Britain's leaders were

"mostly lying" when they claimed that Iraq had WMD before the war.

18. "As New Dangers Loom, More Think the U.S. Does 'Too Little' to Solve World Problems," Pew Research Center, August 28, 2014, www.people-press.org/2014/08/28/as-new-dangers-loom-more-think-the-u-s-does-too-little-to-solve-world-problems.

ABOUT THE AUTHOR

Judith Miller is an investigative reporter formerly with the *New York Times.* She was part of a team that won a Pulitzer for articles before 9/11 on Osama bin Laden. Miller is coauthor of the #1 *New York Times* bestsellers *Germs: Biological Weapons and America's Secret War* and *Saddam Hussein and the Crisis in the Gulf* and author of *God Has Ninety-nine Names: Reporting from a Militant Middle East* and *One, by One, by One: Facing the Holocaust.* Miller is an adjunct fellow at the Manhattan Institute for Policy Research, contributing editor of *City Journal,* and a theater critic for *Tablet* magazine. Since 2008, she has been a commentator for Fox News. She lives in New York City and Sag Harbor with her husband, Jason Epstein.

The employees of Thorndike Press hope you have enjoyed this Large Print book. All our Thorndike, Wheeler, and Kennebec Large Print titles are designed for easy reading, and all our books are made to last. Other Thorndike Press Large Print books are available at your library, through selected bookstores, or directly from us.

For information about titles, please call:
  (800) 223-1244

or visit our Web site at:
  http://gale.cengage.com/thorndike

To share your comments, please write:
Publisher
Thorndike Press
10 Water St., Suite 310
Waterville, ME 04901